Embedded Media Processing

Embedded Media Processing

by David J. Katz and Rick Gentile

AMSTERDAM • BOSTON • HEIDELBERG • LONDON
NEW YORK • OXFORD • PARIS • SAN DIEGO
SAN FRANCISCO • SINGAPORE • SYDNEY • TOKYO

Newnes is an imprint of Elsevier

ELSEVIER

Newnes

Newnes is an imprint of Elsevier
30 Corporate Drive, Suite 400, Burlington, MA 01803, USA
Linacre House, Jordan Hill, Oxford OX2 8DP, UK

 Recognizing the importance of preserving what has been written, Elsevier prints its books on acid-free paper whenever possible.

Library of Congress Cataloging-in-Publication Data

Katz, David J.
  Embedded media processing / by David Katz and Rick Gentile.
    p. cm.
  Includes index.
  ISBN-13: 978-0-7506-7912-1 (pbk. : alk. paper)
  ISBN-10: 0-7506-7912-3 (pbk. : alk. paper)
  1. Signal processing--Digital techniques. 2. Embedded computer systems.
I. Gentile, Rick. II. Title.
  TK5102.9.K39 2005
  004.16--dc22

                    2005013672

British Library Cataloguing-in-Publication Data
A catalogue record for this book is available from the British Library.

For information on all Newnes publications visit our website at www.books.elsevier.com.

Transferred to Digital Printing in 2012

Printed in the United States of America

Cover design by Dan Testen

To Jill, Joseph and Lena—for their love, support and
good humor during this project and always;

To my parents—for their guidance, and for encouraging me
to follow my interests in writing and engineering.

— DK

■

To Emily and Meaghan—thank you both very much
for your patience and love;

To my parents—thank you for your unending
encouragement and support.

— RG

Contents

Contents

Preface

History of This Book

This effort arose out of our experience as part of Analog Devices' Embedded Processor Applications Group. The group has a long history of supporting both fixed-point and floating-point digital signal processors (DSPs). However, when Intel Corporation and Analog Devices collaborated to introduce the Micro Signal Architecture (MSA) in 2000, the result was a processor uniting microcontroller (MCU) and DSP functionality into a single high-performance "convergent processing" device—a rather unique entry into the marketplace. What transpired with the MSA-based Blackfin® family was that a new class of application spaces opened up, from video-enabled handheld gadgets, to control-intensive industrial applications, to operating system/ number-crunching combos running on a single processor core. Consequently, we began fielding questions of a different nature than the signal-processing ones to which we had been accustomed. Now customers were wondering how to partition memory intelligently, organize data flows, and divide processing tasks across multiple cores.

From our interactions with customers, it became clear that the same types of complex questions kept surfacing. So we said, "Why not encapsulate these basic ideas in a book?" We focused the text on embedded media processing (EMP) because that is the "sweet spot" today of high-performance, low-power, small-footprint processing—an area in which the Blackfin® Processor sits squarely. EMP is a relatively new application area, because it requires performance levels only recently attainable.

In this book, we assume that you have a working understanding of microcontroller and DSP fundamentals, and even that you have a halfway decent comprehension of programming methodologies. However, for the complex media systems about which we concern ourselves here, we feel it's our job to give you the tools you need to advance your knowledge toward successful implementation of EMP systems.

Although this book discusses media processing systems in general, it often grounds the discussion in concrete examples, and for this purpose it is useful to discuss a specific processor architecture. As such, we'll use the Blackfin processor family as a basis for examples and architectural discussion. That said, we strive not to lose the generality of concepts as they may apply to other processors or solutions.

We draw on our experience with hundreds of customers across varied application spaces, in a quest to help designers understand how to start designing their EMP systems, and where to look if things aren't going as planned.

Chapter Overviews

Chapter 1: Embedded Media Processing

This chapter introduces the concept of embedded media processing and describes how it presents new design challenges. In doing so, it discusses how the Convergent Processor fills a void created by the application of conventional processing solutions to portable multimedia devices that require high clock rates, low power dissipation, small board footprint and low cost.

A discussion on the system aspects of an EMP application ensues, followed by an architectural discussion of the Blackfin processor that serves as a foundation for much of the conceptual and practical discussions in this book.

Chapter 2: Memory Systems

This chapter provides a combination of information and examples to shed some light on the wide array of current and upcoming memory technologies. It also elucidates the tradeoffs in "architecting" memory for a complex embedded system. For example, we'll cover what types of memory to use, as well as how to connect them in a system. We'll talk about internal (on-chip) versus external memories, synchronous versus asynchronous memories, and volatile versus nonvolatile storage.

Chapter 3: Direct Memory Access (DMA)

This chapter describes Direct Memory Access and relates why it's crucial in an embedded multimedia system. We'll provide numerous examples to show how the DMA controller can intelligently move data to save extra passes through the system. Additionally, we'll describe some helpful DMA constructs that can efficiently move data buffers, as well as advanced DMA controller features that further facilitate management of complex data flows.

Chapter 4: System Resource Partitioning and Code Optimization

This chapter focuses on processor architectural features that are crucial to understand when developing a complex multimedia system. These features include event generation and handling, instruction pipelines, native addressing modes and specialized instructions, among others. We concentrate on using these features, supplemented with a bevy of compiler "tips and tricks," to make the process of porting existing C/C++ code to a new embedded processor as painless as possible.

Additionally, this chapter furthers the memory and DMA concepts discussed in the previous two chapters, providing guidance on advanced topics such as choosing between cache and DMA for code and data management, and the "physics" of external memory flows.

Chapter 5: Basics of Embedded Audio Processing

This chapter serves as a starting point for any embedded system that requires audio processing. We first provide you with a short introduction to the human auditory system and sampling theory. Then, we describe how to connect your embedded processor to audio converters or other inputs and outputs. We devote a detailed section to the importance of dynamic range and data-type emulation on fixed-point processors. Subsequently, we discuss audio processing building blocks, basic programming techniques and fundamental algorithms. We conclude this chapter with an overview of the widely used audio and speech compression standards.

Chapter 6: Basics of Embedded Video and Image Processing

This section deals with a basic differentiator between today's media processors and their recent forebears—the ability to process high-quality video streams in real time. We try here to put the "need to know" video basics in a single place without getting bogged down by format variations, geographic differences, legacy formats, etc. Our aim is to inaugurate the user into video from a media processing standpoint, providing only the details most relevant to accomplishing the tasks at hand.

After an overview of human visual perception as it relates to video, we review video standards, color spaces and pixel formats. We then proceed to a discussion of video sources and displays that also includes an outline of the basic processing steps in an image pipeline. Next, we turn our attention to the media processor itself and walk through an example video application, from raw input through processed display output. We finish with a high-level discussion of image and video compression.

Chapter 7: Media Processing Frameworks

In this chapter, we'll target the problem of how to port media algorithms from larger processors, where memory and bandwidth are "free," to embedded systems that don't have unlimited resources. In portable embedded media applications, some straightforward steps can make a big difference in performance. We will describe a variety of programming frameworks that allow you to optimize performance for a given application without needlessly increasing the complexity of the programming model. We will focus on setting up data movement infrastructures that are well-suited for a wide range of media-based applications involving both single-core and dual-core processors. Moreover, we'll describe benchmarking techniques that will help you adapt a framework to best fit a target application.

Chapter 8: Power Management for Embedded Systems

This chapter will acquaint you with the many facets of power management on high-performance processors. It includes a detailed discussion of "Dynamic Power Management," a suite of processor functionality that allows flexible voltage and frequency tuning to meet performance goals while maximizing power savings.

The discussion then turns to voltage regulation, starting with an overview of linear regulators and proceeding to step-down switching regulators. It provides recommendations for component selection to aid circuit design and maximize regulator efficiency. After a discussion on battery technologies for portable devices, it closes with an analysis of system power dissipation.

Chapter 9: Application Examples

In this chapter, we pick a few key areas of media processing and delve into some detail on the implementation of an algorithm, framework, or system. In doing so, we leverage the knowledge base of the previous chapters, with the intent of showing how the concepts tie together into coherent entities that you can apply to your own embedded media projects.

Acknowledgments

We are indebted to Tomasz Lukasiak, who authored Chapter 5 and contributed to many other areas of this book.

Additionally, we'd like to express our gratitude to the many associates who provided source material for topics we discussed. These contributors include Alan Anderson, Joe Barry, Joe Beauchemin, Brian Erisman, John Hayden, Marc Hoffman, Robert Hoffman, Larry Hurst, Bin Huo, Walt Kester, Paul Kettle, Steve Kilbane, Greg Koker, Benno Kusstatscher, Ching Lam, Dave Lannigan, Dan Ledger, Bob Libert, Fabian Lis, Thorsten Lorenzen, Chris Mayer, Wayne Meyer, Brian Mitchell, Ke Ning, Glen Ouellette, Bob Peloquin, Jim Potts, Rich Schubert, Jim Sobol, John Tomarakos and Gabby Yi.

We'd also like to thank ADI management—especially Rob DeRobertis and Tulika Hainsworth—for supporting this project. Additionally, many thanks to Bob Berube, Becky Fulker, Kelly Johnson, Carol Lewis, Jessen Wehrwein and Scott Williams for their support and facilitation of the entire writing process.

Finally, we'd like to extend special thanks to Michael Forster and Tiffany Gasbarrini of Reed Elsevier, and to Scott Wayne of Analog Devices, for their excellent assistance, guidance, and encouragement throughout the publication process.

So now that we've dispensed with the formalities and you've had a chance to see what this book is about, let's get going!

Acronyms

ADC	Analog-to-Digital Converter
AFE	Analog Front End
ASIC	Application-Specific Integrated Circuit
ASSP	Application-Specific Standard Product
CCD	Charge-Coupled Device
CCLK	Processor Core Clock
CIF	Common Intermediate Format, a video display resolution
CMOS	Complementary Metal Oxide Semiconductor
CYMK	Cyan-Yellow-Magenta-blacK color space
D-1	Digital 1, a broadcast display format
DAC	Digital-to-Analog Converter
DCT	Discrete Cosine Transform
DDR	Double Data Rate SDRAM
DMA	Direct Memory Access
DSP	Digital Signal Processor
EMP	Embedded Media Processing
FFT	Fast Fourier Transform

FIFO	First-In, First-Out (buffer device)
FPGA	Field-Programmable Gate Array
Fps	Frames per second (video)
I/O	Input/Output
kbps, kb/s	Kilobits per second (thousands of bits per second)
kBps, kB/s	Kilobytes per second (thousands of bytes per second)
Mbps, Mb/s	Megabits per second (millions of bits per second)
MBps, MB/s	Megabytes per second (millions of bytes per second)
MCU	Microcontroller
MIPS	Millions of Instructions Per Second (MCU benchmark)
MMACS	Millions of Multiply-Accumulates per Second (DSP benchmark)
NTSC	National Television System Committee television broadcast standard
OS	Operating System
PAL	Phase Alternation Line television broadcast standard
PLL	Phase-Locked Loop
PPI	Parallel Peripheral Interface
PWM	Pulse-Width Modulation
QCIF	Quarter-CIF, a video display resolution
QVGA	Quarter-VGA, a graphics display resolution
RGB	Red-Green-Blue color space
RISC	Reduced Instruction Set Computer/Computing
RTC	Real-Time Clock
RTOS	Real-Time Operating System
SCLK	Processor System Clock (Peripheral Clock)
SDRAM	Synchronous Dynamic Random Access Memory

SPORT	Synchronous Serial Port
SRAM	Static Random Access Memory
UART	Universal Asynchronous Receiver/Transmitter
VDSP	VisualDSP++® software development tools suite
VGA	Video Graphics Array, a graphics display resolution

About the Authors

David Katz has nearly 15 years of experience in analog, digital and embedded systems design. Currently, he is a Senior Applications Engineer at Analog Devices, Inc., where he is involved in specifying new media processors. He has published internationally close to 100 embedded processing articles, and he has presented several conference papers in the field. Previously, he worked at Motorola, Inc., as a senior design engineer in cable modem and factory automation groups. David holds both a B.S. and an M. Eng. in Electrical Engineering from Cornell University.

Rick Gentile has over 15 years of experience in embedded systems, specializing in software development and signal processing. He currently leads the Blackfin Processor Applications Group at Analog Devices, Inc. He is widely published and is a frequent speaker at technical conferences. Previously, Rick was a Member of the Technical Staff at MIT Lincoln Laboratory, leading several large software teams and designing embedded signal processing systems used in a wide range of radar sensors. He received a B.S. from the University of Massachusetts at Amherst and an M.S. from Northeastern University, both in Electrical and Computer Engineering.

What's on the (Companion website)?

Included on the enclosed (Companion website) is a VisualDSP++® Test Drive from Analog Devices, Inc. This is a free, fully functional 90-day trial of the VisualDSP++ 4.0 integrated development and debug environment for Blackfin Processors.

VisualDSP++ allows complete and efficient management of embedded processing projects from within a single interface. Additionally, it allows quick and easy transitioning between editing, building, and debugging activities. Key features include the native C/C++ compiler, advanced graphical plotting tools, statistical profiling, and the VisualDSP++ Kernel (VDK). Other features include an assembler, a linker, cycle-accurate and function-accurate compiled simulators, emulator support, and much more.

This material is now available from the link below: http://www.elsevierdirect.com/companions/9780750679121

Please feel free to visit this book's companion website, http://www.theEMPbook.com. Here you will find lots of useful information on embedded media processing, including application notes, code examples, white papers, and many other resources.

Embedded Media Processing

Why Are You Reading This Book?

Well, assuming that you find your pleasure reading elsewhere, we hope you're reading this book for at least one of the following reasons:

- You'd like to understand more about what embedded media processing entails, and what demands it places on designers who are more familiar with conventional systems based on microcontrollers (MCUs) or digital signal processors (DSPs).

- You need to design an embedded multimedia system and want to know how to choose the proper processor for the application.

- You've already chosen a processor, and you want to know how to start architecting your system so that you can avoid problems at the outset.

- You're in the middle of designing a multimedia system, but you've run into some snags with trying to get all of your data flows and memory accesses to line up properly.

- You're related to one of the authors.

In this book we concern ourselves with *embedded media processing* (EMP) systems—that is, applications involving large data blocks (whether image, video, audio, speech, or some combination of these), a need for signal processing, and (often) a real-time nature. By "embedded," we mean a specialized processor that's part of a larger system and is targeted for a specific application (as opposed to a personal computer, which is intended to do some of everything). A further requirement of many

EMP systems is portability, so battery life is a key factor, and it's often necessary to reach a compromise between power dissipation and computational performance.

So What's All the Excitement About Embedded Multimedia Systems?

With the multimedia revolution in full swing, we're becoming accustomed to toting around cell phones, PDAs, cameras and MP3 players, concentrating our daily interactions into the palms of our hands. But given the usefulness of each gadget, it's surprising how often we upgrade to "the latest and greatest" device. This is, in part, due to the fact that the cell phone we bought last year can't support the new video clip playback feature touted in this year's TV ads.

After all, who isn't frustrated after discovering that his portable audio player gets tangled up over the latest music format? And which overworked couple has the time, much less the inclination, to figure out how to get the family vacation travelogue off their Mini-DV camcorder and onto a DVD or hard disk?

As Figure 1.1 implies, we've now reached the point where a single gadget can serve as a phone, a personal organizer, a camera, an audio player, and a web-enabled portal to the rest of the world.

But still, we're not happy.

Let's add a little perspective: we used to be satisfied just to snap a digital picture and see it on our computer screen. Just 10 years ago, there were few built-in digital camera features, the photo resolution was comparatively low, and only still pictures were an option. Not that we were complaining, since previously our only digital choice involved scanning 35-mm prints into the computer.

In contrast, today we expect multi-megapixel photos, snapped several times per second, that are automatically white-balanced and color-corrected. What's more, we demand seamless transfer between our camera and other media nodes, a feature made practical only because the camera can compress the images before moving them.

Clearly, consumer appetites demand steady improvement in the "media experience." That is, people want high-quality video and audio streams in small form factors, with

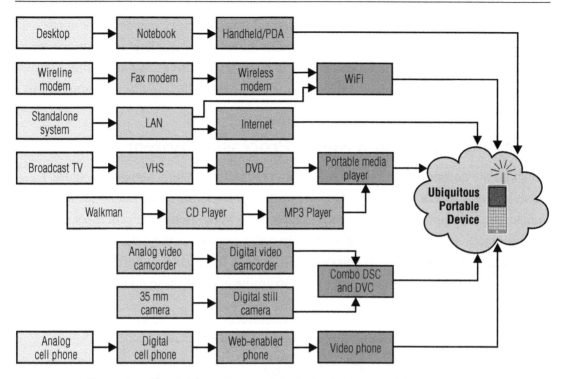

Figure 1.1 **The "ultimate" portable device is almost within our grasp**

low power requirements (for improved battery life) and at low cost. This desire leads to constant development of better compression algorithms that reduce storage requirements while increasing audio/video resolution and frame rates.

To a large extent, the Internet drives this evolution. After all, it made audio, images and streaming video pervasive, forcing transport algorithms to become increasingly clever at handling ever-richer media across the limited bandwidth available on a network. As a result, people today want their portable devices to be Net-connected, high-speed conduits for a never-ending information stream and media show. Unfortunately, networking infrastructure is upgraded at a much slower rate than bandwidth demands grow, and this underscores the importance of excellent compression ratios for media-rich streams.

It may not be readily apparent, but behind the scenes, processors have had to evolve dramatically to meet these new and demanding requirements. They now need to run at very high clock rates (to process video in real time), be very power efficient (to prolong battery life), and comprise very small, inexpensive single-chip solutions (to save board real estate and keep end products price-competitive). What's more, they need to be software-reprogrammable, in order to adapt to the rapidly changing multimedia standards environment.

A Simplified Look at a Media Processing System

Consider the components of a typical media processing system, shown in Figure 1.2. Here, an input source presents a data stream to a processor's input interface, where it is manipulated appropriately and sent to a memory subsystem. The processor core(s) then interact with the memory subsystem in order to process the data, generating intermediate data buffers in the process. Ultimately, the final data buffer is sent to its destination via an output subsystem. Let's examine each of these components in turn.

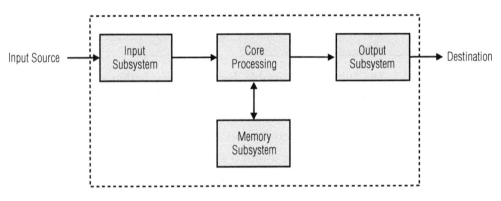

Figure 1.2 **Components of a typical media processing system**

Core Processing

Multimedia processing—that is, the actual work done by the media processor core—boils down into three main categories: format coding, decision operating and overlaying.

Software *format coders* separate into three classifications. *Encoders* convert raw video, image, audio and/or voice data into a compressed format. A digital still camera (DSC) provides a good example of an encoding framework, converting raw image sensor data into compressed JPEG format. *Decoders*, on the other hand, convert a compressed stream into an approximation (or exact duplicate) of the original uncompressed content. In playback mode, a DSC decodes the compressed pictures stored in its file system and displays them on the camera's LCD screen. *Transcoders* convert one media format into another one, for instance MP3 into Windows Media Audio 9 (WMA9).

Unlike the coders mentioned above, *decision operators* process multimedia content and arrive at some result, but do not require the original content to be stored for later retrieval. For instance, a pick-and-place machine vision system might snap pictures of electronic components and, depending on their orientation, size and location, rotate the parts for proper placement on a circuit board. However, the pictures themselves are not saved for later viewing or processing. Decision operators represent the fastest growing segment of image and video processing, encompassing applications as diverse as facial recognition, traffic light control, and security systems.

Finally, *overlays* blend multiple media streams together into a single output stream. For example, a time/date stamp might be instantiated with numerous views of surveillance footage to generate a composited output onto a video monitor. In another instance, graphical menus and icons might be blended over a background video stream for purposes of annotation or user input.

Considering all of these system types, the input data varies widely in its bandwidth requirements. Whereas raw audio might be measured in tens of kilobits/second (kb/s), compressed video could run several megabits per second (Mbps), and raw video could entail tens of megabytes per second (Mbytes/s). Thus, it is clear that the media processor needs to handle different input formats in different ways. That's where the processor's peripheral set comes into play.

Input/Output Subsystems—Peripheral Interfaces

Peripherals are classified in many ways, but a particularly useful generalization is to stratify them into functional groups like those in Table 1.1. Basically, these interfaces act to help control a subsystem, assist in moving and storing data, or enable connectivity with other systems or modules in an application.

Table 1.1 **Classes of peripherals and representative examples**

Subsystem Control	Storage	Connectivity	Data Movement
• Low-speed Serial Interfaces	• Asynchronous Memory Interface	• USB 2.0 On-the-Go/Host/Device	• Low-speed Serial Interfaces
• Programmable Timers	• ATAPI / Serial ATA	• PCI	• USB 2.0 Full Speed (12 Mbps)
• General-purpose I/O	• Flash Storage Card Interfaces	• IEEE 802.3 (Ethernet)	• 10BaseT Ethernet
• Real-Time Clock	• SDRAM/DDR Interface	• IEEE 802.11 a/b/g (WiFi)	• IEEE 802.11b
• Watchdog Timer		• IEEE 1394 (Firewire)	• Synchronous Serial Audio/Data Ports
• Host Interface		• Asynchronous Memory Interface	• Host Interface
		• Flash Storage Card Interfaces	• IEEE 802.11a/g
			• 100BaseT Ethernet
			• USB 2.0 High Speed (480 Mbps)
			• IEEE 1394 (Firewire)
			• Parallel Video/Data Ports
			• Gigabit Ethernet
			• PCI
			• PCI Express

Let's look now at some examples of each interface category.

Subsystem Control

Low-Speed Serial Interfaces

UART—*Universal Asynchronous Receiver/Transmitter*—As its name suggests, this full-duplex interface needs no separate clock or frame synchronization lines. Instead, these are decoded from the bit stream in the form of start bit, data bits, stop bits, and optional parity bits. UARTs are fairly low-speed (kbps to Mbps) and have high overhead, since every data word has control and error checking bits associated with it. UARTs can typically support RS-232 modem implementations, as well as IrDA™ functionality for close-range infrared transfer.

SPI—*Serial Peripheral Interface*—This is a synchronous, moderate-speed (tens of Mbps), full-duplex master/slave interface developed by Motorola. The basic interface consists of a clock line, an enable line, a data input ("Master In, Slave Out") and a data output ("Master Out, Slave In"). SPI supports both multimaster and multislave environments. Many video and audio codecs have SPI control interfaces, as do many EEPROMs. We'll talk more about SPI in Chapter 5.

I²C—*Inter-IC Bus*—Developed by Philips, this synchronous interface requires only two wires (clock and data) for communication. The phase relationships between the two lines determines the start and completion of data transfer. There are primarily three speed levels: 100 kbps, 400 kbps and 3.4 Mbps. Like SPI, I²C is very commonly used for the control channel in video and audio converters, as well as in some ROM-based memories.

Programmable Timers—These multifunction blocks can generate programmable pulse-width modulated (PWM) outputs that are useful for one-shot or periodic timing waveform generation, digital-to-analog conversion (with an external resistor/capacitor network, for instance), and synchronizing timing events (by starting several PWM outputs simultaneously). As inputs, they'll typically have a width-capture capability that allows precise measurement of an external pulse, referenced to the processor's system clock or another timebase. Finally, they can act as event counters, counting external events or internal processor clock cycles (useful for operating system ticks, for instance).

Real-Time Clock (RTC)—This circuit is basically a timer that uses a 32.768 kHz crystal or oscillator as a time base, where every 2^{15} ticks equals one second. In order to use more stable crystals, sometimes higher frequencies are employed instead; the most common are 1.048 MHz and 4.194 MHz. The RTC can track seconds, minutes, hours, days, and even years—with the functionality to generate a processor alarm interrupt at a particular day, hour, minute, second combination, or at regular intervals (say, every minute). For instance, a real-time clock might wake up a temperature sensor to sample the ambient environment and relay information back to the MCU via I/O pins. Then, a timer's pulse-width modulated (PWM) output could increase or decrease the speed of a fan motor accordingly.

Programmable Flags/GPIO (General Purpose Inputs/Outputs)—These all-purpose pins are the essence of flexibility. Configured as inputs, they convey status information from the outside world, and they can be set to interrupt upon receiving an edge-based or level-based signal of a given polarity. As outputs, they can drive high or low to control external circuitry. GPIO can be used in a "bit-banging" approach to simulate interfaces like I²C, detect a keypress through a key matrix arrangement, or send out parallel chunks of data via block writes to the flag pins.

Watchdog Timer—This peripheral provides a way to detect if there's a system software malfunction. It's essentially a counter that is reset by software periodically with a count value such that, in normal system operation, it never actually expires. If, for some reason, the counter reaches 0, it will generate a processor reset, a nonmaskable interrupt, or some other system event.

Host Interface—Often in multimedia applications an external processor will need to communicate with the media processor, even to the point of accessing its entire internal/external memory and register space. Usually, this external host will be the conduit to a network, storage interface, or other data stream, but it won't have the performance characteristics that allow it to operate on the data in real time. Therefore the need arises for a relatively high-bandwidth "host port interface" on the media processor. This port can be anywhere from 8 bits to 32 bits wide and is used to control the media processor and transfer data to/from an external processor.

Storage

External Memory Interface (Asynchronous and SDRAM)—An external memory interface can provide both asynchronous memory and SDRAM memory controllers. The asynchronous memory interface facilitates connection to FLASH, SRAM, EE-PROM and peripheral bridge chips, whereas SDRAM provides the necessary storage for computationally intensive calculations on large data frames. We'll talk much more about these memory interfaces in Chapter 2.

It should be noted that, while some designs may employ the external memory bus as a means to read in raw multimedia data, this is often a suboptimal solution. Because the external bus is intimately involved in processing intermediate frame buffers, it will be hard pressed to manage the real-time requirements of reading in a raw data stream while writing and reading intermediate data blocks to and from L1 memory. This is why the video port needs to be decoupled from the external memory interface, with a separate data bus.

ATAPI/Serial ATA—These are interfaces used to access mass storage devices like hard disks, tape drives, and optical drives (CD/DVD). Serial ATA is a newer standard that encapsulates the venerable ATAPI protocol, yet in a high-speed serialized form, for increased throughput, better noise performance, and easier cabling. We'll talk more about these interfaces in Chapter 2.

Flash Storage Card Interfaces—These peripherals originally started as memory cards for consumer multimedia devices like cameras and PDAs. They allow very small footprint, high density storage and connectivity, from mass storage to I/O functions like wireless networking, Bluetooth and Global Positioning System (GPS) receivers. They include CompactFlash, Secure Digital (SD), MemoryStick, and many others. Given their rugged profile, small form factor and low power requirements, they're perfect for embedded media applications. We'll discuss these cards further in Chapter 2.

Connectivity

Interfacing to PCs and PC peripherals remains essential for most portable multimedia devices, because the PC constitutes a source of constant Internet connectivity and near-infinite storage. Thus, a PC's 200-Gbyte hard drive might serve as a "staging ground" and repository for a portable device's current song list or video clips. To facilitate interaction with a PC, a high-speed port is mandatory, given the substantial file sizes of multimedia data. Conveniently, the same transport channel that allows portable devices to converse in a peer-to-peer fashion often lets them dock with the "mother ship" as a slave device.

Universal Serial Bus (USB) 2.0—*Universal Serial Bus* is intended to simplify communication between a PC and external peripherals via high-speed serial communication. USB 1.1 operated only up to 12 Mbps, and USB 2.0 was introduced in 2000 to compete with IEEE 1394, another high-speed serial bus standard. USB 2.0 supports Low Speed (1.5 Mbps), Full Speed (12 Mbps) and High Speed (480 Mbps) modes, as well as Host and On-the-Go (OTG) functionality. Whereas a USB 2.0 Host can master up to 127 peripheral connections simultaneously, OTG is meant for a peer-to-peer host/device capability, where the interface can act as an ad hoc host to a single peripheral connected to it. Thus, OTG is well-suited to embedded applications where a PC isn't needed. Importantly, USB supports *Plug-and-Play* (automatic configuration of a plugged-in device), as well as *hot pluggability* (the ability to plug in a device without first powering down). Moreover, it allows for bus-powering of a plugged-in device from the USB interface itself.

PCI—Peripheral Component Interconnect—This is a local bus standard developed by Intel Corporation and used initially in personal computers. Many media processors use PCI as a general-purpose "system bus" interface to bridge to several different types of devices via external chips (e.g., PCI to hard drive, PCI to 802.11, etc.). PCI can offer the extra benefit of providing a separate internal bus that allows the PCI bus master to send or retrieve data from an embedded processor's memory without loading down the processor core or peripheral interfaces.

Network Interface—In wired applications, Ethernet (IEEE 802.3) is the most popular physical layer for networking over a LAN (via TCP/IP, UDP and the like), whereas IEEE 802.11a/b/g is emerging as the prime choice for wireless LANs. Many Ethernet solutions are available either on-chip or bridged through another peripheral (like asynchronous memory or USB).

IEEE 1394 ("Firewire")—IEEE 1394, better known by its Apple Computer trademark "Firewire," is a high-speed serial bus standard that can connect with up to 63 devices at once. 1394a supports speeds up to 400 Mbps, and 1394b extends to 800 Mbps. Like USB, IEEE 1394 features hot pluggability and Plug-and-Play capabilities, as well as bus-powering of plugged-in devices.

Data Movement

Synchronous Serial Audio/Data Port—Sometimes called a "SPORT," this interface can attain full-duplex data transfer rates above 65 Mbps. The interface itself includes a data line (receive or transmit), clock, and frame sync. A SPORT usually supports many configurations of frame synchronization and clocking (for instance, "receive mode with internally generated frame sync and externally supplied clock"). Because of its high operating speeds, the SPORT is quite suitable for DSP applications like connecting to high-resolution audio codecs. It also features a multichannel mode that allows data transfer over several time-division-multiplexed channels, providing a very useful mode for high-performance telecom interfaces. Moreover, the SPORT easily supports transfer of compressed video streams, and it can serve as a convenient high bandwidth control channel between processors.

Parallel Video/Data Port—This is a parallel port available on some high-performance processors. Although implementations differ, this port can, for example, gluelessly transmit and receive video streams, as well as act as a general-purpose 8- to 16-bit I/O port for high-speed analog-to-digital (A/D) and digital-to-analog (D/A) converters.

Moreover, it can act as a video display interface, connecting to video encoder chips or LCD displays. On the Blackfin processor, this port is known as the "Parallel Peripheral Interface," or "PPI."

Memory Subsystem

As important as it is to get data into (or send it out from) the processor, even more important is the structure of the memory subsystem that handles the data during processing. It's essential that the processor core can access data in memory at rates fast enough to meet the demands of the application. Unfortunately, there's a tradeoff between memory access speed and physical size of the memory array.

Because of this, memory systems are often structured with multiple tiers that balance size and performance. Level 1 (L1) memory is closest to the core processor and executes instructions at the full core-clock rate. L1 memory is often split between Instruction and Data segments for efficient utilization of memory bus bandwidth. This memory is usually configurable as either SRAM or cache. Additional on-chip L2 memory and off-chip L3 memory provide additional storage (code and data)— with increasing latency as the memory gets further from the processor core.

In multimedia applications, on-chip memory is normally insufficient for storing entire video frames, although this would be the ideal choice for efficient processing. Therefore, the system must rely on L3 memory to support relatively fast access to large buffers. As we'll see in Chapter 7, the processor interface to off-chip memory constitutes a major factor in designing efficient media frameworks, because L3 access patterns must be planned to optimize data throughput.

Laying the Groundwork for an EMP Application

OK, so you're starting a brand new application, and your boss mumbled something about "…streaming media gadget that's better than our competition's." Not surprisingly, selecting a processor for multimedia applications is a complex endeavor. It involves a thorough analysis of the processor's core architecture and peripheral set, a solid understanding of how video and audio data flows through the system, and an appreciation for what level of processing is attainable at an acceptable level of power dissipation.

What Kind(s) of Media Am I Dealing With?

This is a central question, because it drives many other decisions. Here, you need to answer questions about data bandwidth, whether the data pattern is bursty or sustained, and the formats or protocols you'll need to support.

What Do I Need to Do With the Data?

This question relates to the processor performance. Among the first measures that system designers should analyze when evaluating a processor for its performance are the number of instructions performed each second, the number of operations accomplished in each processor clock cycle and the efficiency of the computation units.

As processing demands outpace technological advances in processor core evolution, there comes a point at which a single processor will not suffice for certain applications. This is one reason to consider using a *dual-core* processor. Adding another processor core not only effectively doubles the computational load capability of the processor, but also has some surprising structural benefits that aren't immediately obvious. We'll consider these in Chapter 7.

The merits of each of the aforementioned metrics can be determined by running a representative set of benchmarks on the processors under evaluation. The results will indicate whether the real-time processing requirements exceed the processor's capabilities and, equally as important, whether there will be sufficient capacity available to handle new or evolving system requirements.

Are My System Needs Likely to Change Over Time, or Will This Be a Static System?

If changes will likely be necessary to accommodate new media formats, user interface features, or the like, then a programmable solution (e.g., DSP, MCU, FPGA, Convergent Processor) will probably be required. If system requirements are firm and unlikely to change, a fixed-function ASIC might be suitable instead.

Is This a Portable Application?

Battery-powered systems dictate a whole new set of application requirements. They necessitate a power-efficient processing solution in a compact form factor. Often, this restriction involves a tradeoff between processing performance and power efficiency, and this is a realm where processors not explicitly suited for multimedia applications will tend to fall short, since they'll burn more power in accomplishing tasks for which they're not optimized.

Choosing the proper battery system for the application is also key—for energy density considerations, as well as for the weight of the end product, time between recharges, and even safety concerns.

Does my Application Require a Fixed-Point or Floating-Point Device?

Processor computation arithmetic is divided into two broad categories: fixed-point and floating-point. In general, the cutting-edge fixed-point families tend to be faster, more power-conscious and cost-sensitive, while floating-point processors offer high precision at a wide dynamic range. *Dynamic range* refers to the ratio between the largest and smallest numbers that can be represented in a numeric format, whereas *precision* refers to the granularity with which a fraction can be defined.

As illustrated in Figure 1.3, designers whose applications require only a small amount of floating-point functionality are caught in a "gray zone," often forced to move to higher-cost floating-point devices. Today, however, some fixed-point processors

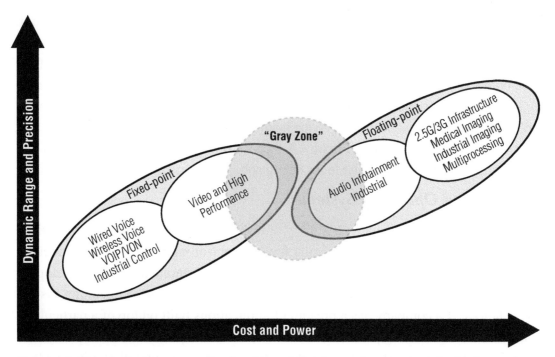

Figure 1.3 **The choice between a fixed-point and floating-point processor isn't always clear**

are running at such high clock speeds that, given the right architecture, it becomes possible to emulate floating-point operations. This approach allows the designer to trade off floating-point computational efficiency for low cost and low-power operation. Obviously, this approach will not work for a truly float-intensive application, but it presents an appealing opportunity for designers "stuck in the gray zone." We'll talk much more about fixed-point versus floating-point in Chapter 5, because audio is a typical "gray zone" application that can often be implemented in either format.

How Does the Data Get Into and/or Out of the Chip?

The right peripheral mix saves time and money by eliminating the need for external circuitry to support the required interfaces. The processor of choice should have a flexible, ample peripheral set. Refer to the "Peripheral Interfaces" discussion earlier in this chapter.

How Do I Develop on the Processor?

This is a very important question that depends as much on the needs of the individual developers as it does on the final application. Many companies have built an experience base with certain development tools packages, and they may have constructed a large code repository that they would like to leverage. Also, a strong development tools suite can dramatically increase productivity and decrease development and debug time. For instance, a powerful C/C++ compiler can facilitate easy porting of existing source code onto a new platform, and multiple optimization choices (for example, optimize for speed, power, or code density) can help designers achieve their development goals without having to invest heavily in understanding the finer points of a processor's instruction set and architecture. Figure 1.4 shows a screenshot of the VisualDSP++ development environment available for debug and development on Blackfin processors.

Do I Need an Operating System?

Operating systems perform a wide variety of tasks, from recognizing and processing high-level I/O, to tracking and managing files, to controlling multiple simultaneous processes and ensuring that they don't interfere with one another. As with development tools, many developers have strong preferences with regard to operating system (OS) choices. If a company has a breadth of applications built on top of a particular OS, there's likely a strong preference to choose their next processor based partly on that OS's availability on the new platform. Often, an application will require an OS

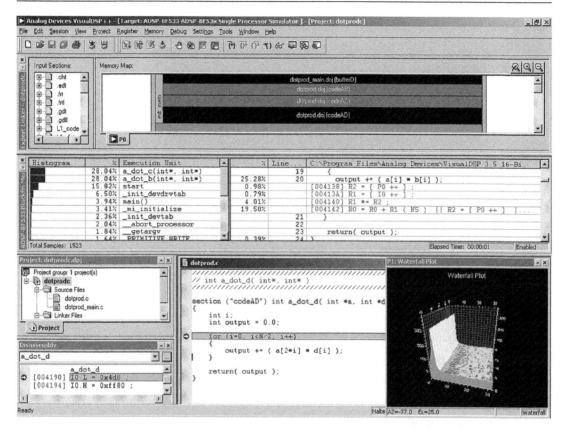

Figure 1.4 **VisualDSP++ development environment**

that's designed for a particular type of environment. For instance, some operating systems guarantee low latency (for time-critical applications), control multiple simultaneously running applications (multitasking), allow multiple users concurrent access to the system (multiuser), and/or allow several instances of an application to run at the same time (multithreading). Of course, many applications don't require an OS at all, so this issue is not always a chief concern.

What Are the Different Ways to Benchmark a Processor?

There are many different kinds of benchmarks that can be run for comparison. The problem is, it's very hard to find uniformity among all processors in a space, as far as the ways that vendors measure performance. Couple that with the fact that there are myriad ways to perform the same task on a single processor, and you can see how hard it can be to get a true objective measure of performance differences between candidate devices. That's why a good approach is to evaluate performance from several different angles:

- *Independent organizations.* These companies or consortiums attempt to create objective benchmarks for processor comparisons for specific groups of tasks. For instance, Berkeley Design Technologies, Inc. (BDTI) has a suite of signal processing kernels that are widely used for comparing DSP performance of processors. Likewise, EEMBC, the Embedded Microprocessor Benchmark Consortium, measures the capabilities of embedded processors according to several application-specific algorithms.

- *Vendor collateral.* Vendor-supplied data sheets, application notes and code examples might be the most obvious way to obtain comparative information. Unfortunately, however, you'll be hard pressed to find two vendors who run identical tests, in large part because each wants to make their processor stand out against the competition. Therefore, you might find that they've taken shortcuts in algorithm kernels or made somewhat unrealistic assumptions in power measurements. On the other hand, some vendors go to great lengths to explain how measurements were taken and how to extrapolate that data for your own set of conditions.

- *Bench testing.* If you want something done right, do it yourself! There are certain basic performance measurements that you can make across processor platforms that will give you a good idea of data flow limitations, memory access latencies, and processor bottlenecks. We'll discuss this further in Chapter 7.

Also, keep in mind that benchmarks don't always tell the whole story. Sometimes, slightly tweaking an algorithm to eliminate potentially unnecessary restrictions can make a huge difference in performance. For instance, true IEEE 854 floating-point emulation can be very expensive in terms of fixed-point computing power. However, relaxing a few constraints (such as representation of special-case numbers) can improve the floating-point emulation benchmarks considerably, as we'll see in Chapter 5.

How Much Am I Willing to Spend?

This is an important question, but you're likely to arrive at a misleading answer unless you consider the total *system design cost*. That is, Processor A might cost more than

Processor B at face value, but it could offer more peripheral connectivity (whereas B requires add-on interface chips), come in a package allowing two-layer board design (contrasted with B's package, which mandates expensive four or six-layer boards in order to route effectively), and have extra processing power that gives more headroom for future expandability.

OK, So What Processor Choices Do I Have?

Glad you asked. But there's no short answer…

There are lots of processor options to consider for embedded media applications. Each has its own pros and cons, and device selection is a crucial milestone in designing the system. In other words, you should not just make a "default" decision to use whatever processor you've used in the past. Although reflexively using a "familiar" part can speed development time, this approach can also lead to design limitations that are often unforeseen until it's too late in the process to address them appropriately. Let's review the basic device choices available:

- Application-Specific Integrated Circuit (ASIC)
- Application-Specific Standard Product (ASSP)
- Field-Programmable Gate Array (FPGA)
- Microcontroller (MCU)
- Digital Signal Processor (DSP)
- DSP/MCU Combinations (discrete or unified)

ASIC and ASSP

ASICs are "hardwired" to fit an exact application space. Because of this, they can be optimized for both power and performance as part of the design process. The ASIC usually evolves from a prototype solution. After market requirements stabilize, an ASIC can be developed to reduce the cost of the end application for high unit volumes. Thus, for markets based on stable technologies and requirements, the ASIC is often a good choice.

A cousin of the ASIC is the ASSP. The ASSP is dedicated to a specific application market but sold to many customers within that market, whereas an ASIC is usually designed and sold to a specific company. As a result, support collateral for ASSPs is usually much more extensive than with ASICs and, because of this, ASSPs are often preferred over ASICs for companies with little in-house ASIC design expertise. ASICs and ASSPs are about equal in size and cost for a given application.

While a fixed-function ASIC/ASSP might very well embody an optimal solution for a specific EMP application—including the exact peripheral set necessary to succeed in the end market—its limited flexibility hinders its ability to accommodate new features or evolving requirements. This lack of programmability, in turn, limits a consumer's options in the breadth of media formats available for recording or playback, for example.

Given today's somewhat volatile mix of old, new and emerging media formats and standards, the decision to choose an ASIC at the outset is not so clear-cut. Evolving standards do not lend themselves to ASIC implementations. Neither do complicated algorithms requiring very high processor clock speeds. After all, software mistakes on a programmable processor can be rectified with just a "recompile," but ASIC mistakes may mean a new chip spin at very high cost.

To keep pace with evolving performance, power and size requirements, there is a natural push towards developing devices in smaller silicon process geometries. However, as these geometries continue to shrink, ASIC development costs grow exponentially. Approaching 90-nanometer feature sizes, for instance, the IC mask set alone can cost around $1 million. This hefty development price tag, coupled with long design lead times, has given pause to companies pursuing an ASIC development path, as it makes it hard to keep pace in custom hardware design. In fact, this is a prime reason why EMP system developers are looking toward more programmable solutions.

FPGA (Field-Programmable Gate Array)

FPGAs help speed product development (thus shortening time to market), as there is a huge base of standard library cells available for signal and control processing applications. Because they basically comprise a string of optimized hardware blocks for a given collection of functions, they can achieve performance exceeding that of programmable processors. For instance, it's common on FPGAs to do massively parallel computation that's limited in scope, but not achievable on a standard microcontroller or DSP.

However, FPGAs are typically large, expensive, and power-hungry, when compared to programmable processing solutions and ASICs. Thus, although ideal for prototyping EMP designs, they aren't well suited as the main processor for portable multimedia applications. Also, while they afford considerable reconfigurability in implementing and modifying application blocks, FPGAs run up against a performance ceiling that is dictated by the number of gates in the package.

That said, it's hard to beat an FPGA for flexibility in interfacing a system to the outside world. Most popular peripherals and industry-standard interfaces are available as standard blocks from FPGA vendors, and the configurable nature of FPGA logic serves as a "Get Out of Jail Free card" for adapting timing and logic nuances to allow the media processor to talk nicely with any external device. Finally, an additional advantage of FPGAs is that it's straightforward to create an ASIC based on an FPGA implementation.

MCU

The typical MCU acts as a system controller. It excels in scenarios that involve many conditional operations, with frequent changes in program flow. MCU code is usually written in C or C++, and code density is paramount—algorithms are measured in terms of compiled code size. Memory systems are cache-based—automatically managing the flow of instructions into the core for execution—and the system usually runs from large memories with higher latencies than L1 memory.

Microcontrollers run the gamut in performance from 4-bit, 32 kHz models up beyond 32-bit, 500 MHz devices. However, the need to connect to media sources and targets often rules out any MCUs that aren't 32-bit capable.

To understand why the 32-bit MCU is growing so popular in the multimedia arena, first consider that the 8-bit MCU does not possess the bandwidth and computational power required to guarantee real-time operation in these systems. This is not to say that 8-bit MCUs are not useful. On the contrary, they are still very popular across a wide array of markets, from cars to cameras. Their chief selling points are very low power consumption, tiny package, excellent code density, and dirt-cheap pricing ($1.00–$2.00). Many 8-bit MCUs today have added integrated flash memory, as well as Ethernet connectivity, making them very attractive for a wide range of small, focused tasks. Moreover, they often act as a companion to a 32-bit processor in more complex systems.

What about 16-bit microcontrollers? After all, these devices do offer an increase in throughput, performance, and integration. In addition, they consume low standby current and typically offer a larger on-chip memory than their 8-bit competitors.

As a natural countermeasure to the competition presented by the 32-bit MCU, 16-bit MCU vendors have tried to expand their internal bus sizes to allow faster operation without increasing the final cost of the solution. While this approach helps somewhat, the basic gap in performance still exists, because a fundamental problem for 8/16-bit MCUs, even those running at "fast" speeds, is that they still have limited processing capability and a small memory addressing range. For instance, some 8-bit MCUs have only a few data registers, with no separate accumulator. The presence of complete register files is very important because it eliminates the requirement to frequently transfer data between memory and the accumulator.

While 16-bit MCUs (starting around $2) might cost only about twice as much as 8-bit MCUs, it's difficult to leverage legacy 8-bit design collateral. 16-bit devices usually require a completely new code development effort, as well as a new software tools suite. Given a transition from 8-bit MCUs, many developers would rather skip over the 16-bit path and jump straight to 32-bit devices (starting around $5), since they have to embark on a new learning curve and incur development cost anyway.

Viewed in this light, the actual cost of implementing a 32-bit MCU-based system is on par with that of many 16-bit solutions available today, while the performance advantage over the 16-bit MCU is significant. While the cost differential between 32-bit and 16-bit devices can be $3 or more, this gap is narrowed through increased peripheral integration and the built-in flexibility associated with much more computational headroom. Let's explore further some reasons why 32-bit devices are increasing in popularity.

As Figure 1.5 indicates, many ubiquitous peripherals (high-speed USB 2.0, PCI, etc.) support such high data rates that it becomes unwieldy or impossible to handle these data streams on 8- and 16-bit MCUs. For example, in the area of network connectivity, a maximum data register size of 8 bits, or even 16 bits, hampers the ability to support a full set of network protocols. Additionally, with multiple 32-bit data address generation registers, great increases in performance can be achieved. These 32-bit MCU features result in denser compiled code, higher continuous bandwidth, and a more flexible programming model.

This point merits more explanation. With more bits in the processor's data path and a 32-bit data and address register file, compiler support is greatly enhanced. In addition, a 32-bit device often supports both 16- and 32-bit opcodes. This allows more flexibility in the instruction set architecture, which yields improvements in code density and allows many operations to be completed in a single processor clock cycle.

These features, in turn, reduce the dependency on hand-crafted assembly code, so that developers can program primarily in a high-level language like C. A C-based programming model translates directly into lower development and maintenance costs. It also allows a company's legacy application code to transition into the 32-bit MCU environment in a much smoother manner.

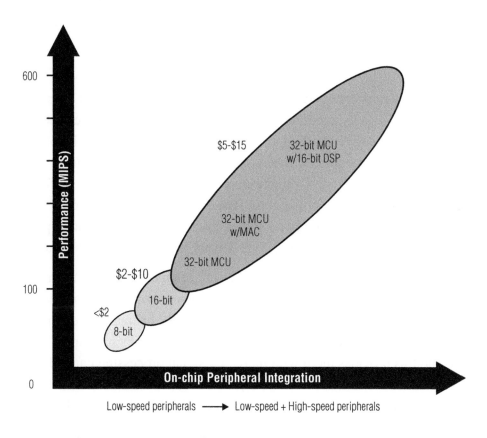

(MIPS = Millions of Instructions Per Second)

Figure 1.5 **Broad range of MCUs available**

In an EMP application, MCUs can play one of many roles. For lower-end systems, they can serve as the sole system processor, mainly doing video decode and display for modest display resolutions (often QVGA or less) and video formats (MPEG-4 Simple Profile, for example, but not H.264). For mid- to high-end systems, a DSP or an MCU with specialized accelerators is needed to perform the massive high-speed computations necessary for supporting higher resolutions and more complex formats. However, the MCU still can serve as system controller in these applications, running an operating system and managing tasks throughout the system. Furthermore, because of their rich peripheral mix, they are often instrumental in bridging between the media processor and the outside world.

DSP

Digital signal processors emerged to address the performance gap that became evident in trying to apply MCUs to compute-intensive applications. DSPs have specialized architectural constructs specifically optimized to run in tight, efficient loops, performing as many multiply-accumulate (MAC) operations as possible in a single clock cycle. A DSP is ideal for high-performance number-crunching on data buffers such as those prevalent in multimedia applications. Achieving DSP performance goals usually requires writing optimized assembly code. Because DSP algorithms can typically fit in small, low-latency on-chip memory, code density is not generally of great concern.

DSPs can run at very high clock rates, and they are often compared in terms of how many millions of MAC operations they can perform per second. This metric is known as "mega MACS," or MMACS. The MAC is a basic DSP operation used in digital filters, fast Fourier transforms (FFTs), and the like. Many DSPs have more than one MAC unit, and this provides them with increased signal processing capability. Figure 1.6 shows the recent strides made in signal processing performance, such that the cost per MMAC has plummeted, and the quantity of MMACS achievable on a single processor has skyrocketed.

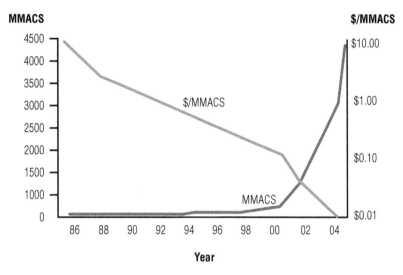

MMACS

4500
4000
3500
3000
2500
2000
1500
1000
0

$/MMACS

$10.00
$1.00
$0.10
$0.01

$/MMACS

MMACS

86 88 90 92 94 96 98 00 02 04

Year

Source: Analog Devices, Inc.
1 MMACS = 1 Million Multiply-Accumulate operations/Second, a measure of processor performance

Figure 1.6 **The sharply declining costs of embedded processing performance**

Discrete DSP + MCU

In the world of multimedia processing, a DSP is not an ideal standalone processor. It is too focused on its math routines to "run the whole show," so it relies on the slower, yet more "managerial," microcontroller (MCU) to provide asynchronous system control functionality like a user interface and an operating system.

A few different design paths have emerged that incorporate an MCU and DSP into a system design solution. For starters, you can always use a separate DSP chip and MCU chip in the design. While this might be a little pricey and take up a fair amount of real estate, it allows maximum flexibility to size each chip appropriately to the system's needs. Alternatively, some chip manufacturers take a heterogeneous multi-core approach and couple separate DSP and MCU processors in a single package.

A limitation of these approaches, however, is that the designer must partition to a fixed share of control and DSP functions; once the DSP is "maxed out," for instance, the MCU will be unable to take up the computational slack. Consequently, the final product might be highly integrated, yet inadequately structured to handle the latest media requirements. Another complexity this introduces is that separate DSP and MCU cores require separate sets of development tools, thus complicating the design environment.

A trend emerging in parallel with the growth of faster 32-bit MCUs is the drive to incorporate more DSP functionality, such as instruction set extensions and MAC units, into the microcontroller device. This philosophy is only appropriate for straightforward signal processing applications, however, because MCU clock speeds and computation architectures are fundamentally not well suited for media-rate number crunching, and therefore these MCU+DSP add-on approaches lack the essential architectural basis required to serve as platforms for advanced media processing applications.

Convergent Processor

A processor design ideal for EMP applications combines an MCU and a DSP into a single device with a unified architecture optimized not only for computation on real-time multimedia data flows, but also for control-oriented tasks. Other key features of this *Convergent Processor* are high clock rate, low power dissipation per unit of processing (mW/MMACS), small form factor (high volumetric efficiency per unit of processing), and flexible programming model.

It is important to understand that this processor is not a DSP with an enhanced instruction set, nor is it a microcontroller with DSP extensions. Instead, it is an equally high-performance media processor and compiler-friendly processor to which both classes of developers can relate.

A Convergent Processor functions simultaneously as a 16-bit DSP and a 32-bit MCU, with the ability to devote all of its resources to control tasks, to computation tasks, or to some division between the two, depending on the real-time needs of the system. It replaces a two-chip solution, saving power and board space, as well as reducing system cost and complexity. For the consumer, this means smaller, cheaper multimedia gadgets with longer battery lives.

In today's design paradigm, MCU and DSP programmers often inhabit two totally separate groups, interacting only at the "system boundary" level where their two functional worlds meet. This makes some sense, as the two groups of developers have evolved their own sets of design practices. For instance, the signal processing developer may relish the nitty-gritty details of the processor architecture and thrive on implementing tips and tricks to improve performance. On the other hand, the MCU programmer might well prefer a model of just turning on the device and letting it do the work.

The Convergent Processor satisfies both classes of engineers by supporting both direct memory access (DMA) and cache memory controllers for moving data through the system. Multiple high-speed DMA channels shuttle data between peripherals and memory systems, allowing the fine tuning controls sought by DSP programmers. Conversely, on-chip configurable instruction and data caches allow a hands-off approach of managing code and data in a manner very familiar to MCU programmers. Often, at the system integration level a combination of both approaches is ideal.

Another reason for the historical separation of MCU and DSP development groups is that the two processors have two separate sets of design imperatives. From a technical standpoint, engineers responsible for architecting a system are sometimes hesitant to mix a "control" application with signal processing on the same device. Their most common fear is that non-real-time tasks will interfere with time-critical tasks. For instance, the programmer who handles functions such as the graphical user interface (GUI) or the networking stack shouldn't have to worry about hampering the real-time signal processing activities of the system. Of course the definition of "real-time" will vary based on the specific application. In an embedded application, the focus is on the time required to service an interrupt.

While the MCU control code is usually written in C and is library-based, the real-time DSP code is typically written in assembly format and is handcrafted to extract the most possible performance for a given application. Unfortunately, this optimization also limits the portability of an application and therefore propagates the need for divergent skill sets and tools suites between the two programming teams on future projects.

The Convergent Processor approach allows developers to create a C/C++ unified programming code base, leveraging existing application code from previous efforts. Because the processor is optimized for both control and signal-processing operations, compilers can generate code that is both "tight" (from a code density standpoint) and efficient (for computationally intensive signal processing applications). Any gap in compiler performance is closed by the high operating frequencies of these parts. Additionally, targeted assembly coding is still an option for optimizing critical processing loops.

The Convergent Processor allows utilization of a single tool chain for code development on a single, united platform. Thus, developers can learn one instruction set and maintain a single code base running on a single operating system. There's one set of software application programming interfaces (APIs) and drivers, one debugger, one loader, one linker, one language, and so forth. A single learning curve means dramatic improvement in development productivity.

While this unified approach can greatly reduce the requirement of writing code in assembly, this fact alone doesn't necessarily justify the switch to this unified platform. Operating system (OS) support is also key, because this allows software task layering. To achieve targeted performance, a prioritizable event/interrupt controller is crucial, with context switching through hardware-based stack and frame pointer support. With these architectural constructs, the Convergent Processor allows developers to create applications that include both worlds—system control and real-time signal processing—on the same device.

The high processing speeds that Convergent Processors can achieve translate into several tangible benefits. The first is time to market: there can be considerable savings in reducing or bypassing the code optimization effort if there's plenty of processing headroom to spare. A second key benefit is reduced software maintenance, which can otherwise dominate a product's lifecycle cost. Finally, for scalable device architectures, there's the possibility of designing a system on the most capable processing family member, and then "rightsizing" the processor for the computational footprint of the final application.

A Look Inside the Blackfin Processor

If you haven't guessed by now, the Convergent Processor will be our focus as we navigate through the complexities of embedded media processing. Although we will strive to offer generic principles and suggestions, we will use Analog Devices' Blackfin processor as a basis for grounding our discussion in concrete examples. Therefore, let's take a little time now to review some basic Blackfin processor architecture, in order to set the stage for our discussions throughout the rest of this book. If you'd like a more detailed treatment than what we present here, please refer to References 1, 2, and 3 in the Appendix.

System View

Figure 1.7 shows a simplified diagram of a representative Blackfin processor at a "system-on-chip" level. The processor core scales up beyond 600 MHz instruction execution rates. It connects to an on-chip Level 1 (L1) memory subsystem consisting of a mix of high-speed cache and SRAM for both instruction and data storage. Integrated peripherals allow connection to the outside world, and system control blocks aid management of processor operation. A System Interface Unit facilitates access between the core, peripherals, and external synchronous and asynchronous memory chips.

Of course, Figure 1.7 only shows a sample part in the Blackfin family. Variants include dual processor cores (each with their own L1 memory blocks), different on-chip memory configurations, and a multitude of peripheral block combinations.

ADSP-BF533/532/531 Blackfin

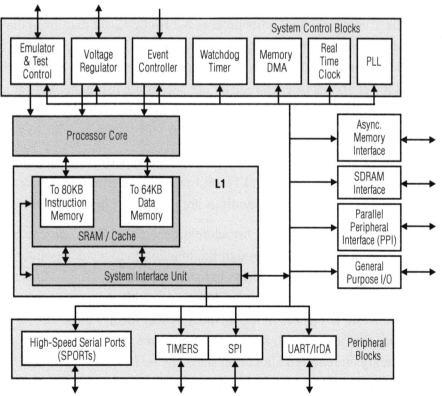

Figure 1.7 **System view of representative single-core Blackfin processor**

Computational Units

Figure 1.8 shows a functional diagram of a representative Blackfin processor core. At the computational heart of the core are two 16-bit multipliers and two 40-bit accumulators, which are collectively called *multiply-accumulate*, or MAC, units. Each MAC can perform a 16-bit by 16-bit multiply per cycle, with accumulation to a 40-bit result. Also, a 32-bit integer multiply can be performed in three cycles.

Additionally (no pun intended), there are two 40-bit *arithmetic logic units* (ALUs), which perform a traditional set of arithmetic and logical operations on 16-bit or 32-bit data.

Blackfin's four 8-bit *video ALUs* perform useful byte-wise image and video manipulations, including byte alignment and packing, 16-bit and 8-bit adds with clipping, 8-bit averaging, and 8-bit subtract/absolute value/accumulate (SAA) operations.

Moreover, a 40-bit *barrel shifter* can deposit data and perform shifting, rotating, normalization, and extraction operations.

All together, these computational units process 8-, 16- or 32-bit data from the *data register file*, which consists of eight registers, R0 through R7. These registers can be used as any combination of sixteen 16-bit data registers or eight 32-bit registers. The upper and lower 16 bits of each register are accessible using the register name followed by ".H" for the upper 16 bits and ".L" for the lower 16 bits. For instance, "R0.L" accesses the lower 16 bits of data register 0.

For some instructions, two 16-bit ALU operations can be performed simultaneously on register pairs (a 16-bit high half and 16-bit low half of a compute register). By also using the second ALU, four 16-bit operations are possible at the same time.

A separate register file is also present for address generation. This *address register file* consists of pointer registers P0 through P5, in addition to a stack pointer (SP) and a frame pointer register (FP). The address registers are capable of 8-, 16- and 32-bit accesses, and they support a wide range of RISC-type addressing operations. A frame and stack can be set up anywhere in the memory space. Ideally these can be located somewhere inside the processor to improve performance, although this is not always practical, depending on required allocation size. The *address arithmetic unit* provides data address generation (DAG) functionality, allowing simultaneous dual fetches from memory. It contains a multi-ported register file consisting of four sets of 32-bit Index,

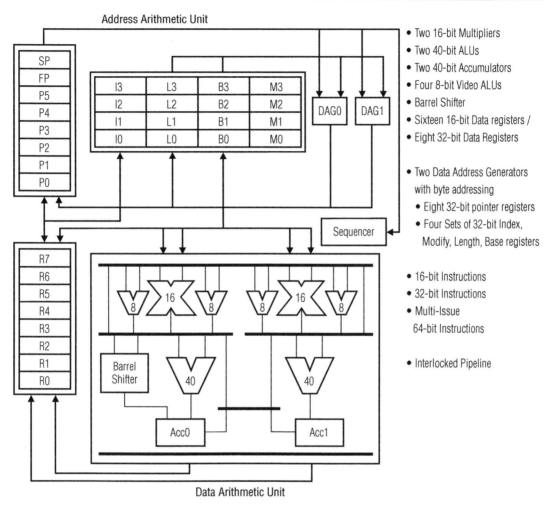

Address Arithmetic Unit

- Two 16-bit Multipliers
- Two 40-bit ALUs
- Two 40-bit Accumulators
- Four 8-bit Video ALUs
- Barrel Shifter
- Sixteen 16-bit Data registers /
- Eight 32-bit Data Registers

- Two Data Address Generators
  with byte addressing
  - Eight 32-bit pointer registers
  - Four Sets of 32-bit Index,
    Modify, Length, Base registers

- 16-bit Instructions
- 32-bit Instructions
- Multi-Issue
  64-bit Instructions

- Interlocked Pipeline

Data Arithmetic Unit

Figure 1.8 **Functional diagram of Blackfin processor core**

Modify, Length, and Base registers (for circular buffering), and eight additional 32-bit pointer registers (for C-style indexed stack manipulation).

Memory Model

Blackfin devices support a modified Harvard architecture in combination with a hierarchical memory structure that views memory as a single, unified 4-Gbyte address space using 32-bit addresses. All resources, including internal memory, external memory, and I/O control registers, occupy separate sections of this common address space.

Taken together, the Blackfin memory space is structured to balance cost and performance between fast, low-latency on-chip memory and larger, lower cost and lower performance off-chip memory systems. L1 on-chip memories typically operate at the full processor speed with little or no latency. At the L1 level, the instruction memory holds instructions only, the data memories hold data, and a dedicated scratchpad data memory stores stack and local variable information. Level 2 (L2) on-chip memories, when present, are usually bigger than L1 memories, but incur longer access latencies. The L2 memory is a unified instruction and data memory and can hold any mixture of code and data required by the system design. Level 3 (L3) external memory is larger and cheaper (per byte), but it has longer latencies than any on-chip memory.

DMA

The Blackfin processor uses direct memory access (DMA) to transfer data within memory spaces or between a memory space and a peripheral. The processor can specify data transfer operations and return to normal processing while the fully integrated DMA controller carries out the data transfers independent of processor activity. The DMA controller can perform data transfers between memory and on-chip peripherals ("Peripheral DMA"), as well as between and within L1/L2/L3 memory spaces ("Memory DMA" or "MemDMA").

DMA transfers can be descriptor-based or register-based. Descriptor-based DMA transfers require a set of parameters stored within memory to initiate a DMA sequence. This sort of transfer allows the chaining together of multiple DMA sequences. In descriptor-based DMA operations, a DMA channel can be programmed to automatically set up and start another DMA transfer after the current sequence completes. Register-based DMA, on the other hand, allows the processor to directly program DMA registers to initiate a DMA transfer. Upon transfer completion, these registers can be automatically updated with their original setup values for continuous transfer, if needed.

The DMA engine is crucial to the successful operation of an EMP application. As such, we will be discussing DMA in much greater detail throughout the course of this book. We even devote an entire chapter to it—Chapter 3.

Instruction Flow

The *program sequencer* controls the instruction execution flow, including instruction alignment and decoding. The instruction pipeline, which holds the addresses of all instructions currently being fetched, decoded and executed, is fully interlocked. This means that it automatically inserts stalls to guarantee correct operation when executing instructions that depend on data that's not yet available (e.g., a result of a previous operation that hasn't yet completed).

The program sequencer determines the next instruction address by examining both the current instruction being executed and the current state of the processor. Generally, the processor executes instructions from memory in sequential order by incrementing the look-ahead address. However, when encountering one of the following structures, the processor will execute an instruction that is not at the next sequential address:

- *Loops.* One sequence of instructions executes several times with zero overhead. Dedicated loop registers are available to support nested loops without having to continually fetch the loop start and end addresses.

- *Subroutines.* The processor temporarily interrupts sequential flow to execute instructions from another part of memory.

- *Jumps.* Program flow transfers permanently to another part of memory.

- *Interrupts and Exceptions.* A runtime event or instruction triggers the execution of a subroutine.

- *Idle.* This instruction causes the processor to stop operating and hold its current state until an interrupt or wakeup occurs. Then, if appropriate, the processor services the interrupt and continues normal execution.

Event Handler

Like many microcontrollers, Blackfin processors allow both interrupts and exceptions. Both kinds of events cause pipelined instructions to suspend execution in favor of servicing the triggering event. An interrupt is an event that changes normal processor instruction flow and is asynchronous to program flow. In contrast, an exception is a software-initiated event whose effects are synchronous to program flow. By trapping exceptions, the end system can guard against invalid or illegal programming.

The event management system supports nesting and prioritization. Consequently, several service routines may be active at any time, and a low priority event may be pre-empted by one of higher priority. The architecture employs a two-level event control mechanism. The system interrupt controller (SIC) works with the core event controller (CEC) to prioritize and control all system interrupts. The SIC provides a mapping between the many peripheral interrupt sources and the prioritized general-purpose interrupt inputs of the core. This mapping is programmable, and individual interrupt sources can be masked in the SIC.

We'll talk more about event handling in Chapter 4.

Protection of Resources

An important aspect of system control is task management. Increasingly, a real-time operating system (RTOS) is employed to handle the wide range of ongoing, concurrent tasks in a complex system. The RTOS simplifies the programming model by providing support for task scheduling and management, and it usually runs on an MCU, since DSPs do not have all of the RTOS-friendly features needed for efficient implementation.

Blackfin's architecture, however, facilitates RTOS development with several important features. One is the provision of separate stack and frame pointers to reduce latency of OS calls and interrupt/exception handling. Another is the ability to restrict access to protected or reserved memory locations. This allows one task, via a paging mechanism, to block memory or instruction accesses by another task. An exception is generated whenever unauthorized access is made to a protected area of memory. The kernel will service this exception and take the appropriate action.

Yet a third RTOS-friendly feature is the existence of separate Supervisor and User modes. Supervisor mode has unrestricted use of all system and core resources, whereas User mode can only access a subset of system resources, thus providing a protected software environment. These crucial protection features prevent users from unknowingly or maliciously accessing or affecting shared parts of the system.

DSPs usually operate in the equivalent of Supervisor mode, allowing full access to all system resources at all times, whereas MCUs provide the analog of a User mode that allows applications to run on top of an OS. On a Blackfin device, both operating modes coexist under one unified architecture, so that a system can restrict user applications to accessing system resources only through the OS.

Programming Model

The Blackfin software development model enables high-performance DSP functionality within a framework matching that of typical RISC MCU devices. System-level and product-level application code can be written in C/C++ and layered on top of multiple standard real-time operating systems. Lower-level code, such as raw data movement and processing, can be optimized in mixed assembly and C/C++ code, utilizing hand-tuned assembly libraries. Blackfin can be just as easily programmed in assembler (using an intuitive algebraic assembly language), compiled C/C++ code, or a mixture of both.

The Blackfin instruction set is optimized so that 16-bit opcodes represent the most frequently used instructions. Complex DSP instructions are encoded into 32-bit opcodes as multifunction instructions. A 64-bit multi-issue capability allows a 32-bit instruction to execute in parallel with two 16-bit instructions. This allows the programmer to use many of the core resources in a single instruction cycle.

Power Management

Along with the increased performance levels of embedded media processing applications comes higher clocking rates and, thus, higher power dissipation. This is why the processor needs an intelligent way to dynamically tailor its clock frequency commensurate with the tasks it's performing. Consider a portable media player, for instance, profiled in Figure 1.9. The processor might need to run at 600 MHz for video processing, but only need about 200 MHz performance for audio processing. Therefore, if the device is acting as an MP3 player, why should it run at 600 MHz and discharge the battery faster? Moreover, lowering clock frequency allows a processor to run at lower operating voltage, thus maximizing battery life.

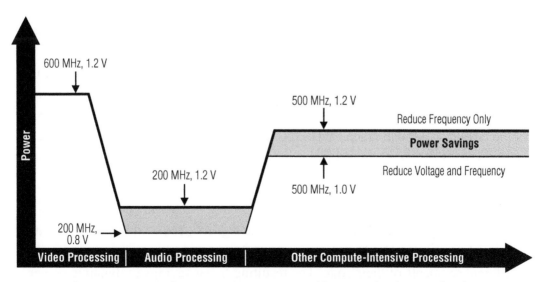

Figure 1.9 **Dynamic Power Management achieves optimal power levels by allowing both voltage and frequency tuning for the task at hand**

Control of power dissipation has long been a feature of embedded controllers. However, when the system requires DSP functionality as well, the power choices have been less than ideal. If discrete MCU and DSP chips are used in power-sensitive applications, a separate switching regulator must often be provided for each one, because the core voltages of the two devices frequently differ. This results in decreased power conversion efficiency and an increased design footprint, ultimately increasing layout complexity and solution cost. Moreover, when separate MCU and DSP cores are combined on one chip, the power solution is inherently nonoptimal, because it must service the needs of two completely independent processors with different loading profiles.

In contrast, the Blackfin processor contains an integrated dynamic power management (DPM) controller. Several intrinsic power modes are available to support a range of system performance levels. Additionally, clocks to unused peripherals and L2 memory are automatically disabled. The operating frequency can be adjusted over a wide range to satisfy stratifications in DSP/MCU processing needs. Finally, the voltage can be adjusted (either externally or through an integrated switching controller) to offer exponential savings in power dissipation.

Blackfin's clock generation unit houses the phase-locked loop (PLL) and associated control circuitry. The PLL is highly programmable, allowing the user to control the processor's performance characteristics and power dissipation dynamically.

Figure 1.10 shows a simplified block diagram of the clock generation unit. Generally speaking, an input crystal or oscillator signal (10 to 40 MHz) is applied to the CLKIN pin to generate f_{ref}. A selectable 1x-to-64x multiplier then multiplies this signal to generate the VCO frequency. Then, separate dividers independently generate core-clock (CCLK) and system/peripheral-clock (SCLK) frequencies. Depending on the specific device, CCLK can reach rates exceeding 600 MHz, while SCLK can attain a maximum of 133 MHz. Control logic ensures that the system clock frequency will not exceed the core-clock frequency.

The great advantage in this approach is that CCLK and SCLK can be changed "on-the-fly," with very little cycle overhead. Thus, designers needn't think twice about changing clock frequencies in order to meet different performance requirements for different segments of their code. The resulting linear savings in dynamic power dissipation comes at no implementation cost, from the designer's perspective.

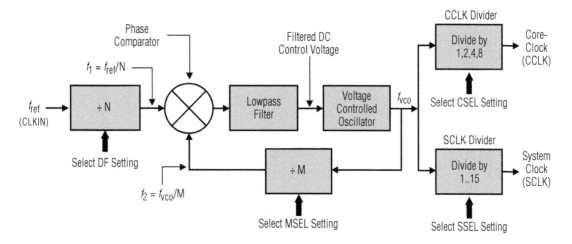

Note that when the loop is phase-locked, $f_1 = f_2$. Hence $f_{vco} = M f_{ref}/N$.
DF, MSEL, CSEL, SSEL are Blackfin PLL configuration fields.

Figure 1.10 **Functional block diagram of Blackfin's clock generation unit**

Another feature of the Clock Generation Unit is that it can be bypassed to allow the CLKIN signal to pass straight through to CCLK. This capability permits use of a very low frequency CCLK during inactive operation intervals, to further reduce overall power dissipation.

We'll elaborate much more on these power management details in Chapter 8. For now, we primarily wanted to introduce you to the CCLK and SCLK functionality and terminology, because we use it extensively in the chapters to come.

What's Next? ·

We hope that this chapter has given you an overview of the nature of embedded media applications, what processing choices are available for EMP applications, and how to drive toward your final device decision from a "top-down" approach, guided by answering key questions about the application requirements. Furthermore, we introduced basic architectural concepts for the Convergent Processor model on which we'll focus in subsequent chapters. In the next chapter, we'll start by digging into the memory subsystem of a processor in an EMP application.

Memory Systems

Introduction

To attain maximum performance, an embedded processor should have independent bus structures to fetch data and instructions concurrently. This feature is a fundamental part of what's known as a *Harvard architecture*. Nomenclature aside, it doesn't take a Harvard grad to see that, without independent bus structures, every instruction or data fetch would be in the critical path of execution. Moreover, instructions would need to be fetched in small increments (most likely one at a time), because each data access the processor makes would need to utilize the same bus. In the end, performance would be horrible.

With separate buses for instructions and data, on the other hand, the processor can continue to fetch instructions while data is accessed simultaneously, saving valuable cycles. In addition, with separate buses a processor can pipeline its operations. This leads to increased performance (higher attainable core-clock speeds) because the processor can initiate future operations before it has finished its currently executing instructions.

So it's easy to understand why today's high-performance devices have more than one bus each for data and instructions. In Blackfin processors, for instance, each core can fetch up to 64 bits of instructions and two 32-bit data words in a single core-clock (CCLK) cycle. Alternately, it can fetch 64 bits of instructions and one data word in the same cycle as it writes a data word.

There are many excellent references on the Harvard architecture, such as Reference 6 in the Appendix. However, because it is a straightforward concept, we will instead focus on the memory hierarchy underlying the Harvard architecture.

Memory Spaces

Embedded processors have hierarchical memory architectures that strive to balance several levels of memory with differing sizes and performance levels. The memory closest to the core processor (known as Level 1, or L1, memory) operates at the full core-clock rate. The use of the term "closest" is literal, in that L1 memory is physically close to the core processor on the silicon die, so as to achieve the highest

(a) **L1 Instruction Memory**

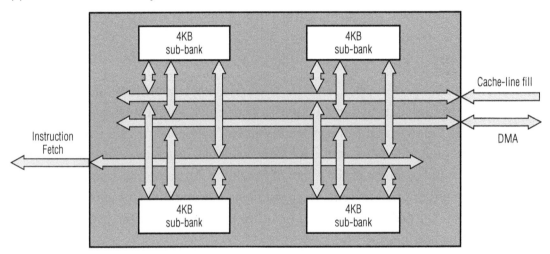

(b) **L1 Data Memory**

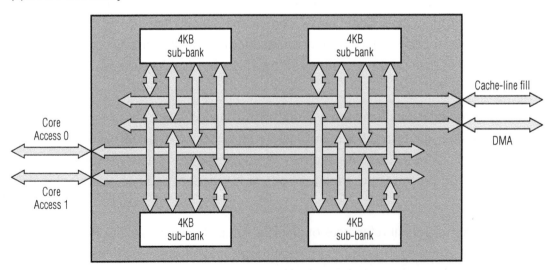

Figure 2.1 **L1 memory architecture**

operating speeds. L1 memory is most often partitioned into instruction and data segments, as shown in Figure 2.1, for efficient utilization of memory bus bandwidth. L1 instruction memory supports instruction execution in a single cycle; likewise, L1 data memory runs at the full core-clock rate and supports single-cycle accesses.

Of course, L1 memory is necessarily limited in size. For systems that require larger code sizes, additional on-chip and off-chip memory is available—with increased latency. Larger on-chip memory is called Level 2 (L2) memory, and we refer to external memory as Level 3 (L3) memory. Figure 2.2 shows a summary of how these memory types vary in terms of speed and size. While the L1 memory size usually comprises tens of kbytes, the L2 memory on-chip is measured in hundreds of kbytes. What's more, while Harvard-style L1 requires us to partition our code and data into separate places, L2 and L3 provide a "unified" memory space. By this, we mean that the instruction and data fetch units of the processor can both access a common memory space.

In addition, note the operating speed of each memory block. L1 memory runs at the CCLK rate. L2 memory does as well, except that accesses typically take multiple CCLK cycles. With L3 memory, the fastest access we can achieve is measured in system clock (SCLK) cycles, usually much slower than the CCLK rate.

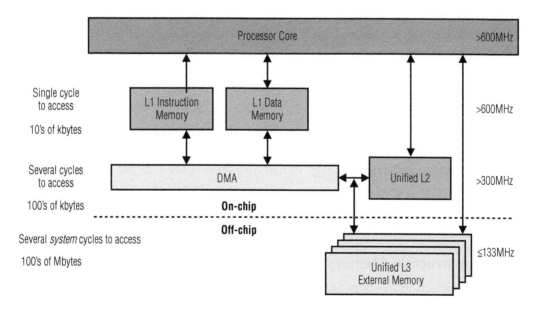

Figure 2.2 **Memory level summary**

On Blackfin processors, L1 and L2 memories are each further divided into sub-banks to allow concurrent core and DMA access in the same cycle. For dual-core devices, the core path to L2 memory is multiplexed between both cores, and the various DMA channels arbitrate for the DMA path into L2 memory. Don't worry too much about DMA right now; we'll focus on it in Chapter 3. For now, it is just important to think of it as a resource that can compete with the processor for access to a given memory space.

As we mentioned earlier, L3 memory is defined as "off-chip memory." In general, multiple internal data paths lead to the external memory interface. For example, one or two core access paths, as well as multiple DMA channels, all can contend for access to L3 memory. When SDRAM is used as external memory, some subset of the processor's external memory interface can be shared with asynchronous memory, such as flash or external SRAM. However, using DDR-SDRAM necessitates a separate asynchronous interface because of the signal integrity and bus loading issues that accompany DDR. Later in this chapter, we will review the most popular L3 memory types.

L1 Instruction Memory

Compared with data fetches, instruction fetches usually occur in larger block sizes. The instructions that run on a processor may range in size in order to achieve the best code density. For instance, the most frequently used Blackfin instructions are encoded in 16 bits, but Blackfin instruction sizes also come in 32-bit and 64-bit variants. The instruction fetch size is 64 bits, which matches the largest instruction size. When the processor accesses instructions from internal memory, it uses 64-bit bus structures to ensure maximum performance.

What happens when code runs from L3 memory that is less than 64 bits wide? In this case, the processor still issues a fetch of 64 bits, but the external memory interface will have to make multiple accesses to fill the request. Take a look at Figure 2.3 to see how instructions might actually align in memory. You'll see that the 64-bit fetch can contain as many as four instructions or as few as one. When the processor reads from memory instructions that are different in size, it must align them in order to prevent problems accessing those instructions later.

Using L1 Instruction Memory for Data Placement

In general, instruction memory is meant to be used only for instructions, because in a Harvard architecture, data can't be accessed from this memory directly. However, due to the code efficiency and low byte count that some applications require, data

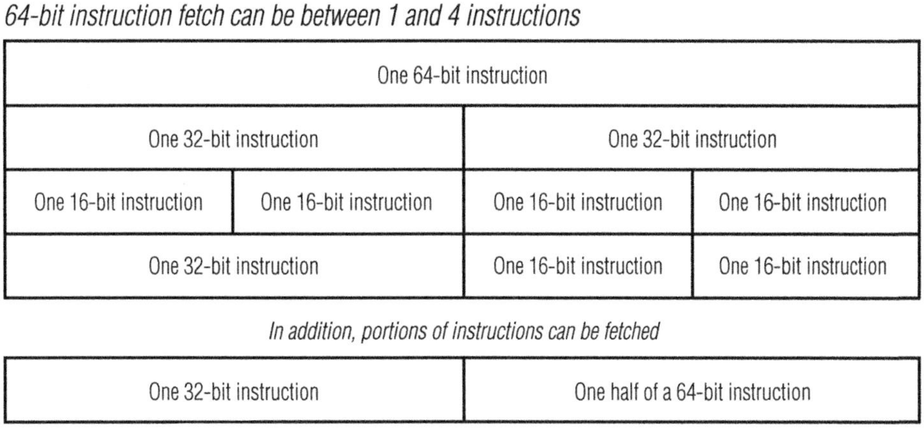

64-bit instruction fetch can be between 1 and 4 instructions

One 64-bit instruction			
One 32-bit instruction		One 32-bit instruction	
One 16-bit instruction	One 16-bit instruction	One 16-bit instruction	One 16-bit instruction
One 32-bit instruction		One 16-bit instruction	One 16-bit instruction

In addition, portions of instructions can be fetched

One 32-bit instruction	One half of a 64-bit instruction

Figure 2.3 **Instruction alignment**

is sometimes staged in L1 instruction memory. In these cases, the DMA controller moves the data between instruction and data memories. While this is not standard practice, it can help in situations where you'd otherwise have to add more external memory. In general, the primary ways of accessing instruction memory are via instruction fetches and via the DMA controller. A back-door method is frequently provided as well, as we will learn in our Chapter 4 discussion on working with cache.

L1 Data Memory

L1 data memory exists as the complement to L1 instruction memory. As you might expect from our L1 instruction memory discussion, the processor can access L1 data memory in a single cycle. As stated earlier, internal memory banks usually are constructed of multiple sub-banks to allow concurrent access between multiple resources.

On the Blackfin processor, L1 data memory banks consist of four 4-kbyte sub-banks, each with multiple ports as shown in Figure 2.1b. In a given cycle, the core can access data in two of the four sub-banks, while the DMA controller can access a third one. Also, when the core accesses two data words on different 32-bit boundaries, it can fetch data (8, 16 or 32 bits in size) from the same sub-bank in a single cycle while the DMA controller accesses another sub-bank in the same cycle. See Figure 2.4 to get a better picture of how using sub-banks can increase performance. In the "un-optimized" diagram, all of the buffers are packed into two sub-banks. In the "optimized" diagram, the buffers are spread out to take advantage of all four sub-banks.

Partitioning Data in L1 Data Memory Sub-Banks

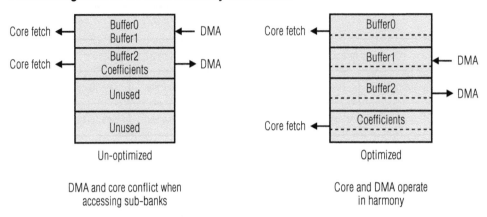

Figure 2.4 **Memory bank structure and corresponding bus structure**

We've seen that there are two separate internal buses for data accesses, so up to two fetches can be performed from L1 memory in a single cycle. When fetching to a location outside L1 memory, however, the accesses occur in a pipelined fashion. In this case, the processor has both fetch operations in the same instruction. The second fetch initiates immediately after the first fetch starts. This creates a *head start* condition that improves performance by reducing the cycle count for the entire instruction to execute.

Cache Overview

By itself, a multilevel memory hierarchy is only moderately useful, because it could force a high-speed processor to run at much slower speeds in order to accommodate larger applications that only fit in slower external memory. To improve performance, there's always the option of manually moving important code into and out of internal SRAM. We'll review this "code overlay" concept in Chapter 4. But there's also a simpler option—cache.

On the Blackfin processor, portions of L1 data and instruction memory can be configured as either SRAM or cache, while other portions are always SRAM. When L1 memory is configured as cache, it is no longer directly accessible for reads or writes as addressable memory.

What Is Cache?

You may be wondering, "Why can't more L1 memory be added to my processor?" After all, if all of a processor's memory ran at the same speed as L1, caches and external memory would not be required. Of course, the reason is that L1 memory is expensive in terms of silicon size, and big L1 memories drive up processor prices.

Enter the cache. Specifically, cache is a smaller amount of advanced memory that improves performance of accesses to larger amounts of slower, less-expensive memories.

By definition, a cache is a set of memory locations that can store something for fast access when the application actually needs it. In the context of embedded processors, this "something" can be either data or instructions. We can map a relatively small cache to a very large cacheable memory space. Because the cache is much smaller than the overall cacheable memory space, the cacheable addresses alias into locations in cache, as shown in Figure 2.5. The high-level goal of cache is to maximize

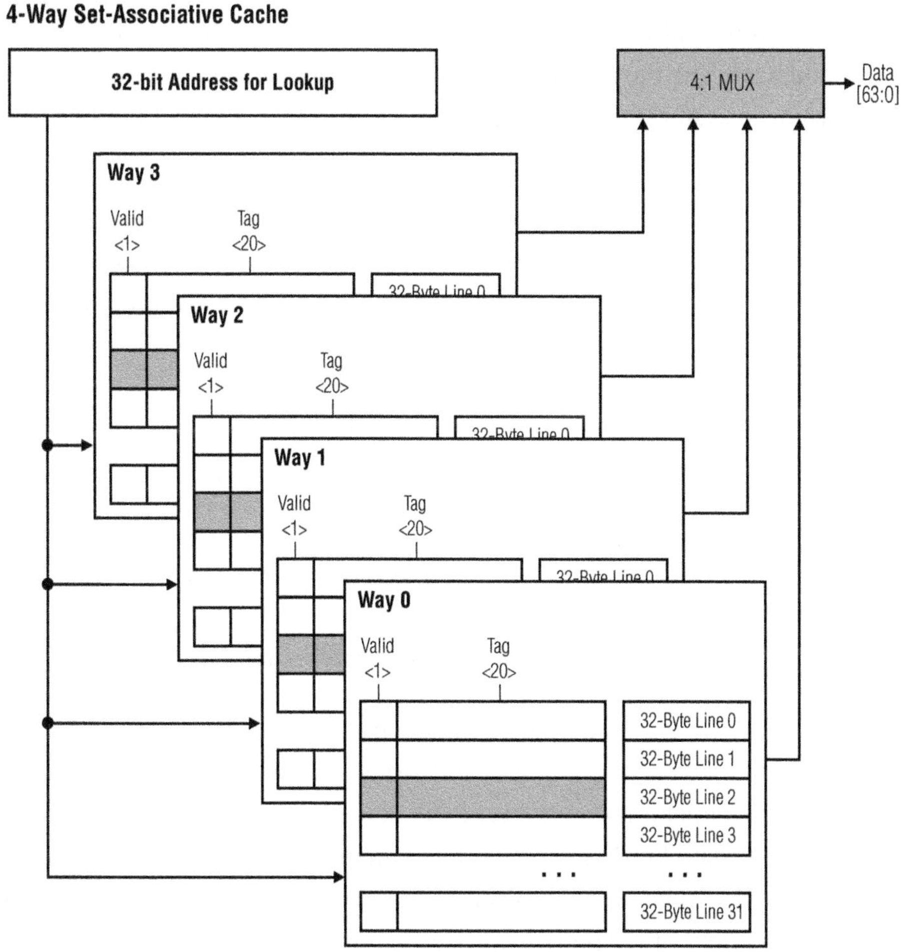

4-Way Set-Associative Cache

Figure 2.5 **Cache concept diagram**

the percentage of "hits," which are instances when the processor finds what it needs in cache instead of having to wait until it gets fetched from slower memory.

Actually, cache increases performance in two ways. First, code that runs most often will have a higher chance of being in single-cycle memory when the processor needs it. Second, fills done as a result of cache line misses will help performance on linear code and data accesses, because by the time the first new instruction or data block has been brought into the cache, the next set of instructions (or data) is also already on its way into cache. Therefore, any cycles associated with a cache-line miss are spread out across multiple accesses.

We will include some rough performance estimates in Chapter 4 with and without cache enabled to give you some idea of how it can help. Just as a sneak peek, instruction cache almost always helps improve performance, whereas data cache is sometimes beneficial. The only time that instruction cache can cause problems is in the highest performance systems that tax the limits of processor bus bandwidths. We will discuss this particular case in Chapter 7 as part of the "Performance-based framework."

Each sub-bank of cache consists of something called *ways*. Each way is made up of *lines*, the fundamental components of cache. Each cache line consists of a collection of consecutive bytes. On Blackfin devices, a cache line is 32 bytes long. Figure 2.6 shows how Blackfin instruction and data caches are organized.

(a) **Instruction Cache**

- One 16KB bank
- Four 4KB sub-banks
- Four ways per sub-bank
- Each 1KB way has 32 lines
- There are 32 bytes per line

(b) **Data Cache**

- Two 16KB banks
- Four sub-banks per bank
- Two ways per sub-bank
- Each 2KB way has 64 lines
- There are 32 bytes per line

Figure 2.6 **Blackfin cache organization**

Ways and lines combine to form locations in cache where instructions and data are stored. As we mentioned earlier, memory locations outside the cache alias to specific ways and lines, depending on the type of cache that is implemented. Let's talk now about the three main kinds of cache: direct-mapped, fully associative, and set-associative. Figure 2.7 illustrates the basic differences between types. It is important to understand the variety of cache your processor employs, because this determines how the cacheable memory aliases to the actual cache memory.

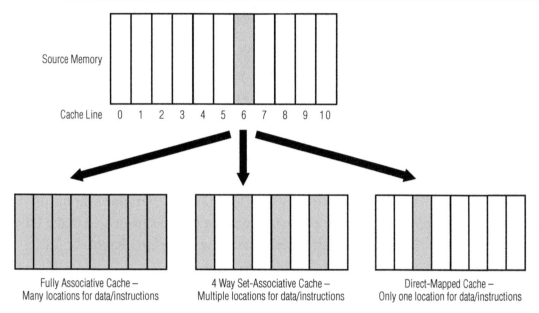

Figure 2.7 **Cache architectures**

Direct-Mapped Cache

When we talk about a cache that is *direct-mapped,* we mean that each memory location maps to a single cache line that it shares with many other memory locations. Only one of the many addresses that share this line can use it at a given time. While this is the simplest scheme to implement, it provides the lowest percentage of performance increase. Since there is only one site in the cache for any given external memory location, code that has lots of branches will always result in cache line misses. Direct mapping only helps when code flow is very linear, a situation that does not fit the control nature of the typical embedded application.

The primary problem with this type of cache is that the probability the desired code or data is actually in cache is the lowest of the three cache models we describe. *Thrashing* occurs when a line in cache is constantly being replaced with another line. This is much more common in a direct-mapped cache than in other cache architectures.

Fully Associative Cache

In a *fully associative* cache, any memory location can be cached in any cache line. This is the most complicated (and costly) scheme to implement in silicon, but performance will always be the best. Essentially, this implementation greatly reduces the number of cache line misses in steady-state operation. Because all addresses map to all sites in the cache, the probability increases that what you want to be in cache will actually be there.

N-Way Set-Associative Cache

The previous two cache designs represent the two ends of the performance spectrum. The final design we will discuss is actually the most common implementation. It is called the *N-way set-associative* cache, where *N* is typically 2 or 4. This scheme represents a compromise between the two previously mentioned types of cache. In this scenario, the cache is comprised of sets of *N* lines each, and any memory address can be cached in any of those *N* lines within a set. This improves hit ratios over the direct-mapped cache, without the added design complexity and silicon area of the fully associative design. Even so, it achieves performance very close to that of the fully associative model.

In Blackfin processors, the data cache is 2-way set-associative, and instruction cache is 4-way set-associative. This mostly has to do with the typical profile of execution and data access patterns in an embedded application. Remember, the number of ways increases the number of locations within the cache to which each address can alias, so it makes sense to have more for instruction cache, where addressing normally spans a larger range.

More Cache Details

As we saw in Figure 2.6, a cache structure is made up of lines and ways. But there's certainly more to cache than this. Let's take a closer look.

Each line also has a "tag array" that the processor uses to find matches in the cache. When an instruction executes from a cached external memory location, the processor first checks the tag array to see if the desired address is in cache. It also checks the "validity bit" to determine whether a cache line is *valid* or *invalid*. If a line is valid, this means the contents of this cache line contain values that can be used directly. On the other hand, when the line is invalid, its contents can't be used. We will review an example in Chapter 4 to illustrate how and why cache lines become valid and invalid.

As we stated before, a *cache hit* refers to the case when the data (or instruction) the core wants to access is already in the cache. Likewise, a *cache miss* refers to the case when the processor needs information from the cache that is not yet present. When this happens, a *cache-line fill* commences.

As noted earlier, the information in the tag array determines whether a match exists or not. At the simplest level, a cache-line fill is just a series of fetches made from cacheable memory. The difference is that when cache is off, the core fetches only what it needs, and when cache is on, the core may actually fetch more than it needs (or hopefully, what it will need soon!).

So, as an example, let's assume cache is enabled and the location being accessed has been configured as cacheable. The first time a processor accesses a specific location in, say, L3 memory, a cache miss will generate a cache-line fill. Once something is brought into cache, it stays there until it is forced out to make room for something else that the core needs. Alternatively, as we will soon see, it is sometimes prudent to manually *invalidate* the cache line.

As we noted earlier, Blackfin processors fetch instructions 64 bits at a time. When instruction cache is enabled and a cache miss occurs, the cache-line fill returns four 64-bit words, beginning with the address of the missed instruction. As Figure 2.8 illustrates, each cache line aligns on a fixed 32-byte boundary. If the instruction is in the last 64-bit word in a cache line, that will be the first value returned. The fill always wraps back around to the beginning of the line and finishes the fetch. From a performance standpoint this is preferable, because we wouldn't want the processor to wait for the three unwanted 64-bit fetches to come back before receiving the desired instruction.

Cache Line Replacement

Cache line fill begins with requested word

Target Word	Fetching Order for Next Three Words
WD0	WD0, WD1, WD2, WD3
WD1	WD1, WD2, WD3, WD0
WD2	WD2, WD3, WD0, WD1
WD3	WD3, WD0, WD1, WD2

Figure 2.8 **Cache line boundaries**

When a cache hit occurs, the processor treats the access as if it were in L1 memory—that is, it fetches the data/instruction in a single CCLK cycle. We can compute the cache *hit rate* as the percentage of time the processor has a cache hit when it tries to fetch data or instructions. This is an important measure because if the hit rate is too low, performance will suffer. A hit rate over 90% is desirable. You can imagine that, as the hit rate drops, performance starts to approach a system where everything to which the core needs access resides in external memory.

Actually, when the hit rate is too low, performance will be worse than the case where everything is in external memory and cache is off. This is due to the fact that the cache-line size is larger than the data or instruction being fetched. When cache misses are more common than cache hits, the core will end up waiting for unwanted instructions or data to come into the system. Of course, this situation degrades performance and, fortunately, it's hard to create a case where this happens.

As a rule of thumb, the more associative a cache is, the higher the hit rate an application can achieve. Also, as the cache size grows, the number of cache ways has less of an impact upon hit rate, but performance still does increase.

As more items are brought into cache, the cache itself becomes full with valid data and/or instructions. When the cache has an open line, new fetches that are part of cache-line fills populate lines that are invalid. When all the lines are valid, something has to be replaced to make room for new fetches. How is this replacement policy determined?

A common method is to use a "least recently used (LRU)" algorithm, which simply targets for replacement the data or instruction cache line that has not been accessed for the longest time. This replacement policy yields great performance, because applications tend to run small amounts of code more frequently. This is true even when application code approaches Mbytes in size. We will talk more about performance improvements that cache can achieve in Chapter 4.

Write-Through and Write-Back Data Cache

Data cache carries with it some additional important concepts. There are generally two modes of operation for data cache, *write-through* and *write-back,* as shown in Figure 2.9.

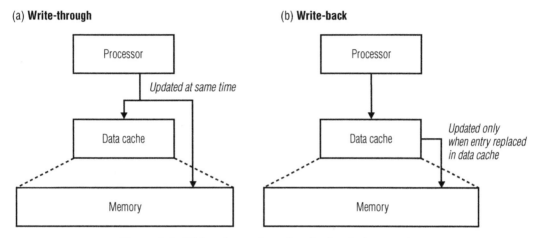

Figure 2.9 **Write-through and write-back data cache**

The term *write-through* means that the information is written both to the cache *and* to the source memory at the time it is modified, as shown in Figure 2.9a. This means that if a data element is brought into cache and modified a million times while the processor is executing an algorithm, the data is written to the source memory a million times as well. In this case, the term "source memory" refers to the actual location being cached in L2 or L3 memory. As you can see, write-through mode can result in lots of traffic on the bus between cache and the source memory. This activity can impact performance when other resources are accessing the memory.

Write-through data cache does have one advantage over write-back, however. It helps keep buffers in source memory coherent when more than one resource has access to them. For example, in a dual-core device with shared memory, a cache configured as write-through can help ensure the shared buffer has the latest data in it. Assume core A modifies the buffer, and then core B needs to make subsequent changes to the same buffer. In this case, core A would notify core B when the initial processing was complete, and core B would have access to the latest data.

The term "write-back" means that the information is written only to the cache, until it is being replaced, as we show in Figure 2.9b. Only then is the modified data written back to source memory. Therefore, if a data value is modified a million times, the result is only written locally to the cache until its cache entry is replaced, at which point source memory will be written a single time. Using our dual-core example again, coherency can still be maintained if core A manually "flushes" the cache when it is done processing the data. The flush operation forces the data in cache to be written out to source memory, even though it is not being replaced in cache, which is normally the only time this data would be written to source memory.

While these two modes each have merit, write-back mode is usually faster because the processor does not need to write to source memory until absolutely necessary. Which one should you choose? The choice depends on the application, and you should try both ways to see which will give the best performance. It is important to try these options multiple times in your development cycle. This approach will let you see how the system performs once peripherals are integrated into your application. Employing the write-back mode (versus write-through mode) can usually increase performance between 10 and 15%.

These write policy concepts don't apply to instruction memory, because modifying code in cached instruction memory isn't a typical programming model. As a result, instruction cache is not designed with this type of feature.

Before we move on, let's look at one additional write-back mode mechanism. Figure 2.10 illustrates what comprises a cache-line. Specifically, there is an address tag that precedes the set of four 64-bit words (in the case of Blackfin devices). The cache array tags possess a *dirty bit* to mark data that has changed in cache under write-back mode. For example, if we read a value from memory that ends up in cache, and the value is subsequently modified by the processor, it is marked as "dirty." This bit is used by the cache as a reminder that before the data is completely removed from cache, it needs to be written out to its source memory. Processors often have a *victim buffer* that holds data that was replaced in the cache. Let's consider why and how this helps performance.

When a data miss occurs in write-back mode and the entire cache contains valid data, something must be removed from the cache to hold the data about to be fetched. Recall that when this happens, the cache (assuming an LRU policy) will replace the data least recently used. What if there's "dirty" data in the line that is replaced—that is, data which has changed and needs to be updated in the source memory? The processor is most immediately interested in obtaining data for the currently executing

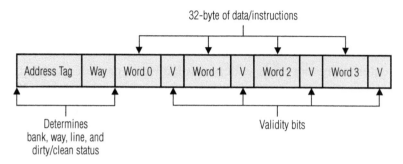

Figure 2.10 **Cache array with tags**

instruction. If it had to wait for the dirty data to be written back to source memory, and then wait again for the new data to be fetched, the core would stall longer than desired. This is where the victim buffer comes in; it holds the data that needs to be written back, while the core gets its new data quickly. Once the cache-line fill completes, the victim buffer empties and the source memory is current.

More Cache in Our Future

In Chapter 4, we'll review some additional twists with cache. For instance, cache coherency becomes important with the presence of a DMA controller, as well as when a second core is present. Additionally, we'll cover the mechanics of cache line fills, the benefits of locking cache lines and the capabilities of a memory management unit (MMU). We will also take a look at some performance numbers with and without instruction cache on, as well as some performance metrics for write-back and write-through caches.

External Memory

So far in this chapter, our discussions have centered on internal memory resources. Let's now focus on the many storage options available external to the processor. While we generically refer to external memory as "L3" throughout this text, you will soon see that the choices for L3 memory vary considerably in terms of how they operate and what their primary uses are. They all can play an important role in media-based applications. We will start with the highest performance volatile memories and move to various nonvolatile options. It is important to note here that the synchronous and asynchronous memories described below are directly memory-mapped to a processor's memory space. Some of the other memories we'll discuss later in this chapter, such as NAND flash, are also mapped to an external memory bank, but they have to be indirectly accessed.

Synchronous Memory

We will begin our discussion with synchronous memory because it is the highest performance external memory. It's widely available and provides a very cost-effective way to add large amounts of memory without completely sacrificing performance. We will focus on SDRAM technology to provide a good foundation for understanding, but then we'll proceed to an overview of current and near-term follow-ons to SDRAM: DDR-SDRAM 1 and 2.

Both SDRAM and DDR are widely available and very cost-effective because the personal computer industry uses this type of memory in standard DIMM modules.

SDRAM

SDRAM is synchronous addressable memory composed of banks, rows and columns. All reads and writes to this memory are locked to a processor-sourced clock. Once the processor initializes SDRAM, the memory must be continually refreshed to ensure it retains its state.

Clock rates vary for SDRAM, but the most popular industry specifications are PC100 and PC133, indicating a 100 MHz and 133 MHz maximum clock, respectively. Today's standard SDRAM devices operate at voltages between 2.5V and 3.3V, with the PC133 memory available at 3.3V.

Memory modules are specified in terms of some number of Mbits, in addition to a variety of data bus sizes (e.g., ×8, ×16, ×32). This sometimes causes confusion, but it is actually a straightforward nomenclature. For example, the ×16 designation on a 256-Mbit device implies an arrangement of 16 Mbits × 16. Likewise, for a ×32 bus width, a 256-Mbit device would be configured as 8 Mbits × 32. This is important when you are selecting your final memory size. For example, if the external bus on your processor is 32 bits wide, and you want 128 Mbytes of total memory, you might connect two 32 Mbits × 16 modules.

At its lowest level, SDRAM is divided into rows and columns. To access an element in an SDRAM chip, the row must first be "opened" to become "active." Next, a column within that row is selected, and the data is transferred from or written to the referenced location. The process of setting up the SDRAM can take several processor system clock cycles. Every access requires that the corresponding row be active.

Once a row is active, it is possible to read data from an entire row without re-opening that row on every access. The address within the SDRAM will automatically increment once a location is accessed. Because the memory uses a high-speed synchronous clock, the fastest transfers occur when performing accesses to contiguous locations, in a burst fashion.

Figure 2.11 shows a typical SDRAM controller (SDC), with the required external pins to interface properly to a memory device. The data access size might be 8, 16, or 32 bits. In addition, the actual addressable memory range may vary, but an SDC can often address hundreds of Mbytes or more.

SDRAMs are composed of internal banks—most commonly, four equally sized banks. So if you connect 64 Mbytes of SDRAM to a processor, the SDRAM would consist of four 16-Mbyte internal banks. This is important to remember because, as we'll discuss in Chapter 4, you'll derive performance benefits from partitioning your application across the internal banks. Another thing to note—the term "bank" is unfortunately used to describe both the internal structure of an SDRAM and an entire SDRAM module (as viewed from the system level). For example, two 64-Mbyte *external* SDRAM banks may connect to a processor, and each 64-Mbyte module may consist of four 16-Mbyte *internal* banks each.

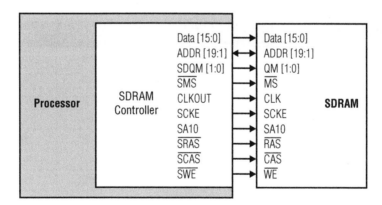

Figure 2.11 **Representative SDRAM controller**

The SDRAM controller uses the external pins shown in Figure 2.11 to issue a series of commands to the SDRAM. Table 2.1 provides a brief description of each of the pins, and Table 2.2 shows how the pins work in concert to send commands to the SDRAM. It generates these commands automatically based on writes and reads by the processor or DMA controller.

Table 2.1 **SDRAM pin description**

ADDR	External Address Bus
DATA	External Data Bus
SRAS	SDRAM Row Address Strobe (Connect to SDRAM's RAS pin.)
SCAS	SDRAM Column Address Strobe (Connect to SDRAM's CAS pin.)
SWE	SDRAM Write Enable pin (Connect to SDRAM's WE pin.)
SDQM	SDRAM Data Mask pins (Connect to SDRAM's DQM pins.)
SMS	Memory select pin of external memory bank configured for SDRAM
SA10	SDRAM A10 pin (Used for SDRAM refreshes; connect to SDRAM's A[10] pin.)
SCKE	SDRAM Clock Enable pin (Connect to SDRAM's CKE pin.)
CLKOUT	SDRAM Clock pin (Connect to SDRAM's CLK pin. Operates at SCLK frequency.)

Table 2.2 **SDRAM commands**

Command	SMS	SCAS	SRAS	SWE	SCKE	SA10
Precharge All	low	high	low	low	high	high
Single Precharge	low	high	low	low	high	low
Bank Activate	low	high	low	high	high	—
Load Mode Register	low	low	low	low	high	—
Load Extended Mode Register	low	low	low	low	high	low
Read	low	low	high	high	high	low
Write	low	low	high	low	high	low
Auto-Refresh	low	low	low	high	high	—
Self-Refresh	low	low	low	high	low	—
NOP (No Operation)	low	high	high	high	high	—
Command Inhibit	high	high	high	high	high	—

Figure 2.12 illustrates an SDRAM transation in a simplified manner. First, the higher bits of the address are placed on the bus and /RAS is asserted. The lower address bits of the address are then placed on the bus and /CAS is asserted. The number of rows and columns will depend on the device you select for connection.

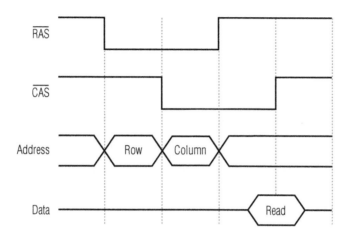

Figure 2.12 **Basic SDRAM timing diagram**

It is important to consider how your processor's SDC multiplexes SDRAM addresses. Consider two possibilities shown in Figure 2.13 as an example. In Figure 2.13b, the SDRAM row addresses are in the higher bit positions. In Figure 2.13a, the bank address lines are in the higher bit positions, which can result in better performance,

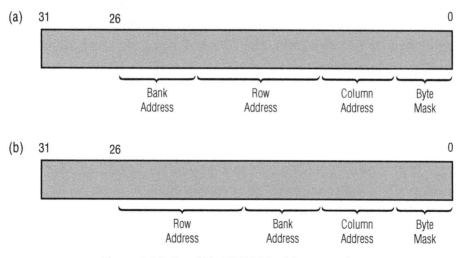

Figure 2.13 **Possible SDRAM address muxing**

depending on the application. Why is this the case? The SDRAM can keep four pages open across four internal banks, thus reducing page opening/closing latency penalties. If your system is connected as shown in Figure 2.13b, it would be very hard to partition your code and data to take advantage of this feature. Specifically, you would have to slice up your data and code and essentially interleave it in memory to make use of all open rows.

Let's now discuss briefly some of the key commands that the SDRAM controller uses to interface with the memory device.

The *Bank Activate* command causes the SDRAM to open an internal bank (specified by the bank address) in a row (specified by the row address). The pins that are used for the bank and row addresses depend on the mappings of Figure 2.13. When the SDC issues the Bank Activate command, the SDRAM opens a new row address in the dedicated bank. The memory in the open internal bank and row is referred to as the "open page." The Bank Activate command must be applied before issuing a read or write command.

The *Precharge* command closes a specific internal bank in the active page, or all internal banks in the page.

The *Precharge All* command precharges all internal banks at the same time before executing an auto-refresh.

A *Read/Write* command executes if the next read/write access is in the present active page. During the *Read* command, the SDRAM controller drives the column address. The delay between Bank Activate and Read commands is determined by the t_{RCD} parameter in the SDRAM data sheet. The SDRAM then makes data available after the CAS latency period described below.

In the *Write* command, the SDRAM controller drives the column address. The write data becomes valid in the same cycle. The delay between Bank Activate and Write commands is determined by the t_{RCD} parameter in the SDRAM data sheet.

Whenever a page miss occurs (an access to a location on a row that is not open), the SDC executes a Precharge command followed by a Bank Activate command before executing the Read or Write command. If there is a page hit, the Read or Write command can be issued immediately without requiring the Precharge command.

The *Command Inhibit* and *NOP* commands are similar in that they have no effect on the current operations of the SDRAM. The only difference between the two is that the *NOP* is used when the actual SDRAM bank has been selected.

The *Load Mode* command is used to initialize an SDRAM chip. *Load Extended Mode* is an additional initialization command that's used for mobile SDRAMs.

Auto-Refresh and *Self-Refresh* commands regulate how the contents of the SDRAM are refreshed periodically. We'll talk more about them shortly.

CAS Latency

SDRAM data sheets are swimming in numbers that specify the performance of the device. What do all these parameters really mean?

The *Column Address Strobe (CAS) latency*, abbreviated as CL2 or CL3, is the delay in clock cycles between when the SDRAM detects a Read command and when it provides the data at its output pins. This CAS latency is an important selection parameter. A common term used to identify SDRAM devices is either *CAS2* or *CAS3*. These actually represent CL2 or CL3, since they refer to *CAS Latency* timings (e.g., two system clocks versus three system clocks). An SDRAM with a CAS latency of two cycles will likely yield better throughput than one with a three-cycle latency. This is based on the fact that for random accesses, a cycle will be saved each time an access is made. You should specify this parameter based on application needs. Does the extra performance of the faster device justify the extra cost? For high-performance systems, the answer is usually "Yes."

The CAS latency of a device must be greater than or equal to its column access time (t_{CAC}) and its frequency of operation (t_{CLK}). That is, the selection of CL must satisfy Equation 2.1:

$$CL \times t_{CLK} \geq t_{CAC} \hspace{4cm} \text{Equation 2.1}$$

For example, if t_{CLK} is 7.5 ns (133 MHz system clock) and t_{CAC} is 15 ns, then you can select a CL2 device. If t_{CAC} is 20 ns, then you must choose CL3. The PC133 SDRAM specification only allows for CAS latency values of 1, 2 or 3.

Sometimes you will see memory devices described as "3-2-2" or "2-2-2". These numbers represent the CAS Latency, RAS-to-CAS delay (t_{RCD}) and Row Precharge (t_{RP}) values, respectively, in clock cycles at 100 MHz. Note that for any other speed of operation, such as 66 MHz or 133 MHz, these numbers would change. For example, let's assume that for a given module, t_{CAC} is 25 ns, t_{RCD} is 20 ns and t_{RP} is 20 ns. This would indicate 3-2-2 timings at 100 MHz (substituting t_{RCD} or t_{RP} for t_{CAC} in Equation 2.1 as appropriate), but what would they be at 133 MHz? Since 133 MHz corresponds to a 7.5 ns clock cycle (t_{CLK}), Equation 2.1 gives timings of 4-3-3, which would be invalid for the SDRAM, since the CAS latency cannot be higher than 3. Therefore, you would not be able to operate this module at 133 MHz.

One more point to understand about the CAS latency figure (CAS2 or CAS3) is that SDRAM suppliers often advertise their top PC100 SDRAM as CAS2. Recall that the CAS latency number is derived from t_{CAC}. Unfortunately, the vendor doesn't provide you with the t_{CAC} value. Imagine a CL2 part with a 20-ns t_{CAC} and a CL3 part with a 21-ns t_{CAC}. At 133 MHz (7.5-ns clock period), both parts would have a CAS latency value of 3. This means that while a CL2 part may be designed to handle a faster system clock speed than a CL3 part, you won't always see a performance difference. Specifically, if you don't plan on running your SDRAM faster than 125 MHz, the device with the lower value of CL doesn't provide any additional benefit over the device with the higher CL value.

Refreshing the SDRAM

SDRAM controllers have a refresh counter that determines when to issue refresh commands to the SDRAM. When the SDC refresh counter times out, the SDC precharges all banks of SDRAM and then issues an Auto-Refresh command to them. This causes the SDRAM to generate an internal refresh cycle. When the internal refresh completes, all internal SDRAM banks are precharged.

In power-saving modes where SDRAM data needs to be maintained, it is sometimes necessary to place the SDRAM in self-refresh mode. Self-refresh is also useful when you want to buffer the SDRAM while the changes are made to the SDRAM controller configuration. Moreover, the self-refresh mode is useful when sharing the memory bus with another resource. As we will see in Chapter 4, it can prevent conflicts on shared pins until the first processor regains ownership of the bus.

When you place the SDRAM in self-refresh mode, it is the SDRAM's internal timer that initiates auto-refresh cycles periodically, without external control input. Current draw when the SDRAM is in self-refresh mode is on the order of a few milliamps, versus the typical "on" current of 100 mA.

The SDC must issue a series of commands, including the Self-Refresh command, to put the SDRAM into this low power mode, and it must issue another series of commands to exit self-refresh mode. Entering self-refresh mode is controlled by software in an application. Any access made by the processor or the DMA controller to the SDRAM address space causes the SDC to remove the SDRAM from self-refresh mode.

It is important to be aware that core or DMA accesses to SDRAM are held off until an in-process refresh cycle completes. This is significant because if the refresh rate is too high, the potential number of accesses to SDRAM decreases, which means that SDRAM throughput declines as well. Programming the refresh rate to a higher value than necessary is a common mistake that programmers make, especially on processors that allow frequency modification on the fly. In other words, they forget to adjust the Refresh Control register to a level commensurate with the newly programmed system clock frequency. As long as the effective refresh rate is not too slow, data will not be lost, but performance will suffer if the rate is too high.

Mobile SDRAM

A variant of SDRAM that targets the portable device realm is called *Mobile SDRAM*. It comes in a smaller form factor and smaller memory sizes than its traditional cousin, and it can operate down to 2.5V or 1.8V, greatly reducing SDRAM power consumption. Mobile SDRAM is also known as LP SDRAM, or low-power SDRAM. It is worth mentioning that mobile SDRAM devices typically specify a supply voltage and an I/O voltage. For the most power-sensitive applications, the supply voltage is at 2.5V while the I/O supply is 1.8V.

In addition to a reduced form factor and greatly reduced power budget, mobile SDRAM has three key JEDEC-specified features that set it apart from SDRAM. The first is a temperature compensated self-refresh mode. The second is a partial array self-refresh capability, and the third is a "deep power-down" mode.

The temperature-compensated self-refresh capability allows you to program the mobile SDRAM device to automatically adjust its refresh rate in self-refresh mode to accommodate case temperature changes. Some mobile devices assume you will connect a temperature sensor to the case and adjust the parameters associated with this feature. Others have a built-in temperature sensor. Either way, the goal is to save power by adjusting the frequency of self-refresh to the minimum level necessary to retain the data.

The partial array self-refresh feature allows you to control which banks within a mobile SDRAM are actually refreshed when the device is in self-refresh mode. You can program the device so that 100%, 50% or 25% of the banks are kept in self-refresh mode. Obviously, any data you need to keep must reside in a bank that is self-refreshed. The other banks are then used for data that does not need to be retained during power-saving modes.

Finally, the deep power-down feature allows you to remove power from the device via a write to the control register of the SDRAM chip to prevent any current draw during self-refresh mode (thus saving hundreds of µA). Of course, all data is lost when you do this, but this mode can be very useful in applications where the entire board is not powered down (e.g., some components are operational and are powered by the same regulator), but you want to extend the battery life as long as possible.

Double Data Rate (DDR) SDRAM/DDR1

SDRAM and mobile SDRAM chips provide the bulk of today's synchronous memory in production. This is quickly changing, however, as an evolved synchronous memory architecture provides increased performance. Double data rate (DDR) SDRAM provides a direct path to double memory bandwidth in an application. In addition, while the industry has more or less skipped 2.5V SDRAM devices (with the notable exception of mobile SDRAM), standard DDR1 chips are all at 2.5V.

While the traditional SDRAM controller often shares processor pins with various types of asynchronous memory, the DDR specification is much tighter to allow for much faster operation. As such, a DDR memory module will not share pins with other types of memory. Additionally, DDR memories require a DDR controller to interface with them; a processor's SDRAM controller is incompatible with DDR memory.

As the name suggests, a key difference between SDRAM and DDR is that while SDRAM allows synchronous data access on each clock cycle, DDR allows synchronous access on both edges of the clock—hence the term *double data rate*. This results in an immediate increase in peak performance when using DDR in an application.

As an example, whereas the peak transfer rate of a PC133 SDRAM running at 133 MHz would be 4 bytes × 133 MHz, the maximum peak transfer rate of the equivalent DDR1 module running at the same frequency is 4 bytes × 266 MHz.

Another important advantage DDR has over SDRAM is the size of the "prefetch" it accepts. DDR1 has a prefetch size of 2n, which means that data accesses occur in pairs. When reads are performed, each access results in a fetch of two data words. The same is true for a single write access—that is, two data words must be sent.

What this means is that the minimum burst size of DDR1 is two external data words. For reads, the DDR controller can choose to ignore either of the words, but the cycles associated with both will still be spent. So you can see that while this feature greatly enhances performance of sequential accesses, it erodes performance on random accesses.

DDR SDRAM also includes a strobe-based data bus. The device that drives the data signals also drives the data strobes. This device is the DDR module for reads and the DDR controller for writes. These strobes allow for higher data rates by eliminating the synchronous clock model to which SDRAM adheres.

When all of these DDR feature enhancements are combined, performance really shines. For example, at 400 MHz, DDR1 increases memory bandwidth to 3.2 Gbytes/s, compared to PC133 SDRAM theoretical bandwidth of 133 MHz × 4 bytes, or 532 Mbytes/s.

Just as a low-power version of SDRAM exists, mobile DDR1 also exists, with many similarities to mobile SDRAM. Mobile DDR1 devices run as low as 1.8V. Another advantage of Mobile DDR1 is that there is no minimum clock rate of operation. This compares favorably to standard DDR1, whose approximate 80 MHz minimum operating frequency can cause problems in power-sensitive applications.

DDR2 SDRAM

DDR2 SDRAM is the second generation of DDR SDRAM. It offers data rates of up to 6.4 Gbytes/s, lower power consumption, and improvements in packaging. It achieves this higher level of performance and lower power consumption through faster clocks, 1.8V operation and signaling, and a simplified command set. Like DDR1, DDR2 has a mobile variety as well, targeted for handheld devices.

Table 2.3 shows a summary of the differences between DDR1, Mobile DDR1 and DDR2. It should be noted that DDR1 is not compatible with a conventional SDRAM interface, and DDR2 is not compatible with DDR1. However, DDR2 is planned to be forward-compatible with next-generation DDR technology.

Table 2.3 **Comparison of DDR1 and DDR2**

Feature	DDR1	Mobile DDR1	DDR2
Data Transfer Rate	266, 333, 400 MHz	200, 250, 266, 333 MHz	400, 533, 667, 800 MHz
Operating Voltage	2.5 V	1.8 V	1.8 V
Densities	128Mb-1Gb	128Mb–512Mb, 1Gb(future)	256Mb-4Gb
Internal Banks	4	4	4 and 8
Prefetch	2	2	4
CAS Latency	2, 2.5, 3	2, 3	3, 4, 5, 6
Additive Latency	no	no	0, 1, 2, 3, 4, 5
READ Latency	CAS Latency	CAS Latency	Additive Latency + CAS Latency
WRITE Latency	Fixed = 1 cycle	Fixed = 1 cycle	READ Latency − 1 cycle
I/O width	x4, x8, x16	x4, x8, x16, x32	x4, x8, x16
On-Die Termination	no	no	selectable
Off Chip Driver	no	no	yes
Burst Length	2, 4, 8	2, 4, 8, 16, full page	4, 8
Burst Terminate Command	yes	yes	no
Partial Array Self-Refresh	no	Full, 1/2, 1/4, 1/8, 1/16	no
Temperature Compensated Self-Refresh	no	supported	no
Deep Power-Down	no	supported	no

Asynchronous Memory

As we have just finished describing, SDRAM and its successors both are accessed in a synchronous manner. Asynchronous memory, as you can guess, does not operate synchronously to a clock. Each access has an associated read and write latency. While burst operations are always available with synchronous memory, the same can't be said of asynchronous memory.

The asynchronous bus of today has evolved from buses that were popular in the past, such as IBM's *Industry Standard Architecture* (ISA) bus. Asynchronous devices come in many different flavors. The most common include Static RAM (SRAM), which is volatile, and nonvolatile memories like PROM and Flash. SRAM can substitute for the pricier SDRAM when high performance isn't required.

Processors that have an asynchronous memory controller (AMC) typically share its data and address pins with the SDRAM controller. As we mentioned earlier, because DDR has much tighter capacitive loading requirements, an AMC would not share pins with a DDR controller.

A characteristic AMC is shown in Figure 2.14. It contains read and write enable pins that can interface to memory devices. Table 2.4 shows a summary of the common AMC pins. Several memory-select lines allow the AMC to choose which of several connected devices it's talking to at a given point in time. The AMC has programmable

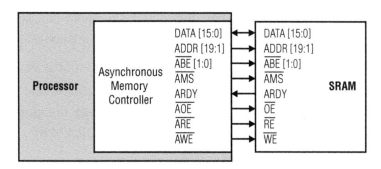

Figure 2.14 **Typical Asynchronous Memory Controller (AMC)**

Table 2.4 **Typical AMC pins**

ADDR	External Address Bus (outputs)
DATA	External Data Bus (inputs/outputs)
AMS	Asynchronous Memory Selects (outputs)
AWE	Asynchronous Memory Write Enable (output)
ARE	Asynchronous Memory Read Enable (output)
AOE	Asynchronous Memory Read Enable (output)
ARDY	Asynchronous Memory Ready Response (input)
ABE[1:0]	Byte Enables (outputs)

wait states and setup/hold timing for each connected device, to accommodate a wide array of asynchronous memories.

The AMC is especially useful because, in addition to interfacing with memory devices, it allows connection to many other types of components. For example, FIFOs and FPGAs easily map to an asynchronous bank. Chip sets for USB and Ethernet, as well as bridges to many other popular peripherals, also easily interface to the asynchronous memory interface.

When connecting a nonmemory device to an AMC, it is always best to use a DMA channel to move data into and out of the device, especially when the interface is shared with SDRAM. Access to these types of components usually consumes multiple system clock cycles, whereas an SDRAM access can occur in a single system clock cycle. Be aware that, when the AMC and SDC share the same L3 memory bus, slow accesses on an asynchronous bank could hold off access to a SDRAM bank considerably.

Synchronous random access memory (synchronous SRAM) is also available for higher performance than traditional SRAMs provide, at increased cost. Synchronous SRAM devices are capable of either pipelined or flow-through functionality. These devices take the asynchronous devices one step closer to SDRAM by providing a burst capability.

While synchronous SRAM provides for higher performance than ordinary SRAM, other technologies allow for lower power. Pseudo-SRAM (and a variant called CellularRAM) connect to a processor via an SDRAM-like interface. Additionally, they sport an I/O supply requirement in line with other processor I/O (2.5V or 3.3V, for instance), while powering the Vcc supply of the memory itself at 1.8V. This presents a good compromise that allows processors to take advantage of some power savings even when they don't have 1.8V-capable I/O.

Figure 2.15 shows a high-level view of how several representative types of external memory compare from the dual standpoints of performance and capacity.

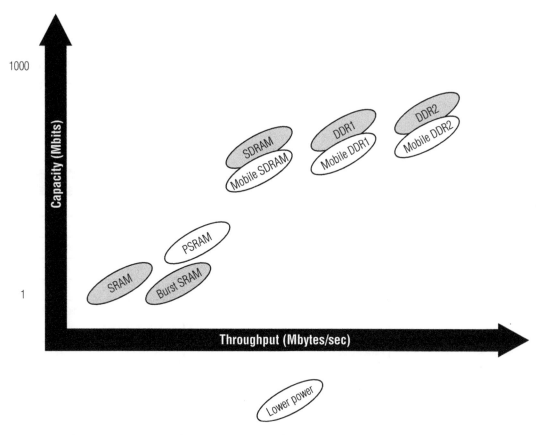

Figure 2.15 **External memory comparison of performance and capacity**

Nonvolatile Memories

Nonvolatile memories—memories that retain their contents even when not powered—come in several forms. The simplest, a ROM (read-only memory), is written once (at the factory) but can be read many times. A PROM, or Programmable ROM, also can only be written once, but this can be done in the field, not just at the time of manufacture. An erasable PROM (EPROM) can be reprogrammed after erasing its contents via ultraviolet light exposure. An electrically erasable PROM (EEPROM), commonly used today, needs only electricity for erasure. A Flash EEPROM takes this technology one step further by allowing data to be stored and erased in blocks, rather than in byte-sized increments. This significantly speeds up access rates to flash memories when compared with regular EEPROM access times. Finally, a Burst-Mode Flash sharply reduces read access times for sequential bytes by adding a few extra control pins to the standard Flash interface.

NAND and NOR Flash Memories

The two main types of nonvolatile flash memory widely used today are NOR-based and NAND-based. There are many differences between these two technologies, and they are each optimal for certain classes of usage. Table 2.5 gives a rundown of their major characteristics.

Table 2.5 **Summary of NOR and NAND flash characteristics**

Trait	NOR Flash	NAND Flash
Capacity/Bit Density	Low (<64 MB)	High (16 MB – 512 MB)
Directly Execute Code From?	Yes	No
Erase performance	Very slow (5 sec)	Fast (3 ms)
Write performance	Slow	Fast
Read performance	Fast	Medium
Reliability	OK	Low – requires error checking and bad-block checking
Erase Cycles	10K-100K	100K-1000K
Life Span	OK	Excellent (10x NOR)
Interface	ISA-like/MCU-friendly (Addr+Data+Control), Serial (SPI or I2C)	I/O only (command sequence)
Pin Count	High	Low
Access Method	Random	Sequential
Ease-of-use	Easy; memory-mapped address+data scheme	Difficult (File System needed)
Cost/bit	High	Low
Primary Usage	Low-density, high-speed code access, some data storage:	High-density data block storage
Bootable?	Yes	Not generally
Power/Energy Dissipation	Higher (due to long program and erase cycles)	Lower

Fundamentally, NAND and NOR flash technologies differ in the structure of their respective memory cell arrays. In NOR devices, memory cells are connected in parallel between a bit line and ground, such that selecting any number of memory cells can end up grounding a bit line. Because this is similar to a wired-OR configuration, it is termed "NOR flash." This arrangement enables very fast read times and thus makes NOR flash a good candidate for random access—a trait associated with processor code.

NAND realizes a more efficient cell architecture that results in only about half of the space taken by a NOR cell. However, this space-saving layout connects memory cells in series, sharing bit-select lines across several cells. In order to ground a bit line, an entire group of memory cells must be turned on simultaneously. This makes NAND flashes a poor choice for random accesses, but it provides excellent cell compactness. What's more, it allows several NAND cells to be programmed simultaneously, providing very fast write performance compared to NOR devices.

While NOR flash holds the edge in read access speed, NAND is superior in programming and erasing speeds. Erase time is especially crucial, because flash devices must all be erased (each bit set to 1) before programming occurs (selectively setting bits back to 0). Therefore, erasing is an integral part of writing to a flash device. Moreover, NAND flashes can tolerate many more erase cycles than NOR flashes can, usually on the order of tenfold, thus providing much longer life spans than NOR devices.

One intricacy of NAND flashes is that a file system is necessary in order to use them. This is because, in order to maintain high yields, NAND flashes are shipped with randomly located bad blocks. It is the file system's job (running on the embedded processor) to find these bad blocks, tag them, and avoid using them. Usually, the memory vendor has already scanned and marked the bad blocks at the factory, and the file system just needs to maintain a table of where these are located, keeping in mind that some additional bad blocks will be formed over the lifetime of the part. The good news is that, because each block is independent of all others, the failure of one block has no impact on the operation of others.

As it turns out, NOR flash can also have bad blocks, but manufacturers typically allocate extra blocks on the chip to substitute for any bad blocks discovered during factory test. NAND has no such spare blocks, because it's assumed that a file system is necessary anyway for the mass storage systems of which NAND devices are a part.

As another consideration, NAND is somewhat prone to bit errors due to periodic programming (one bit error out of every 10 billion bits programmed). Therefore, error-correcting codes (Hamming codes, usually) are employed by the file system to detect and correct bit errors.

As far as processor interface, NOR devices have a couple of options. For one, they hook directly up to the asynchronous memory controller of microprocessors, with the conventional address and data bus lines, as well as write/read/select control. Depending on the address space desired, this interface can encompass a large number of pins. As a slower, lower pin-count alternative, serial flash devices can connect through just a few wires via an SPI or I²C interface. Here, the address and data is multiplexed on the serial bus to achieve memory access rates only a fraction of those attainable using parallel address/data buses.

Interfacing to NAND devices is more complex and occurs indirectly, requiring a sequence of commands on the 8-bit bus to internal command and address registers. Data is then accessed in pages, usually around 528 bytes in length. Although this indirect interface makes NAND not suitable for booting, this approach provides a fixed, low pin-count interface that remains static as higher density devices are substituted. In this respect (and many others), NAND flash acts like a conventional hard disk drive. This accounts for the similar structure and access characteristics between the two storage technologies.

In fact, NAND flash devices were specifically intended to replace magnetic hard disk drives in many embedded applications. To their advantage, they are solid-state devices, meaning that they have no moving parts. This leads to more rugged, reliable devices than magnetic disk drives, as well as much less power dissipation.

NAND flash serves as the basis for all of the most popular removable solid-state mass storage cards: CompactFlash, SmartMedia, Secure Digital/Multimedia Card (SD/MMC), Extreme Digital Picture Card (xD), MemoryStick, and the like. With the exception of SmartMedia, all of these cards have built-in controllers that simplify access to the NAND memory on the device. These products find wide use in consumer electronics (like cameras, PDAs, cell phones, etc.) and other embedded applications requiring mass storage. Table 2.6 provides a high-level comparison of these storage cards.

Devices like SD, MemoryStick, and CompactFlash also have an I/O layer, which makes them quite attractive as interfaces on embedded processors. They enable a wide range of peripherals through these interfaces, including Bluetooth, 802.11b, Ethernet transceivers, modems, FM radio, and the like.

Table 2.6 **Storage card comparison**

	SmartMedia	MMC	CompactFlash	Secure Digital (SD)	MemoryStick	xD	TransFlash/Micro SD
Developer	Toshiba	Infineon,SanDisk	SanDisk	SanDisk, Panasonic, Toshiba	Sony (later with SanDisk)	Fujifilm, Olympus	SanDisk, Motorola
Variants		MMCplus HS-MMC (High Speed) RS-MMC (Reduced Size) SecureMMC MMCmobile		mini-SD	MemoryStick Pro MemoryStick Duo Memory Stick Pro Duo		
Volume (mm³)	1265	1075 605 (RS-MMC, MMCmobile)	5141 (Type I) 7790 (Type II)	1613 (SD) 602 (mini-SD)	3010 992 (Duo & Pro Duo)	850	165
Weight (g)	2	1.5	11.4	2 (1 for mini-SD)	4 (2 for Duo & Pro Duo)	2	0.4
Interface pins	22	7-13	50	9	10	18	8
Present Capacity	128 MB	1 GB	8 GB	2 GB (1GB for mini-SD)	128 MB 4 GB (Pro & Pro Duo)	1 GB	512 MB
Content Security	ID Copy Protection	Depends on variant	No	CPRM, SD	MagicGate	ID Copy Protection	CPRM, SD
Max Data Transfer Rate	1MB/s Write 3.5 MB/s Read	up to 52 MB/s (depends on variant)	66 MB/s	10 MB/s	1.8 MB/s Write 2.5 MB/s Read 20 MB/s (Pro & Pro Duo)	3 MB/s Write 5 MB/s Read	1.8 MB/s typical
Comments	no on-board controller, limited capacity	small form factor, compatible with SD interfaces	IDE-compatible	mini-SD has adapter to fit SD card slot	mostly Sony products, supports real-time DVD-quality video transfer	adapters available to other card types	bridges between embedded and removable memory worlds
I/O Capability?	No	No	Yes	Yes	Yes	No	No
Voltage	3.3V/5V	3.3V (1.8V/3.3V for MMCplus and MMCmobile)	3.3V/5V	3.3V	3.3V	3.3V	3.3V
Interface	8-bit I/O	SPI, MMC	IDE	SPI, SD	MemoryStick	NAND Flash	SPI, SD

Photos courtesy of Sandisk Corporation

Hard Disk Storage—IDE, ATA and ATAPI

The terms IDE and ATA actually refer to the same general interface, but they mean different things, and people often get confused and use the terms interchangeably. For simplicity, we'll just refer to the interface as ATA or ATAPI, as explained below.

IDE is short for Integrated Drive Electronics, which refers to a pivotal point in the PC storage market when the disk drive controllers were integrated directly on the hard disk itself, rather than as a separate board inside the PC. This reduced the cost of the interface and increased reliability considerably. IDE drives can support a master and a slave device on each IDE channel.

ATA stands for AT Attachment, dating back to the days of the IBM PC/AT. It describes a device interface for hooking up to hard disk drives. ATAPI stands for ATA Packet Interface, which specifies a way to hook up to CD-ROM, DVD and tape drives, which communicate by means of packetized commands and data. While the packet layer of ATAPI adds considerable complexity, it still maintains the same electrical interface as ATA. ATA is such a ubiquitous standard for mass storage (dwarfing SCSI, for instance) that ATA-compliant storage has found its way into the PC-MCIA and CompactFlash worlds as well.

The ATA interface specifies how commands are passed through to the hard drive controller, interpreted, and processed. The interface consists of eight basic registers: seven are used by the processor's I/O subsystem to set up a read or write access, and the eighth one is used to perform block reads/writes in 512-byte chunks called sectors. Each sector has 256 words, and each access utilizes a 16-bit data bus.

The original scheme for addressing drive data followed a CHS method of accessing a particular *c*ylinder, *h*ead and *s*ector of the hard disk. A more intuitive mode known as Logical Block Addressing (LBA) was soon added, in which each sector on a hard disk has its own unique identification number. LBA led the way toward breaking through the 8 GB addressing barrier inherent in the CHS approach (which allows for only 1,024 cylinders, 256 heads, and 63 sectors).

ATA lays down timing requirements for control and data accesses. It offers two modes of data access—Programmed I/O (PIO) and DMA—each offering various levels of performance. PIO modes operate in analogous fashion to direct processor accesses to the hard drive. That is, the processor has to schedule time out of what it's doing to set up and complete a data processing cycle. DMA modes, on the other hand, allow data transfer between the drive and processor memory to occur without core intervention, much the same as we discuss in Chapter 3. The term Ultra DMA refers to higher-performance levels of DMA that involve double-edge clocking, where data is transferred on both the rising and falling edges of the clock. Ultra DMA usually requires an 80-conductor IDE cable (instead of the standard 40-pin one for parallel ATA drives) for better noise immunity at the higher transfer rates, and it also incorporates cyclical redundancy checking (CRC) for error reduction.

Table 2.7 lists the several different levels of ATA, starting with ATA-1 and extending to ATA/ATAPI-7, which is still under development. At Level 4, ATAPI was introduced, so every level from 4 onwards is designated ATA/ATAPI. The levels differ mainly in I/O transfer rates, DMA capability and reliability. All new drives at a given ATA level are supposed to be backward-compatible to the previous ATA levels.

Table 2.7 **ATAPI summary**

ATA Version	Max PIO Transfer Rate (MB/s)	Max DMA Transfer Rate (MB/s)	Added Features
ATA-1	8.3	8.3	Original standard for IDE drives
ATA-2	16.7	16.7	Logical Block Addressing Block Transfers
ATA-3	16.7	16.7	Improved reliability, Drive security, SMART (self-monitoring)
ATA/ATAPI-4	16.7	33.3	Packet Interface extension, Ultra DMA (80-conductor ribbon cable), CRC error checking and correction
ATA/ATAPI-5	16.7	66.7	Faster Ultra DMA transfer modes
ATA/ATAPI-6	16.7	100	Support for drives larger than 137 GB
ATA/ATAPI-7	16.7	133	SATA and DVR support

Other Hard Drive Interfaces

Serial ATA (SATA)

SATA is a follow-on to ATA that serializes the parallel ATA data interface, thus reducing electrical noise and increasing performance while allowing for longer, skinnier cabling. SATA uses differential signaling at very high clock rates to achieve data transfer rates of several hundred megabytes per second. SATA sheds the legacy 5V power supply baggage that parallel ATA carries, and its differential signaling operates in the range of 200–300 mV. More good news: it's software-compatible with parallel ATA. This allows simple SATA-to-parallel-ATA converters to translate between the two technologies in the near term, without disturbing the software layer underneath the different physical layers. On the downside, SATA allows only for point-to-point connections between a controller and a device, although external port multipliers are available to effect a point-to-multipoint scheme.

SATA is targeted primarily at the PC market, to improve reliability and increase data transfer speeds. It will slowly make its way into embedded applications, first targeting those systems where the storage density of solid state flash cards isn't adequate, leaving parallel or serial ATA as the only options. But as flash card densities grow into the several-Gbyte range, they will maintain a firm foothold in a wide swath of embedded applications due to the increased reliability of their solid-state nature and their small form factors.

SCSI

SCSI stands for Small Computer Systems Interface, and it's a high-end interconnect that outperforms ATA, but is also much more complex. It offers expandability to many more devices than ATA and has a feature set geared toward higher performance. SCSI is more expensive than ATA for the same storage capacity, and it's typically the realm of niche applications, not very popular in the embedded world.

Microdrive

The Microdrive is an actual miniature hard disk in a CompactFlash Type II form factor. Invented by IBM, the product line is now owned and propagated by Hitachi. Whereas CompactFlash is a solid-state memory, Microdrives are modeled after conventional magnetically based hard drives, with tiny spinning platters. For this reason, they are not as rugged and reliable as CompactFlash memory, and they also consume more power. Presently, they are available at capacities up to several gigabytes.

USB/Firewire

These drives are nothing more than Parallel ATA disk drives with a USB 2.0 high-speed or Firewire (IEEE 1394) front-end, usually used to facilitate access to a PC. However, in the embedded world, where USB and Firewire are gaining traction, these interfaces provide a handy way to add storage to a system.

USB pen drives, also called keychain drives, are not related to these ATA drives. Instead, they are flash memory devices with a USB front-end, similar in all respects to the NAND memory devices described above.

Emerging Nonvolatile Memory Technologies

There are some exciting new technologies on the horizon that will probably be very important in embedded multimedia applications. Two of particular interest are FRAM and MRAM. FRAM, or Ferroelectric RAM, uses electric field orientation to store charge. This gives it almost infinite write capability. By comparison, conventional EEPROMs can only be written on the order of 10,000 times. MRAM, or Magnetore-sistive RAM, uses electron spin to store information. It represents the best of several memory domains: it's nonvolatile, it has bit densities rivaling DRAM, and it operates at SRAM-like speeds.

What's Next?

This chapter provided some important context for memory transactions and data buffer movements. In the next chapter, we'll add another dimension to these discussions, detailing how direct memory access (DMA) works with a processor's memory subsystem to move data between memories and peripherals, independent of the core's computational activities.

Direct Memory Access

Introduction

The processor core is capable of doing multiple operations in a single cycle, including calculations, data fetches, data stores and pointer increments/decrements. In addition, the core can orchestrate data transfer between internal and external memory spaces by moving data into and out of the register file.

All this sounds great, but in reality you can only achieve optimum performance in your application if data can move around without constantly bothering the core to perform the transfers.

This is where a direct memory access (DMA) controller comes into play. Processors need DMA capability to relieve the core from these transfers between internal/external memory and peripherals, or between memory spaces. There are two main types of DMA controllers. "Cycle-stealing" DMA uses spare (idle) core cycles to perform data transfers. This is not a workable solution for systems with heavy processing loads like multimedia flows. Instead, it is much more efficient to employ a DMA controller that operates independently from the core.

Why is this so important? Well, imagine if a processor's video port has a FIFO that needs to be read every time a data sample is available. In this case, the core has to be interrupted tens of millions of times each second. As if that's not disruptive enough, the core has to perform an equal amount of writes to some destination in memory. For every core processing cycle spent on this task, a corresponding cycle would be lost in the processing loop.

We know from experience that PC-based software designers transitioning to the embedded world are hesitant to rely on a DMA controller for moving data around in an application. This usually stems from their impression that the complexity of the programming model increases exponentially when DMA is factored in. Yes, it is true that a DMA controller adds another dimension to your solution. We will, in fact, explore some intricacies that DMA introduces—such as contention for shared resources and new challenges in maintaining coherency between data buffers. Our goal, however, is to put your mind at ease, to show you how DMA is truly your friend. In this chapter, we'll focus on the DMA controller itself. In Chapter 4, we'll show you how to optimize performance using the DMA controller, and in Chapter 7, we'll offer ideas on how best to manage the DMA controller as part of an overall framework.

DMA Controller Overview

Because you'll typically configure a DMA controller during code initialization, the core should only need to respond to interrupts after data set transfers are complete. You can program the DMA controller to move data in parallel with the core, while the core is doing its basic processing tasks—the jobs on which it's supposed to be focused! In an optimized application, the core would never have to move any data, but rather only access it in L1 memory. The core wouldn't need to wait for data to arrive, because the DMA engine would have already made it available by the time the core was ready to access it. Figure 3.1 shows a typical interaction between the processor and the DMA controller. The steps allocated to the processor involve setting up the transfer, enabling interrupts, and running code when an interrupt is generated. The dashed lines/arrows between memory and the peripheral indicate operations the DMA controller makes to move data independent of the processor. Finally, the interrupt input back to the processor can be used to signal that data is ready for processing.

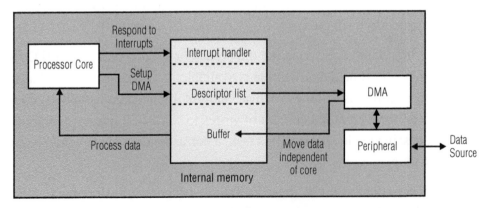

Figure 3.1 **DMA controller**

In addition to moving to and from peripherals, data also needs to move from one memory space to another. For example, source video might flow from a video port straight to L3 memory, because the working buffer size is too large to fit into internal memory. We don't want to make the processor fetch pixels from external memory every time we need to perform a calculation, so a memory-to-memory DMA (MemDMA for short) can bring pixels into L1 or L2 memory for more efficient access times. Figure 3.2 shows some typical DMA data flows.

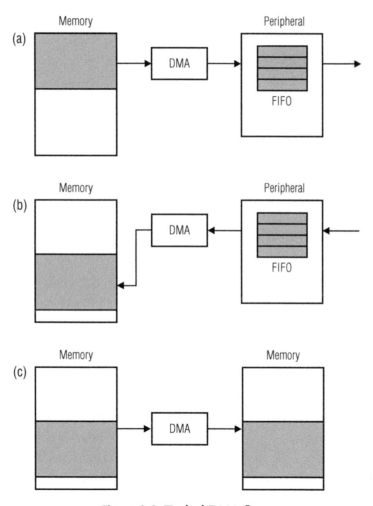

Figure 3.2 **Typical DMA flows**

So far we've focused on data movement, but a DMA transfer doesn't always have to involve data. We can use code overlays to improve performance, configuring the DMA controller to move code into L1 instruction memory before execution. The code is usually staged in larger external memory. We describe this technique in Chapter 4.

In this chapter, we will use the Blackfin Processor's DMA controller as a model to illustrate the basic concepts of direct memory access and how it can boost system performance. We will also offer some helpful ways to manage the DMA controller and review examples of "two-dimensional" transfers that can save valuable data passes by markedly reducing the time an application spends traversing a data buffer.

More on the DMA Controller

A DMA controller is a unique peripheral devoted to moving data around a system. Think of it as a controller that connects internal and external memories with each DMA-capable peripheral via a set of dedicated buses. It is a peripheral in the sense that the processor programs it to perform transfers. It is unique in that it interfaces to both memory and selected peripherals. Notably, only peripherals where data flow is significant (kbytes per second or greater) need to be DMA-capable. Good examples of these are video, audio and network interfaces. Lower-bandwidth peripherals can also be equipped with DMA capability, but it's less of an imposition on the core to step in and assist with data transfer on these interfaces.

In general, DMA controllers will include an address bus, a data bus, and control registers. An efficient DMA controller will possess the ability to request access to any resource it needs, without having the processor itself get involved. It must have the capability to generate interrupts. Finally, it has to be able to calculate addresses within the controller.

A processor might contain multiple DMA controllers. Each controller has multiple DMA channels, as well as multiple buses that link directly to the memory banks and peripherals, as shown in Figure 3.3. There are two types of DMA controllers in the Blackfin processor. The first category, usually referred to as a System DMA controller, allows access to any resource (peripherals and memory). Cycle counts for this type of controller are measured in *system clocks* (SCLKs) at frequencies up to 133 MHz. The second type, an Internal Memory DMA (IMDMA) controller, is dedicated to accesses between internal memory locations. Because the accesses are internal (L1 to L1, L1 to L2, or L2 to L2), cycle counts are measured in *core clocks* (CCLKs), which can exceed 600 MHz rates.

Figure 3.3 also shows the Blackfin DMA bus structure, where the DMA External Bus (DEB) connects the DMA controller to external memory, the DMA Core Bus (DCB) connects the controller to internal memory, and the DMA Access Bus (DAB) connects to the peripherals. An additional DMA bus set is also available when L2 memory is present, in order to move data within the processor's internal memory spaces.

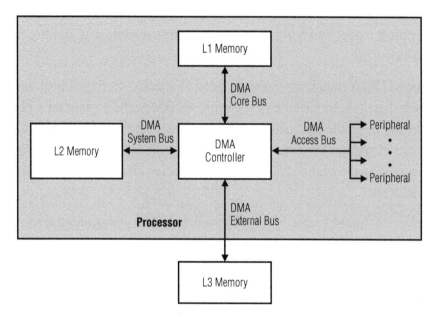

Figure 3.3 **System and internal memory DMA architecture**

Each DMA channel on a Blackfin DMA controller has a programmable priority associated with it. If more than one channel requests the DMA bus in a single cycle, the highest priority channel wins access. For memory DMA channels, a "round-robin" access capability exists. That is, one memory channel can access the bus for a programmable number of cycles before turning the bus over to the next MemDMA channel, which also gets the same number of cycles on the bus. When more than one DMA controller is present on a processor, the channels from one controller can run at the same time as channels on the other controller. This is possible, for example, when a memory-to-memory transfer takes place from L3 to L2 memory while the second controller feeds a peripheral from L1 memory. If both DMA controllers try to access the same resource (L3 memory, for example), arbitration must take place. In this case, one of the controllers can be programmed to a higher priority than the other.

Each DMA controller has a set of FIFOs that act as a buffer between the DMA subsystem and peripherals or memory. For MemDMA, a FIFO exists on both the source and destination sides of the transfer. The FIFO improves performance by providing a place to hold data while busy resources are preventing a transfer from completing.

Programming the DMA Controller

Let's take a look at what options we have in specifying DMA activity. We will start with the simplest model and build up to more flexible models that, in turn, increase in setup complexity.

For any type of DMA transfer, we always need to specify starting source and destination addresses for data. In the case of a peripheral DMA, the peripheral's FIFO serves as either the source or the destination. When the peripheral serves as the source, a memory location (internal or external) serves as the destination address. When the peripheral serves as the destination, a memory location (internal or external) serves as the source address.

In the simplest MemDMA case, we need to tell the DMA controller the source address, the destination address and the number of words to transfer. With a peripheral DMA, we specify either the source or the destination, depending on the direction of the transfer. The word size of each transfer can be either 8, 16 or 32 bits. This type of transaction represents a simple one-dimensional (1D) transfer with a unity "stride." As part of this transfer, the DMA controller keeps track of the source and destination addresses as they increment. With a unity stride, as in Figure 3.4a, the address increments by 1 byte for 8-bit transfers, 2 bytes for 16-bit transfers, and 4 bytes for 32-bit transfers.

We can add more flexibility to a one-dimensional DMA simply by changing the stride, as in Figure 3.4b. For example, with nonunity strides, we can skip addresses in multiples of the transfer sizes. That is, specifying a 32-bit transfer and striding by 4 samples results in an address increment of 16 bytes (four 32-bit words) after each transfer.

Couching this discussion in Blackfin DMA controller lingo, we have now described the operations of the XCOUNT and XMODIFY registers. XCOUNT is the number of *transfers* that need to be made. Note that this is not necessarily the same as the number of *bytes* to transfer. XMODIFY is the number of bytes to increment the address pointer after the DMA controller moves the first data element. Regardless of the transfer word

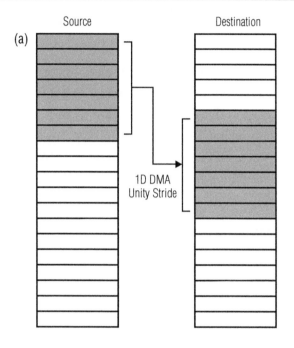

(a)

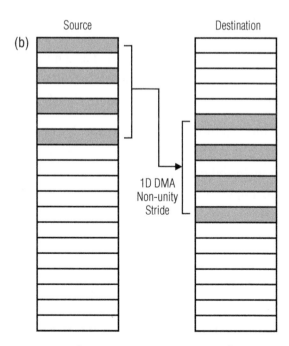

(b)

Figure 3.4 **1D DMA examples**
(a) 1D DMA with unity stride
(b) 1D DMA with non-unity stride

size, XMODIFY is always expressed in bytes. XMODIFY can also take on the value of 0, which has its own advantage, as we'll see later in this chapter.

While the 1D DMA capability is widely used, the two-dimensional (2D) capability is even more useful, especially in video applications. The 2D feature is a direct extension to what we discussed for 1D DMA. In addition to an XCOUNT and XMODIFY value, we also program corresponding YCOUNT and YMODIFY values. It is easiest to think of the 2D DMA as a nested loop, where the inner loop is specified by XCOUNT and XMODIFY, and the outer loop is specified by YCOUNT and YMODIFY. A 1D DMA can then be viewed simply as an "inner loop" of the 2D transfer of the form:

```
for y = 1 to YCOUNT STEP YMODIFY /* 2D with outer loop */
     for x = 1 to XCOUNT STEP XMODIFY /* 1D inner loop */
          {
                  /*Loop goes here */
          }
```

While XMODIFY determines the stride value the DMA controller takes every time XCOUNT decrements, YMODIFY determines the stride taken whenever YCOUNT decrements. As is the case with XCOUNT and XMODIFY, YCOUNT is specified in terms of the number of transfers, while YMODIFY is specified as a number of bytes. Notably, YMODIFY can be negative, which allows the DMA controller to wrap back around to the beginning of the buffer. We'll explore this feature shortly.

For a peripheral DMA, the "memory side" of the transfer can be either 1D or 2D. On the peripheral side, though, it is always a 1D transfer. The only constraint is that the total number of bytes transferred on each side (source and destination) of the DMA must be the same. For example, if we were feeding a peripheral from three 10-byte buffers, the peripheral would have to be set to transfer 30 bytes using any possible combination of supported transfer width and transfer count values available.

MemDMA offers a bit more flexibility. For example, we can set up a 1D-to-1D transfer, a 1D-to-2D transfer, a 2D-to-1D transfer, and of course a 2D-to-2D transfer, as shown in Figure 3.5. The only constraint is that the total number of bytes being transferred on each end of the DMA transfer block has to be the same.

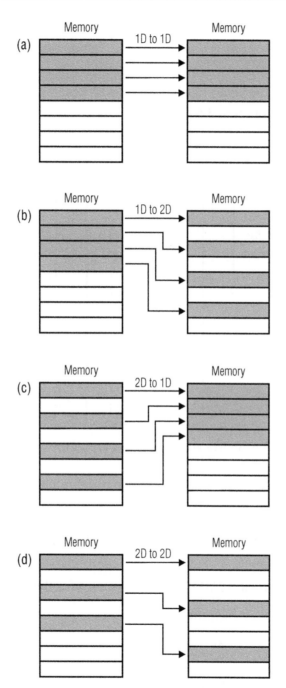

Figure 3.5 **Possible Memory DMA configurations**

Let's now look at some DMA transfer examples:

Example 3.1

Consider a 4-pixel (per line) × 5-line array, with byte-sized pixel values, ordered as shown in Figure 3.6a.

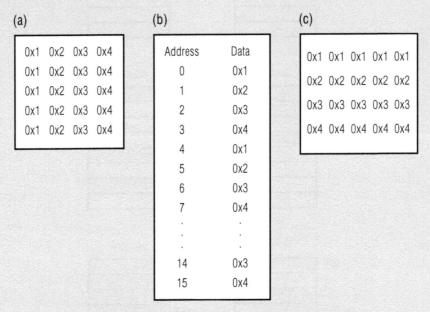

Figure 3.6 **Source and destination arrays for Example 3.1**

While this data is shown as a matrix, it appears consecutively in memory as shown in Figure 3.6b.

We now want to create the array shown in Figure 3.6c using the DMA controller.

The source and destination DMA register settings for this transfer are:

Source	Destination
XCOUNT = 5	XCOUNT = 20
XMODIFY = 4	XMODIFY = 1
YCOUNT = 4	YCOUNT = 0
YMODIFY = −15	YMODIFY = 0

Source and destination word transfer size = 1 byte per transfer.

Let's walk through the process. In this example, we can use a MemDMA, with a 2D-to-1D transfer configuration. Since the source is 2D, it should be clear that the source channel's XCOUNT and YCOUNT are 5 and 4, respectively, since the array size is 5 lines × 4 pixels/line. Because we will use a 1D transfer to fill the destination buffer, we only need to program XCOUNT and XMODIFY on the destination side. In this case, the value of XCOUNT is set to 20, because that is the number of bytes that will be transferred. The YCOUNT value for the destination side is simply 0, and YMODIFY is also 0. You can see that the count values obey the rule we discussed earlier (e.g., $4 \times 5 = 20$ bytes).

Now let's talk about the correct values for XMODIFY and YMODIFY for the source buffer. We want to take the first value (0x1) and skip 4 bytes to the next value of 0x1. We will repeat this five times (Source XCOUNT = 5). The value of the source XMODIFY is 4, because that is the number of bytes the controller skips over to get to the next pixel (including the first pixel). XCOUNT decrements by 1 every time a pixel is collected. When the DMA controller reaches the end of the first row, XCOUNT decrements to 0, and YCOUNT decrements by 1. The value of YMODIFY on the source side then needs to bring the address pointer back to the second element in the array (0x2). At the instant this happens, the address pointer is still pointing to the last element in the first row (0x1). Counting back from that point in the array to the second pixel in the first row, we traverse back by 15 elements. Therefore, the source YMODIFY = –15.

If the core carried out this transfer without the aid of a DMA controller, it would consume valuable cycles to read and write each pixel. Additionally, it would have to keep track of the addresses on the source and destination sides, tracking the stride values with each transfer.

Here's a more complex example involving a 2D-to-2D transfer:

Example 3.2

Let's assume now we start with the array that has a border of 0xFF values, shown in Figure 3.7.

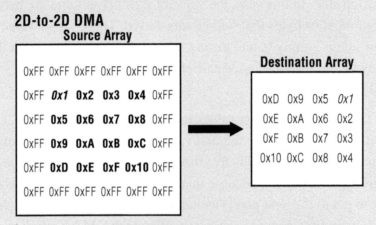

Figure 3.7 **Source and destination arrays for Example 3.2**

We want to keep only the inner square of the source matrix (shown in bold), but we also want to rotate the matrix 90 degrees as shown in Figure 3.7.

The register settings below will produce the transformation shown in this example, and now we will explain why.

Source	Destination
XCOUNT = 4	XCOUNT = 4
XMODIFY = 1	XMODIFY = 4
YCOUNT = 4	YCOUNT = 4
YMODIFY = 3	YMODIFY = −13

As a first step, we need to determine how to access data in the source array. As the DMA controller reads each byte from the source array, the destination builds the output array 1 byte at a time.

How do we get started? Well, let's look at the first byte that we want to move in the input array. It is shown in italics as *0x1*. This will help us select the start address of the source buffer. We then want to sequentially read the next three bytes before we skip over the "border" bytes. The transfer size is assumed to be 1 byte for this example.

Because the controller reads 4 bytes in a row before skipping over some bytes to move to the next line in the array, the source XCOUNT is 4. Because the controller increments the address by 1 as it collects 0x2, 0x3, and 0x4, the source XMODIFY = 1. When the controller finishes the first line, the source YCOUNT decrements by 1. Since we are transferring four lines, the source YCOUNT = 4. Finally, the source YMODIFY = 3, because as we discussed earlier, the address pointer does not increment by XMODIFY after XCOUNT goes from 1 to 0. Setting YMODIFY = 3 ensures the next fetch will be 0x5.

On the destination side of the transfer, we will again program the location of the *0x1* byte as the initial destination address. Since the second byte fetched from the source address was 0x2, the controller will need to write this value to the destination address next. As you can in see in the destination array in Figure 3.7, the destination address has to first be incremented by 4, which defines the destination XMODIFY value. Since the destination array is 4 × 4 in size, the values of both the destination XCOUNT and YCOUNT are 4. The only value left is the destination YMODIFY. To calculate this value, we must compute how many bytes the destination address moves back in the array. After the destination YCOUNT decrements for the first time, the destination address is pointing to the value 0x4. The resulting destination YMODIFY value of −13 will ensure that a value of 0x5 is written to the desired location in the destination buffer.

In Chapter 7, we'll review some data flows that involve a dual-core processor. For some applications, it is desirable to split data between both cores. The DMA controller can be configured to spool data to different memory spaces for the most efficient processing.

Example 3.3

Consider when the processor is connected to a dual-channel sensor that multiplexes alternating video samples into a single output stream. In this example,
each channel transfers four 8-bit samples packed as a 32-bit word. The
samples are arranged such that a "packed" sample from Channel 2 follows
a "packed" sample from Channel 1, and so on, as shown in Figure 3.8. Here
the peripheral serves as the source of the DMA, and L2 memory serves as the
destination. We want to spread the data out in L2 memory to take advantage of
its internal bank structures, as this will consequently allow the processor and
the DMA controller access to different banks simultaneously.

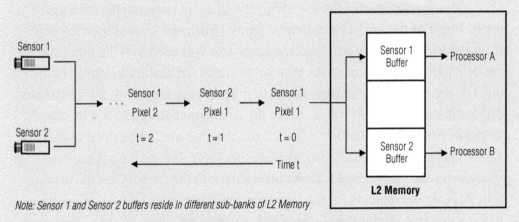

Figure 3.8 **Multiplexed stream from two sensors**

Because a sample is sent from each sensor, we set the destination XCOUNT to 2
(one word each from Sensor 1 and Sensor 2). The value of XMODIFY is set to
the separation distance of the sensor buffers, in bytes. The controller will then
write the first 4 bytes to the beginning of Sensor 1 buffer, skip XMODIFY bytes,
and write the first 4 bytes of Sensor 2 buffer. The value of YCOUNT is based on
the number of transfers required for each line. For a QVGA-sized image, that
would be 320 pixels per line × 2 bytes per pixel / 4 bytes per transfer, or 160
transfers per line. The value of YMODIFY depends on the separation of the two
buffers. In this example, it would be negative (buffer separation + number of
line transfers − 1, which already accounts for the fact that the pointer doesn't
increment when XCOUNT goes to 0).

Earlier, we mentioned that it's useful in some applications to set XMODIFY to 0. A short example will illustrate this concept.

Example 3.4

Consider the case where we want to zero-fill a large section—say 1024 bytes—of L3 memory. To do so, we can first create a 32-bit buffer in internal memory that contains all zeros, and then perform core writes to the block of external memory, but then the core would not be available to do more useful tasks.

So why not use a simple 1D DMA instead? In this case, if we assume a 32-bit word transfer size, the XCOUNT values for the source and destination are (1024 bytes / 4 bytes per transfer), or simply 256 transfers. The XMODIFY value for the destination will be 4 bytes. The source value of XMODIFY can be set to 0 to ensure that the address of the source pointer stays on the same 32-bit word in the source buffer, meaning that only a single 32-bit "zero word" is needed in L1 memory. This will cause the source side of the DMA to continually fetch the value of 0x0000 from the same L1 location, which is subsequently written to the buffer in external memory.

The previous examples show how the DMA controller can move data around without bothering the core to calculate the source and destination addresses. Everything we have shown so far can be accomplished by programming the DMA controller at system initialization.

The next example will provide some insight into implications of transfer sizes in a DMA operation. The DMA bus structure consists of individual buses that are either 16- or 32-bits wide. When 8-bit data is not packed into 16-bit or 32-bit words (by either the memory or peripheral subsystems), some portion of the bus in question goes unused. Example 3.5 considers the scenario where a video port sends 8-bit YCbCr data straight into L2 memory. (Don't worry if you are not too familiar with the term "YCbCr"—you will be after reading Chapter 6!).

Example 3.5

Assume we have Field 1 of a 4:2:2 YCbCr video buffer in L2 memory as shown in Figure 3.9a.

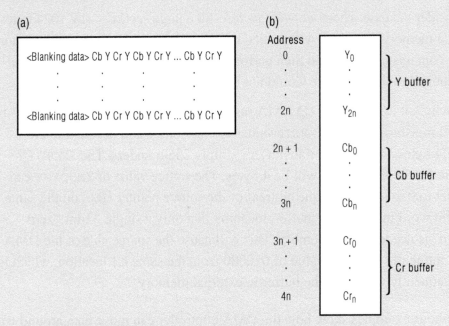

Figure 3.9 **Source and destination buffers for Example 3.5**

We would like to separate the data into discrete Y, Cb and Cr buffers in L3 memory where we can fit the entire field of data, since L2 memory can't hold the entire field for large image sizes. The peripheral sends data to L2 memory in the same order in which the camera sends it. Because there is no re-ordering of the data on the first pass into L2 memory, the word transfer size should be maximized (e.g., to 32 bits). This ensures that the best performance is achieved when the data enters the processor.

How should we separate the buffers? One viable option is to set up three 2D-to-1D DMAs for each line—one each for Y, Cb and Cr pixel components. Because the data that needs to be separated is spread out in the array, 8-bit transfers must be used. Since there are twice as many values of Y as there are of Cr and Cb, the XCOUNT for the source and destination would be twice that of the Cb buffer, and twice that of the Cr buffer as well. On the source side,

XCOUNT would be the number of Y values in each line, and YCOUNT would be the number of lines in the source buffer. This is typically some subset of a video field size. The source XMODIFY = 2, which is the number of bytes to increment the address to reach the next Y value. For Cb or Cr transfers, the source XMODIFY = 4. YMODIFY is simply the number of bytes in the horizontal blanking data that precedes each line.

The destination parameters for the Y buffer in L3 memory are much simpler. Since the destination side of the transfer is one-dimensional, only XCOUNT and XMODIFY are needed. The value of XCOUNT on the destination side is equal to the product of the source XCOUNT and YCOUNT values. The XMODIFY value is simply 1.

This example is important because transfers to L3 memory are not efficient when they are made in byte-sized increments. It is much more efficient to move data into external memory at the maximum transfer size (typically 16 or 32 bits). As such, in this case it is better to create new data buffers from one L2 buffer using the technique we just described. Once the separate buffers are created in L2 memory as shown in Figure 3.9b, three 1D DMAs can transfer them to L3 memory. As you can see, in this case we have created an extra pass of the data (Peripheral to L2, L2 to L3, versus Peripheral to L2 to L3). On the surface, you may think this is something to avoid, because normally we try to reduce data movement passes.

In reality, however, bandwidth of external memory is often more valuable than that of internal memory. The reason the extra pass is more efficient is that the final transfer to L3 memory can be accomplished using 32-bit transfers, which is far more efficient than using 8-bit transfers. When doing four times as many 8-bit transfers, the number of times the DMA bus has to change directions, as well as the number of actual transfers on the bus, eats into total available bandwidth. You may also recall that the IMDMA controller is available to make the intermediate pass in L2 memory, and thus the transfers can be made at the CCLK rate.

DMA Classifications

There are two main classes of DMA transfer configuration: Register mode and Descriptor mode. Regardless of the class of DMA, the same type of information depicted in Table 3.1 makes its way into the DMA controller. When the DMA runs in Register mode, the DMA controller simply uses the values contained in the DMA channel's registers. In the case of Descriptor mode, the DMA controller looks in memory for its configuration values.

Table 3.1 **DMA registers**

Next Descriptor Pointer (lower 16 bits)	Address of next descriptor
Next Descriptor Pointer (upper 16 bits)	Address of next descriptor
Start Address (lower 16 bits)	Start address (source or destination)
Start Address (upper 16 bits)	Start address (source or destination)
DMA Configuration	Control information (enable, interrupt selection, 1D vs. 2D)
X_Count	Number of transfers in inner loop
X_Modify	Number of bytes between each transfer in inner loop
Y_Count	Number of transfers in outer loop
Y_Modify	Number of bytes between end of inner loop and start of outer loop

Register-Based DMA

In a register-based DMA, the processor directly programs DMA control registers to initiate a transfer. Register-based DMA provides the best DMA controller performance, because registers don't need to keep reloading from descriptors in memory, and the core does not have to maintain descriptors.

Register-based DMA consists of two sub-modes: *Autobuffer mode* and *Stop mode*. In Autobuffer DMA, when one transfer block completes, the control registers automatically reload to their original setup values, and the same DMA process restarts, with zero overhead.

As we see in Figure 3.10, if we set up an Autobuffer DMA to transfer some number of words from a peripheral to a buffer in L1 data memory, the DMA controller would reload the initial parameters immediately upon completion of the 1024th word transfer. This creates a "circular buffer," because after a value is written to the last location in the buffer, the next value will be written to the first location in the buffer.

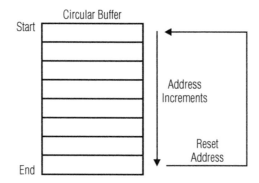

Figure 3.10 **Implementing a Circular Buffer**

Autobuffer DMA especially suits performance-sensitive applications with continuous data streams. The DMA controller can read in the stream independent of other processor activities and then interrupt the core when each transfer completes. While it's possible to stop Autobuffer mode gracefully, if a DMA process needs to be started and stopped regularly, it doesn't make sense to use this mode.

Let's take a look at an Autobuffer example.

Example 3.6

Consider an application where the processor operates on 512 audio samples at a time, and the codec sends new data at the audio clock rate. Autobuffer DMA is the perfect choice in this scenario, because the data transfer occurs at such periodic intervals.

Drawing on this same model, let's assume we want to "double-buffer" the incoming audio data. That is, we want the DMA controller to fill one buffer while we operate on the other. The processor must finish working on a particular data buffer before the DMA controller wraps around to the beginning of it, as shown in Figure 3.11. Using Autobuffer mode, configuration is simple.

The total count of the Autobuffer DMA must comprise the size of two data buffers via a 2D DMA. In this example, each data buffer size corresponds to the size of the inner loop on a 2D DMA. The number of buffers corresponds to the outer loop. Therefore, we keep XCOUNT = 512. Assuming the audio data element size is 4 bytes, we program the word transfer size to 32 bits and set

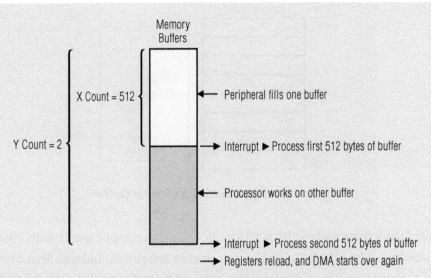

Figure 3.11 **Double buffering**

XMODIFY = 4. Since we want two buffers, we set YCOUNT = 2. If we want the two buffers to be back-to-back in memory, we must set YMODIFY = 1. However, for the reasons we've discussed in Chapter 2, in many cases it's smarter to separate the buffers. This way, we avoid conflicts between the processor and the DMA controller in accessing the same sub-banks of memory. To separate the buffers, YMODIFY can be increased to provide the proper separation.

In a 2D DMA transfer, we have the option of generating an interrupt when XCOUNT expires and/or when YCOUNT expires. Translated to this example, we can set the DMA interrupt to trigger every time XCOUNT decrements to 0 (i.e., at the end of each set of 512 transfers). Again, it is easy to think of this in terms of receiving an interrupt at the end of each inner loop.

Stop mode works identically to Autobuffer DMA, except registers don't reload after DMA completes, so the entire DMA transfer takes place only once. Stop mode is most useful for one-time transfers that happen based on some event—for example, moving data blocks from one location to another in a nonperiodic fashion, as is the case for buffer initialization. This mode is also useful when you need to synchronize events. For example, if one task has to complete before the next transfer is initiated, Stop mode can guarantee this sequencing.

Descriptor-Based DMA

DMA transfers that are descriptor-based require a set of parameters stored within memory to initiate a DMA sequence. The descriptor contains all of the same parameters normally programmed into the DMA control register set. However, descriptors also allow the chaining together of multiple DMA sequences. In descriptor-based DMA operations, we can program a DMA channel to automatically set up and start another DMA transfer after the current sequence completes. The descriptor-based model provides the most flexibility in managing a system's DMA transfers.

Blackfin processors offer two main descriptor models—a *Descriptor Array* scheme and a *Descriptor List* method. The goal of these two models is to allow a tradeoff between flexibility and performance. Let's take a look at how this is done.

In the Descriptor Array mode, descriptors reside in consecutive memory locations. The DMA controller still fetches descriptors from memory, but because the next descriptor immediately follows the current descriptor, the two words that describe where to look for the next descriptor (and their corresponding descriptor fetches) aren't necessary. Because the descriptor does not contain this Next Descriptor Pointer entry, the DMA controller expects a group of descriptors to follow one another in memory like an array.

A Descriptor List is used when the individual descriptors are not located "back-to-back" in memory. There are actually multiple sub-modes here, again to allow a tradeoff between performance and flexibility. In a "small descriptor" model, descriptors include a single 16-bit field that specifies the lower portion of the Next Descriptor Pointer field; the upper portion is programmed separately via a register and doesn't change. This, of course, confines descriptors to a specific 64K (= 2^{16}) page in memory. When the descriptors need to be located across this boundary, a "large" model is available that provides 32 bits for the Next Descriptor Pointer entry.

Regardless of the descriptor mode, using more descriptor values requires more descriptor fetches. This is why Blackfin processors specify a "flex descriptor model" that tailors the descriptor length to include only what's needed for a particular transfer, as shown in Figure 3.12. For example, if 2D DMA is not needed, the YMODIFY and YCOUNT registers do not need to be part of the descriptor block.

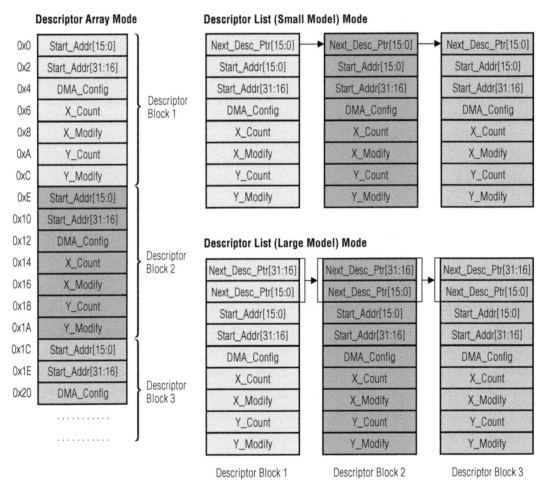

Figure 3.12 **DMA descriptor models**

Descriptor Management

So what's the best way to manage a descriptor list? Well, the answer is application-dependent, but it is important to understand what alternatives exist.

The first option we will describe behaves very much like an Autobuffer DMA. It involves setting up multiple descriptors that are chained together as shown in Figure

3.13a. The term "chained" implies that one descriptor points to the next descriptor, which is loaded automatically once the data transfer specified by the first descriptor block completes. To complete the chain, the last descriptor points back to the first descriptor, and the process repeats. One reason to use this technique rather than the Autobuffer mode is that descriptors allow more flexibility in the size and direction of the transfers. In our YCbCr example (Example 3.5), the Y buffer is twice as large as the other buffers. This can be easily described via descriptors and would be much harder to implement with an Autobuffer scheme.

(a) **Linked List of Descriptors**

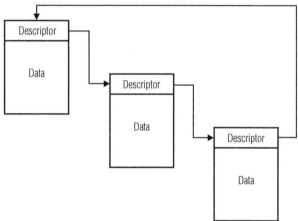

(b) **"Throttled" Descriptor Management**

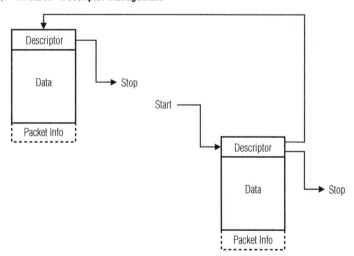

Figure 3.13 **DMA descriptor throttled by the processor**

The second option involves the processor manually managing the descriptor list. Recall that a descriptor is really a structure in memory. Each descriptor contains a configuration word, and each configuration word contains an "Enable" bit which can regulate when a transfer starts. Let's assume we have four buffers that have to move data over some given task interval. If we need to have the processor start each transfer specifically when the processor is ready, we can set up all of the descriptors in advance, but with the "Enable" bits cleared. When the processor determines the time is right to start a descriptor, it simply updates the descriptor in memory and then writes to a DMA register to start the stalled DMA channel. Figure 3.13b shows an example of this flow.

When is this type of transfer useful? As we will see in Chapter 7, EMP applications often require us to synchronize an input stream to an output stream. For example, we may receive video samples into memory at a rate that is different from the rate at which we display output video. This will happen in real systems even when you attempt to make the streams run at exactly the same clock rate. In cases where synchronization is an issue, the processor can manually regulate the DMA descriptors corresponding to the output buffer. Before the next descriptor is enabled, the processor can synchronize the stream by adjusting the current output descriptor via a semaphore mechanism. We will talk more about semaphores in Chapter 4, but for now, just consider them tools that guarantee only one entity at a time accesses a shared resource.

When using internal DMA descriptor chains or DMA-based streams between processors, it can also be useful to add an extra word at the end of the transferred data block that helps identify the packet being sent, including information on how to handle the data and, possibly, a time stamp. The dashed area of Figure 3.13b shows an example of this scheme.

Most sophisticated applications have a "DMA Manager" function implemented in software. This may be provided as part of an operating system or real-time kernel, but it can also run without either of these. In both cases, an application submits DMA descriptor requests to the DMA Queue Manager, whose responsibility it is to handle each request. Usually, an address pointer to a "callback" function is part of the system as well. This function carries out the work you want the processor to perform when a data buffer is ready, without needlessly making the core linger in a high-priority interrupt service routine. We will review this concept in more detail in Chapters 4 and 7.

There are two general methods for managing a descriptor queue using interrupts. The first is based on interrupting upon the completion of every descriptor. Use this method only if you can guarantee that each interrupt event will be serviced separately, with no interrupt overrun. The second involves interrupting only on completion of the work transfer specified by the last descriptor of a work block. A work block is a collection of one or more descriptors.

To maintain synchronization of the descriptor queue, you need to maintain in software a count of descriptors added to the queue, while the interrupt handler maintains a count of completed descriptors removed from the queue. The counts are then equal only when the DMA channel pauses after having processed all the descriptors.

We will expand more on this concept in Chapter 7, where we tie together descriptor-based and register-based DMAs running in concert within an application.

Advanced DMA Features

System Performance Tuning

To effectively use DMA in a multimedia system, there must be enough DMA channels to support the processor's peripheral set fully, with more than one pair of Memory DMA streams. This is an important point, because there are bound to be raw media streams incoming to external memory (via high-speed peripherals), while at the same time data blocks will be moving back and forth between external memory and L1 memory for core processing. What's more, DMA engines that allow direct data transfer between peripherals and external memory, rather than requiring a stopover in L1 memory, can save extra data passes in numerically intensive algorithms.

As data rates and performance demands increase, it becomes critical to have "system performance tuning" controls at your disposal. For example, the DMA controller might be optimized to transfer a data word on every clock cycle. When there are multiple transfers ongoing in the same direction (e.g., all from internal memory to external memory), this is usually the most efficient way to operate the controller because it prevents idle time on the DMA bus.

But in cases involving multiple bidirectional video and audio streams, "direction control" becomes obligatory in order to prevent one stream from usurping the bus entirely. For instance, if the DMA controller always granted the DMA bus to any peripheral that was ready to transfer a data word, overall throughput would degrade when using SDRAM. In situations where data transfers switch direction on nearly every cycle, the latency associated with turn-around time on the SDRAM bus will lower throughput significantly. As a result, DMA controllers that have a channel-programmable burst size hold a clear advantage over those with a fixed transfer size. Because each DMA channel can connect a peripheral to either internal or external memory, it is also important to be able to automatically service a peripheral that may issue an urgent request for the bus.

Other important DMA features include the ability to prioritize DMA channels to meet current peripheral task requirements, as well as the capacity to configure the corresponding DMA interrupts to match these priority levels. These functions help insure that data buffers do not overflow due to DMA activity on other peripherals, and they provide the programmer with extra degrees of freedom in optimizing the entire system based on the data traffic on each DMA channel.

External DMA

Let's close out this chapter by spending a few minutes discussing how to DMA data between the processor and a memory-mapped external device. When a device is memory-mapped to an asynchronous memory bank, a MemDMA channel can move data into and out of the external chip via the DMA FIFOs we described earlier. If the destination for this data is another external memory bank in SDRAM, for example, the bus turns around when a few samples have entered the DMA FIFO, and these samples are then written back out over the same external bus, to another memory bank. This process repeats for the duration of the transfer period.

Normally, these Memory DMA transfers are performed at maximum speed. Once a MemDMA starts, data transfers continuously until the data count expires or the DMA channel is halted. This works well when the transfer is being made as a memory-to-memory transfer, but if one of the ends of the transfer is a memory-mapped device, this can cause the processor to service the transactions constantly, or impede the memory-mapped device from making transfers effectively.

When the data source and/or destination is external to the processor, a separate "Handshake DMA" mode can help throttle the MemDMA transfer, as well as improve performance by removing the processor from having to be involved in every transfer. In this mode, the Memory DMA does not transfer data automatically when it is enabled. Rather, it waits for an external trigger from another device. Once a trigger event is detected, a user-specified portion of data is transferred, and then the Mem-DMA channel halts and waits for the next trigger.

The handshake mode can be used to control the timing of memory-to-memory transfers. In addition, it enables the Memory DMA to operate efficiently with asynchronous FIFO-style devices connected to the external memory bus. In the Blackfin processor, the external interface acknowledges a Handshake DMA request by performing a programmable number of read or write operations. It is up to the device connected to the designated external pins to de-assert or assert the "DMA request" signal.

The Handshake DMA configuration registers control how many data transfers are performed upon every DMA request. When set to 1, the peripheral times every individual data transfer. If greater than 1, the external peripheral must possess sufficient buffer size to provide or consume the number of words programmed. Once the handshake transfer commences, no flow control can hold off the DMA from transferring the entire data block.

In the next chapter, we will discuss "speculative fetches." These are fetches that are started but not finished. Normally, speculative fetches can cause problems for external FIFOs, because the FIFO can't tell the difference between an aborted access and a real access, and it increments its read/write pointers in either case. Handshake DMA, however, eliminates this issue, because all DMA accesses that start always finish.

What's Next?

Now that you have a thorough understanding of memory and DMA concepts, we'll integrate these topics in Chapter 4 as part of an overall discussion of system performance tuning. We will also focus on how a processor's core architectural features can sharply improve performance in an EMP application.

System Resource Partitioning and Code Optimization

Introduction

In an ideal situation, we can select an embedded processor for our application that provides maximum performance for minimum extra development effort. In this utopian environment, we could code everything in a high-level language like C, we wouldn't need an intimate knowledge of our chosen device, it wouldn't matter where we placed our data and code, we wouldn't need to devise any data movement subsystem, the performance of external devices wouldn't matter... In short, everything would just work.

Alas, this is only the stuff of dreams and marketing presentations. The reality is, as embedded processors evolve in performance and flexibility, their complexity also increases. Depending on the time-to-market for your application, you will have to walk a fine line to reach your performance targets. The key is to find the right balance between getting the application to work and achieving optimum performance. Knowing when the performance is "good enough" rather than optimal can mean getting your product out on time versus missing a market window.

In this chapter, we want to explain some important aspects of processor architectures that can make a real difference in designing a successful multimedia system. Once you understand the basic mechanics of how the various architectural sections behave, you will be able to gauge where to focus your efforts, rather than embark on the noble yet unwieldy goal of becoming an expert on all aspects of your chosen processor.

We discussed the basic components of the Blackfin architecture in Chapter 1. Here, we'll explore in detail some Blackfin processor architectural constructs. Again, keep in mind that much of our discussion generalizes to other processor families from different vendors as well.

We will begin with what should be key focal points in any complex application: interrupt and exception handling and response times.

Event Generation and Handling

Nothing in an application should make you think "performance" more than event management. If you have used a microprocessor, you know that "events" encompass two categories: interrupts and exceptions. An interrupt is an event that happens asynchronous to processor execution. For example, when a peripheral completes a transfer, it can generate an interrupt to alert the processor that data is ready for processing.

Exceptions, on the other hand, occur synchronously to program execution. An exception occurs based on the instruction about to be executed. The change of flow due to an exception occurs prior to the offending instruction actually being executed. Later in this chapter, we'll describe the most widely used exception handler in an embedded processor—the handler that manages pages describing memory attributes. Now, however, we will focus on interrupts rather than exceptions, because managing interrupts plays such a critical role in achieving peak performance.

System Interrupts

System level interrupts (those that are generated by peripherals) are handled in two stages—first in the system domain, and then in the core domain. Once the system interrupt controller (SIC) acknowledges an interrupt request from a peripheral, it compares the peripheral's assigned priority to all current activity from other peripherals to decide when to service this particular interrupt request. The most important peripherals in an application should be mapped to the highest priority levels. In general, the highest-bandwidth peripherals need the highest priority. One "exception" to this rule (pardon the pun!) is where an external processor or supervisory circuit uses a nonmaskable interrupt (NMI) to indicate the occurrence of an important event, such as powering down.

When the SIC is ready, it passes the interrupt request information to the core event controller (CEC), which handles all types of events, not just interrupts. Every interrupt from the SIC maps into a priority level at the CEC that regulates how to service interrupts with respect to one another, as Figure 4.1 shows. The CEC checks the "vector" assignment for the current interrupt request, to find the address of the appropriate interrupt service routine (ISR). Finally, it loads this address into the processor's execution pipeline to start executing the ISR.

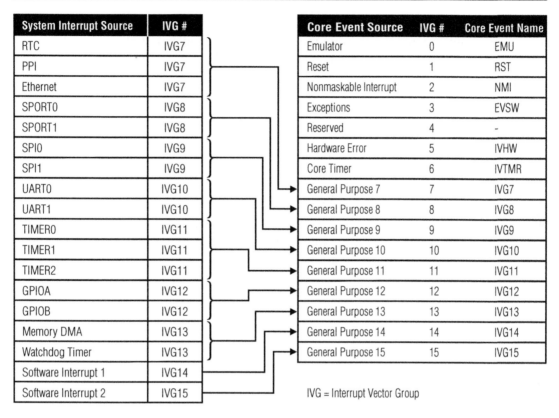

System Interrupt Source	IVG #
RTC	IVG7
PPI	IVG7
Ethernet	IVG7
SPORT0	IVG8
SPORT1	IVG8
SPI0	IVG9
SPI1	IVG9
UART0	IVG10
UART1	IVG10
TIMER0	IVG11
TIMER1	IVG11
TIMER2	IVG11
GPIOA	IVG12
GPIOB	IVG12
Memory DMA	IVG13
Watchdog Timer	IVG13
Software Interrupt 1	IVG14
Software Interrupt 2	IVG15

Core Event Source	IVG #	Core Event Name
Emulator	0	EMU
Reset	1	RST
Nonmaskable Interrupt	2	NMI
Exceptions	3	EVSW
Reserved	4	-
Hardware Error	5	IVHW
Core Timer	6	IVTMR
General Purpose 7	7	IVG7
General Purpose 8	8	IVG8
General Purpose 9	9	IVG9
General Purpose 10	10	IVG10
General Purpose 11	11	IVG11
General Purpose 12	12	IVG12
General Purpose 13	13	IVG13
General Purpose 14	14	IVG14
General Purpose 15	15	IVG15

IVG = Interrupt Vector Group

Figure 4.1 **Sample system-to-core interrupt mapping**

There are two key interrupt-related questions you need to ask when building your system. The first is, "How long does the processor take to respond to an interrupt?" The second is, "How long can any given task afford to wait when an interrupt comes in?"

The answers to these questions will determine what your processor can actually perform within an interrupt or exception handler.

For the purposes of this discussion, we define interrupt response time as the number of cycles it takes from when the interrupt is generated at the source (including the time it takes for the current instruction to finish executing) to the time that the first instruction is executed in the interrupt service routine. In our experience, the most common method software engineers use to evaluate this interval for themselves is to set up a programmable flag to generate an interrupt when its pin is triggered by an externally generated pulse. The first instruction in the interrupt service routine then performs a write to a different flag pin. The resulting time difference is then measured on an oscilloscope. This method only provides a rough idea of the time taken to service interrupts, including the time required to latch an interrupt at the peripheral, propagate the interrupt through to the core, and then vector the core to the first instruction in the interrupt service routine. Thus, it is important to run a benchmark that more closely simulates the profile of your end application. We'll consider some more detailed scenarios in Chapter 7.

Once the processor is running code in an ISR, other higher priority interrupts are held off until the return address associated with the current interrupt is saved off to the stack. This is an important point, because even if you designate all other interrupt channels as higher priority than the currently serviced interrupt, these other channels will all be held off until you save the return address to the stack. The mechanism to re-enable interrupts kicks in automatically when you save the return address. When you program in C, any register the ISR uses will automatically be saved to the stack. Before exiting the ISR, the registers are restored from the stack. This also happens automatically, but depending on where your stack is located and how many registers are involved, saving and restoring data to the stack can take a significant amount of cycles.

Interrupt service routines often perform some type of processing. For example, when a line of video data arrives into its destination buffer, the ISR might run code to filter or downsample it. For this case, when the handler does the work, other interrupts are held off (provided that nesting is disabled) until the processor services the current interrupt.

When an operating system or kernel is used, however, the most common technique is to service the interrupt as soon as possible, release a semaphore, and perhaps make a call to a callback function, which then does the actual processing. The semaphore in this context provides a way to signal other tasks that it is okay to continue or to assume control over some resource.

For example, we can allocate a semaphore to a routine in shared memory. To prevent more than one task from accessing the routine, one task takes the semaphore while it is using the routine, and the other task has to wait until the semaphore has been relinquished before it can use the routine. A Callback Manager can optionally assist with this activity by allocating a callback function to each interrupt. This adds a protocol layer on top of the lowest layer of application code, but in turn it allows the processor to exit the ISR as soon as possible and return to a lower-priority task. Once the ISR is exited, the intended processing can occur without holding off new interrupts.

We already mentioned that a higher-priority interrupt can break into an existing ISR once you save the return address to the stack. However, some processors (like Blackfin) also support self-nesting of core interrupts, where an interrupt of one priority level can interrupt an ISR of the same level, once the return address is saved. This feature can be useful for building a simple scheduler or kernel that uses low-priority software-generated interrupts to preempt an ISR and allow the processing of ongoing tasks.

There are two additional performance-related issues to consider when you plan out your interrupt usage. The first is the placement of your ISR code. For interrupts that run most frequently, every attempt should be made to locate these in L1 instruction memory. On Blackfin processors, this strategy allows single-cycle access time. Moreover, if the processor were in the midst of a multi-cycle fetch from external memory, the fetch would be interrupted, and the processor would vector to the ISR code.

Keep in mind that before you re-enable higher priority interrupts, you have to save more than just the return address to the stack. Any register used inside the current ISR must also be saved. This is one reason why the stack should be located in the fastest available memory in your system. An L1 "scratchpad" memory bank, usually smaller in size than the other L1 data banks, can be used to hold the stack. This allows the fastest context switching when taking an interrupt.

Programming Methodology

It's nice not to have to be an expert in your chosen processor, but even if you program in a high-level language, it's important to understand certain things about the architecture for which you're writing code.

One mandatory task when undertaking a signal-processing-intensive project is deciding what kind of programming methodology to use. The choice is usually between assembly language and a high-level language (HLL) like C or C++. This decision revolves around many factors, so it's important to understand the benefits and drawbacks each approach entails.

The obvious benefits of C/C++ include modularity, portability and reusability. Not only do the majority of embedded programmers have experience with one of these high-level languages, but also a huge code base exists that can be ported from an existing processor domain to a new processor in a relatively straightforward manner. Because assembly language is architecture-specific, reuse is typically restricted to devices in the same processor family. Also, within a development team it is often desirable to have various teams coding different system modules, and an HLL allows these cross-functional teams to be processor-agnostic.

One reason assembly has been difficult to program is its focus on actual data flow between the processor register sets, computational units and memories. In C/C++, this manipulation occurs at a much more abstract level through the use of variables and function/procedure calls, making the code easier to follow and maintain.

The C/C++ compilers available today are quite resourceful, and they do a great job of compiling the HLL code into tight assembly code. One common mistake happens when programmers try to "outsmart" the compiler. In trying to make it easier for the compiler, they in fact make things more difficult! It's often best to just let the optimizing compiler do its job. However, the fact remains that compiler performance is tuned to a specific set of features that the tool developer considered most important. Therefore, it cannot exceed handcrafted assembly code performance in all situations.

The bottom line is that developers use assembly language only when it is necessary to optimize important processing-intensive code blocks for efficient execution. Compiler features can do a very good job, but nothing beats thoughtful, direct control of your application data flow and computation.

Architectural Features for Efficient Programming

In order to achieve high performance media processing capability, you must understand the types of core processor structures that can help optimize performance. These include the following capabilities:

- Multiple operations per cycle

- Hardware loop constructs

- Specialized addressing modes

- Interlocked instruction pipelines

These features can make an enormous difference in computational efficiency. Let's discuss each one in turn.

Multiple Operations per Cycle

Processors are often benchmarked by how many millions of instructions they can execute per second (MIPS). However, for today's processors, this can be misleading because of the confusion surrounding what actually constitutes an instruction. For example, multi-issue instructions, which were once reserved for use in higher-cost parallel processors, are now also available in low-cost, fixed-point processors. In addition to performing multiple ALU/MAC operations each core processor cycle, additional data loads and stores can be completed in the same cycle. This type of construct has obvious advantages in code density and execution time.

An example of a Blackfin multi-operation instruction is shown in Figure 4.2. In addition to two separate MAC operations, a data fetch and data store (or two data fetches) can also be accomplished in the same processor clock cycle. Correspondingly, each address can be updated in the same cycle that all of the other activities are occurring.

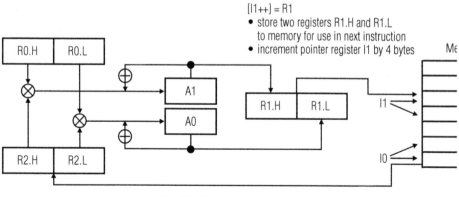

Instruction:
R1.H=(A1+=R0.H*R2.H), R1.L=(A0+=R0.L*R2.L) || R2 = [I0--] || [I1++] = R1;

R1.H=(A1+=R0.H*R2.H), R1.L=(A0+=R0.L*R2.L)
• multiply R0.H*R2.H, accumulate to A1, store to R1.H
• multiply R0.L*R2.L, accumulate to A0, store to R1.L

[I1++] = R1
• store two registers R1.H and R1.L
  to memory for use in next instruction
• increment pointer register I1 by 4 bytes

R2 = [I0 - -]
• load two 16-bit registers R2.H and R2.L from
  memory for use in next instruction
• decrement pointer register I0 by 4 bytes

Figure 4.2 **Example of single-cycle, multi-issue instruction**

Hardware Loop Constructs

Looping is a critical feature in real-time processing algorithms. There are two key looping-related features that can improve performance on a wide variety of algorithms: *zero-overhead hardware loops* and *hardware loop buffers*.

Zero-overhead loops allow programmers to initialize loops simply by setting up a count value and defining the loop bounds. The processor will continue to execute this loop until the count has been reached. In contrast, a software implementation would add overhead that would cut into the real-time processing budget.

Many processors offer zero-overhead loops, but hardware loop buffers, which are less common, can really add increased performance in looping constructs. They act as a kind of cache for instructions being executed in the loop. For example, after the first time through a loop, the instructions can be kept in the loop buffer, eliminating the need to re-fetch the same code each time through the loop. This can produce a significant savings in cycles by keeping several loop instructions in a buffer where they can be accessed in a single cycle. The use of the hardware loop construct comes at no cost to the HLL programmer, since the compiler should automatically use hardware looping instead of conditional jumps.

Let's look at some examples to illustrate the concepts we've just discussed.

Example 4.1 Dot Product

The dot product, or scalar product, is an operation useful in measuring orthogonality of two vectors. It's also a fundamental operator in digital filter computations. Most C programmers should be familiar with the following implementation of a dot product:

```
short dot(const short a[], const short b[], int size) {
```

/* Note: It is important to declare the input buffer arrays as const, because this gives the compiler a guarantee that neither "a" nor "b" will be modified by the function. */

```
    int i;
    int output = 0;

    for(i=0; i<size; i++) {
        output += (a[i] * b[i]);
```

```
    }
    return output;


}
```

Below is the main portion of the equivalent assembly code:

```
/* P0 = Loop Count, P1 & I0 hold starting addresses of a & b
   arrays */
A1 = A0 = 0;                  /* A0 & A1 are accumulators */
LSETUP (loop1,loop1) LC0 = P0 ;     /* Set up hardware loop
   starting and ending at label loop1 */
loop1: A1 += R1.H * R0.H , A0 += R1.L * R0.L || R1 = [ P1 ++ ]
   || R0 = [ I0 ++ ] ;
```

The following points illustrate how a processor's architectural features can facilitate this tight coding.

Hardware loop buffers and loop counters eliminate the need for a jump instruction at the end of each iteration. Since a dot product is a summation of products, it is implemented in a loop. Some processors use a JUMP instruction at the end of each iteration in order to process the next iteration of the loop. This contrasts with the assembly program above, which shows the LSETUP instruction as the only instruction needed to implement a loop.

Multi-issue instructions allow computation and two data accesses with pointer updates in the same cycle. In each iteration, the values a[i] and b[i] must be read, then multiplied, and finally written back to the running summation in the variable output. On many microcontroller platforms, this effectively amounts to four instructions. The last line of the assembly code shows that all of these operations can be executed in one cycle.

Parallel ALU operations allow two 16-bit instructions to be executed simultaneously. The assembly code shows two accumulator units (A0 and A1) used in each iteration. This reduces the number of iterations by 50%, effectively halving the original execution time.

Specialized Addressing Modes

Byte Addressability

Allowing the processor to access multiple data words in a single cycle requires substantial flexibility in address generation. In addition to the more signal-processing-centric access sizes along 16- and 32-bit boundaries, byte addressing is required for the most efficient processing. This is important for multimedia processing because many video-based systems operate on 8-bit data. When memory accesses are restricted to a single boundary, the processor may spend extra cycles to mask off relevant bits.

Circular Buffering

Another beneficial addressing capability is *circular buffering*. We have already discussed this concept in Chapter 3 from a DMA perspective. We will now look at it from the processor's perspective. For maximum efficiency, this feature must be supported directly by the processor, with no special management overhead. Circular buffering allows a programmer to define buffers in memory and stride through them automatically. Once the buffer is set up, no special software interaction is required to navigate through the data. The address generator handles nonunity strides and, more importantly, handles the "wrap-around" feature illustrated in Figure 4.3. Without this automated address generation, the programmer would have to manually keep track of buffer pointer positions, thus wasting valuable processing cycles.

Many optimizing compilers will automatically use hardware circular buffering when they encounter array addressing with a modulus operator.

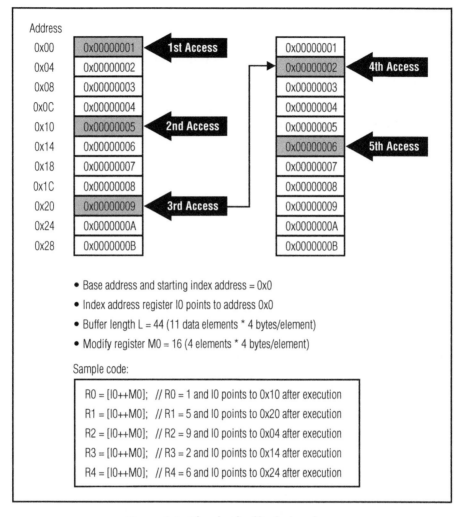

Figure 4.3 **Circular buffer in hardware**

Example 4.2. Single-Sample FIR

The finite impulse response filter is a very common filter structure equivalent to the convolution operator. A straightforward C implementation follows:

```
// sample the signal into a circular buffer
x[cur] = sampling_function();
cur = (cur+1)%TAPS; // advance cur pointer in circular fashion

// perform the multiply-addition
y = 0;
for (k=0; k<TAPS; k++) {
  y += h[k] * x[(cur+k)%TAPS];
}
```

The essential part of an FIR kernel written in assembly is shown below.

```
/* the samples are stored in the R0 register, while the
   coefficients are stored in the R1 register */
LSETUP (loop_begin, loop_end) LC0 = P0;   /* loop counter set to
   traverse the filter */
loop_begin: A1+=R0.H*R1.L, A0+=R0.L*R1.L || R0.L = [I0++] ;
   /* perform MAC and fetch next data */
loop_end: A1+=R0.L*R1.H, A0+=R0.H*R1.H || R0.H = [I0++] || R1 =
   [I1++];/* perform MAC and fetch next data */
```

In the C code snippet, the % (modulus) operator provides a mechanism for circular buffering. As shown in the assembly kernel, this modulus operator does not get translated into an additional instruction inside the loop. Instead, the Data Address Generator registers I0 and I1 are configured outside the loop to automatically wrap around to the beginning upon hitting the buffer boundary.

Bit Reversal

An essential addressing mode for efficient signal-processing operations such as the FFT and DCT is bit reversal. Just as the name implies, bit reversal involves reversing the bits in a binary address. That is, the least significant bits are swapped in position with the most significant bits. The data ordering required by a radix-2 butterfly is in "bit-reversed" order, so bit-reversed indices are used to combine FFT stages. It is possible to calculate these bit-reversed indices in software, but this is very inefficient. An example of bit reversal address flow is shown in Figure 4.4.

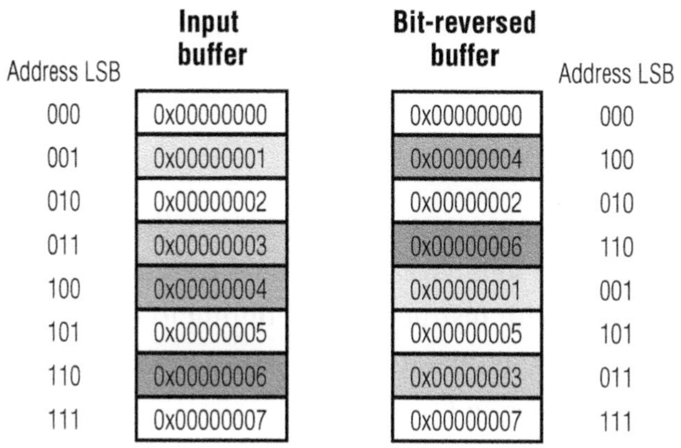

Address LSB	Input buffer	Bit-reversed buffer	Address LSB
000	0x00000000	0x00000000	000
001	0x00000001	0x00000004	100
010	0x00000002	0x00000002	010
011	0x00000003	0x00000006	110
100	0x00000004	0x00000001	001
101	0x00000005	0x00000005	101
110	0x00000006	0x00000003	011
111	0x00000007	0x00000007	111

Sample code:

```
LSETUP(start,end) LC0 = P0;          //Loop count = 8
start: R0 = [I0] || I0 += M0 (BREV) ;  // I0 points to input buffer, automatically incremented in
                                       //bit-reversed progression
end:[I2++] = R0;                       // I2 points to bit-reversed buffer
```

Figure 4.4 **Bit reversal in hardware**

Since bit reversal is very specific to algorithms like fast Fourier transforms and discrete Fourier transforms, it is difficult for any HLL compiler to employ hardware bit reversal. For this reason, comprehensive knowledge of the underlying architecture and assembly language are key to fully utilizing this addressing mode.

Example 4.3 FFT

A fast Fourier transform is an integral part of many signal-processing algorithms. One of its peculiarities is that if the input vector is in sequential time order, the output comes out in bit-reversed order. Most traditional general-purpose processors require the programmer to implement a separate routine to unscramble the bit-reversed output. On a media processor, bit reversal is often designed into the addressing engine.

Allowing the hardware to automatically bit-reverse the output of an FFT algorithm relieves the programmer from writing additional utilities, and thus improves performance.

Interlocked Instruction Pipelines

As processors increase in speed, it is necessary to add stages to the processing pipeline. For instances where a high-level language is the sole programming language, the compiler is responsible for dealing with instruction scheduling to maximize performance through the pipeline. That said, the following information is important to understand even if you're programming in C.

On older processor architectures, pipelines are usually not interlocked. On these architectures, executing certain combinations of neighboring instructions can yield incorrect results. Interlocked pipelines like the one in Figure 4.5, on the other hand, make assembly programming (as well as the life of compiler engineers) easier by automatically inserting stalls when necessary. This prevents the assembly programmer from scheduling instructions in a way that will produce inaccurate results. It should be noted that, even if the pipeline is interlocked, instruction rearrangement can still yield optimization improvements by eliminating unnecessary stalls.

Let's take a look at stalls in more detail. Stalls will show up for one of four reasons:

1. The instruction in question may itself take more than one cycle to execute. When this is the case, there isn't anything you can do to eliminate the stall. For example, a 32-bit integer multiply might take three core-clock cycles to execute on a 16-bit processor. This will cause a "bubble" in two pipeline stages for a three-cycle instruction.

IF1-3: Instruction Fetch
DC: Decode
AC: Address Calculation
EX1-4: Execution
WB: Writeback

		Pipeline Stage								
	IF1	**IF2**	**IF3**	**DC**	**AC**	**EX1**	**EX2**	**EX3**	**EX4**	**WB**
1	Inst1									
2	Inst2	Inst1								
3	Inst3	Inst2	Inst1							
4	Inst4	Inst3	Inst2	Inst1						
5	Inst5	Inst4	Inst3	Inst2	Inst1					
6	Branch	Inst5	Inst4	Inst3	Inst2	Inst1				
7	Stall	Branch	Inst5	Inst4	Inst3	Inst2	Inst1			
8	Stall	Stall	Branch	Inst5	Inst4	Inst3	Inst2	Inst1		
9	Stall	Stall	Stall	Branch	Inst5	Inst4	Inst3	Inst2	Inst1	
10	Stall	Stall	Stall	Stall	Branch	Inst5	Inst4	Inst3	Inst2	Inst1

Time (vertical label on left)

Figure 4.5 **Example of interlocked pipeline architecture with stalls inserted**

2. The second case involves the location of one instruction in the pipeline with respect to an instruction that follows it. For example, in some instructions, a stall may exist because the result of the first instruction is used as an operand of the following instruction. When this happens and you are programming in assembly, it is often possible to move the instruction so that the stall is not in the critical path of execution.

Here are some simple examples on Blackfin processors that demonstrate these concepts.

Register Transfer/Multiply latencies (One stall, due to R0 being used in the multiply):

```
R0 = R4;   /* load R0 with contents of R4 */
<STALL>
R2.H = R1.L * R0.H;   /* R0 is used as an operand */
```

In this example, any instruction that does not change the value of the operands can be placed in-between the two instructions to hide the stall.

When we load a pointer register and try to use the content in the next instruction, there is a latency of three stalls:

```
P3 = [SP++];   /* Pointer register loaded from stack  */
<STALL>
<STALL>
<STALL>
R0 = P3;   /* Use contents of P3 after it gets its value
    from earlier instruction */
```

3. The third case involves a change of flow. While a deeper pipeline allows increased clock speeds, any time a change of flow occurs, a portion of the pipeline is flushed, and this consumes core-clock cycles. The branching latency associated with a change of flow varies based on the pipeline depth. Blackfin's 10-stage pipeline yields the following latencies:

Instruction flow dependencies (Static Prediction):

Correctly predicted branch	(4 stalls)
Incorrectly predicted branch	(8 stalls)
Unconditional branch	(8 stalls)
"Drop-through" conditional branch	(0 stalls)

The term "predicted" is used to describe what the sequencer does as instructions that will complete ten core-clock cycles later enter the pipeline. You can see that when the sequencer does not take a branch, and in effect "drops through" to the next instruction after the conditional one, there are no added cycles. When an unconditional branch occurs, the maximum number of stalls occurs (eight cycles). When the processor predicts that a branch occurs and it actually is taken, the number of stalls is four. In the case where it predicted no branch, but one is actually taken, it mirrors the case of an unconditional branch.

One more note here. The maximum number of stalls is eight, while the depth of the pipeline is ten. This shows that the branching logic in an architecture does not implicitly have to match the full size of the pipeline.

4. The last case involves a conflict when the processor is accessing the same memory space as another resource (or simply fetching data from memory

other than L1). For instance, a core fetch from SDRAM will take multiple core-clock cycles. As another example, if the processor and a DMA channel are trying to access the same memory bank, stalls will occur until the resource is available to the lower-priority process.

Compiler Considerations for Efficient Programming

Since the compiler's foremost task is to create correct code, there are cases where the optimizer is too conservative. In these cases, providing the compiler with extra information (through pragmas, built-in keywords, or command-line switches) will help it create more optimized code.

In general, compilers can't make assumptions about what an application is doing. This is why pragmas exist—to let the compiler know it is okay to make certain assumptions. For example, a pragma can instruct the compiler that variables in a loop are aligned and that they are not referenced to the same memory location. This extra information allows the compiler to optimize more aggressively, because the programmer has made a guarantee dictated by the pragma.

In general, a four-step process can be used to optimize an application consisting primarily of HLL code:

1. Compile with an HLL-optimizing compiler.

2. Profile the resulting code to determine the "hot spots" that consume the most processing bandwidth.

3. Update HLL code with pragmas, built-in keywords, and compiler switches to speed up the "hot spots."

4. Replace HLL procedures/functions with assembly routines in places where the optimizer did not meet the timing budget.

For maximum efficiency, it is always a good idea to inspect the most frequently executed compiler-generated assembly code to make a judgment on whether the code could be more vectorized. Sometimes, the HLL program can be changed to help the compiler produce faster code through more use of multi-issue instructions. If this still fails to produce code that is fast enough, then it is up to the assembly programmer to fine-tune the code line-by-line to keep all available hardware resources from idling.

Choosing Data Types

It is important to remember how the standard data types available in C actually map to the architecture you are using. For Blackfin processors, each type is shown in Table 4.1.

Table 4.1 **C data types and their mapping to Blackfin registers**

C type	Blackfin equivalent
char	8-bit signed
unsigned char	8-bit unsigned
short	16-bit signed integer
unsigned short	16-bit unsigned integer
int	32-bit signed integer
unsigned int	32-bit unsigned integer
long	32-bit signed integer
unsigned long	32-bit unsigned integer

The **float** (32-bit), **double** (32-bit), **long long** (64-bit) and **unsigned long long** (64-bit) formats are not supported natively by the processor, but these can be emulated.

Arrays versus Pointers

We are often asked whether it is better to use arrays to represent data buffers in C, or whether pointers are better. Compiler performance engineers always point out that arrays are easier to analyze. Consider the example:

```
void array_example(int a[], int b[], int sum[], int n)
{
        int i;
        for (i = 0; i < n; ++i)
        sum[i] = a[i] + b[i];
}
```

Even though we chose a simple example, the point is that these constructs are very easy to follow.

Now let's look at the same function using pointers. With pointers, the code is "closer" to the processor's native language.

```
void pointer_example(int a[], int b[], int sum[], int n) {
    int i;
    for (i = 0; i < n; ++i)
        *out++ = *a++ + *b++ ;
}
```

Which produces the most efficient code? Actually, there is usually very little difference. It is best to start by using the array notation because it is easier to read. An array format can be better for "alias" analysis in helping to ensure there is no overlap between elements in a buffer. If performance is not adequate with arrays (for instance, in the case of tight inner loops), pointers may be more useful.

Division

Fixed-point processors often do not support division natively. Instead, they offer division primitives in the instruction set, and these help accelerate division.

The "cost" of division depends on the range of the inputs. There are two possibilities: You can use division primitives where the result and divisor each fit into 16 bits. On Blackfin processors, this results in an operation of ~ 40 cycles. For more precise, bitwise 32-bit division, the result is ~ 10x more cycles.

If possible, it is best to avoid division, because of the additional overhead it entails. Consider the example:

```
if   ( X/Y > A/B )
```

This can easily be rewritten as:

```
if ( X * B > A * Y )
```

to eliminate the division.

Keep in mind that the compiler does not know anything about the data precision in your application. For example, in the context of the above equation rewrite, two 12-bit inputs are "safe," because the result of the multiplication will be 24 bits maximum. This quick check will indicate when you can take a shortcut, and when you have to use actual division.

Loops

We already discussed hardware looping constructs. Here we'll talk about software looping in C. We will attempt to summarize what you can do to ensure best performance for your application.

1. Try to keep loops short. Large loop bodies are usually more complex and difficult to optimize. Additionally, they may require register data to be stored in memory, decreasing code density and execution performance.

2. Avoid loop-carried dependencies. These occur when computations in the present iteration depend on values from previous iterations. Dependencies prevent the compiler from taking advantage of loop overlapping (i.e., nested loops).

3. Avoid manually unrolling loops. This confuses the compiler and cheats it out of a job at which it typically excels.

4. Don't execute loads and stores from a noncurrent iteration while doing computations in the current loop iteration. This introduces loop-carried dependencies. This means avoiding loop array writes of the form:

   ```
   for (i = 0; i < n; ++i)
        a[i] = b[i] * a[c[i]]; /* has array dependency*/
   ```

5. Make sure that inner loops iterate more than outer loops, since most optimizers focus on inner loop performance.

6. Avoid conditional code in loops. Large control-flow latencies may occur if the compiler needs to generate conditional jumps.

   As an example,

   ```
   for {
           if  { ….. } else {…..}
           }
   ```

   should be replaced, if possible, by:

   ```
   if {
           for {…..}
       } else {
           for  {…..}
               }
   ```

7. Don't place function calls in loops. This prevents the compiler from using hardware loop constructs, as we described earlier in this chapter.

8. Try to avoid using variables to specify stride values. The compiler may need to use division to figure out the number of loop iterations required, and you now know why this is not desirable!

Data Buffers

It is important to think about how data is represented in your system. It's better to pre-arrange the data in anticipation of "wider" data fetches—that is, data fetches that optimize the amount of data accessed with each fetch. Let's look at an example that represents complex data.

One approach that may seem intuitive is:

```
short Real_Part[ N ];
short Imaginary_Part [ N ];
```

While this is perfectly adequate, data will be fetched in two separate 16-bit accesses. It is often better to arrange the array in one of the following ways:

```
short Complex [ N*2 ];
    or
long Complex [ N ];
```

Here, the data can be fetched via one 32-bit load and used whenever it's needed. This single fetch is faster than the previous approach.

On a related note, a common performance-degrading buffer layout involves constructing a 2D array with a column of pointers to **malloc**'d rows of data. While this allows complete flexibility in row and column size and storage, it may inhibit a compiler's ability to optimize, because the compiler no longer knows if one row follows another, and therefore it can see no constant offset between the rows.

Intrinsics and In-lining

It is difficult for compilers to solve all of your problems automatically and consistently. This is why you should, if possible, avail yourself of "in-line" assembly instructions and intrinsics.

In-lining allows you to insert an assembly instruction into your C code directly. Sometimes this is unavoidable, so you should probably learn how to in-line for the compiler you're using.

In addition to in-lining, most compilers support intrinsics, and their optimizers fully understand intrinsics and their effects. The Blackfin compiler supports a comprehensive array of 16-bit intrinsic functions, which must be programmed explicitly. Below is a simple example of an intrinsic that multiplies two 16-bit values. Chapters 5 and 9 contain some more examples of these **fract** intrinsics.

```
#include <fract.h>
fract32 fdot(fract16 *x, fract16 *y, int n)
{
    fract32 sum = 0;
    int i;
    for (i = 0; i < n; i++)
        sum = add_fr1x32(sum, mult_fr1x32(x[i], y[i]));
    return sum;
}
```

Here are some other operations that can be accomplished through intrinsics:

- Align operations
- Packing operations
- Disaligned loads
- Unpacking
- Quad 8-bit add/subtract
- Dual 16-bit add/clip
- Quad 8-bit average
- Accumulator extract with addition
- Subtract/absolute value/accumulate

The intrinsics that perform the above functions allow the compiler to take advantage of video-specific instructions that improve performance but that are difficult for a compiler to use natively.

When should you use in-lining, and when should you use intrinsics? Well, you really don't have to choose between the two. Rather, it is important to understand the results of using both, so that they become tools in your programming arsenal. With regard to in-lining of assembly instructions, look for an option where you can include in the in-lining construct the registers you will be "touching" in the assembly instruction. Without this information, the compiler will invariably spend more cycles, because it's limited in the assumptions it can make and therefore has to take steps that can result in lower performance. With intrinsics, the compiler can use its knowledge to improve the code it generates on both sides of the intrinsic code. In addition, the fact that the intrinsic exists means someone who knows the compiler and architecture very well has already translated a common function to an optimized code section.

Volatile Data

The **volatile** data type is essential for peripheral-related registers and interrupt-related data.

Some variables may be accessed by resources not visible to the compiler. For example, they may be accessed by interrupt routines, or they may be set or read by peripherals.

The **volatile** attribute forces all operations with that variable to occur exactly as written in the code. This means that a variable is read from memory each time it is needed, and it's written back to memory each time it's modified. The exact order of events is preserved. Missing a **volatile** qualifier is the largest single cause of trouble when engineers port from one C-based processor to another. Architectures that don't require **volatile** for hardware-related accesses probably treat all accesses as volatile by default and thus may perform at a lower performance level than those that require you to state this explicitly. When a C program works with optimization turned off but doesn't work with optimization on, a missing **volatile** qualifier is usually the culprit.

System and Core Synchronization

Earlier we discussed the importance of an interlocked pipeline, but we also need to discuss the implications of the pipeline on the different operating domains of a processor. On Blackfin devices, there are two synchronization instructions that help manage the relationship between when the core and the peripherals complete specific instructions or sequences. While these instructions are very straightforward, they are sometimes used more than necessary. The CSYNC instruction prevents any other instructions from entering the pipeline until all pending core activities have completed. The SSYNC behaves in a similar manner, except that it holds off new instructions until all pending system actions have completed. The performance impact from a CSYNC is measured in multiple CCLK cycles, while the impact of an SSYNC is measured in multiple SCLKs. When either of these instructions is used too often, performance will suffer needlessly.

So when do you need these instructions? We'll find out in a minute. But first we need to talk about memory transaction ordering.

Load/Store Synchronization

Many embedded processors support the concept of a Load/Store data access mechanism. What does this mean, and how does it impact your application? "Load/Store" refers to the characteristic in an architecture where memory operations (loads and stores) are intentionally separated from the arithmetic functions that use the results of fetches from memory operations. The separation is made because memory operations, especially instructions that access off-chip memory or I/O devices, take multiple cycles to complete and would normally halt the processor, preventing an instruction execution rate of one instruction per core-clock cycle. To avoid this situation, data is brought into a data register from a source memory location, and once it is in the register, it can be fed into a computation unit.

In write operations, the "store" instruction is considered complete as soon as it executes, even though many clock cycles may occur before the data is actually written to an external memory or I/O location. This arrangement allows the processor to execute one instruction per clock cycle, and it implies that the synchronization between when writes complete and when subsequent instructions execute is not guaranteed. This synchronization is considered unimportant in the context of most memory operations. With the presence of a write buffer that sits between the processor and external memory, multiple writes can, in fact, be made without stalling the processor.

For example, consider the case where we write a simple code sequence consisting of a single write to L3 memory surrounded by five NOP ("no operation") instructions. Measuring the cycle count of this sequence running from L1 memory shows that it takes six cycles to execute. Now let's add another write to L3 memory and measure the cycle count again. We will see the cycle count increase by one cycle each time, until we reach the limits of the write buffer, at which point it will increase substantially until the write buffer is drained.

Ordering

The relaxation of synchronization between memory accesses and their surrounding instructions is referred to as "weak ordering" of loads and stores. Weak ordering implies that the timing of the actual completion of the memory operations—even the order in which these events occur—may not align with how they appear in the sequence of a program's source code.

In a system with weak ordering, only the following items are guaranteed:

- Load operations will complete before a subsequent instruction uses the returned data.

- Load operations using previously written data will use the updated values, even if they haven't yet propagated out to memory.

- Store operations will eventually propagate to their ultimate destination.

Because of weak ordering, the memory system is allowed to prioritize reads over writes. In this case, a write that is queued anywhere in the pipeline, but not completed, may be deferred by a subsequent read operation, and the read is allowed to be completed before the write. Reads are prioritized over writes because the read operation has a dependent operation waiting on its completion, whereas the processor considers the write operation complete, and the write does not stall the pipeline if it takes more cycles to propagate the value out to memory.

For most applications, this behavior will greatly improve performance. Consider the case where we are writing to some variable in external memory. If the processor performs a write to one location followed by a read from a different location, we would prefer to have the read complete before the write.

This ordering provides significant performance advantages in the operation of most memory instructions. However, it can cause side effects—when writing to or reading from non-memory locations such as I/O device registers, the order of how read and write operations complete is often significant.

For example, a read of a status register may depend on a write to a control register. If the address in either case is the same, the read would return a value from the write buffer rather than from the actual I/O device register, and the order of the read and write at the register may be reversed. Both of these outcomes could cause undesirable side effects. To prevent these occurrences in code that requires precise (strong) ordering of load and store operations, synchronization instructions like CSYNC or SSYNC should be used.

The CSYNC instruction ensures all pending core operations have completed and the core buffer (between the processor core and the L1 memories) has been flushed before proceeding to the next instruction. Pending core operations may include any pending interrupts, speculative states (such as branch predictions) and exceptions. A CSYNC is typically required after writing to a control register that is in the core domain. It ensures that whatever action you wanted to happen by writing to the register takes place before you execute the next instruction.

The SSYNC instruction does everything the CSYNC does, and more. As with CSYNC, it ensures all pending operations have to be completed between the processor core and the L1 memories. SSYNC further ensures completion of all operations between the processor core, external memory and the system peripherals. There are many cases where this is important, but the best example is when an interrupt condition needs to be cleared at a peripheral before an interrupt service routine (ISR) is exited. Somewhere in the ISR, a write is made to a peripheral register to "clear" and, in effect, acknowledge the interrupt. Because of differing clock domains between the core and system portions of the processor, the SSYNC ensures the peripheral clears the interrupt before exiting the ISR. If the ISR were exited before the interrupt was cleared, the processor might jump right back into the ISR.

Load operations from memory do not change the state of the memory value itself. Consequently, issuing a speculative memory-read operation for a subsequent load instruction usually has no undesirable side effect. In some code sequences, such as a conditional branch instruction followed by a load, performance may be improved by speculatively issuing the read request to the memory system before the conditional branch is resolved.

For example,

```
IF CC JUMP away_from_here
RO = [P2];

...

away_from_here:
```

If the branch is taken, then the load is flushed from the pipeline, and any results that are in the process of being returned can be ignored. Conversely, if the branch is not taken, the memory will have returned the correct value earlier than if the operation were stalled until the branch condition was resolved.

However, this could cause an undesirable side effect for a peripheral that returns sequential data from a FIFO or from a register that changes value based on the number of reads that are requested. To avoid this effect, use an SSYNC instruction to guarantee the correct behavior between read operations.

Store operations never access memory speculatively, because this could cause modification of a memory value before it is determined whether the instruction should have executed.

Atomic Operations

We have already introduced several ways to use semaphores in a system. While there are many ways to implement a semaphore, using atomic operations is preferable, because they provide noninterruptible memory operations in support of semaphores between tasks.

The Blackfin processor provides a single atomic operation: TESTSET. The TESTSET instruction loads an indirectly addressed memory word, tests whether the low byte is zero, and then sets the most significant bit of the low memory byte without affecting any other bits. If the byte is originally zero, the instruction sets a status bit. If the byte is originally nonzero, the instruction clears the status bit. The sequence of this memory transaction is atomic—hardware bus locking insures that no other memory operation can occur between the test and set portions of this instruction. The TESTSET instruction can be interrupted by the core. If this happens, the TESTSET instruction is executed again upon return from the interrupt. Without something like this TESTSET facility, it is difficult to ensure true protection when more than one entity (for example, two cores in a dual-core device) vies for a shared resource.

Memory Architecture—The Need for Management

In Chapter 2, we discussed the various types of memory available. Now we will discuss how to best use this memory in your application.

Memory Access Tradeoffs

Embedded media processors usually have a small amount of fast, on-chip memory, whereas microcontrollers usually have access to large external memories. A hierarchical memory architecture combines the best of both approaches, providing several tiers of memory with different performance levels. For applications that require the most determinism, on-chip SRAM can be accessed in a single core-clock cycle. Systems with larger code sizes can utilize bigger, higher-latency on-chip and off-chip memories.

On its own, the hierarchy we described in Chapter 2 is only part of the answer, since most complex programs today are large enough to require external memory, and this would dictate an unacceptably slow execution speed. As a result, programmers would be forced to manually move key code in and out of internal SRAM. However, by adding data and instruction caches into the architecture, external memory becomes much more manageable. The cache reduces the manual movement of instructions and data into the processor core, thus greatly simplifying the programming model.

Figure 4.6 demonstrates a typical memory configuration where instructions are brought in from external memory as they are needed. Instruction cache usually operates with some type of least recently used (LRU) algorithm, insuring that instructions that run more often get replaced less often. The figure also illustrates that having the ability to configure some on-chip data memory as cache and some as SRAM can optimize performance. DMA controllers can feed the core directly, while data from tables can be brought into the data cache as they are needed.

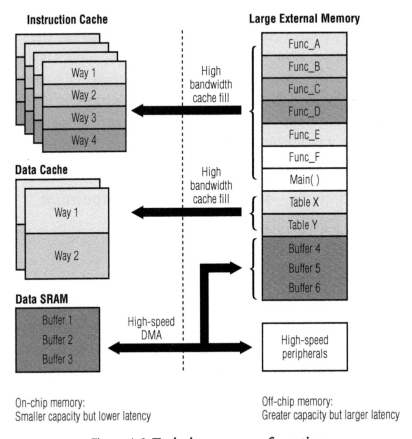

Figure 4.6 **Typical memory configuration**

When porting existing applications to a new processor, "out-of-the-box" performance is important. As we saw earlier, there are many features compilers exploit that require minimal developer involvement. Yet, there are many other techniques that, with a little extra effort by the programmer, can have a big impact on system performance.

Proper memory configuration and data placement always pays big dividends in improving system performance. On high-performance media processors, there are typically three paths into a memory bank. This allows the core to make multiple accesses in a single clock cycle (e.g., a load and store, or two loads). By laying out an intelligent data flow, a developer can avoid conflicts created when the core processor and DMA vie for access to the same memory bank.

Instruction Memory Management—To Cache or To DMA?

Maximum performance is only realized when code runs from internal L1 memory. Of course, the ideal embedded processor would have an unlimited amount of L1 memory, but this is not practical. Therefore, programmers must consider several alternatives to take advantage of the L1 memory that exists in the processor, while optimizing memory and data flows for their particular system. Let's examine some of these scenarios.

The first, and most straightforward, situation is when the target application code fits entirely into L1 instruction memory. For this case, there are no special actions required, other than for the programmer to map the application code directly to this memory space. It thus becomes intuitive that media processors must excel in code density at the architectural level.

In the second scenario, a caching mechanism is used to allow programmers access to larger, less expensive external memories. The cache serves as a way to automatically bring code into L1 instruction memory as needed. The key advantage of this process is that the programmer does not have to manage the movement of code into and out of the cache. This method is best when the code being executed is somewhat linear in nature. For nonlinear code, cache lines may be replaced too often to allow any real performance improvement.

The instruction cache really performs two roles. For one, it helps pre-fetch instructions from external memory in a more efficient manner. That is, when a cache miss occurs, a cache-line fill will fetch the desired instruction, along with the other instructions contained within the cache line. This ensures that, by the time the first instruction in the line has been executed, the instructions that immediately follow have also been fetched. In addition, since caches usually operate with an LRU algorithm, instructions that run most often tend to be retained in cache.

Some strict real-time programmers tend not to trust cache to obtain the best system performance. Their argument is that if a set of instructions is not in cache when needed for execution, performance will degrade. Taking advantage of cache-locking mechanisms can offset this issue. Once the critical instructions are loaded into cache, the cache lines can be locked, and thus not replaced. This gives programmers the ability to keep what they need in cache and to let the caching mechanism manage less-critical instructions.

In a final scenario, code can be moved into and out of L1 memory using a DMA channel that is independent of the processor core. While the core is operating on one section of memory, the DMA is bringing in the section to be executed next. This scheme is commonly referred to as an overlay technique.

While overlaying code into L1 instruction memory via DMA provides more deter-minism than caching it, the tradeoff comes in the form of increased programmer involvement. In other words, the programmer needs to map out an overlay strategy and configure the DMA channels appropriately. Still, the performance payoff for a well-planned approach can be well worth the extra effort.

Data Memory Management

The data memory architecture of an embedded media processor is just as important to the overall system performance as the instruction clock speed. Because multiple data transfers take place simultaneously in a multimedia application, the bus structure must support both core and DMA accesses to all areas of internal and external memo-ry. It is critical that arbitration between the DMA controller and the processor core be handled automatically, or performance will be greatly reduced. Core-to-DMA interac-tion should only be required to set up the DMA controller, and then again to respond to interrupts when data is ready to be processed.

A processor performs data fetches as part of its basic functionality. While this is typi-cally the least efficient mechanism for transferring data to or from off-chip memory, it provides the simplest programming model. A small, fast scratchpad memory is some-times available as part of L1 data memory, but for larger, off-chip buffers, access time will suffer if the core must fetch everything from external memory. Not only will it take multiple cycles to fetch the data, but the core will also be busy doing the fetches.

It is important to consider how the core processor handles reads and writes. As we detailed above, Blackfin processors possess a multi-slot write buffer that can allow the core to proceed with subsequent instructions before all posted writes have completed. For example, in the following code sample, if the pointer register P0 points to an address in external memory and P1 points to an address in internal memory, line 50 will be executed before R0 (from line 46) is written to external memory:

```
...
Line 45: R0 =R1+R2;
Line 46: [P0] = R0;   /* Write the value contained in R0 to slower
    external memory */
Line 47: R3 = 0x0 (z);
Line 48: R4 = 0x0 (z);
Line 49: R5 = 0x0 (z);
Line 50: [P1] = R0;   /* Write the value contained in R0 to faster
    internal memory */
```

In applications where large data stores constantly move into and out of external DRAM, relying on core accesses creates a difficult situation. While core fetches are inevitably needed at times, DMA should be used for large data transfers, in order to preserve performance.

What About Data Cache?

The flexibility of the DMA controller is a double-edged sword. When a large C/C++ application is ported between processors, a programmer is sometimes hesitant to integrate DMA functionality into already-working code. This is where data cache can be very useful, bringing data into L1 memory for the fastest processing. The data cache is attractive because it acts like a mini-DMA, but with minimal interaction on the programmer's part.

Because of the nature of cache-line fills, data cache is most useful when the processor operates on consecutive data locations in external memory. This is because the cache doesn't just store the immediate data currently being processed; instead, it prefetches data in a region contiguous to the current data. In other words, the cache mechanism assumes there's a good chance that the current data word is part of a block of neighboring data about to be processed. For multimedia streams, this is a reasonable conjecture.

Since data buffers usually originate from external peripherals, operating with data cache is not always as easy as with instruction cache. This is due to the fact that coherency must be managed manually in "non-snooping" caches. "Non-snooping" means that the cache is not aware of when data changes in source memory unless it makes the change directly. For these caches, the data buffer must be invalidated before making any attempt to access the new data. In the context of a C-based application, this type of data is "volatile." This situation is shown in Figure 4.7.

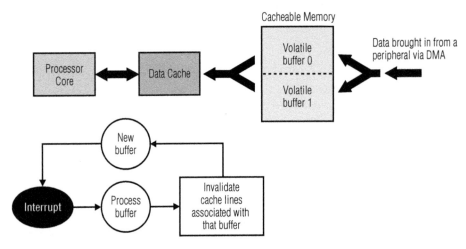

Figure 4.7 **Data cache and DMA coherency**

In the general case, when the value of a variable stored in cache is different from its value in the source memory, this can mean that the cache line is "dirty" and still needs to be written back to memory. This concept does not apply for volatile data. Rather, in this case the cache line may be "clean," but the source memory may have changed without the knowledge of the core processor. In this scenario, before the core can safely access a volatile variable in data cache, it must invalidate (but not flush!) the affected cache line.

This can be performed in one of two ways. The cache tag associated with the cache line can be directly written, *or* a "Cache Invalidate" instruction can be executed to invalidate the target memory address. Both techniques can be used interchangeably, but the direct method is usually a better option when a large data buffer is present (e.g., one greater in size than the data cache size). The Invalidate instruction is always preferable when the buffer size is smaller than the size of the cache. This is true even when a loop is required, since the Invalidate instruction usually increments by the size of each cache line instead of by the more typical 1-, 2- or 4-byte increment of normal addressing modes.

From a performance perspective, this use of data cache cuts down on improvement gains, in that data has to be brought into cache each time a new buffer arrives. In this case, the benefit of caching is derived solely from the pre-fetch nature of a cache-line fill. Recall that the prime benefit of cache is that the data is present the second time through the loop.

One more important point about volatile variables, regardless of whether or not they are cached—if they are shared by both the core processor and the DMA controller, the programmer must implement some type of semaphore for safe operation. In sum, it is best to keep volatiles out of data cache altogether.

System Guidelines for Choosing Between DMA and Cache

Let's consider three widely used system configurations to shed some light on which approach works best for different system classifications.

Instruction Cache, Data DMA

This is perhaps the most popular system model, because media processors are often architected with this usage profile in mind. Caching the code alleviates complex instruction flow management, assuming the application can afford this luxury. This works well when the system has no hard real-time constraints, so that a cache miss would not wreak havoc on the timing of tightly coupled events (for example, video refresh or audio/video synchronization).

Also, in cases where processor performance far outstrips processing demand, caching instructions is often a safe path to follow, since cache misses are then less likely to cause bottlenecks. Although it might seem unusual to consider that an "oversized" processor would ever be used in practice, consider the case of a portable media player that can decode and play both compressed video and audio. In its audio-only mode, its performance requirements will be only a fraction of its needs during video playback. Therefore, the instruction/data management mechanism could be different in each mode.

Managing data through DMA is the natural choice for most multimedia applications, because these usually involve manipulating large buffers of compressed and uncompressed video, graphics and audio. Except in cases where the data is quasi-static (for instance, a graphics icon constantly displayed on a screen), caching these buffers makes little sense, since the data changes rapidly and constantly. Furthermore, as discussed above, there are usually multiple data buffers moving around the chip at one time—unprocessed blocks headed for conditioning, partly conditioned sections headed for temporary storage, and completely processed segments destined for external display or storage. DMA is the logical management tool for these buffers, since it allows the core to operate on them without having to worry about how to move them around.

Instruction Cache, Data DMA/Cache

This approach is similar to the one we just described, except in this case part of L1 data memory is partitioned as cache, and the rest is left as SRAM for DMA access. This structure is very useful for handling algorithms that involve a lot of static coefficients or lookup tables. For example, storing a sine/cosine table in data cache facilitates quick computation of FFTs. Or, quantization tables could be cached to expedite JPEG encoding or decoding.

Keep in mind that this approach involves an inherent tradeoff. While the application gains single-cycle access to commonly used constants and tables, it relinquishes the equivalent amount of L1 data SRAM, thus limiting the buffer size available for single-cycle access to data. A useful way to evaluate this tradeoff is to try alternate scenarios (Data DMA/Cache versus only DMA) in a Statistical Profiler (offered in many development tools suites) to determine the percentage of time spent in code blocks under each circumstance.

Instruction DMA, Data DMA

In this scenario, data and code dependencies are so tightly intertwined that the developer must manually schedule when instruction and data segments move through the chip. In such hard real-time systems, determinism is mandatory, and thus cache isn't ideal.

Although this approach requires more planning, the reward is a deterministic system where code is always present before the data needed to execute it, and no data blocks are lost via buffer overruns. Because DMA processes can link together without core involvement, the start of a new process guarantees that the last one has finished, so that the data or code movement is verified to have happened. This is the most efficient way to synchronize data and instruction blocks.

The Instruction/Data DMA combination is also noteworthy for another reason. It provides a convenient way to test code and data flows in a system during emulation and debug. The programmer can then make adjustments or highlight "trouble spots" in the system configuration.

An example of a system that might require DMA for both instructions and data is a video encoder/decoder. Certainly, video and its associated audio need to be deterministic for a satisfactory user experience. If the DMA signaled an interrupt to the core after each complete buffer transfer, this could introduce significant latency into the system, since the interrupt would need to compete in priority with other events. What's more, the context switch at the beginning and end of an interrupt service routine would consume several core processor cycles. All of these factors interfere with the primary objective of keeping the system deterministic. We'll look at possible solutions to this problem in Chapter 7.

Figures 4.8 and 4.9 provide guidance in choosing between cache and DMA for instructions and data, as well as how to navigate the tradeoff between using cache and using SRAM, based on the guidelines we discussed previously.

As a real-world illustration of these flowchart choices, Tables 4.2 and 4.3 provide actual benchmarks for G.729 and GSM AMR algorithms running on a Blackfin processor under various cache and DMA scenarios. You can see that the best performance can be obtained when a balance is achieved between cache and SRAM.

In short, there is no single answer as to whether cache or DMA should be the mechanism of choice for code and data movement in a given multimedia system. However, once developers are aware of the tradeoffs involved, they should settle into the "middle ground," the perfect optimization point for their system.

Table 4.2 **Benchmarks (relative cycles per frame) for G.729A algorithm with cache enabled**

	L1 banks configured as SRAM		L1 banks configured as cache			Cache + SRAM
	All L2	L1	Code only	Code + DataA	Code + DataB	DataA cache, DataB SRAM
Coder	1.00	0.24	0.70	0.21	0.21	0.21
Decoder	1.00	0.19	0.80	0.20	0.19	0.19

Table 4.3 **Benchmarks (relative cycles per frame) for GSM AMR algorithm with cache enabled**

	L1 banks configured as SRAM		L1 banks configured as cache			Cache + SRAM
	All L2	L1	Code	Code + DataA	Code + DataB	DataA cache, DataB SRAM
Coder	1.00	0.34	0.74	0.20	0.20	0.20
Decoder	1.00	0.42	0.75	0.23	0.23	0.23

Instruction Cache vs Code Overlay decision flow

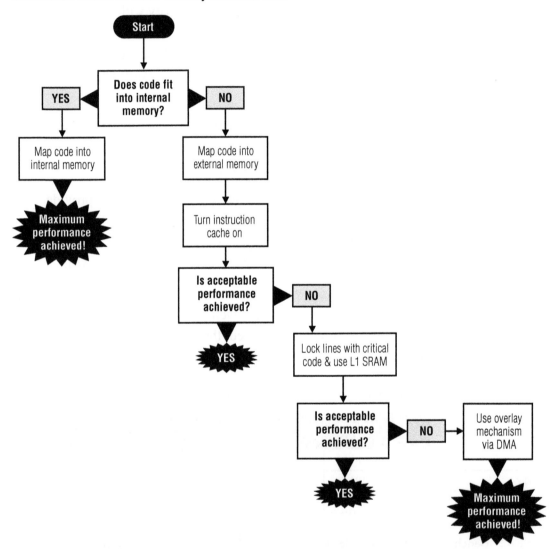

Figure 4.8 **Checklist for choosing between instruction cache and DMA**

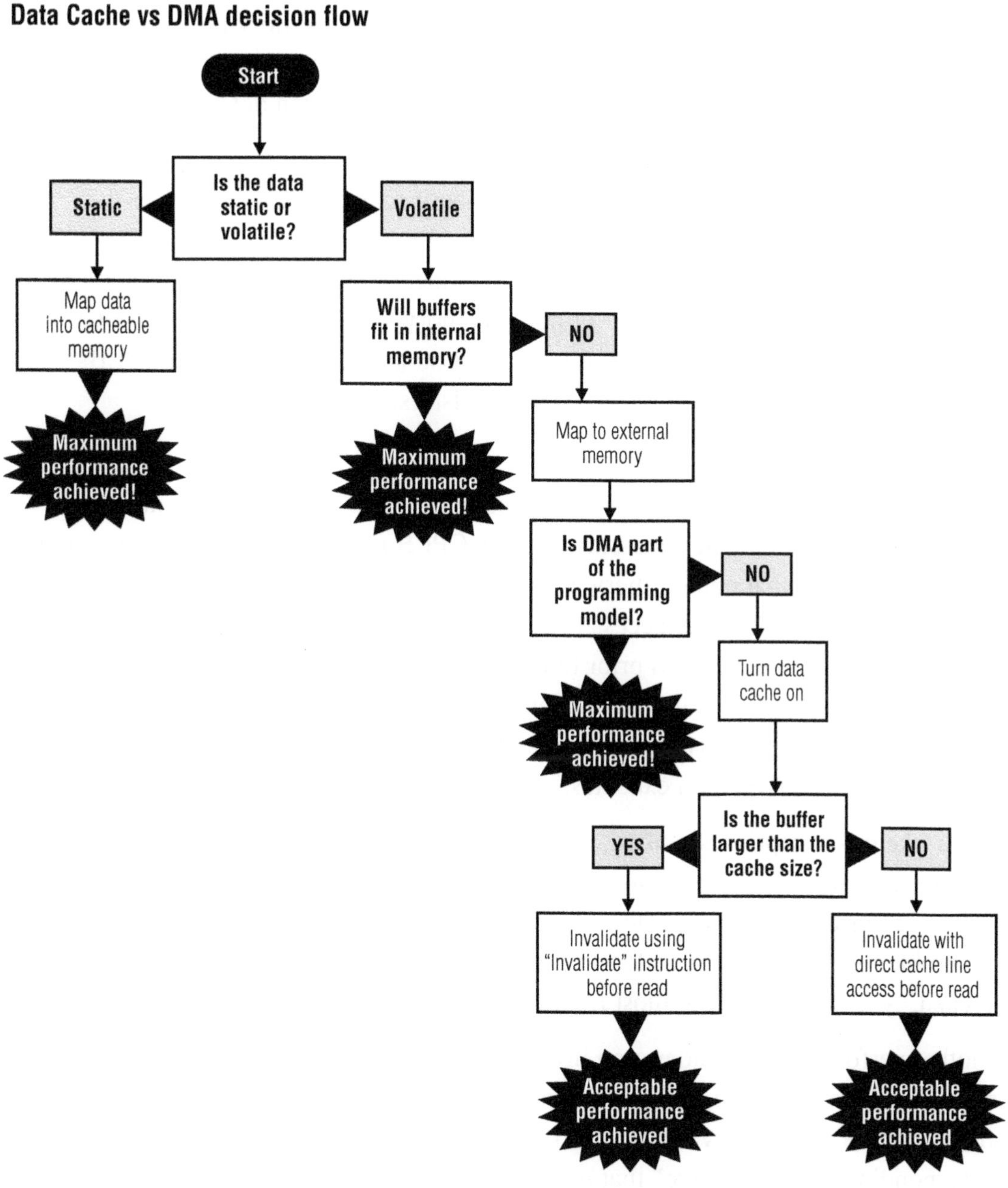

Data Cache vs DMA decision flow

Figure 4.9 **Checklist for choosing between data cache and DMA**

Memory Management Unit (MMU)

An MMU in a processor controls the way memory is set up and accessed in a system. The most basic capabilities of an MMU provides for memory protection, and when cache is used, it also determines whether or not a memory page is cacheable. Explicitly using the MMU is usually optional, because you can default to the standard memory properties on your processor.

On Blackfin processors, the MMU contains a set of registers that can define the properties of a given memory space. Using something *called cacheability protection look-aside buffers* (CPLBs), you can define parameters such as whether or not a memory page is cacheable, and whether or not a memory space can be accessed. Because the 32-bit-addressable external memory space is so large, it is likely that CPLBs will have to be swapped in and out of the MMU registers.

CPLB Management

Because the amount of memory in an application can greatly exceed the number of available CPLBs, it may be necessary to use a CPLB manager. If so, it's important to tackle some issues that could otherwise lead to performance degradation. First, whenever CPLBs are enabled, any access to a location without a valid CPLB will result in an exception being executed prior to the instruction completing. In the exception handler, the code must free up a CPLB and re-allocate it to the location about to be accessed. When the processor returns from the exception handler, the instruction that generated the exception then executes.

If you take this exception too often, it will impact performance, because every time you take an exception, you have to save off the resources used in your exception handler. The processor then has to execute code to re-program the CPLB. One way to alleviate this problem is to profile the code and data access patterns. Since the CPLBs can be "locked," you can protect the most frequently used CPLBs from repeated page swaps.

Another performance consideration involves the search method for finding new page information. For example, a "nonexistent CPLB" exception handler only knows the address where an access was attempted. This information must be used to find the corresponding address "range" that needs to be swapped into a valid page. By locking the most frequently used pages and setting up a sensible search based on your memory access usage (for instructions and/or data), exception-handling cycles can be amortized across thousands of accesses.

Memory Translation

A given MMU may also provide memory translation capabilities, enabling what's known as *virtual memory*. This feature is controlled in a manner that is analogous to memory protection. Instead of CPLBs, *translation look-aside buffers* (TLBs) are used to describe physical memory space. There are two main ways in which memory translation is used in an application. As a holdover from older systems that had limited memory resources, operating systems would have to swap code in and out of a memory space from which execution could take place.

A more common use on today's embedded systems still relates to operating system support. In this case, all software applications run thinking they are at the same physical memory space, when, of course, they are not. On processors that support memory translation, operating systems can use this feature to have the MMU translate the actual physical memory address to the same virtual address based on which specific task is running. This translation is done transparently, without the software application getting involved.

Physics of Data Movement

So far, we've seen that the compiler and assembler provide a bunch of ways to maximize performance on code segments in your system. Using of cache and DMA provide the next level for potential optimization. We will now review the third tier of optimization in your system—it's a matter of physics.

Understanding the "physics" of data movement in a system is a required step at the start of any project. Determining if the desired throughput is even possible for an application can yield big performance savings without much initial investment.

For multimedia applications, on-chip memory is almost always insufficient for storing entire video frames. Therefore, the system must usually rely on L3 DRAM to support relatively fast access to large buffers. The processor interface to off-chip memory constitutes a major factor in designing efficient media frameworks, because access patterns to external memory must be well planned in order to guarantee optimal data throughput. There are several high-level steps that can ensure that data flows smoothly through memory in any system. Some of these are discussed below and play a key role in the design of system frameworks.

1. Grouping Like Transfers to Minimize Memory Bus Turnarounds

Accesses to external memory are most efficient when they are made in the same direction (e.g., consecutive reads or consecutive writes). For example, when accessing off-chip synchronous memory, 16 reads followed by 16 writes is always completed sooner than 16 individual read/write sequences. This is because a write followed by a read incurs latency. Random accesses to external memory generate a high probability of bus turnarounds. This added latency can easily halve available bandwidth. Therefore, it is important to take advantage of the ability to control the number of transfers in a given direction. This can be done either automatically (as we'll see here) or by manually scheduling your data movements, which we'll review in Chapter 7.

As we discussed in Chapter 3, a DMA channel garners access according to its priority, signified on Blackfin processors by its channel number. Higher priority channels are granted access to the DMA bus(es) first. Because of this, you should always assign higher priority DMA channels to peripherals with the highest data rates or with requirements for lowest latency.

To this end, MemDMA streams are always lower in priority than peripheral DMA activity. This is due to the fact that with Memory DMA, no external devices will be held off or starved of data. Since a Memory DMA channel requests access to the DMA bus as long as the channel is active, efficient use of any time slots unused by a peripheral DMA are applied to MemDMA transfers. By default, when more than one MemDMA stream is enabled and ready, only the highest priority MemDMA stream is granted.

When it is desirable for the MemDMA streams to share the available DMA bus bandwidth, however, the DMA controller can be programmed to select each stream in turn for a fixed number of transfers.

This "Direction Control" facility is an important consideration in optimizing use of DMA resources on each DMA bus. By grouping same-direction transfers together, it provides a way to manage how frequently the transfer direction changes on the DMA buses. This is a handy way to perform a first level of optimization without real-time processor intervention. More importantly, there's no need to manually schedule bursts into the DMA streams.

When direction control features are used, the DMA controller preferentially grants data transfers on the DMA or memory buses that are going in the same read/write direction as in the previous transfer, until either the direction control counter times out, or until traffic stops or changes direction on its own. When the direction counter reaches zero, the DMA controller changes its preference to the opposite flow direction.

In this case, reversing direction wastes no bus cycles other than any physical bus turnaround delay time. This type of traffic control represents a tradeoff of increased latency for improved utilization (efficiency). Higher block transfer values might increase the length of time each request waits for its grant, but they can dramatically improve the maximum attainable bandwidth in congested systems, often to above 90%.

Here's an example that puts these concepts into some perspective:

Example 4.4

First, we set up a memory DMA from L1 to L3 memory, using 16-bit transfers, that takes about 1100 system clock (SCLK) cycles to move 1024 16-bit words.

We then begin a transfer from a different bank of external memory to the video port (PPI). Using 16-bit unpacking in the PPI, we continuously feed an NTSC video encoder with 8-bit data. Since the PPI sends out an 8-bit quantity at a 27 MHz rate, the DMA bus bandwidth required for the PPI transfer is roughly 13.5M transfers/second.

When we measure the time it takes to complete the same 1024-word MemDMA transfer with the PPI transferring simultaneously, it now takes three times as long.

Why is this? It's because the PPI DMA activity takes priority over the MemDMA channel transactions. Every time the PPI is ready for its next sample, the bus effectively reverses direction. This translates into cycles that are lost both at the external memory interface and on the various internal DMA buses.

When we enable Direction Control, the performance increases because there are fewer bus turn-arounds.

As a rule of thumb, it is best to maximize same-direction contiguous transfers during moderate system activity. For the most taxing system flows, however, it is best to select a block transfer value in the middle of the range to ensure no one peripheral gets locked out of accesses to external memory. This is especially crucial when at least two high-bandwidth peripherals (like PPIs) are used in the system.

In addition to using direction control, transfers among MDMA streams can be alternated in a "round-robin" fashion on the bus as the application requires. With this type of arbitration, the first DMA process is granted access to the DMA bus for some number of cycles, followed by the second DMA process, and then back to the first. The channels alternate in this pattern until all of the data is transferred. This capability is most useful on dual-core processors (for example, when both core processors have tasks that are awaiting a data stream transfer). Without this "round-robin" feature, the first set of DMA transfers will occur, and the second DMA process will be held off until the first one completes. Round-robin prioritization can help insure that both transfer streams will complete back-to-back.

Another thing to note: using DMA and/or cache will always help performance because these types of transactions transfer large data blocks in the same direction. For example, a DMA transfer typically moves a large data buffer from one location to another. Similarly, a cache-line fill moves a set of consecutive memory locations into the device, by utilizing block transfers in the same direction.

Buffering data bound for L3 in on-chip memory serves many important roles. For one, the processor core can access on-chip buffers for pre-processing functions with much lower latency than it can by going off-chip for the same accesses. This leads to a direct increase in system performance. Moreover, buffering this data in on-chip memory allows more efficient peripheral DMA access to this data. For instance, transferring a video frame on-the-fly through a video port and into L3 memory creates a situation where other peripherals might be locked out from accessing the data they need, because the video transfer is a high-priority process. However, by transferring lines incrementally from the video port into L1 or L2 memory, a Memory DMA stream can be initiated that will quietly transfer this data into L3 as a low-priority process, allowing system peripherals access to the needed data.

This concept will be further demonstrated in the "Performance-based framework" in Chapter 7.

2. Understanding Core and DMA SDRAM Accesses

Consider that on a Blackfin processor, core reads from L1 memory take one *core-*clock cycle, whereas core reads from SDRAM consume eight *system* clock cycles. Based on typical CCLK/SCLK ratios, this could mean that eight SCLK cycles equate to

40 CCLKs. Incidentally, these eight SCLKs reduce to only one SCLK by using a DMA controller in a burst mode instead of direct core accesses.

There is another point to make on this topic. For processors that have multiple data fetch units, it is better to use a dual-fetch instruction instead of back-to-back fetches. On Blackfin processors with a 32-bit external bus, a dual-fetch instruction with two 32-bit fetches takes nine SCLKs (eight for the first fetch and one for the second). Back-to-back fetches in separate instructions take 16 SCLKs (eight for each). The difference is that, in the first case, the request for the second fetch in the single instruction is pipelined, so it has a head start.

Similarly, when the external bus is 16 bits in width, it is better to use a 32-bit access rather than two 16-bit fetches. For example, when the data is in consecutive locations, the 32-bit fetch takes nine SCLKs (eight for the first 16 bits and one for the second). Two 16-bit fetches take 16 SCLKs (eight for each).

3. Keeping SDRAM Rows Open and Performing Multiple Passes on Data

Each access to SDRAM can take several SCLK cycles, especially if the required SDRAM row has not yet been activated. Once a row is active, it is possible to read data from an entire row without reopening that row on every access. In other words, it is possible to access any location in memory on every SCLK cycle, as long as those locations are within the same row in SDRAM. Multiple SDRAM clock cycles are needed to close a row, and therefore constant row closures can severely restrict SDRAM throughput. Just to put this into perspective, an SDRAM page miss can take 20–50 CCLK cycles, depending on the SDRAM type.

Applications should take advantage of open SDRAM banks by placing data buffers appropriately and managing accesses whenever possible. Blackfin processors, as an example, keep track of up to four open SDRAM rows at a time, so as to reduce the setup time—and thus increase throughput—for subsequent accesses to the same row within an open bank. For example, in a system with one row open, row activation latency would greatly reduce the overall performance. With four rows open at one time, on the other hand, row activation latency can be amortized over hundreds of accesses.

Let's look at an example that illustrates the impact this SDRAM row management can have on memory access bandwidth:

Figure 4.10 shows two different scenarios of data and code mapped to a single *external* SDRAM bank. In the first case, all of the code and data buffers in external memory fit in a single bank, but because the access patterns of each code and data line are random, almost every access involves the activation of a new row. In the second case, even though the access patterns are randomly interspersed between code and data accesses, each set of accesses has a high probability of being within the same row. For example, even when an instruction fetch occurs immediately before and after a data access, two rows are kept open and no additional row activation cycles are incurred.

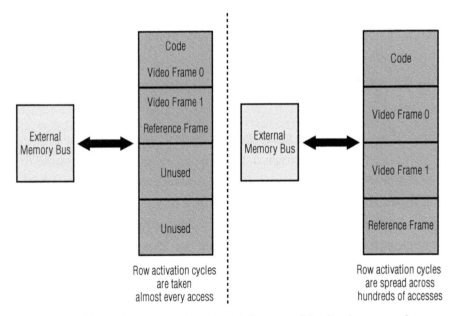

Figure 4.10 **Taking advantage of code and data partitioning in external memory**

When we ran an MPEG-4 encoder from external memory (with both code and data in SDRAM), we gained a 6.5% performance improvement by properly spreading out the code and data in external memory.

4. Optimizing the System Clock Settings and Ensuring Refresh Rates are Tuned for the Speed At Which SDRAM Runs

External DRAM requires periodic refreshes to ensure that the data stored in memory retains its proper value. Accesses by the core processor or DMA engine are held off until an in-process refresh cycle has completed. If the refresh occurs too frequently, the processor can't access SDRAM as often, and throughput to SDRAM decreases as a result.

On the Blackfin processor, the SDRAM Refresh Rate Control register provides a flexible mechanism for specifying the Auto-Refresh timing. Since the clock frequency supplied to the SDRAM can vary, this register implements a programmable refresh counter. This counter coordinates the supplied clock rate with the SDRAM device's required refresh rate.

Once the desired delay (in number of SDRAM clock cycles) between consecutive refresh counter time-outs is specified, a subsequent refresh counter time-out triggers an Auto-Refresh command to all external SDRAM devices.

Not only should you take care not to refresh SDRAM too often, but also be sure you're refreshing it often enough. Otherwise, stored data will start to decay because the SDRAM controller will not be able to keep corresponding memory cells refreshed.

Table 4.4 shows the impact of running with the best clock values and optimal refresh rates. Just in case you were wondering, RGB, CYMK and YIQ are imaging/video formats. Conversion between the formats involves basic linear transformation that is common in video-based systems. Table 4.4 illustrates that the performance degradation can be significant with a non-optimal refresh rate, depending on your actual access patterns. In this example, CCLK is reduced to run with an increased SCLK to

Table 4.4 **Using the optimal refresh rate**

	Sub-optimal SDRAM refresh rate		Optimal SDRAM refresh rate	
CCLK (MHz)	594 MHz	526 MHz	526 MHz	
SCLK (MHz)	119 MHz	132 MHz	132 MHz	
RGB to CMYK Conversion (iterations per second)	226	244	250	
RGB to YIQ Conversion (iterations per second)	266	276	282	Total
Cumulative Improvement		5%	2%	7%

illustrate this point. Doing this improves performance for this algorithm because the code fits into L1 memory and the data is partially in L3 memory. By increasing the SCLK rate, data can be fetched faster. What's more, by setting the optimal refresh rate, performance increases a bit more.

5. Exploiting Priority and Arbitration Schemes Between System Resources

Another important consideration is the priority and arbitration schemes that regulate how processor subsystems behave with respect to one another. For instance, on Blackfin processors, the core has priority over DMA accesses, by default, for transactions involving L3 memory that arrive at the same time. This means that if a core read from L3 occurs at the same time a DMA controller requests a read from L3, the core will win, and its read will be completed first.

Let's look at a scenario that can cause trouble in a real-time system. When the processor has priority over the DMA controller on accesses to a shared resource like L3 memory, it can lock out a DMA channel that also may be trying to access the memory. Consider the case where the processor executes a tight loop that involves fetching data from external memory. DMA activity will be held off until the processor loop has completed. It's not only a loop with a read embedded inside that can cause trouble. Activities like cache line fills or nonlinear code execution from L3 memory can also cause problems because they can result in a series of uninterruptible accesses.

There is always a temptation to rely on core accesses (instead of DMA) at early stages in a project, for a number of reasons. The first is that this mimics the way data is accessed on a typical prototype system. The second is that you don't always want to dig into the internal workings of DMA functionality and performance. However, with the core and DMA arbitration flexibility, using the memory DMA controller to bring data into and out of internal memory gives you more control of your destiny early on in a project. We will explore this concept in more detail in Chapter 7.

What's Next?

Now that we've explored memory and DMA fundamentals, as well as performance tuning in a multimedia system, it's finally time to look at some basics of multimedia. We'll start in the next chapter with a backgrounder on audio as it pertains to embedded media processing.

Basics of Embedded Audio Processing

Introduction

Audio functionality plays a critical role in embedded media processing. While audio takes less processing power in general than video processing, it should be considered equally important.

In this chapter, we will begin with a discussion of sound and audio signals, and then explore how data is presented to the processor from a variety of audio converters. We will also describe the formats in which audio data is stored and processed.

Additionally, we'll discuss some software building blocks for embedded audio systems. Efficient data movement is essential, so we will examine data buffering as it applies to audio algorithms. Finally, we'll cover some fundamental algorithms and finish with a discussion of audio and speech compression.

What Is Sound?

Sound is a longitudinal displacement wave that propagates through air or some other medium. Sound waves are defined using two attributes: amplitude and frequency.

The amplitude of a sound wave is a gauge of pressure change, measured in decibels (dB). The lowest sound amplitude that the human ear can perceive is called the "threshold of hearing," denoted by 0 dBSPL. On this SPL (sound pressure level) scale, the reference pressure is defined as 20 micropascals (20 µPa). The general equation for dBSPL, given a pressure change x, is

$$dBSPL = 20 \times \log (x \text{ µPa} / 20 \text{ µPa})$$

Table 5.1 shows decibel levels for typical sounds. These are all relative to the threshold of hearing (0 dBSPL).

Table 5.1 **Decibel (dBSPL) values for various typical sounds**

Source (distance)	dBSPL
Threshold of hearing	0
Normal conversation (3-5 feet away)	60-70
Busy traffic	70-80
Loud factory	90
Power saw	110
Discomfort	120
Threshold of pain	130
Jet engine (100 feet away)	150

The main point to take away from Table 5.1 is that the range of tolerable audible sounds is about 120 dB (when used to describe ratios without reference to a specific value, the correct notation is dB without the SPL suffix). Therefore, all engineered audio systems can use 120 dB as the upper bound of dynamic range. In case you're wondering why all this is relevant to embedded systems, don't worry—we'll soon relate dynamic range to data formats for embedded media processing.

Frequency, the other key feature of sound, is denoted in Hertz (Hz), or cycles per second. We can hear sounds in the frequency range between 20 and 20,000 Hz, but this ability degrades as we age.

Our ears can hear certain frequencies better than others. In fact, we are most sensitive to frequencies in the area of 2–4 kHz. There are other quirky features about the ear that engineers are quick to exploit. Two useful phenomena, employed in the lossy compression algorithms that we'll describe later, are *temporal masking* and *frequency masking*. In temporal masking (Figure 5.1a), loud tones can drown out softer tones that occur at almost the same time. Frequency masking (Figure 5.1b) occurs when a loud sound at a certain frequency renders softer sounds at nearby frequencies inaudible. The human ear is such a complex organ that only books dedicated to the subject can do it justice. For a more in-depth survey of ear physiology, consult Reference 23 in the Appendix.

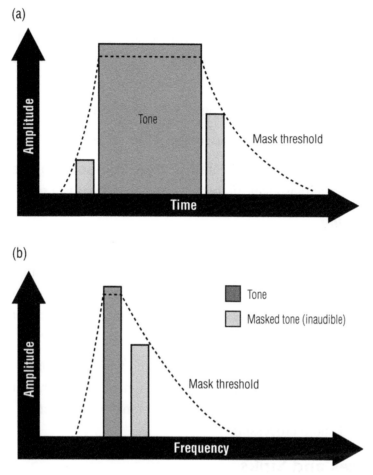

Figure 5.1 **(a) Loud sounds at a specific time can mask out softer sounds in the temporal vicinity (b) Loud sounds at a specific frequency can mask softer sounds at nearby frequencies**

Audio Signals

In order to create an analog signal that represents a sound wave, we must use a transducer to convert the mechanical pressure energy into electrical energy. A more common name for this audio source transducer is a microphone.

All transducers can be described with a sensitivity (or transduction) curve. In the case of a microphone, this curve dictates how well it translates pressure into an electrical signal. Ideal transducers have a linear sensitivity curve—that is, a voltage level is directly proportional to a sound wave's pressure.

Since a microphone converts a sound wave into voltage levels, we now need to use a new decibel scale to describe amplitude. This scale, called dBV, is based on a reference point of 1V. The equation describing the relationship between a voltage level x and dBV is

$$dBV = 20 \times \log (x \text{ volts } / 1.0 \text{ volts})$$

An alternative analog decibel scale is based on a reference of 0.775V and uses dBu units.

In order to create an audible mechanical sound wave from an analog electrical signal, we again need to use a transducer. In this case, the transducer is a speaker or headset.

Speech Processing

Speech processing is an important and complex class of audio processing, and we won't delve too deeply here. However, we'll discuss speech-processing techniques where they are analogous to the more general audio processing methods. The most common use for speech signal processing is in voice telecommunications for such algorithms as echo cancellation and compression.

Most of the energy in typical speech signals is stored within less than 4 kHz of bandwidth, thus making speech a subset of audio signals. However, many speech-processing techniques are based on modeling the human vocal tract, so these cannot be used for general audio processing.

Audio Sources and Sinks

Converting Between Analog and Digital Audio Signals

Assuming we've already taken care of converting sound energy into electrical energy, the next step is to digitize the analog signals. This is accomplished with an analog-to-digital converter (A/D converter or ADC). As you might expect, in order to create an analog signal from a digital one, a digital-to-analog converter (D/A converter or DAC) is used. Since many audio systems are really meant for a full-duplex media flow, the ADC and DAC are available in one package called an "audio codec." The term codec is used here to mean a discrete hardware chip. As we'll discuss later in the section on audio compression, this should not be confused with a software audio codec, which is a software algorithm.

All A/D and D/A conversions should obey the Shannon-Nyquist sampling theorem. In short, this theorem dictates that an analog signal must be sampled at a rate (Nyquist sampling rate) equal to or exceeding twice its highest-frequency component (Nyquist frequency) in order for it to be reconstructed in the eventual D/A conversion. Sampling below the Nyquist sampling rate will introduce aliases, which are low frequency "ghost" images of those frequencies that fall above the Nyquist frequency. If we take a sound signal that is band-limited to 0–20 kHz, and sample it at 2×20 kHz $= 40$ kHz, then the Nyquist Theorem assures us that the original signal can be reconstructed perfectly without any signal loss. However, sampling this 0–20 kHz band-limited signal at anything less than 40 kHz will introduce distortions due to aliasing. Figure 5.2 shows how sampling at less than the Nyquist sampling rate results in an incorrect representation of a signal. When sampled at 40 kHz, a 20 kHz signal is represented correctly (Figure 5.2a). However, the same 20 kHz sine wave that is sampled at a 30 kHz sampling rate actually looks like a lower frequency alias of the original sine wave (Figure 5.2b).

(a)   (b)

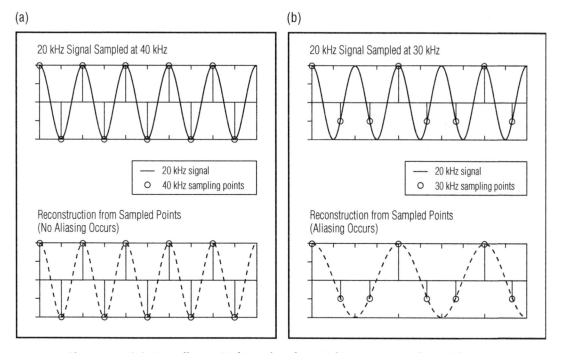

Figure 5.2 **(a) Sampling a 20 kHz signal at 40 kHz captures the original signal correctly (b) Sampling the same 20 kHz signal at 30 kHz captures an aliased (low frequency ghost) signal**

No practical system will sample at exactly twice the Nyquist frequency, however. For example, restricting a signal into a specific band requires an analog low-pass filter, but these filters are never ideal. Therefore, the lowest sampling rate used to reproduce music is 44.1 kHz, not 40 kHz, and many high-quality systems sample at 48 kHz in order to capture the 20 Hz–20 kHz range of hearing even more faithfully. As we mentioned earlier, speech signals are only a subset of the frequencies we can hear; the energy content below 4 kHz is enough to store an intelligible reproduction of the speech signal. For this reason, telephony applications usually use only 8 kHz sampling (= 2 × 4 kHz). Table 5.2 summarizes some sampling rates used by common systems.

Table 5.2 **Commonly used sampling rates**

System	Sampling Frequency
Telephone	8000 Hz
Compact Disc	44100 Hz
Professional Audio	48000 Hz
DVD Audio	96000 Hz (for 6-channel audio)

The most common digital representation for audio is a pulse-code-modulated (PCM) signal. In this representation, an analog amplitude is encoded with a digital level for each sampling period. The resulting digital wave is a vector of snapshots taken to approximate the input analog wave. All A/D converters have finite resolution, so they introduce quantization noise that is inherent in digital audio systems. Figure 5.3 shows a PCM representation of an analog sine wave (Figure 5.3a) converted using an ideal A/D converter, in which the quantization manifests itself as the "staircase effect" (Figure 5.3b). You can see that lower resolution leads to a worse representation of the original wave (Figure 5.3c).

For a numerical example, let's assume that a 24-bit A/D converter is used to sample an analog signal whose range is –2.828V to 2.828V (5.656 Vpp). The 24 bits allow for 2^{24} (16,777,216) quantization levels. Therefore, the effective voltage resolution is 5.656V / 16,777,216 = 337.1 nV. Shortly, we'll see how codec resolution affects the dynamic range of audio systems.

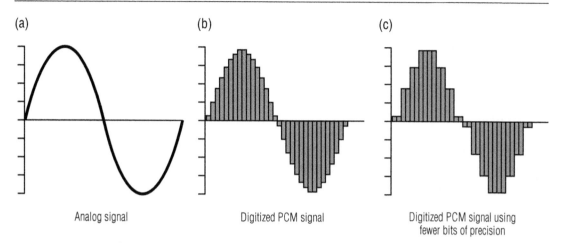

(a) Analog signal

(b) Digitized PCM signal

(c) Digitized PCM signal using fewer bits of precision

Figure 5.3 **(a) An analog signal (b) Digitized PCM signal
(c) Digitized PCM signal using fewer bits of precision**

Background on Audio Converters

Audio ADCs

There are many ways to perform A/D conversion. One traditional approach is a successive approximation scheme, which uses a comparator to test the analog input signal against a number of interim D/A conversions to arrive at the final answer.

Most audio ADCs today, however, are sigma-delta converters. Instead of employing successive approximations to create wide resolutions, sigma-delta converters use 1-bit ADCs. In order to compensate for the reduced number of quantization steps, they are oversampled at a frequency much higher than the Nyquist frequency. Conversion from this super-sampled 1-bit stream into a slower, higher-resolution stream is performed using digital filtering blocks inside these converters, in order to accommodate the more traditional PCM stream processing. For example, a 16-bit 44.1 kHz sigma-delta ADC might oversample at 64x, yielding a 1-bit stream at a rate of 2.8224 MHz. A digital decimation filter (described in more detail later) converts this super-sampled stream to a 16-bit one at 44.1 kHz.

Because they oversample analog signals, sigma-delta ADCs relax the performance requirements of the analog low-pass filters that band-limit input signals. They also have the advantage of reducing peak noise by spreading it over a wider spectrum than traditional converters.

Audio DACs

Just as in the A/D case, sigma-delta designs rule the D/A conversion space. They can take a 16-bit 44.1 kHz signal and convert into a 1-bit 2.8224 MHz stream using an interpolating filter (described later). The 1-bit DAC then converts the super-sampled stream to an analog signal.

A typical embedded digital audio system may employ a sigma-delta audio ADC and a sigma-delta DAC, and therefore the conversion between a PCM signal and an oversampled stream is done twice. For this reason, Sony and Philips have introduced an alternative to PCM, called Direct-Stream Digital (DSD), in their Super Audio CD (SACD) format. This format stores data using the 1-bit high-frequency (2.8224 MHz) sigma-delta stream, bypassing the PCM conversion. The disadvantage is that DSD streams are less intuitive to process than PCM, and they require a separate set of digital audio algorithms, so we will focus only on PCM in this chapter.

Connecting to Audio Converters

An ADC Example

OK, enough background information. Let's do some engineering now. One good choice for a low-cost audio ADC is the Analog Devices AD1871, which features 24-bit conversion at 96 kHz. The functional block diagram of the AD1871 is shown in Figure 5.4a. This converter has left (VINLx) and right (VINRx) input channels, which is really just another way of saying that it can handle stereo data. The digitized audio data is streamed out serially through the data port, usually to a corresponding serial port on a signal processor (like the SPORT interface on Blackfin processors). There is also an SPI (serial peripheral interface) port provided for the host processor to configure the AD1871 via software commands. These commands include ways to set the sampling rate, word width, and channel gain and muting, among other parameters.

As the block diagram in Figure 5.4b implies, interfacing the AD1871 ADC to a Blackfin processor is a glueless connection. The analog representation of the circuit is simplified, since only the digital signals are important in this discussion. The oversampling rate of the AD1871 is achieved with an external crystal. The Blackfin processor shown has two serial ports (SPORTs) and an SPI port used for connecting to the AD1871. The SPORT, configured in I²S mode, is the data link to the AD1871, whereas the SPI port acts as the control link.

(a)

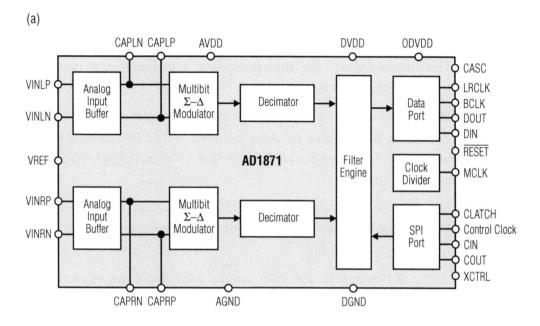

(b)

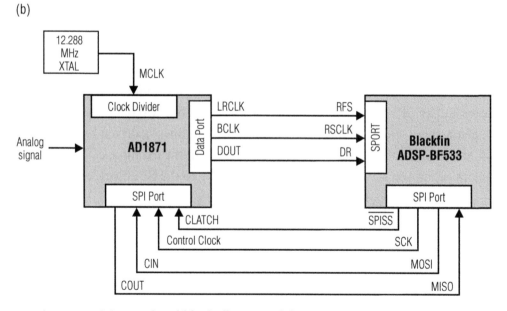

Figure 5.4 **(a) Functional block diagram of the AD1871 audio ADC**
(b) Glueless connection of an ADSP-BF533 media processor to the AD1871

I²S (Inter-IC-Sound)

The I²S protocol is a standard developed by Philips for the digital transmission of audio signals. This standard allows for audio equipment manufacturers to create components that are compatible with each other.

In a nutshell, I²S is simply a three-wire serial interface used to transfer stereo data. As shown in Figure 5.5a, it specifies a bit clock (middle), a data line (bottom), and a left/right synchronization line (top) that selects whether a left or right channel frame is currently being transmitted.

In essence, I²S is a time-division-multiplexed (TDM) serial stream with two active channels. TDM is a method of transferring more than one channel (for example, left and right audio) over one physical link.

In the AD1871 setup of Figure 5.4b, the ADC can use a divided-down version of the 12.288 MHz sampling rate it receives from the external crystal to drive the SPORT clock (RSCLK) and frame synchronization (RFS) lines. This configuration insures that the sampling and data transmission are in sync.

SPI (Serial Peripheral Interface)

The SPI interface, shown in Figure 5.5b, was designed by Motorola for connecting host processors to a variety of digital components. The entire interface between an SPI master and an SPI slave consists of a clock line (SCK), two data lines (MOSI and MISO), and a slave select ($\overline{\text{SPISS}}$) line. One of the data lines is driven by the master (MOSI), and the other is driven by the slave (MISO). In the example of Figure 5.4b, the Blackfin processor's SPI port interfaces gluelessly to the SPI block of the AD1871.

Audio codecs with a separate SPI control port allow a host processor to change the ADC settings on the fly. Besides muting and gain control, one of the really useful settings on ADCs like the AD1871 is the ability to place it in power-down mode. For battery-powered applications, this is often an essential function.

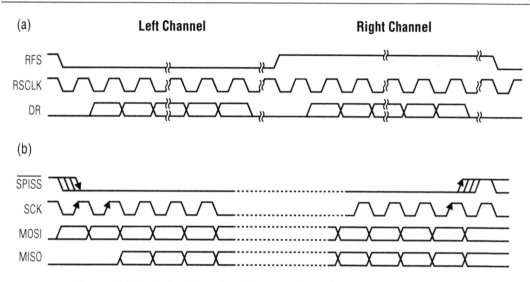

Figure 5.5 **(a) The data signals transmitted by the AD1871 using the I²S protocol (b) The SPI interface used to control the AD1871**

DACs and Codecs

Connecting an audio DAC to a host processor is an identical process to the ADC connection we just discussed. In a system that uses both an ADC and a DAC, the same serial port can hook up to both, if it supports bidirectional transfers.

But if you're tackling full-duplex audio, then you're better off using a single-chip audio codec that handles both the analog-to-digital and digital-to-analog conversions. A good example of such a codec is the Analog Devices AD1836, which features three stereo DACs and two stereo ADCs, and is able to communicate through a number of serial protocols, including I²S.

AC '97 (Audio Codec '97)

I²S is only one audio specification. Another popular one is AC '97, which Intel Corporation created to standardize all PC audio and to separate the analog circuitry from the less-noise-susceptible digital chip. In its simplest form, an AC '97 codec uses a TDM scheme where control and data are interleaved in the same signal. Various timeslots in the serial transfer are reserved for a specific data channel or control word. Most processors with serial ports that support TDM mode can de-multiplex an AC '97 signal at the expense of some software overhead. One example of an AC '97 codec is the AD1847 from Analog Devices.

Speech Codecs

Since speech processing has slightly relaxed requirements compared to hi-fidelity music systems, you may find it worthwhile to look into codecs designed specifically for speech. Among many good choices is the dual-channel 16-bit Analog Devices AD73322, which has a configurable sampling frequency from 8 kHz all the way to 64 kHz.

PWM Output

So far, we've only talked about digital PCM representation and the audio DACs used to get those digital signals to the analog domain. But there is a way to use a different kind of modulation, called pulse-width modulation (PWM), to drive an output circuit directly without any need for a DAC, when a low-cost solution is required.

In PCM, amplitude is encoded for each sample period, whereas it is the duty cycle that describes amplitude in a PWM signal. PWM signals can be generated with general-purpose I/O pins, or they can be driven directly by specialized PWM timers, available on many processors.

To make PWM audio achieve decent quality, the PWM carrier frequency should be at least 12 times the bandwidth of the signal, and the resolution of the timer (i.e., granularity of the duty cycle) should be 16 bits. Because of the carrier frequency requirement, traditional PWM audio circuits were used for low-bandwidth audio, like subwoofers. However, with today's high-speed processors, it's possible to carry a larger audible spectrum.

The PWM stream must be low-pass-filtered to remove the high-frequency carrier. This is usually done in the amplifier circuit that drives a speaker. A class of amplifiers, called Class D, has been used successfully in such a configuration. When amplification is not required, then a low-pass filter is sufficient as the output stage. In some low-cost applications, where sound quality is not as important, the PWM streams can connect directly to a speaker. In such a system, the mechanical inertia of the speaker's cone acts as a low-pass filter to remove the carrier frequency.

Interconnections

Before we end this hardware-centric section, let's review some of the common connectors and interfaces you'll encounter when designing systems with embedded audio capabilities.

Connectors

Microphones, speakers, and other analog equipment connect to an embedded system through a variety of standard connectors (see Figure 5.6). Because of their small size, 1/8" connectors are quite common for portable systems. Many home stereo components support 1/4" connectors. Higher performance equipment usually uses RCA connectors, or even a coaxial cable connector, to preserve signal integrity.

Digital Connections

Some of the systems you'll design actually won't require any ADCs or DACs, because the input signals may already be digital and the output device may accept digital data. A few standards exist for transfer of digital data from one device to another.

The *Sony Digital InterFace* (SDIF-2) protocol is used in some professional products. It requires an unbalanced BNC coaxial connection for each channel. The Audio Engineering Society (AES) introduced the AES3 standard for serial transmission of

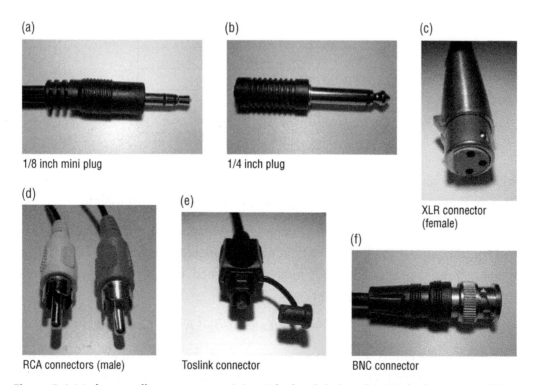

(a)

1/8 inch mini plug

(b)

1/4 inch plug

(c)

XLR connector
(female)

(d)

RCA connectors (male)

(e)

Toslink connector

(f)

BNC connector

Figure 5.6 **Various audio connectors: (a) 1/8 inch mini plug (b) 1/4 inch plug (c) XLR connector (d) Male RCA connectors (e) Toslink connector (f) BNC connector**

data; this one uses an XLR connector. A more ubiquitous standard, the S/PDIF (Sony/ Philips Digital InterFace), is prevalent in consumer and professional audio devices. Two possible S/PDIF connectors are single-ended coaxial cable and the Toslink connector for fiber optic connections.

Dynamic Range and Precision

We promised earlier that we would get into a lot more detail on dynamic range of audio systems. You might have seen dB specs thrown around for various products available on the market today. Table 5.3 lists a few fairly established products along with their assigned signal quality, measured in dB.

Table 5.3 **Dynamic range comparison of various audio systems**

Audio Device	Typical Dynamic Range
AM Radio	48 dB
Analog TV	60 dB
FM Radio	70 dB
16-bit Audio Codecs	90-95 dB
CD Player	92-96 dB
Digital Audio Tape (DAT)	110 dB
20-bit Audio Codecs	110 dB
24-bit Audio Codecs	110-120 dB

So what exactly do those numbers represent? Let's start by getting some definitions down. Use Figure 5.7 as a reference diagram for the following discussion.

As you might remember from the beginning of this chapter, the dynamic range for the human ear (the ratio of the loudest to the quietest signal level) is about 120 dB. In systems where noise is present, dynamic range is described as the ratio of the maximum signal level to the noise floor. In other words,

Dynamic Range (dB) = Peak Level (dB) – Noise Floor (dB)

The noise floor in a purely analog system comes from the electrical properties of the system itself. On top of that, audio signals also acquire noise from ADCs and DACs, including quantization errors due to the sampling of analog data.

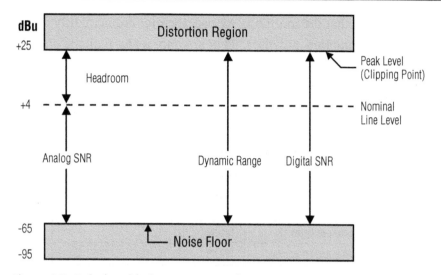

Figure 5.7 **Relationship between some important terms in audio systems**

Another important term is the signal-to-noise ratio (SNR). In analog systems, this means the ratio of the nominal signal to the noise floor, where "line level" is the nominal operating level. On professional equipment, the nominal level is usually 1.228 Vrms, which translates to +4 dBu. The headroom is the difference between nominal line level and the peak level where signal distortion starts to occur. The definition of SNR is a bit different in digital systems, where it is defined as the dynamic range.

Now, armed with an understanding of dynamic range, we can start to discuss how this is useful in practice. Without going into a long derivation, let's simply state what is known as the "6 dB rule". This rule holds the key to the relationship between dynamic range and computational word width. The complete formulation is described in Equation 5.1, but it is used in shorthand to mean that the addition of one bit of precision will lead to a dynamic range increase of 6 dB. Note that the 6 dB rule does not take into account the analog subsystem of an audio design, so the imperfections of the transducers on both the input and the output must be considered separately. Those who want to see the statistical math behind the rule should consult Reference 23 in the Appendix.

$$Dynamic\ Range\ (dB) = 6.02n + 1.76 \approx 6n\ dB$$

$$where\ \mathbf{n} = the\ number\ of\ precision\ bits$$

Equation 5.1 **The 6 dB rule**

The 6 dB rule dictates that the more bits we use, the higher the quality of the system we can attain. In practice, however, there are only a few realistic choices. Most devices suitable for embedded media processing come in three word-width flavors: 16-bit, 24-bit and 32-bit. Table 5.4 summarizes the dynamic ranges for these three types of processors.

Table 5.4 **Dynamic range of various fixed-point architectures**

Computation word width	Dynamic Range (using 6 dB rule)
16-bit fixed-point precision	96 dB
24-bit fixed-point precision	144 dB
32-bit fixed-point precision	192 dB

Since we're talking about the 6 dB rule, it is worth noting something about nonlinear quantization methods typically used for speech signals. A telephone-quality linear PCM encoding requires 12 bits of precision. However, our ears are more sensitive to audio changes at small amplitudes than at high amplitudes. Therefore, the linear PCM sampling is overkill for telephone communications. The logarithmic quantization used by the A-law and μ–law companding standards achieves a 12-bit PCM level of quality using only 8 bits of precision. To make our lives easier, some processor vendors have implemented A-law and μ–law companding into the serial ports of their devices. This relieves the processor core from doing logarithmic calculations.

After reviewing Table 5.4, recall once again that the dynamic range for the human ear is around 120 dB. Because of this, 16-bit data representation doesn't quite cut it for high quality audio. This is why vendors introduced 24-bit processors that extended the dynamic range of 16-bit systems. The 24-bit systems are a bit nonstandard from a C compiler standpoint, so many audio designs these days use 32-bit processing.

Choosing the right processor is not the end of the story, because the total quality of an audio system is dictated by the level of the "lowest-achieving" component. Besides the processor, a complete system includes analog components like microphones and speakers, as well the converters to translate signals between the analog and digital domains. The analog domain is outside of the scope of this discussion, but the audio converters cross into the digital realm.

Let's say that you want to use the AD1871, the same ADC shown in Figure 5.4a, for sampling audio. The datasheet for this converter explains that it is a 24-bit converter, but its dynamic range is not 144 dB—it is 105 dB. The reason for this is that a converter is not a perfect system, and vendors publish only the useful dynamic range in their documentation.

If you were to hook up a 24-bit processor to the AD1871, then the SNR of your complete system would be 105 dB. The conversion error would amount to 144 dB – 105 dB = 39 dB. Figure 5.8 is a graphical representation of this situation. However, there is still another component of a digital audio system that we have not discussed yet: computation on the processor's core.

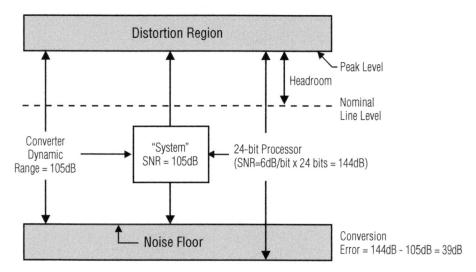

Figure 5.8 **An audio system's SNR consists of the weakest component's SNR**

Passing data through a processor's computation units can potentially introduce rounding and truncation errors. For example, a 16-bit processor may be able to add a vector of 16-bit data and store this in an extended-length accumulator. However, when the value in the accumulator is eventually written to a 16-bit data register, then some of the bits are truncated.

Take a look at Figure 5.9 to see how computation errors can affect a real system. If we take an ideal 16-bit A/D converter (Figure 5.9a), then its signal-to-noise ratio would be $16 \times 6 = 96$ dB. If arithmetic and storage errors did not exist, then 16-bit computation would suffice to keep the SNR at 96 dB. 24-bit and 32-bit systems would dedicate 8 and 16 bits, respectively, to the dynamic range below the noise floor. In essence, those extra bits would be wasted.

However, most digital audio systems do introduce some round-off and truncation errors. If we can quantify this error to take, for example, 18 dB (or 3 bits), then it becomes clear that 16-bit computations will not suffice in keeping the system's SNR at 96 dB (Figure 5.9b). Another way to interpret this is to say that the effective noise floor is raised by 18 dB, and the total SNR is decreased to 96 dB − 18 dB = 78 dB. This leads to the conclusion that having extra bits below the converter's noise floor helps to deal with the nuisance of quantization.

Numeric Formats for Audio

There are many ways to represent data inside a processor. The two main processor architectures used for audio processing are fixed-point and floating-point. Fixed-point processors are designed for integer and fractional arithmetic, and they usually natively support 16-bit, 24-bit, or 32-bit data. Floating-point processors provide excellent performance with native support for 32-bit or 64-bit floating-point data types. However, they are typically more costly and consume more power than their fixed-point counterparts, and most real systems must strike a balance between quality and engineering cost.

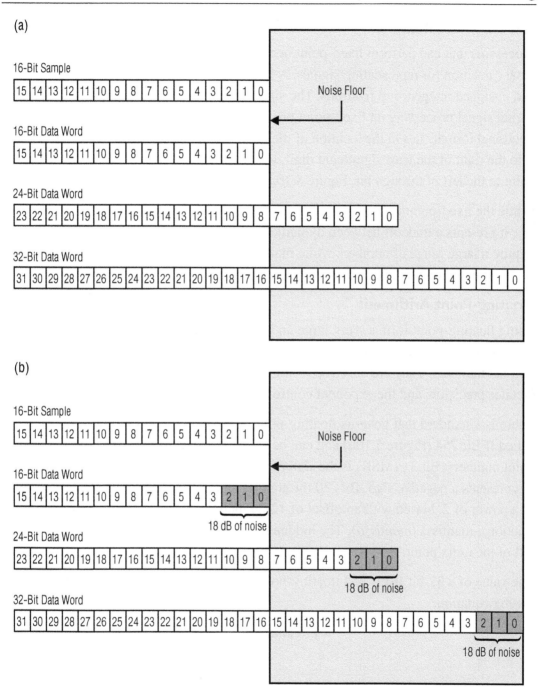

Figure 5.9 **(a) Allocation of extra bits with various word-width computations for an ideal 16-bit, 96 dB SNR system, when quantization error is neglected (b) Allocation of extra bits with various word-width computations for an ideal 16-bit, 96 dB SNR system, when quantization noise is present**

Fixed-Point Arithmetic

Processors that can perform fixed-point operations typically use a twos-complement binary notation for representing signals. A fixed-point format can represent both signed and unsigned integers and fractions. The signed fractional format is most common for digital signal processing on fixed-point processors. The difference between integer and fractional formats lies in the location of the binary point. For integers, the binary point is to the right of the least significant digit, whereas fractions usually have their binary point to the left of the sign bit. Figure 5.10a shows integer and fractional formats.

While the fixed-point convention simplifies numeric operations and conserves memory, it presents a tradeoff between dynamic range and precision. In situations that require a large range of numbers while maintaining high resolution, a radix point that can shift based on magnitude and exponent is desirable.

Floating-Point Arithmetic

Using floating-point format, very large and very small numbers can be represented in the same system. Floating-point numbers are quite similar to scientific notation of rational numbers. They are described with a mantissa and an exponent. The mantissa dictates precision, and the exponent controls dynamic range.

There is a standard that governs floating-point computations of digital machines. It is called IEEE 754 (Figure 5.10b) and can be summarized as follows for 32-bit floating-point numbers. Bit 31 (MSB) is the *sign bit*, where a 0 represents a positive sign and a 1 represents a negative sign. Bits 30 through 23 represent an exponent field (*exp_field*) as a power of 2, biased with an offset of 127. Finally, bits 22 through 0 represent a fractional mantissa (*mantissa*). The hidden bit is basically an implied value of 1 to the left of the radix point.

The value of a 32-bit IEEE 754 floating-point number can be represented with the following equation:

$$(-1)^{sign\_bit} \times (1.mantissa) \times 2^{(exp\_field - 127)}$$

With an 8-bit exponent and a 23-bit mantissa, IEEE 754 reaches a balance between dynamic range and precision. In addition, IEEE floating-point libraries include support for additional features such as $\pm\infty$, 0 and NaN (not a number).

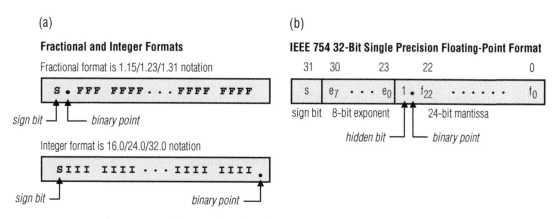

Figure 5.10 **(a) Fractional and integer formats (b) IEEE 754 32-bit single-precision floating-point format**

Table 5.5 shows the smallest and largest values attainable from the common floating-point and fixed-point types.

Table 5.5 **Comparison of dynamic range for various data formats**

Data type	Smallest positive value	Largest positive value
IEEE 754 Floating-Point (single-precision)	$2^{-126} \approx 1.2 \times 10^{-38}$	$2^{128} \approx 3.4 \times 10^{38}$
1.15 16-bit fixed-point	$2^{-15} \approx 3.1 \times 10^{-5}$	$1-2^{-15} \approx 9.9 \times 10^{-1}$
1.23 24-bit fixed-point	$2^{-23} \approx 1.2 \times 10^{-7}$	$1-2^{-23} \approx 9.9 \times 10^{-1}$

Emulation on 16-Bit Architectures

As we explained earlier, 16-bit processing does not provide enough SNR for high quality audio, but this does not mean that you shouldn't choose a 16-bit processor for an audio system. For example, a 32-bit floating-point machine makes it easier to code an algorithm that preserves 32-bit data natively, but a 16-bit processor can also maintain 32-bit integrity through emulation at a much lower cost. Figure 5.11 illustrates some of the possibilities when it comes to choosing a data type for an embedded algorithm.

In the remainder of this section, we'll describe how to achieve floating-point and 32-bit extended-precision fixed-point functionality on a 16-bit fixed-point machine.

Floating-Point Emulation Techniques on a 16-bit Processor

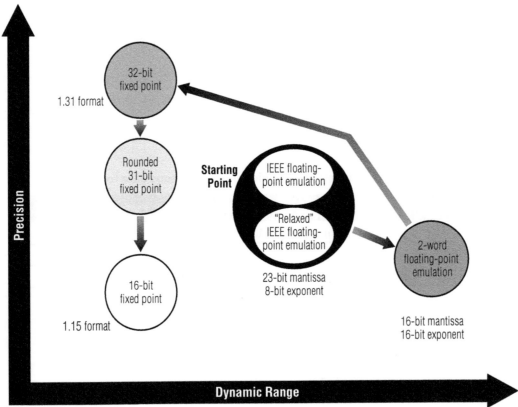

Path of arrows denotes decreasing core cycles required

Figure 5.11 **Depending on the goals of an application, there are many data types that can satisfy system requirements**

Floating-Point Emulation on Fixed-Point Processors

On most 16-bit fixed-point processors, IEEE 754 floating-point functions are available as library calls from either C/C++ or assembly language. These libraries emulate the required floating-point processing using fixed-point multiply and ALU logic. This emulation requires additional cycles to complete. However, as fixed-point processor core-clock speeds venture into the 500 MHz–1 GHz range, the extra cycles required to emulate IEEE 754-compliant floating-point math become less significant.

It is sometimes advantageous to use a "relaxed" version of IEEE 754 in order to reduce computational complexity. This means that the floating-point arithmetic doesn't implement features such ∞ and NaN.

A further optimization is to use a processor's native data register widths for the mantissa and exponent. Take, for example, the Blackfin architecture, which has a register file set that consists of sixteen 16-bit registers that can be used instead as eight 32-bit registers. In this configuration, on every core-clock cycle, two 32-bit registers can source operands for computation on all four register halves. To make optimized use of the Blackfin register file, a two-word format can be used. In this way, one word (16 bits) is reserved for the exponent and the other word (16 bits) is reserved for the fraction.

Double-Precision Fixed-Point Emulation

There are many applications where 16-bit fixed-point data is not sufficient, but where emulating floating-point arithmetic may be too computationally intensive. For these applications, extended-precision fixed-point emulation may be enough to satisfy system requirements. Using a high-speed fixed-point processor will insure a significant reduction in the amount of required processing. Two popular extended-precision formats for audio are 32-bit and 31-bit fixed-point representations.

32-Bit-Accurate Emulation

32-bit arithmetic is a natural software extension for 16-bit fixed-point processors. For processors whose 32-bit register files can be accessed as two 16-bit halves, the halves can be used together to represent a single 32-bit fixed-point number. The Blackfin processor's hardware implementation allows for single-cycle 32-bit addition and subtraction.

For instances where a 32-bit multiply will be iterated with accumulation (as is the case in some algorithms we'll talk about soon), we can achieve 32-bit accuracy with

16-bit multiplications in just three cycles. Each of the two 32-bit operands (R0 and R1) can be broken up into two 16-bit halves (R0.H | R0.L and R1.H | R1.L).

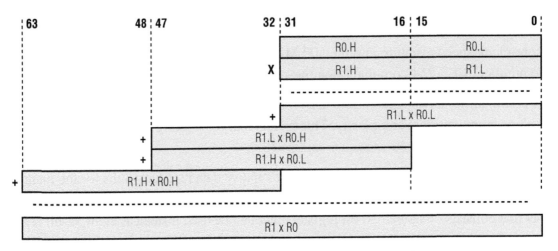

Figure 5.12 **32-bit multiplication with 16-bit operations**

From Figure 5.12, it is easy to see that the following operations are required to emulate the 32-bit multiplication R0 × R1 with a combination of instructions using 16-bit multipliers:

- Four 16-bit multiplications to yield four 32-bit results

  1. R1.L × R0.L

  2. R1.L × R0.H

  3. R1.H × R0.L

  4. R1.H × R0.H

- Three operations to preserve bit place in the final answer (the >> symbol denotes a right shift). Since we are performing fractional arithmetic, the result is 1.62 (1.31 × 1.31 = 2.62 with a redundant sign bit). Most of the time, the result can be truncated to 1.31 in order to fit in a 32-bit data register. Therefore, the result of the multiplication should be in reference to the sign bit, or the most significant bit. This way the least significant bits can be safely discarded in a truncation.

1. $(R1.L \times R0.L) >> 32$

2. $(R1.L \times R0.H) >> 16$

3. $(R1.H \times R0.L) >> 16$

The final expression for a 32-bit multiplication is

$$((R1.L \times R0.L) >> 32 + (R1.L \times R0.H) >> 16) + ((R1.H \times R0.L) >> 16 + R1.H \times R0.H)$$

On the Blackfin architecture, these instructions can be issued in parallel to yield an effective rate of a 32-bit multiplication in three cycles.

31-Bit-Accurate Emulation

We can reduce a fixed-point multiplication requiring at most 31-bit accuracy to just two cycles. This technique is especially appealing for audio systems, which usually require at least 24-bit representation, but where 32-bit accuracy may be a bit excessive. Using the 6 dB rule, 31-bit-accurate emulation still maintains a dynamic range of around 186 dB, which is plenty of headroom even with rounding and truncation errors.

From the multiplication diagram shown in Figure 5.12, it is apparent that the multiplication of the least significant half-word $R1.L \times R0.L$ does not contribute much to the final result. In fact, if the result is truncated to 1.31, then this multiplication can only have an effect on the least significant bit of the 1.31 result. For many applications, the loss of accuracy due to this bit is balanced by the speeding up of the 32-bit multiplication through eliminating one 16-bit multiplication, one shift, and one addition.

The expression for 31-bit accurate multiplication is

$$((R1.L \times R0.H) + (R1.H \times R0.L)) >> 16 + (R1.H \times R0.H)$$

On the Blackfin architecture, these instructions can be issued in parallel to yield an effective rate of two cycles for each 32-bit multiplication.

Audio Processing Methods
Getting Data to the Processor's Core

There are a number of ways to get audio data into the processor's core. For example, a foreground program can poll a serial port for new data, but this type of transfer is uncommon in embedded media processors, because it makes inefficient use of the core.

Instead, a processor connected to an audio codec usually uses a DMA engine to transfer the data from the codec link (like a serial port) to some memory space available to the processor. This transfer of data occurs in the background without the core's intervention. The only overhead is in setting up the DMA sequence and handling the interrupts once the data buffer has been received or transmitted.

Block Processing versus Sample Processing

Sample processing and block processing are two approaches for dealing with digital audio data. In the sample-based method, the processor crunches the data as soon as it's available. Here, the processing function incurs overhead during each sample period. Many filters (like FIR and IIR, described later) are implemented this way, because the effective latency is low.

Block processing, on the other hand, is based on filling a buffer of a specific length before passing the data to the processing function. Some filters are implemented using block processing because it is more efficient than sample processing. For one, the block method sharply reduces the overhead of calling a processing function for each sample. Also, many embedded processors contain multiple ALUs that can parallelize the computation of a block of data. What's more, some algorithms are, by nature, meant to be processed in blocks. For example, the Fourier transform (and its practical counterpart, the fast Fourier transform, or FFT) accepts blocks of temporal or spatial data and converts them into frequency domain representations.

Double-Buffering

In a block-based processing system that uses DMA to transfer data to and from the processor core, a "double buffer" must exist to handle the DMA transfers and the core. This is done so that the processor core and the core-independent DMA engine do not access the same data at the same time, causing a data coherency problem. To facilitate the processing of a buffer of length N, simply create a buffer of length 2 × N. For a bidirectional system, two buffers of length 2 × N must be created. As shown in Figure 5.13a, the core processes the `in1` buffer and stores the result in the `out1` buffer, while the DMA engine is filling `in0` and transmitting the data from `out0`. Figure 5.13b depicts that once the DMA engine is done with the left half of the double buffers, it starts transferring data into `in1` and out of `out1`, while the core processes data from `in0` and into `out0`. This configuration is sometimes called "ping-pong buffering," because the core alternates between processing the left and right halves of the double buffers.

Note that, in real-time systems, the serial port DMA (or another peripheral's DMA tied to the audio sampling rate) dictates the timing budget. For this reason, the block processing algorithm must be optimized in such a way that its execution time is less than or equal to the time it takes the DMA to transfer data to/from one half of a double-buffer.

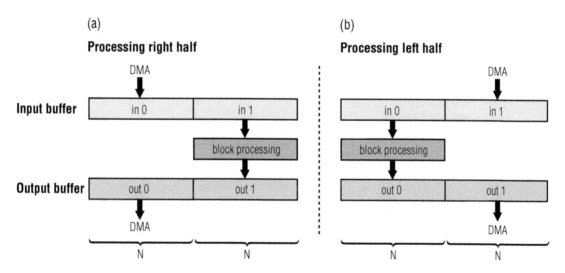

Figure 5.13 **Double-buffering scheme for stream processing**

2D DMA

When data is transferred across a digital link like I²S, it may contain several channels. These may all be multiplexed on one data line going into the same serial port. In such a case, 2D DMA can be used to de-interleave the data so that each channel is linearly arranged in memory. Take a look at Figure 5.14 for a graphical depiction of this arrangement, where samples from the left and right channels are de-multiplexed into two separate blocks. This automatic data arrangement is extremely valuable for those systems that employ block processing.

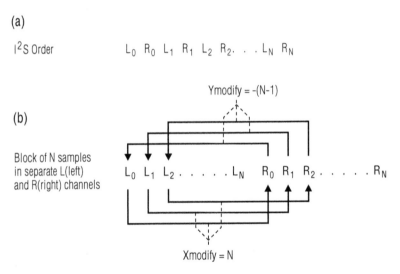

(a)

I²S Order $\qquad L_0 \ R_0 \ L_1 \ R_1 \ L_2 \ R_2 \ldots L_N \ R_N$

Ymodify = -(N-1)

(b)

Block of N samples in separate L(left) and R(right) channels

$L_0 \ L_1 \ L_2 \ldots \ldots L_N \qquad R_0 \ R_1 \ R_2 \ldots \ldots R_N$

Xmodify = N

Figure 5.14 **A 2D DMA engine used to de-interleave (a) I²S stereo data into (b) separate left and right buffers**

Basic Operations

There are three fundamental building blocks in audio processing. They are the summing operation, multiplication, and time delay. Many more complicated effects and algorithms can be implemented using these three elements. A summer has the obvious duty of adding two signals together. A multiplication can be used to boost or attenuate an audio signal. On most media processors, multiple summer and/or multiplier blocks can execute in a single cycle. A time delay is a bit more complicated. In many audio algorithms, the current output depends on a combination of previous inputs and/or outputs. The implementation of this delay effect is accomplished with a delay line, which is really nothing more than an array in memory that holds previous data. For example, an echo algorithm might hold 500 ms of input samples. The current output value can be computed by adding the current input value to a slightly attenuated prior sample. If the audio system is sample-based, then the programmer can simply keep track of an input pointer and an output pointer (spaced at 500 ms worth of samples apart), and increment them after each sampling period.

Since delay lines are meant to be reused for subsequent sets of data, the input and output pointers will need to wrap around from the end of the delay line buffer back to the beginning. In C/C++, this is usually done by appending the modulus operator (%) to the pointer increment.

This wrap-around may incur no extra processing cycles if you use a processor that supports circular buffering (see Figure 5.15). In this case, the beginning address and length of a circular buffer must be provided only once. During processing, the software increments or decrements the current pointer within the buffer, but the hardware takes care of wrapping around to the beginning of the buffer if the current pointer falls outside of the buffer's boundaries. Without this automated address generation, the programmer would have to manually keep track of the buffer, thus wasting valuable processing cycles.

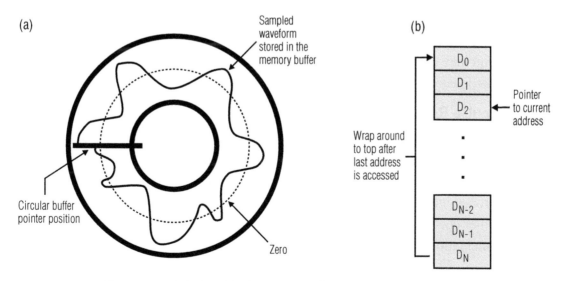

Figure 5.15 **(a) Graphical representation of a delay line using a circular buffer (b) Layout of a circular buffer in memory**

An echo effect derives from an important audio building block called the comb filter, which is essentially a delay with a feedback element. When multiple comb filters are used simultaneously, they can create the effect of reverberation.

Signal Generation

In some audio systems, a signal (for example, a sine wave) might need to be synthesized. Taylor Series function approximations can emulate trigonometric functions. Moreover, uniform random number generators are handy for creating white noise.

However, synthesis might not fit into a given system's processing budget. On fixed-point systems with ample memory, you can use a table lookup instead of generating a signal. This has the side effect of taking up precious memory resources, so hybrid methods can be used as a compromise. For example, you can store a coarse lookup table to save memory. During runtime, the exact values can be extracted from the table using interpolation, an operation that can take significantly less time than computing a full approximation. This hybrid approach provides a good balance between computation time and memory resources.

Filtering and Algorithms

Digital filters are used in audio systems for attenuating or boosting the energy content of a sound wave at specific frequencies. The most common filter forms are high-pass, low-pass, band-pass and notch. Any of these filters can be implemented in two ways. These are the finite impulse response filter (FIR) and the infinite impulse response filter (IIR), and they constitute building blocks to more complicated filtering algorithms like parametric equalizers and graphic equalizers.

Finite Impulse Response (FIR) Filter

The FIR filter's output is determined by the sum of the current and past inputs, each of which is first multiplied by a filter coefficient. The FIR summation equation, shown in Figure 5.16a, is also known as *convolution*, one of the most important operations in signal processing. In this syntax, x is the input vector, y is the output vector, and h holds the filter coefficients. Figure 5.16a also shows a graphical representation of the FIR implementation.

Convolution is such a common operation in media processing that many processors are designed to execute a multiply-accumulate (MAC) instruction along with multiple data accesses (reads and writes) and pointer increments in one cycle.

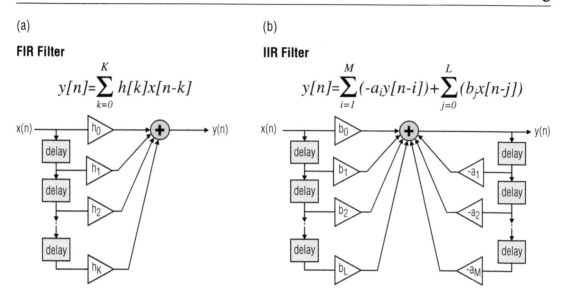

Figure 5.16 (a) FIR filter equation and structure (b) IIR filter equation and structure

Infinite Impulse Response (IIR) Filter

Unlike the FIR, whose output depends only on inputs, the IIR filter relies on both inputs and past outputs. The basic equation for an IIR filter is a difference equation, as shown in Figure 5.16b. Because of the current output's dependence on past outputs, IIR filters are often referred to as *recursive filters*. Figure 5.16b also gives a graphical perspective on the structure of the IIR filter.

Fast Fourier Transform

Quite often, we can do a better job describing an audio signal by characterizing its frequency composition. A Fourier transform takes a time-domain signal and translates it into the frequency domain; the inverse Fourier transform achieves the opposite, converting a frequency-domain representation back into the time domain. Mathematically, there are some nice property relationships between operations in the time domain and those in the frequency domain. Specifically, a time-domain convolution (or an FIR filter) is equivalent to a multiplication in the frequency domain. This tidbit would not be too practical if it weren't for a special optimized implementation of the Fourier transform called the fast Fourier transform (FFT). In fact, it is often more efficient to implement an FIR filter by transforming the input signal and coefficients into the frequency domain with an FFT, multiplying the transforms, and finally transforming the result back into the time domain with an inverse FFT.

There are other transforms that are used often in audio processing. Among them, one of the most common is the modified discrete cosine transform (MDCT), which is the basis for many audio compression algorithms.

Sample Rate Conversion

There are times when you will need to convert a signal sampled at one frequency to a different sampling rate. One situation where this is useful is when you want to decode an audio signal sampled at, say 8 kHz, but the DAC you're using does not support that sampling frequency. Another scenario is when a signal is oversampled, and converting to a lower sampling frequency can lead to a reduction in computation time. The process of converting the sampling rate of a signal from one rate to another is called sampling rate conversion (or SRC).

Increasing the sampling rate is called interpolation, and decreasing it is called decimation. Decimating a signal by a factor of M is achieved by keeping only every Mth sample and discarding the rest. Interpolating a signal by a factor of L is accomplished by padding the original signal with L–1 zeros between each sample.

Even though interpolation and decimation factors are integers, you can apply them in series to an input signal to achieve a rational conversion factor. When you upsample by 5 and then downsample by 3, then the resulting resampling factor is 5/3 = 1.67.

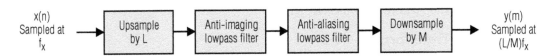

Figure 5.17 **Sample-rate conversion through upsampling and downsampling**

To be honest, we oversimplified the SRC process a bit too much. In order to prevent artifacts due to zero-padding a signal (which creates images in the frequency domain), an interpolated signal must be low-pass-filtered before being used as an output or as an input into a decimator. This anti-imaging low-pass filter can operate at the input sample rate, rather than at the faster output sample rate, by using a special FIR filter structure that recognizes that the inputs associated with the L–1 inserted samples have zero values.

Similarly, before they're decimated, all input signals must be low-pass-filtered to prevent aliasing. The anti-aliasing low-pass filter may be designed to operate at the decimated sample rate, rather than at the faster input sample rate, by using a FIR filter structure that realizes the output samples associated with the discarded samples need not be computed. Figure 5.17 shows a flow diagram of a sample rate converter. Note that it is possible to combine the anti-imaging and anti-aliasing filter into one component for computational savings.

Audio Compression

Even though raw audio requires a lower bit rate than raw video, the amount of data is still substantial. The bit rate required to code a single CD-quality audio channel (44.1 kHz at 16 bits) using the standard PCM method is 705.6 kbps—one minute of stereo sound requires over 10 Mbytes of storage! Sending this much data over a network or a serial connection is inefficient, and sometimes impossible. The solution comes in the form of compression algorithms called audio codecs. These software codecs, not to be confused with hardware ADCs and DACs discussed already, compress raw data either for low-bandwidth transfer or for storage, and decompress for the reverse effect.

There are lossless codecs and lossy codecs available for audio. Lossless codecs are constructed in such a way that a compressed signal can be reconstructed to contain the exact data as the original input signal. Lossless codecs are computationally intensive, and they can reduce audio bit rate by up to about ½. Lossy codecs can compress audio much more (10× or more, depending on desired quality), and the audio decoded from a lossy stream sounds very close to the original, even though information is lost forever in the encoding process. Lossy codecs can throw out data and still preserve audio integrity, because they are based on a psycho-acoustical model that takes advantage of our ears' physiology. In essence, a lossy codec can cheat by dropping data that will not affect how we'll ultimately perceive the signal. This technique is often referred to as "perceptual encoding."

Earlier, we mentioned frequency and temporal masking. Another useful feature for perceptual encoding—called *joint stereo encoding*—deals with multiple channels. The basic premise is that data in two or more channels is correlated. By decoupling unique features of each channel from the shared features, we can drastically reduce the data needed to encode the content. If one channel takes 196 kbps, then an encoder that recognizes the redundancy will allocate much less data than 2×196 kbps for a stereo stream, while still retaining the same perceived sound. The general rule of thumb is that multichannel audio can be efficiently encoded with an amount of data proportional to the square root of the number of channels (see Reference 23 in the Appendix for more details).

In practice, audio encoders use two techniques: sub-band coding and transform coding. Sub-band coding splits the input audio signal into a number of sub-bands, using band-pass filters. A psycho-acoustical model is applied on the sub-bands to define the number of bits necessary to maintain a specified sound quality. Transform coding uses a transform like the FFT or an MDCT on a block of audio data. Then, a psycho-acoustical model is used to determine the proper quantization of the frequency components based on a masking threshold to ensure that the output sounds like the input signal.

Let's take a look at some of the currently available audio codecs. Some of the algorithms are proprietary and require a license before they can be used in a system. Table 5.6 lists common audio coding standards and the organizations responsible for them.

Table 5.6 **Various audio codecs**

Audio Coding Standard	(Licensing/Standardization Organization)
MP3	ISO/IEC
AAC	ISO/IEC
AC-3	Dolby Labs
Windows Media Audio	Microsoft
RealAudio	RealNetworks
Vorbis	Xiph.org
FLAC	Xiph.org

MP3

MP3 is probably the most popular lossy audio compression codec available today. The format, officially known as MPEG-1 Audio Layer 3, was released in 1992 as a complement to the MPEG-1 video standard from the Moving Pictures Experts Group. MPEG is a group of ISO/IEC, an information center jointly operated by the International Organization for Standardization and the International Electrotechnical Commission. MP3 was developed by the German Fraunhofer Institut Integrierte Schaltungen (Fraunhofer IIS), which holds a number of patents for MP3 encoding and decoding. Therefore, you must obtain a license before incorporating the MP3 algorithm into your embedded systems.

MP3 uses polyphase filters to separate the original signal into sub-bands. Then, the MDCT transform converts the signal into the frequency domain, where a psycho-acoustical model quantizes the frequency coefficients. A CD-quality track can be MP3-encoded at a 128–196 kbps rate, thus achieving up to a 12:1 compression ratio.

AAC

Advanced Audio Coding (AAC) is a second-generation codec also developed by Fraunhofer IIS. It was designed to complement the MPEG-2 video format. Its main improvement over MP3 is the ability to achieve lower bit rates at equivalent sound quality.

AC-3

The AC-3 format was developed by Dolby Laboratories to efficiently handle multi-channel audio such as 5.1, a capability that was not implemented in the MP3 standard. The nominal stereo bit rate is 192 kbps, whereas it's 384 kbps for 5.1 surround sound.

A 5.1 surround-sound system contains five full-range speakers, including front left and right, rear left and right, and front center channels, along with a low-frequency (10 Hz–120 Hz) subwoofer.

WMA

Windows Media Audio (WMA) is a proprietary codec developed by Microsoft to challenge the popularity of MP3. Microsoft developed WMA with paid music distribution in mind, so they incorporated Digital Rights Management (DRM) into the codec. Besides the more popular lossy codec, WMA also supports lossless encoding.

RealAudio

RealAudio, developed by RealNetworks, is another proprietary format. It was conceived to allow the streaming of audio data over low bandwidth links. Many Internet radio stations use this format to stream their content. Recent updates to the codec have improved its quality to match that of other modern codecs.

Vorbis

Vorbis was created at the outset to be free of any patents. It is released by the Xiph.org Foundation as a completely royalty-free codec. A full Vorbis implementation for both floating-point and fixed-point processors is available under a free license from Xiph.org. Because it is free, Vorbis is finding its way into increasing numbers of embedded devices.

According to many subjective tests, Vorbis outperforms MP3, and it is therefore in the class of the newer codecs like WMA and AAC. Vorbis also fully supports multi-channel compression, thereby eliminating redundant information carried by the channels. Refer to Chapter 9 for further discussion on the Vorbis codec and its implementation on an embedded processor.

FLAC

FLAC is another open standard from the Xiph.org Foundation. It stands for Free Lossless Audio Codec, and as the name implies, it does not throw out any information from the original audio signal. This, of course, comes at the expense of much smaller achievable compression ratios. The typical compression range for FLAC is 30–70%.

Speech Compression

Speech compression is used widely in real-time communications systems like cell phones, and in packetized voice connections like Internet phones.

Since speech is more band-limited than full-range audio, it is possible to employ audio codecs, taking the smaller bandwidth into account. Almost all speech codecs do, indeed, sample voice data at 8 kHz. However, we can do better than just take advantage of the smaller frequency range. Since only a subset of the audible signals within the speech bandwidth is ever vocally generated, we can drive bit rates even lower. The major goal in speech encoding is a highly compressed stream with good intelligibility and short delays to make full-duplex communication possible.

The most traditional speech coding approach is code-excited linear prediction (CELP). CELP is based on linear prediction coding (LPC) models of the vocal tract and a supplementary residue codebook.

The idea behind using LPC for speech coding is founded on the observation that the human vocal tract can be roughly modeled with linear filters. We can make two basic kinds of sounds: voiced and unvoiced. Voiced sounds are produced when our vocal cords vibrate, and unvoiced sounds are created when air is constricted by the mouth, tongue, lips and teeth. Voiced sounds can be modeled as linear filters driven by a fundamental frequency, whereas unvoiced ones are modeled with random noise sources. Through these models, we can describe human utterances with just a few parameters. This allows LPC to predict signal output based on previous inputs and outputs. To complete the model, LPC systems supplement the idealized filters with residue (i.e., error) tables. The codebook part of CELP is basically a table of typical residues.

In real-time duplex communications systems, one person speaks while the other one listens. Since the person speaking is not contributing anything to the signal, some codecs implement features like voice activity detection (VAD) to recognize silence, and comfort noise generation (CNG) to simulate the natural level of noise without actually encoding it at the transmitting end.

Table 5.7 **Various speech codecs**

Speech Coding Standard	Bit rate	Governing Body
GSM-FR	13 kbps	ETSI
GSM-EFR	12.2 kbps	ETSI
GSM-AMR	4.75, 5.15, 5.90, 6.70, 7.40, 7.95, 10.2, 12.2 kbps	3GPP
G.711	64 kbps	ITU-T
G.723.1	5.3, 6.3 kbps	ITU-T
G.729	6.4, 8, 11.8 kbps	ITU-T
Speex	2 – 44 kbps	Xiph.org

GSM

The GSM speech codecs find use in cell phone systems around the world. The governing body of these standards is the European Telecommunications Standards Institute (ETSI). There is actually an evolution of standards in this domain. The first one was GSM Full Rate (GSM-FR). This standard uses a CELP variant called Regular Pulse Excited Linear Predictive Coder (RPELPC). The input speech signal is divided into 20-ms frames. Each of those frames is encoded as 260 bits, thereby producing a total bit rate of 13 kbps. Free GSM-FR implementations are available for use under certain restrictions.

GSM Enhanced Full Rate (GSM-EFR) was developed to improve the quality of speech encoded with GSM-FR. It operates on 20-ms frames at a bit rate of 12.2 kbps, and it works in noise-free and noisy environments. GSM-EFR is based on the patented Algebraic Code Excited Linear Prediction (ACELP) technology, so you must purchase a license before using it in end products.

The 3rd Generation Partnership Project (3GPP), a group of standards bodies, introduced the GSM Adaptive Multi-Rate (GSM-AMR) codec to deliver even higher quality speech over lower-bit-rate data links by using an ACELP algorithm. It uses 20-ms data chunks, and it allows for multiple bit rates at eight discrete levels between 4.75 kbps and 12.2 kbps. GSM-AMR supports VAD and CNG for reduced bit rates.

The "G-Dot" Standards

The International Telecommunication Union (ITU) was created to coordinate the standards in the communications industry, and the ITU Telecommunication Standardization Sector (ITU-T) is responsible for the recommendations of many speech codecs, known as the G.x standards.

G.711

G.711, introduced in 1988, is a simple standard when compared with the other options presented here. The only compression used in G.711 is companding (using either the μ-law or A-law standards), which compresses each data sample to 8 bits, yielding an output bit rate of 64 kbps.

G.723.1

G.723.1 is an ACELP-based dual-bit-rate codec, released in 1996, that targets Voice-Over-IP (VoIP) applications like teleconferencing. The encoding frame for G.723.1 is 30 ms. Each frame can be encoded in 20 or 24 bytes, thus translating to 5.3 kbps and 6.3 kbps streams, respectively. The bit rates can be effectively reduced through VAD and CNG. The codec offers good immunity against network imperfections like lost frames and bit errors. This speech codec is part of video conferencing applications described by the H.324 family of standards.

G.729

Another speech codec released in 1996 is G.729, which partitions speech into 10-ms frames, making it a low-latency codec. It uses an algorithm called Conjugate Structure ACELP (CS-ACELP). G.729 compresses 16-bit signals sampled at 8 kHz via 10-ms frames into a standard bit rate of 8 kbps, but it also supports 6.4 kbps and 11.8 kbps rates. VAD and CNG are also supported.

Speex

Speex is another codec released by Xiph.org, with the goal of being a totally patent-free speech solution. Like many other speech codecs, Speex is based on CELP with residue coding. The codec can take 8 kHz, 16 kHz, and 32 kHz linear PCM signals and code them into bit rates ranging from 2 to 44 kbps. Speex is resilient to network errors, and it supports voice activity detection. Besides allowing variable bit rates, another unique feature of Speex is stereo encoding. Source code is available from Xiph.org in both a floating-point reference implementation and a fixed-point version.

What's Next?

Now that you've got a backgrounder on audio as it relates to embedded media processing, we'll strive to provide you with a similar level of familiarity with video. Taken together, audio and video provide the core of most multimedia systems, and once we have explored both, we'll start looking at multimedia frameworks in embedded systems.

Basics of Embedded Video and Image Processing

Introduction

As consumers, we're intimately familiar with video systems in many embodiments. However, from the embedded developer's viewpoint, video represents a tangled web of different resolutions, formats, standards, sources and displays. Many references exist that delve into the details of all things video; outstanding among them are References 33 and 34 in the Appendix.

In this chapter, our goal will not be to duplicate such excellent works. Rather, we will strive to untangle some of this intricate web, focusing on the most common circumstances you're likely to face in today's media processing systems. After reviewing the basics of video, we will discuss some common scenarios you may encounter in embedded multimedia design and provide some tips and tricks for dealing with challenging video design issues.

Human Visual Perception

Let's start by discussing a little physiology. Understanding how our eyes work has paved an important path in the evolution of video and imaging. As we'll see, video formats and compression algorithms both rely on the eye's responses to different types of stimuli.

Our eyes contain two types of vision cells: rods and cones. Rods are primarily sensitive to light intensity as opposed to color, and they give us night vision capability. Cones, on the other hand, are not tuned to intensity, but instead are sensitive to wavelengths of light between 400 nm (violet) and 770 nm (red). Thus, the cones provide the foundation for our color perception.

There are three types of cones, each with a different pigment that's either most sensitive to red, green or blue wavelengths, although there's a lot of overlap between the three responses. Taken together, the response of our cones peaks in the green region, at around 555 nm. This is why, as we'll see, we can make compromises in LCD displays by assigning the green channel more bits of resolution than the red or blue channels.

The discovery of the red, green and blue cones ties into the development of the *trichromatic color theory*, which states that almost any color of light can be conveyed by combining proportions of monochromatic red, green and blue wavelengths.

Because our eyes have lots more rods than cones, they are more sensitive to intensity than actual color. This allows us to save bandwidth in video and image representations by *subsampling* the color information.

Our perception of brightness is logarithmic, not linear. In other words, the actual intensity required to produce a 50% gray image (exactly between total black and total white) is only around 18% of the intensity we need to produce total white. This characteristic is extremely important in camera sensor and display technology, as we'll see in our discussion of *gamma correction*. Also, this effect leads to a reduced sensitivity to quantization distortion at high intensities, a trait that many media-encoding algorithms use to their advantage.

Another visual novelty is that our eyes adjust to the viewing environment, always creating their own reference for white, even in low-lighting or artificial-lighting situations. Because camera sensors don't innately act the same way, this gives rise to a *white balance* control in which the camera picks its reference point for absolute white.

The eye is less sensitive to high-frequency information than low-frequency information. What's more, although it can detect fine details and color resolution in still images, it cannot do so for rapidly moving images. As a result, *transform coding* (DCT, FFT, etc.) and *low-pass filtering* can be used to reduce total bandwidth needed to represent an image or video sequence.

Our eyes can notice a "flicker" effect at image update rates less than 50 to 60 times per second (50 to 60 Hz) in bright light. Under dim lighting conditions, this rate drops to about 24 Hz. Additionally, we tend to notice flicker in large uniform regions more so than in localized areas. These traits have important implications for *interlaced* video and display technologies.

What's a Video Signal?

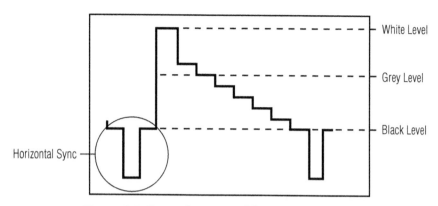

Figure 6.1 **Example composition of Luma signal**

At its root, a video signal is basically just a two-dimensional array of intensity and color data that is updated at a regular frame rate, conveying the perception of motion. On conventional cathode-ray tube (CRT) TVs and monitors, an electron beam modulated by an analog video signal such as that shown in Figure 6.1 illuminates phosphors on the screen in a top-to-bottom, left-to-right fashion. Synchronization signals embedded in the analog signal define when the beam is actively "painting" phosphors and when it is inactive, so that the electron beam can retrace from right to left to start on the next row, or from bottom to top to begin the next video field or frame. These synchronization signals are represented in Figure 6.2.

HSYNC is the horizontal synchronization signal. It demarcates the start of active video on each row (left to right) of a video frame. *Horizontal blanking* is the interval

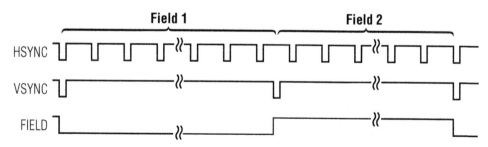

Figure 6.2 **Typical timing relationships between HSYNC, VSYNC, FIELD**

in which the electron gun retraces from the right side of the screen back over to the next row on the left side.

VSYNC is the vertical synchronization signal. It defines the start (top to bottom) of a new video image. *Vertical blanking* is the interval in which the electron gun retraces from the bottom right corner of the screen image back up to the top left corner.

FIELD distinguishes, for interlaced video, which field is currently being displayed. This signal is not applicable for progressive-scan video systems.

The transmission of video information originated as a display of relative luminance from black to white—thus was born the black-and-white television system. The voltage level at a given point in space correlated to the brightness level of the image at that point.

When color TV became available, it had to be backward-compatible with black-and-white systems, so the color burst information was added on top of the existing luminance signal, as shown in Figure 6.3. Color information is also called chrominance. We'll talk more about it in our discussion on color spaces.

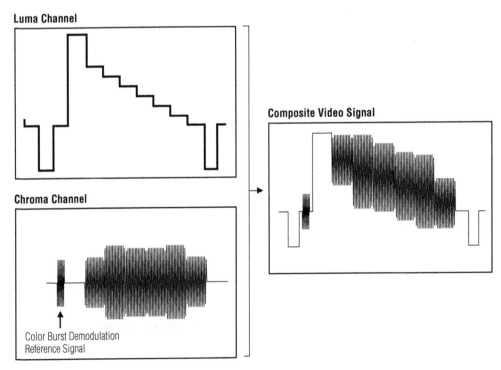

Figure 6.3 **Analog video signal with color burst**

Broadcast TV—NTSC and PAL

Analog video standards differ in the ways they encode brightness and color information. Two standards dominate the broadcast television realm—NTSC and PAL. NTSC, devised by the National Television System Committee, is prevalent in Asia and North America, whereas PAL (Phase Alternation Line) dominates Europe and South America. PAL developed as an offshoot of NTSC, improving on its color distortion performance. A third standard, SECAM, is popular in France and parts of eastern Europe, but many of these areas use PAL as well. Our discussions will center on NTSC systems, but the results relate also to PAL-based systems. Reference 34 in the Appendix provides a thorough discussion of the intricacies of each of these standards, along with which countries use them.

Video Resolution

Horizontal resolution indicates the number of pixels on each line of the image, and vertical resolution designates how many horizontal lines are displayed on the screen to create the entire frame. Standard definition (SD) NTSC systems are interlaced-scan, with 480 lines of active pixels, each with 720 active pixels per line (i.e., 720×480 pixels). Frames refresh at a rate of roughly 30 frames/second (actually 29.97 fps), with interlaced fields updating at a rate of 60 fields/second (actually 59.94 fields/sec).

High-definition (HD) systems often employ progressive scanning and can have much higher horizontal and vertical resolutions than SD systems. We will focus on SD systems rather than HD systems, but most of our discussion also generalizes to the higher frame and pixel rates of the high-definition systems.

When discussing video, there are two main branches along which resolutions and frame rates have evolved. These are computer graphics formats and broadcast video formats. Table 6.1 shows some common screen resolutions and frame rates belonging to each category. Even though these two branches emerged from separate domains with different requirements (for instance, computer graphics uses RGB progressive-scan schemes, while broadcast video uses YCbCr interlaced schemes), today they are used almost interchangeably in the embedded world. That is, VGA compares closely with the NTSC "D-1" broadcast format, and QVGA parallels CIF. It should be noted that, although D-1 is 720 pixels × 486 rows, it's commonly referred to as being 720×480 pixels (which is really the arrangement of the NTSC "DV" format used for DVDs and other digital video).

Table 6.1 **Graphics vs. Broadcast standards**

Origin	Video Standard	Horizontal Resolution (pixels)	Vertical Resolution (pixels)	Total Pixels
Broadcast	QCIF	176	144	25,344
Graphics	QVGA	320	240	76,800
Broadcast	CIF	352	288	101,376
Graphics	VGA	640	480	307,200
Broadcast	NTSC	720	480	345,600
Broadcast	PAL	720	576	414,720
Graphics	SVGA	800	600	480,000
Graphics	XGA	1024	768	786,432
Broadcast	HDTV (720p)	1280	720	921,600
Graphics	SXGA	1280	1024	1,310,720
Graphics	UXGA	1600	1200	1,920,000
Broadcast	HDTV (1080i)	1920	1080	2,073,600

Interlaced versus Progressive Scanning

Interlaced scanning originates from early analog television broadcasts, where the image needed to be updated rapidly in order to minimize visual flicker, but the technology available did not allow for refreshing the entire screen this quickly. Therefore, each frame was "interlaced," or split into two fields, one consisting of odd-numbered scan lines, and the other composed of even-numbered scan lines, as depicted in Figure 6.4. The frame refresh rate for NTSC (PAL) was set at approximately 30 (25) frames/sec. Thus, large areas flicker at 60 (50) Hz, while localized regions flicker at 30 (25) Hz. This was a compromise to conserve bandwidth while accounting for the eye's greater sensitivity to flicker in large uniform regions.

Not only does some flickering persist, but interlacing also causes other artifacts. For one, the scan lines themselves are often visible. Because each NTSC field is a snapshot of activity occurring at 1/60 second intervals, a video frame consists of two temporally different fields. This isn't a problem when you're watching the display, because it presents the video in a temporally appropriate manner. However, converting interlaced fields into progressive frames (a process known as *deinterlacing*) can cause jagged edges when there's motion in an image. Deinterlacing is important because it's often more efficient to process video frames as a series of adjacent lines.

With the advent of digital television, progressive (that is, noninterlaced) scan has become a very popular input and output video format for improved image quality. Here, the entire image updates sequentially from top to bottom, at twice the scan rate of a comparable interlaced system. This eliminates many of the artifacts associated with interlaced scanning. In progressive scanning, the notion of two fields composing a video frame does not apply.

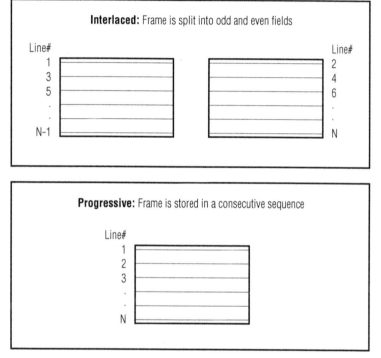

Figure 6.4 **Interlaced scan vs. progressive scan illustration**

Color Spaces

There are many different ways of representing color, and each color system is suited for different purposes. The most fundamental representation is RGB color space.

RGB stands for "Red-Green-Blue," and it is a color system commonly employed in camera sensors and computer graphics displays. As the three primary colors that sum to form white light, they can combine in proportion to create most any color in the visible spectrum. RGB is the basis for all other color spaces, and it is the overwhelming choice of color space for computer graphics.

Just as RGB rules the display graphics world, CYMK reigns in the printing realm. CYMK stands for "Cyan-Yellow-Magenta-blacK," and it is a popular color space for printing and painting. It can be regarded as the inverse of the RGB color system, to the extent that RGB is additive, and CYMK is subtractive. In other words, whereas R, G and B light add together to form white light, C, Y and M inks add together to absorb all white. In other words, they create black. However, because it's difficult to create pure black, given the physical properties of printing media, true black is also added to the color system (hence the fourth letter, "K").

Gamma Correction

"Gamma" is a crucial phenomenon to understand when dealing with color spaces. This term describes the nonlinear nature of luminance perception and display. Note that this is a twofold manifestation: the human eye perceives brightness in a nonlinear manner, and physical output devices (such as CRTs and LCDs) display brightness nonlinearly. It turns out, by way of coincidence, that human perception of luminance sensitivity is almost exactly the inverse of a CRT's output characteristics.

Stated another way, luminance on a display is roughly proportional to the input analog signal voltage raised to the power of gamma. On a CRT or LCD display, this value is ordinarily between 2.2 and 2.5. A camera's precompensation, then, scales the RGB values to the power of (1/gamma).

The upshot of this effect is that video cameras and computer graphics routines, through a process called "gamma correction," prewarp their RGB output stream both to compensate for the target display's nonlinearity and to create a realistic model of how the eye actually views the scene. Figure 6.5 illustrates this process.

Gamma-corrected RGB coordinates are referred to as R'G'B' space, and the luma value Y' is derived from these coordinates. Strictly speaking, the term "luma" should only refer to this gamma-corrected luminance value, whereas the true "luminance" Y is a color science term formed from a weighted sum of R, G, and B (with no gamma correction applied). Reference 33 in the Appendix provides an in-depth discussion of proper terminology related to gamma, luma, and chroma in color systems.

Often when we talk about YCbCr and RGB color spaces in this text, we are referring to gamma-corrected components—in other words, Y'CbCr or R'G'B'. However, because this notation can be distracting and doesn't affect the substance of our

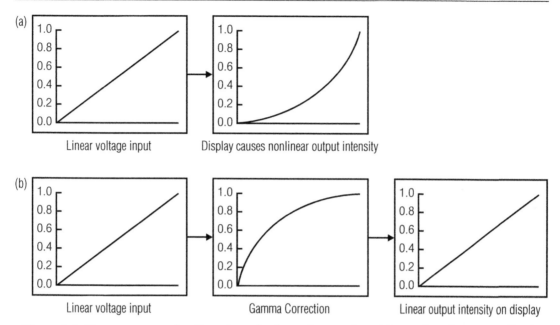

Figure 6.5 **Gamma correction linearizes the intensity produced for a given input amplitude**
(a) Linear input voltage creates a nonlinear brightness characteristic on the display
(b) By precorrecting for this distortion, display intensity follows input voltage linearly

discussion, and since it's clear that gamma correction is essential (whether performed by the processor or by dedicated hardware) at sensor and display interfaces, we will confine ourselves to the YCbCr/RGB nomenclature even in cases where gamma adjustment has been applied. The exception to this convention is when we discuss actual color space conversion equations.

While RGB channel format is a natural scheme for representing real-world color, each of the three channels is highly correlated with the other two. You can see this by independently viewing the R, G, and B channels of a given image—you'll be able to perceive the entire image in each channel. Also, RGB is not a preferred choice for image processing because changes to one channel must be performed in the other two channels as well, and each channel has equivalent bandwidth.

To reduce required transmission bandwidths and increase video compression ratios, other color spaces were devised that are highly uncorrelated, thus providing better compression characteristics than RGB does. The most popular ones—YPbPr, YCbCr, and YUV—all separate a luminance component from two chrominance components. This separation is performed via scaled color difference factors (B´-Y´) and (R´-Y´).

The Pb/Cb/U term corresponds to the (B´-Y´) factor, and the Pr/Cr/V term corresponds to the (R´-Y´) parameter. YPbPr is used in component analog video, YUV applies to composite NTSC and PAL systems, and YCbCr relates to component digital video.

Separating luminance and chrominance information saves image processing bandwidth. Also, as we'll see shortly, we can reduce chrominance bandwidth considerably via subsampling, without much loss in visual perception. This is a welcome feature for video-intensive systems.

As an example of how to convert between color spaces, the following equations illustrate translation between 8-bit representations of Y´CbCr and R´G´B´ color spaces, where Y´, R´, G´ and B' normally range from 16–235, and Cr and Cb range from 16–240.

$$Y´ = (0.299)R´ + (0.587)G´ + (0.114)B´$$
$$Cb = -(0.168)R´ - (0.330)G´ + (0.498)B´ + 128$$
$$Cr = (0.498)R´ - (0.417)G´ - (0.081)B´ + 128$$

$$R´ = Y´ + 1.397(Cr - 128)$$
$$G´ = Y´ - 0.711(Cr - 128) - 0.343(Cb - 128)$$
$$B´ = Y´ + 1.765(Cb - 128)$$

Chroma Subsampling

With many more rods than cones, the human eye is more attuned to brightness and less to color differences. As luck (or really, design) would have it, the YCbCr color system allows us to pay more attention to Y, and less to Cb and Cr. As a result, by subsampling these chroma values, video standards and compression algorithms can achieve large savings in video bandwidth.

Before discussing this further, let's get some nomenclature straight. Before subsampling, let's assume we have a full-bandwidth YCbCr stream. That is, a video source generates a stream of pixel components in the form of Figure 6.6a. This is called "4:4:4 YCbCr." This notation looks rather odd, but the simple explanation is this: the first number is always 4, corresponding historically to the ratio between the luma sampling frequency and the NTSC color subcarrier frequency. The second number corresponds to the ratio between luma and chroma within a given line (horizontally): if there's no downsampling of chroma with respect to luma, this number is 4. The third number relates to the luma/chroma relationship vertically: if there's no downsampling of chroma between lines, this number is also 4. Therefore, 4:4:4 implies that each pixel on every line has its own unique Y, Cr and Cb components.

Now, if we filter a 4:4:4 YCbCr signal by subsampling the chroma by a factor of two horizontally, we end up with 4:2:2 YCbCr. '4:2:2' implies that there are four luma values for every two chroma values on a given video line. Each (Y,Cb) or (Y,Cr) pair represents one pixel value. Another way to say this is that a chroma pair coincides spatially with every other luma value, as shown in Figure 6.6b. Believe it or not, 4:2:2 YCbCr qualitatively shows little loss in image quality compared with its 4:4:4 YCbCr source, even though it represents a savings of 33% in bandwidth over 4:4:4 YCbCr. As we'll discuss soon, 4:2:2 YCbCr is a foundation for the ITU-R BT.601 video recommendation, and it is the most common format for transferring digital video between subsystem components.

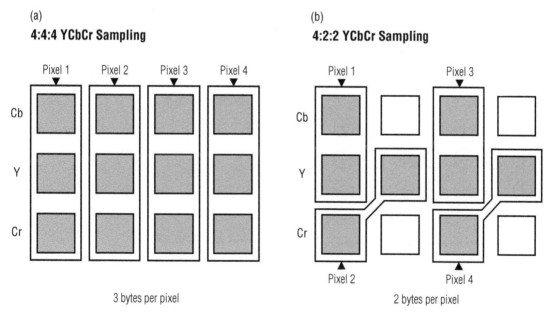

Figure 6.6 **(a) 4:4:4 vs. (b) 4:2:2 YCbCr pixel sampling**

Note that 4:2:2 is not the only chroma subsampling scheme. Figure 6.7 shows others in popular use. For instance, we could subsample the chroma of a 4:4:4 YCbCr stream by a factor of four horizontally, as shown in Figure 6.7c, to end up with a 4:1:1 YCbCr stream. Here, the chroma pairs are spatially coincident with every fourth luma value. This chroma filtering scheme results in a 50% bandwidth savings; 4:1:1 YCbCr is a popular format for inputs to video compression algorithms and outputs from video decompression algorithms.

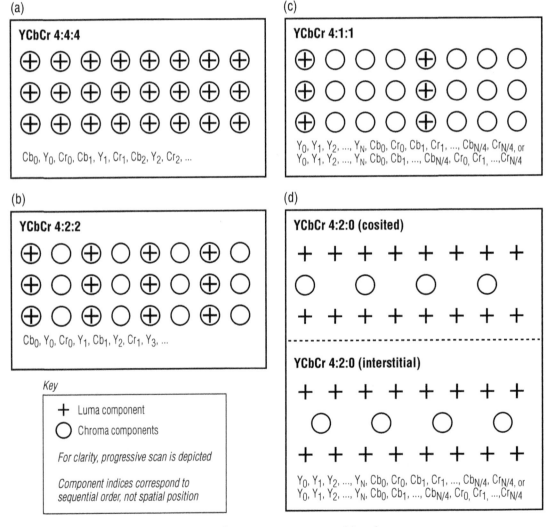

Figure 6.7 **(a)** YCbCr 4:4:4 stream and its chroma-subsampled derivatives **(b)** 4:2:2 **(c)** 4:1:1 **(d)** 4:2:0

Another format popular in video compression/decompression is 4:2:0 YCbCr; it's more complex than the others we've described for a couple of reasons. For one, the Cb and Cr components are each subsampled by 2, horizontally *and* vertically. This means we have to store multiple video lines in order to generate this subsampled stream. What's more, there are two popular formats for 4:2:0 YCbCr. MPEG-2 compression uses a horizontally co-located scheme (Figure 6.7d, top), whereas MPEG-1 and JPEG algorithms use a form where the chroma are centered between Y samples (Figure 6.7d, bottom).

Digital Video

Before the mid-1990s, nearly all video was in analog form. Only then did forces like the advent of MPEG-2 compression, the proliferation of streaming media on the Internet, and the FCC's adoption of a Digital Television (DTV) standard create a "perfect storm" that brought the benefits of digital representation into the video world. These advantages over analog include better signal-to-noise performance, improved bandwidth utilization (fitting several digital video channels into each existing analog channel), and reduction in storage space through digital compression techniques.

At its root, digitizing video involves both *sampling* and *quantizing* the analog video signal. In the 2D context of a video frame, sampling entails dividing the image space, gridlike, into small regions and assigning relative amplitude values based on the intensities of color space components in each region. Note that analog video is already sampled vertically (discrete number of rows) and temporally (discrete number of frames per second).

Quantization is the process that determines these discrete amplitude values assigned during the sampling process. Eight-bit video is common in consumer applications, where a value of 0 is darkest (total black) and 255 is brightest (white), for each color channel (R,G,B or YCbCr). However, it should be noted that 10-bit and 12-bit quantization per color channel is rapidly entering mainstream video products, allowing extra precision that can be useful in reducing received image noise by minimizing roundoff error.

The advent of digital video provided an excellent opportunity to standardize, to a large degree, the interfaces to NTSC and PAL systems. When the International Telecommunication Union (ITU) met to define recommendations for digital video standards, it focused on achieving a large degree of commonality between NTSC and PAL standards, such that the two could share the same coding formats.

They defined two separate recommendations—ITU-R BT.601 and ITU-R BT.656. Together, these two define a structure that enables different digital video system components to interoperate. Whereas BT.601 defines the parameters for digital video transfer, BT.656 defines the interface itself.

ITU-R BT.601 (formerly CCIR-601)

BT.601 specifies methods for digitally coding video signals, employing the YCbCr color space for efficient use of channel bandwidth. It proposes 4:2:2 YCbCr as a preferred format for broadcast video. Synchronization signals (HSYNC, VSYNC, FIELD) and a clock are also provided to delineate the boundaries of active video regions.

Each BT.601 pixel component (Y, Cr, or Cb) is quantized to either 8 or 10 bits, and both NTSC and PAL have 720 pixels of active video per line. However, they differ in their vertical resolution. While 30 frames/sec NTSC has 525 lines (including vertical blanking, or retrace, regions), the 25 frame/sec rate of PAL is accommodated by adding 100 extra lines, or 625 total, to the PAL frame.

BT.601 specifies Y with a nominal range from 16 (total black) to 235 (total white). The color components Cb and Cr span from 16 to 240, but a value of 128 corresponds to no color. Sometimes, due to noise or rounding errors, a value might dip outside the nominal boundaries, but never all the way to 0 or 255.

ITU-R BT.656 (formerly CCIR-656)

Whereas BT.601 outlines how to digitally encode video, BT.656 actually defines the physical interfaces and data streams necessary to implement BT.601. It defines both bit-parallel and bit-serial modes. The bit-parallel mode requires only a 27 MHz clock (for NTSC, 30 frames/sec) and 8 or 10 data lines (depending on the resolution of pixel components). All synchronization signals are embedded in the data stream, so no extra hardware lines are required. Figure 6.8 shows some common timing relationships using embedded frame syncs, including the standard BT.656 4:2:2 YCbCr format, as well as "BT.656-style" 4:4:4 YCbCr and RGB formats.

The bit-serial mode requires only a multiplexed 10-bit-per-pixel serial data stream over a single channel, but it involves complex synchronization, spectral shaping and clock recovery conditioning. Furthermore, the bit clock rate runs close to 300 MHz, so it can be challenging to implement bit-serial BT.656 in many systems. In this chapter, we'll focus our attention on the bit-parallel mode only.

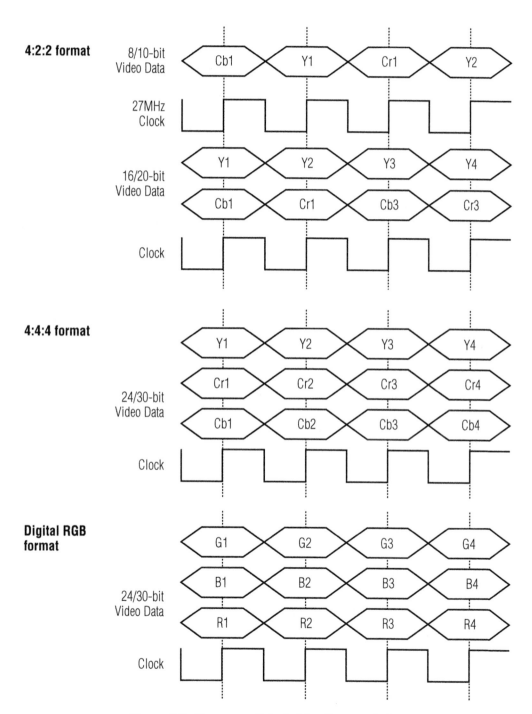

Figure 6.8 **Common digital video format timing**

The frame partitioning and data stream characteristics of ITU-R BT.656 are shown in Figures 6.9 and 6.10, respectively, for 525/60 (NTSC) and 625/50 (PAL) systems.

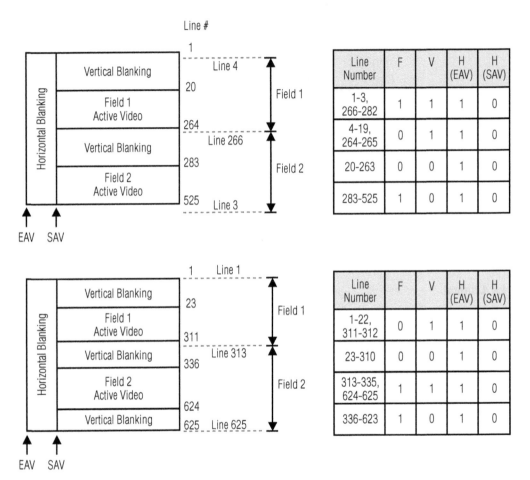

Figure 6.9 **ITU-R BT.656 frame partitioning**

In BT.656, the Horizontal (H), Vertical (V), and Field (F) signals are sent as an embedded part of the video data stream in a series of bytes that form a control word. The Start of Active Video (SAV) and End of Active Video (EAV) signals indicate the beginning and end of data elements to read in on each line. SAV occurs on a 1-to-0 transition of H, and EAV occurs on a 0-to-1 transition of H. An entire field of video is composed of Active Video, Horizontal Blanking (the space between an EAV and SAV code) and Vertical Blanking (the space where V = 1).

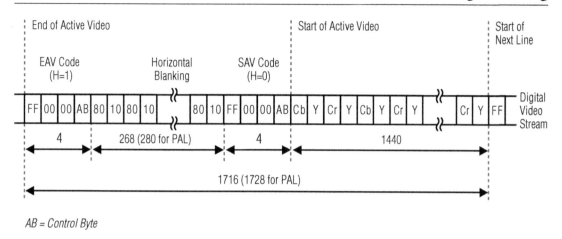

AB = Control Byte

Figure 6.10 **ITU-R BT.656 data stream**

A field of video commences on a transition of the F bit. The "odd field" is denoted by a value of F = 0, whereas F = 1 denotes an even field. Progressive video makes no distinction between Field 1 and Field 2, whereas interlaced video requires each field to be handled uniquely, because alternate rows of each field combine to create the actual video frame.

The SAV and EAV codes are shown in more detail in Figure 6.11. Note there is a defined preamble of 3 bytes (0xFF, 0x00, 0x00 for 8-bit video, or 0x3FF, 0x000, 0x000 for 10-bit video), followed by the Control Byte, which, aside from the F (Field), V (Vertical Blanking) and H (Horizontal Blanking) bits, contains four protection bits for single-bit error detection and correction. Note that F and V are only

	8-bit Data								10-bit Data	
	D9 (MSB)	D8	D7	D6	D5	D4	D3	D2	D1	D0
Preamble	1	1	1	1	1	1	1	1	1	1
	0	0	0	0	0	0	0	0	0	0
	0	0	0	0	0	0	0	0	0	0
Control Byte	1	F	V	H	P3	P2	P1	P0	0	0

P3:P0 = Error detection/correction bits

Figure 6.11 **SAV/EAV preamble codes**

allowed to change as part of EAV sequences (that is, transitions from H = 0 to H = 1). Also, notice that for 10-bit video, the two additional bits are actually the least-significant bits, not the most-significant bits.

The bit definitions are as follows:

- F = 0 for Field 1
- F = 1 for Field 2
- V = 1 during Vertical Blanking
- V = 0 when not in Vertical Blanking
- H = 0 at SAV
- H = 1 at EAV
- P3 = V XOR H
- P2 = F XOR H
- P1 = F XOR V
- P0 = F XOR V XOR H

The vertical blanking interval (the time during which V=1) can be used to send nonvideo information, like audio, teletext, closed-captioning, or even data for interactive television applications. BT.656 accommodates this functionality through the use of ancillary data packets. Instead of the "0xFF, 0x00, 0x00" preamble that normally precedes control bytes, the ancillary data packets all begin with a "0x00, 0xFF, 0xFF" preamble. For further information about ancillary data types and formats, refer to Reference 39 in the Appendix.

Assuming that ancillary data is not being sent, during horizontal and vertical blanking intervals the (Cb, Y, Cr, Y, Cb, Y, ...) stream is (0x80, 0x10, 0x80, 0x10, 0x80, 0x10...). Also, note that because the values 0x00 and 0xFF hold special value as control preamble demarcators, they are not allowed as part of the active video stream. In 10-bit systems, the values (0x000 through 0x003) and (0x3FC through 0x3FF) are also reserved, so as not to cause problems in 8-bit implementations.

A Systems View of Video

Figure 6.12 shows a typical end-to-end embedded digital video system. In one case, a video source feeds into a media processor (after being digitized by a video decoder, if

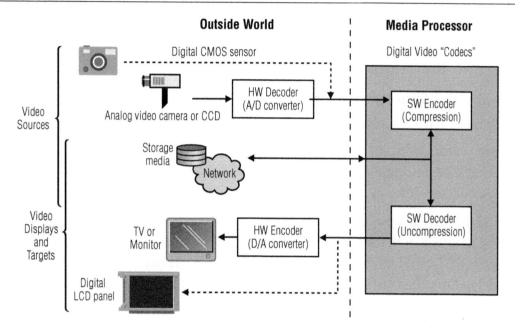

Figure 6.12 System video flow for analog/digital sources and displays

necessary). There, it might be compressed via a software encoder before being stored locally or sent over the network.

In an opposite flow, a compressed stream is retrieved from a network or from mass storage. It is then decompressed via a software decoder and sent directly to a digital output display (like a TFT-LCD panel), or perhaps it is instead converted to analog form by a video encoder for display on a conventional CRT.

Keep in mind that compression and decompression represent only a subset of possible video processing algorithms that might run on the media processor. Still, for our purposes, they set a convenient template for discussion. Let's examine in more detail the video-specific portions of these data flows.

Video Sources

Analog Video Sources

A video decoder chip converts an analog video signal (e.g., NTSC, PAL, CVBS, S-Video) into a digital form (usually of the ITU-R BT.601/656 YCbCr or RGB variety). This is a complex, multi-stage process. It involves extracting timing information from the input, separating luma from chroma, separating chroma into Cr and Cb components, sampling the output data, and arranging it into the appropriate format. A serial interface such as SPI or I²C configures the decoder's operating parameters. Figure 6.13 shows a block diagram of a representative video decoder.

Digital Video Sources

CCDs and CMOS Sensors

Camera sources today are overwhelmingly based on either charge-coupled device (CCD) or CMOS technology. Both of these technologies convert light into electrical signals, but they differ in how this conversion occurs.

In CCD devices, an array of millions of light-sensitive picture elements, or pixels, spans the surface of the sensor. After exposure to light, the accumulated charge over the entire CCD pixel array is read out at one end of the device and then digitized via an Analog Front End (AFE) chip or CCD processor. On the other hand, CMOS sensors directly digitize the exposure level at each pixel site.

In general, CCDs have higher quality and better noise performance, but they are not power-efficient. CMOS sensors are easy to manufacture and have low power dissipation, but at reduced quality. Part of the reason for this is because the transistors at each pixel site tend to occlude light from reaching part of the pixel. However, CMOS has started giving CCD a run for its money in the quality arena, and increasing numbers of mid-tier camera sensors are now CMOS-based.

Regardless of their underlying technology, all pixels in the sensor array are sensitive to grayscale intensity—from total darkness (black) to total brightness (white). The extent to which they're sensitive is known as their "bit depth." Therefore, 8-bit pixels can distinguish between 2^8, or 256, shades of gray, whereas 12-bit pixel values differentiate between 4096 shades. Layered over the entire pixel array is a color filter that segments each pixel into several color-sensitive "subpixels." This arrangement allows a measure of different color intensities at each pixel site. Thus, the color at each pixel location can be viewed as the sum of its red, green and blue channel light content, superimposed in an additive manner. The higher the bit depth, the more colors that can be generated in the RGB space. For example, 24-bit color (8 bits each of R,G,B) results in 2^{24}, or 16.7 million, discrete colors.

Bayer Pattern

In order to properly represent a color image, a sensor needs three color samples— most commonly, red, green and blue—for every pixel location. However, putting

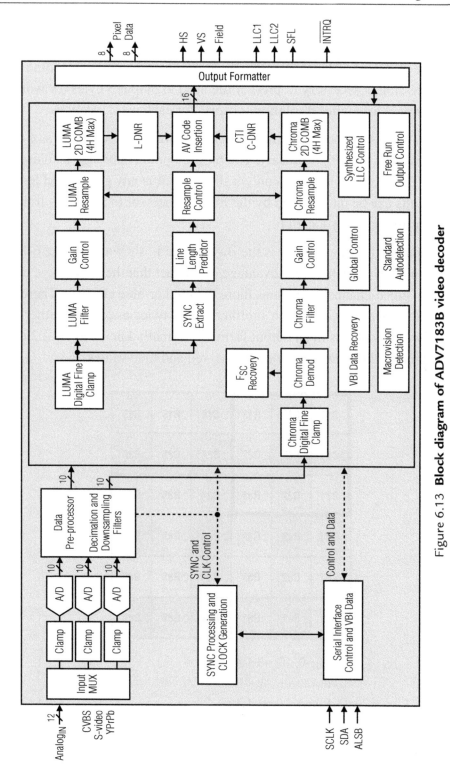

Figure 6.13 **Block diagram of ADV7183B video decoder**

three separate sensors in every camera is not a financially tenable solution (although lately such technology is becoming more practical). What's more, as sensor resolutions increase into the 5–10 megapixel range, it becomes apparent that some form of image compression is necessary to prevent the need to output 3 bytes (or worse yet, three 12-bit words for higher-resolution sensors) for each pixel location.

Not to worry, because camera manufacturers have developed clever ways of reducing the number of color samples necessary. The most common approach is to use a Color Filter Array (CFA), which measures only a single color at any given pixel location. Then, the results can be interpolated by the image processor to appear as if three colors were measured at every location.

The most popular CFA in use today is the Bayer pattern, shown in Figure 6.14. This scheme, invented by Kodak, takes advantage of the fact that the human eye discerns differences in green-channel intensities more than red or blue changes. Therefore, in the Bayer color filter array, the green subfilter occurs twice as often as either the blue or red subfilter. This results in an output format informally known as "4:2:2 RGB," where four green values are sent for every two red and blue values.

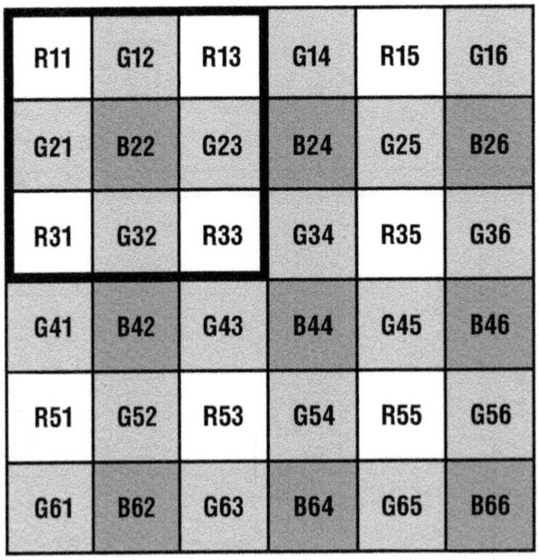

R11	G12	R13	G14	R15	G16
G21	B22	G23	B24	G25	B26
R31	G32	R33	G34	R35	G36
G41	B42	G43	B44	G45	B46
R51	G52	R53	G54	R55	G56
G61	B62	G63	B64	G65	B66

$G_{22}=(G_{12}+G_{21}+G_{23}+G_{32})/4$

$R_{22}=(R_{11}+R_{13}+R_{31}+R_{33})/4$

$B_{22}=B_{22}$, actual sampled value

Figure 6.14 **Bayer pattern image sensor arrangement**

Connecting to Image Sensors

CMOS sensors ordinarily output a parallel digital stream of pixel components in either YCbCr or RGB format, along with horizontal and vertical synchronization signals and a pixel clock. Sometimes, they allow for an external clock and sync signals to control the transfer of image frames out from the sensor.

CCDs, on the other hand, usually hook up to an Analog Front End (AFE) chip, such as the AD9948, that processes the analog output signal, digitizes it, and generates appropriate timing to scan the CCD array. A processor supplies synchronization signals to the AFE, which needs this control to manage the CCD array. The digitized parallel output stream from the AFE might be in 10-bit, or even 12-bit, resolution per pixel component.

Recently, LVDS (low-voltage differential signaling) has become an important alternative to the parallel data bus approach. LVDS is a low-cost, low-pin-count, high-speed serial interconnect that has better noise immunity and lower power consumption than the standard parallel approach. This is important as sensor resolutions and color depths increase, and as portable multimedia applications become more widespread.

Image Pipe

Of course, the picture-taking process doesn't end at the sensor; on the contrary, its journey is just beginning. Let's take a look at what a raw image has to go through before becoming a pretty picture on a display. Sometimes this is done within the sensor electronics module (especially with CMOS sensors), and other times these steps must be performed by the media processor. In digital cameras, this sequence of processing stages is known as the "image processing pipeline," or just "image pipe." Refer to Figure 6.15 for one possible dataflow.

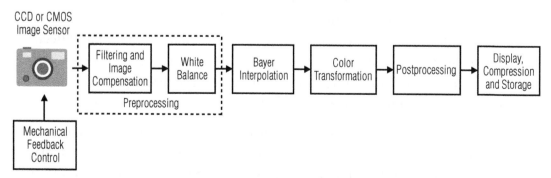

Figure 6.15 **Example image processing pipeline**

Mechanical Feedback Control

Before the shutter button is even released, the focus and exposure systems work with the mechanical camera components to control lens position based on scene characteristics. *Auto-exposure* algorithms measure brightness over discrete scene regions to compensate for overexposed or underexposed areas by manipulating shutter speed and/or aperture size. The net goals here are to maintain relative contrast between different regions in the image and to achieve a target average luminance.

Auto-focus algorithms divide into two categories. Active methods use infrared or ultrasonic emitters/receivers to estimate the distance between the camera and the object being photographed. Passive methods, on the other hand, make focusing decisions based on the received image in the camera.

In both of these subsystems, the media processor manipulates the various lens and shutter motors via PWM output signals. For auto-exposure control, it also adjusts the Automatic Gain Control (AGC) circuit of the sensor.

Preprocessing

As we discussed earlier, a sensor's output needs to be *gamma-corrected* to account for eventual display, as well as to compensate for nonlinearities in the sensor's capture response.

Since sensors usually have a few inactive or defective pixels, a common preprocessing technique is to eliminate these via median filtering, relying on the fact that sharp changes from pixel to pixel are abnormal, since the optical process blurs the image somewhat.

Filtering and Image Compensation

This set of algorithms accounts for the physical properties of lenses that warp the output image compared to the actual scene the user is viewing. Different lenses can cause different distortions; for instance, wide-angle lenses create a "barreling" or "bulging" effect, while telephoto lenses create a "pincushion" or "pinching" effect. Lens *shading distortion* reduces image brightness in the area around the lens. *Chromatic aberration* causes color fringes around an image. The media processor needs to mathematically transform the image in order to correct for these distortions.

Another area of preprocessing is *image stability compensation*, or *hand-shaking correction*. Here, the processor adjusts for the translational motion of the received image, often with the help of external transducers that relate the real-time motion profile of the sensor.

White Balance

Another stage of preprocessing is known as *white balance.* When we look at a scene, regardless of lighting conditions, our eyes tend to normalize everything to the same set of natural colors. For instance, an apple looks deep red to us whether we're indoors under fluorescent lighting or outside in sunny weather. However, an image sensor's "perception" of color depends largely on lighting conditions, so it needs to map its acquired image to appear "lighting-agnostic" in its final output. This mapping can be done either manually or automatically.

In manual systems, you point your camera at an object you determine to be "white," and the camera will then shift the "color temperature" of all images it takes to accommodate this mapping. Automatic White Balance (AWB), on the other hand, uses inputs from the image sensor and an extra white balance sensor to determine what should be regarded as "true white" in an image. It tweaks the relative gains between the R, G and B channels of the image. Naturally, AWB requires more image processing than manual methods, and it's another target of proprietary vendor algorithms.

Bayer Interpolation

Demosaicking, or interpolation of the Bayer data, is perhaps the most crucial and numerically intensive operation in the image pipeline. Each camera manufacturer typically has its own "secret recipe," but in general, the approaches fall into a few main algorithm categories.

Nonadaptive algorithms like bilinear interpolation or bicubic interpolation are among the simplest to implement, and they work well in smooth areas of an image. However, edges and texture-rich regions present a challenge to these straightforward implementations. Adaptive algorithms, those that change behavior based on localized image traits, can provide better results.

One example of an adaptive approach is *edge-directed reconstruction.* Here, the algorithm analyzes the region surrounding a pixel and determines in which direction to perform interpolation. If it finds an edge nearby, it interpolates along the edge, rather than across it. Another adaptive scheme assumes a *constant hue* for an entire object, and this prevents abrupt changes in color gradients within individual objects.

Many other demosaicking approaches exist, some involving frequency-domain analysis, Bayesian probabilistic estimation, and even neural networks. For an excellent survey of the various methods available, refer to Reference 43 in the Appendix.

Color Transformation

In this stage, the interpolated RGB image is transformed to the targeted output color space (if not already in the right space). For compression or display to a television, this will usually involve an RGB → YCbCr matrix transformation, often with another gamma correction stage to accommodate the target display. The YCbCr outputs may also be chroma subsampled at this stage to the standard 4:2:2 format for color bandwidth reduction with little visual impact.

Postprocessing

In this phase, the image is perfected via a variety of filtering operations before being sent to the display and/or storage media. For instance, edge enhancement, pixel thresholding for noise reduction, and color-artifact removal are all common at this stage.

Display/Compression/Storage

Once the image itself is ready for viewing, the image pipe branches off in two different directions. In the first, the postprocessed image is output to the target display, usually an integrated LCD screen (but sometimes an NTSC/PAL television monitor, in certain camera modes). In the second, the image is sent to the media processor's compression algorithm, where industry-standard compression techniques (JPEG, for instance) are applied before the picture is stored locally in some storage medium (usually a nonvolatile flash memory card).

Video Displays

Analog Video Displays

Video Encoder

A video encoder converts a digital video stream into an analog video signal. It typically accepts a YCbCr or RGB video stream in either ITU-R BT.656 or BT.601 format and converts it to a signal compliant with one of several different output standards (e.g., NTSC, PAL, SECAM). A host processor controls the encoder via a serial interface like SPI or I^{2}C, programming such settings as pixel timing, input/output formats, and luma/chroma filtering. Figure 6.16 shows a block diagram of a representative encoder. Video encoders commonly output in one or more of the following analog formats:

CVBS—This acronym stands for Composite Video Baseband Signal (or Composite Video Blanking and Syncs.) Composite video connects through the ubiquitous yellow

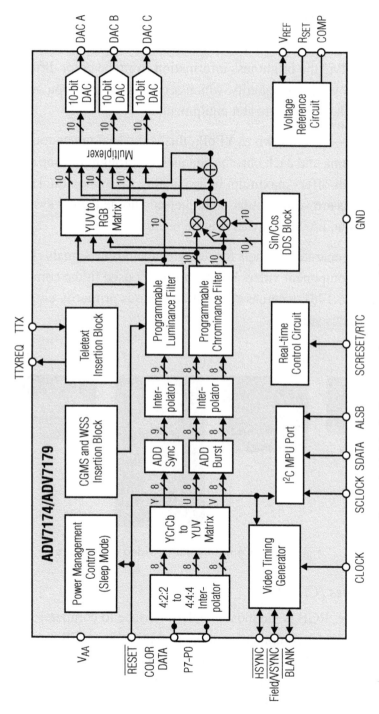

Figure 6.16 **Block diagram of ADV7179 video encoder**

RCA jack shown in Figure 6.17a. It contains luma, chroma, sync and color burst information all on the same wire.

<u>S Video</u>, using the jack shown in Figure 6.17b, sends the luma and chroma content separately. Separating the brightness information from the color difference signals dramatically improves image quality, which accounts for the popularity of S Video connections on today's home theater equipment.

<u>Component Video</u>—Also known as YPbPr, this is the analog version of YCbCr digital video. Here, the luma and each chroma channel are brought out separately, each with its own timing. This offers maximum image quality for analog transmission. Component connections are very popular on higher-end home theater system components like DVD players and A/V receivers (Figure 6.17c).

<u>Analog RGB</u> has separate channels for red, green and blue signals. This offers similar image quality to component video, but it's normally used in the computer graphics realm (see Figure 6.17d), whereas component video is primarily employed in the consumer electronics arena.

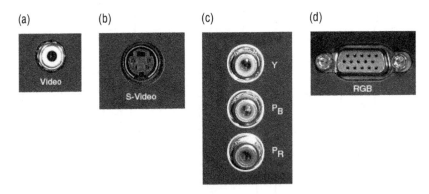

Figure 6.17 **Common analog video connectors**

Cathode Ray Tubes (CRTs)

On the display side, RGB is the most popular interface to computer monitors and LCD panels. Most older computer monitors accept analog RGB inputs on three separate pins from the PC video card and modulate three separate electron gun beams to generate the image. Depending on which beam(s) excite a phosphor point on the screen, that point will glow either red, green, blue, or some combination of these colors. This is different from analog television, where a composite signal, one that includes all color information superimposed on a single input, modulates a single electron beam. Newer computer monitors use DVI, or Digital Visual Interface, to accept RGB information in both digital and analog formats.

The main advantages of CRTs are that they're very inexpensive and can produce more colors than a comparably sized LCD panel. Also, unlike LCDs, they can be viewed from any angle. On the downside, CRTs are very bulky, emit considerable electro-magnetic radiation, and can cause eyestrain due to their refresh-induced flicker.

Digital Video Displays

Liquid Crystal Display (LCD) Panels

There are two main categories of LCD technology: passive matrix and active matrix. In the former (whose common family members include STN, or Super Twisted Nematic, derivatives), a glass substrate imprinted with rows forms a "liquid crystal sandwich" with a substrate imprinted with columns. Pixels are constructed as row-column intersections. Therefore, to activate a given pixel, a timing circuit energizes the pixel's column while grounding its row. The resultant voltage differential untwists the liquid crystal at that pixel location, which causes it to become opaque and block light from coming through.

Straightforward as it is, passive matrix technology does have some shortcomings. For one, screen refresh times are relatively slow (which can result in "ghosting" for fast-moving images). Also, there is a tendency for the voltage at a row-column intersection to bleed over into neighboring pixels, partly untwisting the liquid crystals and block-ing some light from passing through the surrounding pixel area. To the observer, this blurs the image and reduces contrast. Moreover, viewing angle is relatively narrow.

Active matrix LCD technology improves greatly upon passive technology in these respects. Basically, each pixel consists of a capacitor and transistor switch. This ar-rangement gives rise to the more popular term, "Thin-Film Transistor Liquid Crystal Display (TFT-LCD)." To address a particular pixel, its row is enabled, and then a voltage is applied to its column. This has the effect of isolating only the pixel of inter-est, so others in the vicinity don't turn on. Also, since the current to control a given pixel is reduced, pixels can be switched at a faster rate, which leads to faster refresh rates for TFT-LCDs over passive displays. What's more, modulating the voltage level applied to the pixel allows many discrete levels of brightness. Today, it is common to have 256 levels, corresponding to 8 bits of intensity.

Connecting to a TFT-LCD panel can be a confusing endeavor due to all of the different components involved. First, there's the *panel* itself, which houses an array of pixels arranged for strobing by row and column, referenced to the pixel clock frequency.

The *Backlight* is often a CCFL (Cold Cathode Fluorescent Lamp), which excites gas molecules to emit bright light while generating very little heat. CCFLs exhibit durability, long life, and straightforward drive requirements. LEDs are also a popular backlight method, mainly for small- to mid-sized panels. They have the advantages of low cost, low operating voltage, long life, and good intensity control. However, for larger panel sizes, LED backlights can draw a lot of power compared with comparable CCFL solutions.

An *LCD Controller* contains most of the circuitry needed to convert an input video signal into the proper format for display on the LCD panel. It usually includes a timing generator that controls the synchronization and pixel clock timing to the individual pixels on the panel. However, in order to meet LCD panel size and cost requirements, sometimes timing generation circuitry needs to be supplied externally. In addition to the standard synchronization and data lines, timing signals are needed to drive the individual rows and columns of the LCD panel. Sometimes, spare general-purpose PWM (pulse-width modulation) timers on a media processor can substitute for this separate chip, saving system cost.

Additional features of LCD controller chips include on-screen display support, graphics overlay blending, color lookup tables, dithering and image rotation. The more elaborate chips can be very expensive, often surpassing the cost of the processor to which they're connected.

An *LCD Driver* chip is necessary to generate the proper voltage levels to the LCD panel. It serves as the "translator" between the output of the LCD Controller and the LCD Panel. The rows and columns are usually driven separately, with timing controlled by the timing generator. Liquid crystals must be driven with periodic polarity inversions, because a dc current will stress the crystal structure and ultimately deteriorate it. Therefore, the voltage polarity applied to each pixel varies either on a per-frame, per-line, or per-pixel basis, depending on the implementation.

With the trend toward smaller, cheaper multimedia devices, there has been a push to integrate these various components of the LCD system. Today, integrated TFT-LCD modules exist that include timing generation and drive circuitry, requiring only a data bus connection, clocking/synchronization lines, and power supplies. Some panels are also available with a composite analog video input, instead of parallel digital inputs.

OLED (Organic Light-Emitting Diode) Displays

The "Organic" in OLED refers to the material that's encased between two electrodes. When charge is applied through this organic substance, it emits light. This display technology is still very new, but it holds promise by improving upon several deficiencies in LCD displays. For one, it's a self-emissive technology and does not require a backlight. This has huge implications for saving panel power, cost and weight—an OLED panel can be extremely thin. Additionally, it can support a wider range of colors than comparable LCD panels can, and its display of moving images is also superior to that of LCDs. What's more, it supports a wide viewing angle and provides high contrast. OLEDs have an electrical signaling and data interface similar to that of TFT-LCD panels.

For all its advantages, so far the most restrictive aspect of the OLED display is its limited lifetime. The organic material breaks down after a few thousand hours of use, although this number has now improved in some displays to over 10,000 hours—quite suitable for many portable multimedia applications. It is here where OLEDs have their brightest future—in cellphones, digital cameras, and the like. However, it is also quite possible that we'll ultimately see televisions or computer monitors based on OLED technology.

Embedded Video Processing Considerations

Video Port Features

To handle video streams, processors must have a suitable interface that can maintain a high data transfer rate into and out of the part. Some processors accomplish this through an FPGA and/or FIFO connected to the processor's external memory interface. Typically, this device will negotiate between the constant, relatively slow stream of video into and out of the processor, and the sporadic but speedy bursting nature of the external memory controller.

However, there are problems with this arrangement. For example, FPGAs and FIFOs are expensive, often costing as much as the video processor itself. Additionally, using the external memory interface for video transfer steals bandwidth from its other prime use in these systems—moving video buffers back and forth between the processor core and external memory.

Therefore, a dedicated video interface is highly preferable for media processing systems. On Blackfin processors, this is the Parallel Peripheral Interface (PPI). The PPI is a multifunction parallel interface that can be configured between 8 and 16 bits in width. It supports bidirectional data flow and includes three synchronization lines and a clock pin for connection to an externally supplied clock. The PPI can gluelessly decode ITU-R BT.656 data and can also interface to ITU-R BT.601 video streams. It is flexible and fast enough to serve as a conduit for high-speed analog-to-digital converters (ADCs) and digital-to-analog converters (DACs). It can also emulate a host interface for an external processor. It can even act as a glueless TFT-LCD controller.

The PPI has some built-in features that can reduce system costs and improve data flow. For instance, in BT.656 mode the PPI can decode an input video stream and automatically ignore everything except active video, effectively reducing an NTSC input video stream rate from 27 Mbytes/s to 20 Mbytes/s, and markedly reducing the amount of off-chip memory needed to handle the video. Alternately, it can ignore active video regions and only read in ancillary data that's embedded in vertical blanking intervals. These modes are shown pictorially in Figure 6.18.

Likewise, the PPI can ignore every other field of an interlaced stream; in other words, it will not forward this data to the DMA controller. While this instantly decimates input bandwidth requirements by 50%, it also eliminates 50% of the source content, so sometimes this tradeoff might not be acceptable. Nevertheless, this can be a useful feature when the input video resolution is much greater than the required output resolution.

On a similar note, the PPI allows "skipping" of odd- or even-numbered elements, again saving DMA bandwidth for the skipped pixel elements. For example, in a 4:2:2 YCbCr stream, this feature allows only luma or chroma elements to be read in, providing convenient partitioning of an algorithm between different processors; one can read in the luma, and the other can read the chroma. Also, it provides a simple way to convert an image or video stream to grayscale (luma-only). Finally, in high-speed converter applications with interleaved I/Q data, this feature allows partitioning between these in-phase and quadrature components.

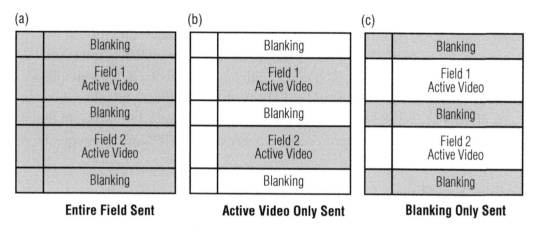

(a) (b) (c)

Entire Field Sent   **Active Video Only Sent**   **Blanking Only Sent**

Figure 6.18 **Selective masking of BT.656 regions in PPI**

Importantly, the PPI is format-agnostic, in that it is not hardwired to a specific video standard. It allows for programmable row lengths and frame sizes. This aids applications that need, say, CIF or QCIF video instead of standard NTSC/PAL formats. In general, as long as the incoming video has the proper EAV/SAV codes (for BT.656 video) or hardware synchronization signals (for BT.601 video), the PPI can process it.

Packing

Although the BT.656 and BT.601 recommendations allow for 10-bit pixel elements, this is not a very friendly word length for processing. The problem is, most processors are very efficient at handling data in 8-bit, 16-bit or 32-bit chunks, but anything in-between results in data movement inefficiencies. For example, even though a 10-bit pixel value is only 2 bits wider than an 8-bit value, most processors will treat it as a 16-bit entity with the 6 most significant bits (MSBs) set to 0. Not only does this consume bandwidth on the internal data transfer (DMA) buses, but it also consumes a lot of memory—a disadvantage in video applications, where several entire frame buffers are usually stored in external memory.

A related inefficiency associated with data sizes larger than 8 bits is nonoptimal packing. Usually, a high-performance media processor will imbue its peripherals with a data packing mechanism that sits between the outside world and the internal data movement buses of the processor, and its goal is to minimize the overall bandwidth burden that the data entering or exiting the peripheral places on these buses.

Therefore, an 8-bit video stream clocking into a peripheral at 27 Mbytes/s might be packed onto a 32-bit internal data movement bus, thereby requesting service from this bus at a rate of only 27/4, or 6.75 MHz. Note that the overall data transfer rate remains the same (6.75 MHz × 32 bits = 27 Mbytes/s). In contrast, a 10-bit video stream running at 27 Mbytes/s would only be packed onto the 32-bit internal bus in two 16-bit chunks, reducing the overall transfer rate to 27/2, or 13.5 MHz. In this case, since only 10 data bits out of every 16 are relevant, 37.5% of the internal bus bandwidth is not used efficiently.

Possible Data Flows

It is instructive to examine some ways in which a video port connects in multimedia systems, to show how the system as a whole is interdependent on each component. In Figure 6.19a, an image source sends data to the PPI. The DMA engine then dispositions it to L1 memory, where the data is processed to its final form before being sent out through a high-speed serial port. This model works very well for low-resolution video processing and for image compression algorithms like JPEG, where small blocks of video (several lines worth) can be processed and are subsequently never needed again. This flow also can work well for some data converter applications.

In Figure 6.19b, the video data is not routed to L1 memory, but instead is directed to L3 memory. This configuration supports algorithms such as MPEG-2 and MPEG-4, which require storage of intermediate video frames in memory in order to perform temporal compression. In such a scenario, a bidirectional DMA stream between L1 and L3 memories allows for transfers of pixel macroblocks and other intermediate data.

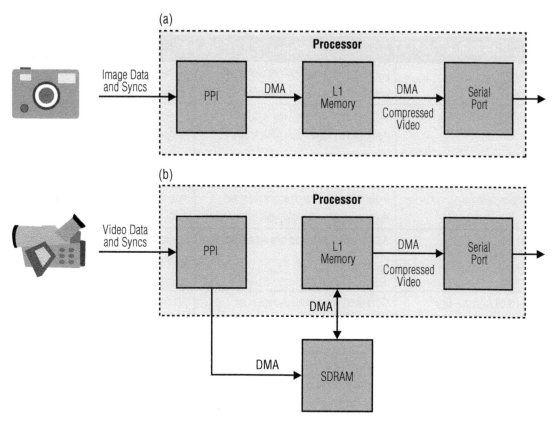

Figure 6.19 **Possible video port data transfer scenarios**

Video ALUs

Most video applications need to deal with 8-bit data, since individual pixel components (whether RGB or YCbCr) are usually byte quantities. Therefore, 8-bit video ALUs and byte-based address generation can make a huge difference in pixel manipulation. This is a nontrivial point, because embedded media processors typically operate on 16-bit or 32-bit boundaries.

As we discussed in Chapter 4, the Blackfin processor has some instructions that are geared to processing 8-bit video data efficiently. Table 6.2 shows a summary of the specific instructions that can be used together to handle a variety of video operations.

Let's look at a few examples of how these instructions can be used.

The Quad 8-bit Subtract/Absolute/Accumulate (SAA) instruction is well-suited for block-based video motion estimation. The instruction subtracts 4 pairs of bytes, takes

Table 6.2 **Native Blackfin video instructions**

Instruction	Description	Algorithm Use
Byte Align	Copies a contiguous four-byte unaligned word from a combination of two data registers.	Useful for aligning data bytes for subsequent SIMD instructions.
Dual 16-Bit Add/Clip	Adds two 8-bit unsigned values to two 16-bit signed values, then limits to an 8-bit unsigned range.	Used primarily for video motion compensation algorithms.
Dual 16-Bit Accumulator Extraction w/Addition	Adds together the upper half words and lower half words of each accumulator and loads into a destination register.	Used in conjunction with the Quad SAA instruction for motion estimation.
Quad 8-Bit Add	Adds two unsigned quad byte number sets.	Useful for providing packed data arithmetic typical in video processing applications.
Quad 8-Bit Average – Byte	Computes the arithmetic average of two quad byte number sets byte-wise.	Supports binary interpolation used in fractional motion search and motion estimation.
Quad 8-Bit Average – Half Word	Computes the arithmetic average of two quad byte number sets byte-wise and places results on half word boundaries.	Supports binary interpolation used in fractional motion search and motion estimation.
Quad 8-Bit Pack	Packs four 8-bit values into one 32-bit register.	Prepares Data for ALU operation.
Quad 8-Bit Subtract	Subtracts two quad byte number sets, byte-wise.	Provides packed data arithmetic in video applications.
Quad 8-Bit Subtract – Absolute - Accumulate	Subtracts four pairs of values, takes that absolute value, and accumulates.	Useful for block-based video motion estimation.
Quad 8-Bit Unpack	Copies four contiguous bytes from a pair of source registers.	Unpacks data after ALU operation.

the absolute value of each difference, and accumulates the results. This all happens within a single cycle. The actual formula is shown below:

$$SAA = \sum_{i=0}^{N-1} \sum_{j=0}^{N-1} \left| a(i,j) - b(i,j) \right|$$

Consider the macroblocks shown in Figure 6.20a. The reference frame of 16 pixels × 16 pixels can be further divided into four groups. A very reasonable assumption is that neighboring video frames are correlated to each other. That is, if there is motion, then pieces of each frame will move in relation to macroblocks in previous frames. It takes less information to encode the movement of macroblocks than it does to encode each video frame as a separate entity—MPEG compression uses this technique.

This motion detection of macroblocks decomposes into two basic steps. Given a *reference macroblock* in one frame, we can search all surrounding macroblocks (*target macroblocks*) in a subsequent frame to determine the closest match. The offset in location between the reference macroblock (in Frame n) and the best-matching target macroblock (in Frame n + 1) is the motion vector.

Figure 6.20b shows how this can be visualized in a system.

- Circle = some object in a video frame
- Solid square = reference macroblock

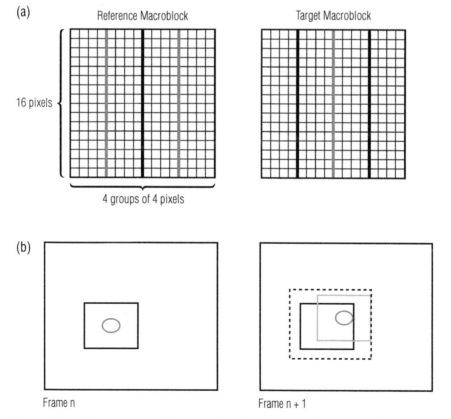

Figure 6.20 **Illustration of Subtract-Absolute-Accumulate (SAA) instruction**

- Dashed square = search area for possible macroblocks

- Gray square = best-matching target macroblock (i.e., the one representing the motion vector of the circle object)

The SAA instruction on a Blackfin processor is single-cycle because it utilizes four 8-bit ALUs in each clock cycle. We can implement the following loop to iterate over each of the four entities shown in Figure 6.20.

```
/* used in a loop that iterates over an image block   */
/* I0 and I1 point to the pixels being operated on */

SAA (R1:0,R3:2) || R1 = [I0++]  || R2 = [I1++]; /* compute
    absolute difference and accumulate */
SAA (R1:0,R3:2) (R) || R0 = [I0++] || R3 = [I1++];
SAA (R1:0,R3:2) || R1 = [I0 ++ M3] || R2 = [I1++M1]; /* after
    fetch of 4th word of target block, pointer is made to point to
    the next row */
SAA (R1:0,R3:2) (R) || R0 = [I0++] || R2 = [I1++];
```

Let's now consider another example, the 4-Neighborhood Average computation whose basic kernel is shown in Figure 6.21a. Normally, four additions and one division (or multiplication or shift) are necessary to compute the average. The BYTEOP2P instruction can accelerate the implementation of this filter.

The value of the center pixel of Figure 6.21b is defined as:

$$x = \text{Average}(xN, xS, xE, xW)$$

The BYTEOP2P can perform this kind of average on two pixels (Figures 6.21c,d) in one cycle. So, if $x1 = \text{Average}(x1N, x1S, x1E, x1W)$, and $x2 = \text{Average}(x2N, x2S, x2E, x2W)$, then

```
R3 = BYTEOP2P(R1:0, R3:2);
```

will compute both pixel averages in a single cycle, assuming the x1 (N, S, E, W) information is stored in registers R1 and R0, and the x2 (N, S, E, W) data is sourced from R3 and R2.

(a)

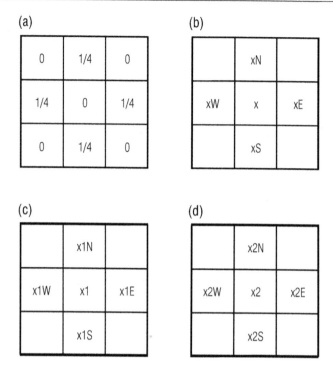

Figure 6.21 **Neighborhood Average computation**

DMA Considerations

A feature we discussed in Chapter 3, *two-dimensional DMA* capability, offers several system-level benefits. For starters, two-dimensional DMA can facilitate transfers of macroblocks to and from external memory, allowing data manipulation as part of the actual transfer. This eliminates the overhead typically associated with transferring noncontiguous data. It can also allow the system to minimize data bandwidth by selectively transferring, say, only the desired region of an image, instead of the entire image.

As another example, 2D DMA allows data to be placed into memory in a sequence more natural to processing. For example, as shown in Figure 6.22, RGB data may enter a processor's L2 memory from a CCD sensor in interleaved RGB888 format, but using 2D DMA, it can be transferred to L3 memory in separate R, G and B planes. Interleaving/deinterleaving color space components for video and image data saves additional data moves prior to processing.

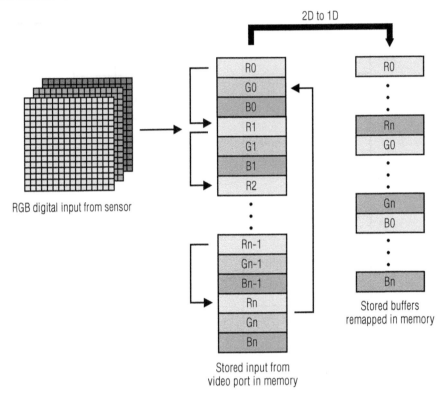

Figure 6.22 **Deinterleaving data with 2D DMA**

Planar versus Interleaved Buffer Formats

How do you decide whether to structure your memory buffers as interleaved or planar? The advantage to interleaved data is that it's the natural output format of image sensors, and the natural input format for video encoders. However, planar buffers (that is, separate memory regions for each pixel component) are often more effective structures for video algorithms, since many of them (JPEG and MPEG included) work on luma and chroma channels separately. What's more, accessing planar buffers in L3 is more efficient than striding through interleaved data, because the latency penalty for SDRAM page misses is spread out over a much larger sample size when the buffers are structured in a planar manner. Refer back to Chapter 4 for more discussion on this topic.

Double-Buffering

We have previously discussed the need for double-buffering as a means of ensuring that current data is not overwritten by new data until you're ready for this to happen. Managing a video display buffer serves as a perfect example of this scheme.

Normally, in systems involving different rates between source video and the final displayed content, it's necessary to have a smooth switchover between the old content and the new video frame. This is accomplished using a double-buffer arrangement. One buffer points to the present video frame, which is sent to the display at a certain refresh rate. The second buffer fills with the newest output frame. When this latter buffer is full, a DMA interrupt signals that it's time to output the new frame to the display. At this point, the first buffer starts filling with processed video for display, while the second buffer outputs the current display frame. The two buffers keep switching back and forth in a "ping-pong" arrangement. We discuss this model in more detail in Chapter 7.

It should be noted that multiple buffers can be used, instead of just two, in order to provide more margin for synchronization, and to reduce the frequency of interrupts and their associated latencies.

Classification of Video Algorithms

Video processing algorithms fall into two main categories: spatial and temporal. It is important to understand the different types of video processing in order to discern how the data is treated efficiently in each case. Many algorithms use a combination of spatial and temporal techniques (dubbed "spatiotemporal processing") to achieve their desired results. We'll talk in detail about video data flows in Chapter 7. For now, let's gain some exposure to the different classifications of image and video processing algorithms.

Spatial processing can either be pixel-wise or block-based. Pixel-by-pixel processing is spatially local. Every pixel is touched in turn to create a single output, and no result accumulation is necessary from previous (or future) pixels to generate the output. An example of pixel-wise processing is color space conversion from RGB to YCbCr. Often, this type of computation can be performed on the fly as the data arrives, without the need to store source image data to external memory.

Block-based algorithms, while spatially localized, typically need a group of pixel data in order to generate a result. A simple example of this is an averaging engine, where a given pixel is low-pass filtered by averaging its value with those of its neighbors. A more complex example is a 5×5 2D convolution kernel used to detect edge information in an image frame, drawing on the information from a wide neighborhood of surrounding pixels. In these block-based algorithms, there needs to be some source image storage in memory, but the entire video frame doesn't necessarily need to be saved, since it might be acceptable to operate on a few lines of video at a time. This could make the difference between needing external SDRAM for frame storage versus using faster, smaller on-chip L1 or L2 memory as a line buffer.

Thus far, we've considered only spatially *local* processing. However, another class of algorithms involves spatially *global* processing. These routines operate on an entire image or video frame at a time, and usually need to traverse often between an L3 frame buffer and L1 storage of source data and intermediate results. Examples of spatially global algorithms include the Discrete Cosine Transform (DCT), the Hough Transform that searches for line segments within an image, and histogram equalization algorithms that depend on analysis of the entire image before modifying the image based on these results.

Temporal processing algorithms strive to exploit changes or similarities in specific pixels or pixel regions between frames. One example of temporal processing is conversion of an interlaced field to a progressive scan format via line doubling and/ or filtering. Here, the assumption is that two interlaced fields are temporally similar enough to allow one field's content alone to be used to generate the "missing" field. When this is not the case—for instance, on motion boundaries or scene changes— there will be an aberration in the video output, but the preprocessing serves to soften this effect.

Another example where temporal processing is important is in video surveillance systems. Here, each frame is compared to the preceding one(s) to determine if there are enough differences to warrant an "alarm condition." In other words, an algorithm determines if something moved, vanished or appeared unexpectedly across a sequence of frames.

The majority of widely used video compression algorithms combine spatial and temporal elements into a category called spatiotemporal processing. Spatially, each image frame is divided into macroblocks of, say, 16 × 16 pixels. Then, these macroblocks are tracked and compared frame-to-frame to derive motion estimation and compensation approximations.

Bandwidth Calculations

Let's spend a few minutes going through some rough bandwidth calculations for video, in order to bring to light some important concepts about estimating required throughput.

First, we'll consider a progressive-scan VGA (640 × 480) CMOS sensor that connects to a processor's video port, sending 8-bit 4:2:2 YCbCr data at 30 frames/sec.

(640 × 480 pixels/frame)(2 bytes/pixel)(30 frames/sec) ≈ 18.4 Mbytes/second

This represents the raw data throughput into the processor. Often, there will also be blanking information transmitted on each row, such that the actual pixel clock here would be somewhere around 24 MHz. By using a sensor mode that outputs 16 bits at a time (luma and chroma on one clock cycle), the required clock rate is halved, but the total throughput will remain unchanged, since the video port takes in twice as much data on each clock cycle.

Now, let's switch over to the display side. Let's consider a VGA LCD display with a "RGB565" characteristic. That is, each RGB pixel value is packed into 2 bytes for display on an LCD screen with 6-bit R, G, and B components. The nuance here is that LCDs usually require a refresh rate somewhere in the neighborhood of 50 to 80 Hz. Therefore, unless we use a separate LCD controller chip with its own frame memory, we need to update the display at this refresh rate, even though our sensor input may only be changing at a 30 frames/sec rate. So we have, for example,

(640 × 480 pixels/frame)(2 bytes/pixel)(75 frames/sec refresh) = 46.08 Mbytes/second

Since we typically transfer a parallel RGB565 word on every clock cycle, our pixel clock would be somewhere in the neighborhood of 25 MHz (accounting for blanking regions).

Sample Video Application Walk-Through

Let's walk through the sample system of Figure 6.23 to illustrate some fundamental video processing steps present in various combinations in an embedded video application. In the diagram, an interlaced-scan CMOS sensor sends a 4:2:2 YCbCr video stream through the processor's video port, at which point it is deinterlaced and scan-rate converted. Then it passes through some computational algorithm(s) and is prepared for output to an LCD panel. This preparation involves chroma resampling, gamma correction, color conversion, scaling, blending with graphics, and packing into the appropriate output format for display on the LCD panel. Note that this system is only provided as an example, and not all of these components are necessary in a given system. Additionally, these steps may occur in different order than shown here.

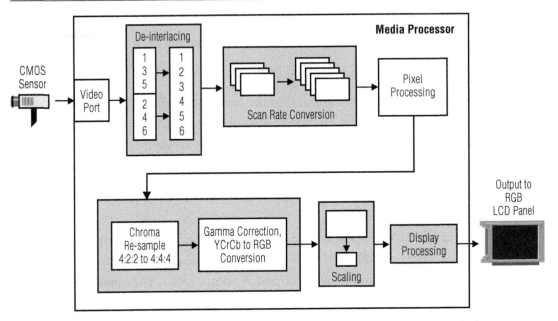

Figure 6.23 **Example flow of Video In to LCD Out, with processing stages in-between**

Deinterlacing

When taking video source data from a camera that outputs interlaced NTSC data, it's often necessary to deinterlace it so that the odd and even lines are interleaved in memory, instead of being located in two separate field buffers. Deinterlacing is not only needed for efficient block-based video processing, but also for displaying interlaced video in progressive format (for instance, on an LCD panel). There are many ways to deinterlace, each with its own benefits and drawbacks. We'll review some methods here, but for a good discussion of deinterlacing approaches, refer to Reference 45 in the Appendix.

Perhaps the most obvious solution would be to simply read in Field 1 (odd scan lines) and Field 2 (even scan lines) of the source data and interleave these two buffers to create a sequentially scanned output buffer. While this technique, called *weave*, is commonly used, it has the drawback of causing artifacts related to the fact that the two fields are temporally separated by 60 Hz, or about 16.7 ms. Therefore, while this scheme may suit relatively static image frames, it doesn't hold up well in scenes with high motion content.

To mitigate these artifacts and conserve system bandwidth, sometimes it's acceptable to just read in Field 1 and duplicate it into Field 2's row locations in the output buffer. This "line doubling" approach understandably reduces image resolution and causes blockiness in the output image, so more processing-intensive methods are often used. These include linear interpolation, median filtering and motion compensation.

Averaging lines, known as *bob*, determines the value of a pixel on an even line by averaging the values of the pixels on the adjacent odd lines, at the identical horizontal index location. This method can be generalized to linear interpolation, using weighted averages of pixels on neighboring lines (with highest weights ascribed to the closest pixels) to generate the missing lines of pixels. This is akin to an FIR filter in the vertical dimension.

Instead of an FIR filter, a median filter can be employed for better deinterlacing results. Median filtering replaces each pixel's luma value with the median gray-scale value of its immediate neighbors to help eliminate high-frequency noise in the image.

As an alternative deinterlacing approach, motion detection and compensation can be employed to adapt deinterlacing techniques based on the extent of motion in a given sequence of frames. These are the most advanced deinterlacing techniques in general use today.

Scan Rate Conversion

Once the video has been deinterlaced, a scan-rate conversion process may be necessary, in order to insure that the input frame rate matches the output display refresh rate. In order to equalize the two, fields may need to be dropped or duplicated. Of course, as with deinterlacing, some sort of filtering is preferable in order to smooth out high-frequency artifacts caused by creating abrupt frame transitions.

A special case of frame rate conversion that's employed to convert a 24 frame/sec stream (common for 35-mm and 70-mm movie recordings) to the 30 frame/sec required by NTSC video is *3:2 pulldown*. For instance, motion pictures recorded at 24 fps would run 25% faster (= 30/24) if each film frame is used only once in an NTSC video system. Therefore, 3:2 pulldown was conceived to adapt the 24 fps stream into a 30 fps video sequence. It does so by repeating frames in a certain periodic pattern, shown in Figure 6.24.

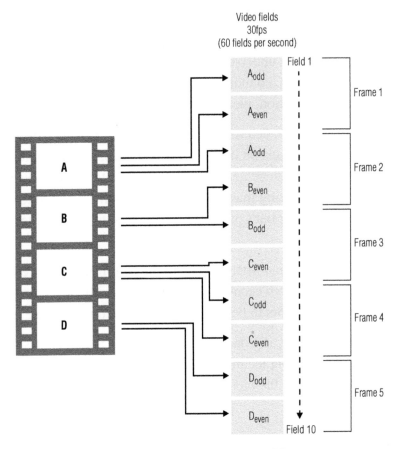

Figure 6.24 **3:2 pulldown frame repetition pattern**

Pixel Processing

As we discussed above, there are lots of video algorithms in common use, and they're stratified into spatial and temporal classifications. One particularly common video operator is the two-dimensional (2D) convolution kernel, which is used for many different forms of image filtering. We'll discuss the basics of this kernel here, and we'll get into more specifics in Chapter 9, as part of the Automotive Safety application example. Chapter 9 also includes further discussion on other important pixel processing algorithms, including the Discrete Cosine Transform (DCT) and the Hough Transform.

2D Convolution

Since a video stream is really an image sequence moving at a specified rate, image filters need to operate fast enough to keep up with the succession of input images. Thus, it is imperative that image filter kernels be optimized for execution in the lowest possible number of processor cycles. This can be illustrated by examining a simple image filter set based on two-dimensional convolution.

Convolution is one of the fundamental operations in image processing. In a two-dimensional convolution, the calculation performed for a given pixel is a weighted sum of intensity values from pixels in its immediate neighborhood. Since the neighborhood of a mask is centered on a given pixel, the mask usually has odd dimensions. The mask size is typically small relative to the image, and a 3 × 3 mask is a common choice, because it is computationally reasonable on a per-pixel basis, but large enough to detect edges in an image. However, it should be noted that 5 × 5, 7 × 7 and beyond are also widely used. Camera image pipes, for example, can employ 11 × 11 (and larger!) kernels for extremely complex filtering operations.

The basic structure of the 3 × 3 kernel is shown in Figure 6.25a. As an example, the output of the convolution process for a pixel at row 20, column 10 in an image would be:

$$Out(20,10) = A \times (19,9) + B \times (19,10) + C \times (19,11) + D \times (20,9) + E \times (20,10) + F \times (20,11) + G \times (21,9) + H \times (21,10) + I \times (21,11)$$

(a) 3x3 Convolution Kernel

0	0	0
0	1	0
0	0	0

(b) Delta

-1	0	1
-1	0	1
-1	0	1

(c) Edge Detection

1	1	1
0	0	0
-1	-1	-1

(d) Smoothing

1/8	1/8	1/8
1/8	0	1/8
1/8	1/8	1/8

(e) Edge Enhancement

-1/8	-1/8	-1/8
-1/8	1	-1/8
-1/8	-1/8	-1/8

Figure 6.25 **The 3 × 3 convolution mask and how it can be used**

It is important to choose coefficients in a way that aids computation. For instance, scale factors that are powers of 2 (including fractions) are preferred because multiplications can then be replaced by simple shift operations.

Figures 6.25b–e shows several useful 3 × 3 kernels, each of which is explained briefly below.

The Delta Function shown in Figure 6.25b is among the simplest image manipulations, passing the current pixel through without modification.

Figure 6.25c shows two popular forms of an edge detection mask. The first one detects vertical edges, while the second one detects horizontal edges. High output values correspond to higher degrees of edge presence.

The kernel in Figure 6.25d is a smoothing filter. It performs an average of the 8 surrounding pixels and places the result at the current pixel location. This has the result of "smoothing," or low-pass filtering, the image.

The filter in Figure 6.25e is known as an "unsharp masking" operator. It can be considered as producing an edge-enhanced image by subtracting from the current pixel a smoothed version of itself (constructed by averaging the 8 surrounding pixels).

Dealing With Image Boundaries

What happens when a function like 2D convolution operates on pixels near an image's border regions? To properly perform pixel filtering requires pixel information "outside" these boundaries. There are a couple of remedies for this situation. The simplest is just to ignore these edge regions. That is, consider that a 5 × 5 convolution kernel needs 2 pixels to the left, top, bottom and right of the current pixel in order to perform properly. Therefore, why not just shave two rows off of the image in each direction, so as to guarantee that the kernel will always act on real data? Of course, this isn't always an ideal approach, since it throws out real image data. Also, in cases where filters are strung together to create more complex pixel manipulations, this scheme will continually narrow the input image with every new filter stage that executes.

Other popular ways of handling the image boundary quandary are to duplicate rows and/or columns of pixels, or to wrap around from the left (top) edge back to the previous right (bottom) edge. While these might be easy to implement in practice, they create data that didn't exist before, and therefore they corrupt filtering results to some extent.

Perhaps the most straightforward, and least damaging, method for dealing with image boundaries is to consider everything that lies outside of the actual image to be zero-valued, or black. Although this scheme, too, distorts filtering results, it is not as invasive as creating lines of potentially random nonzero-valued pixels.

Chroma Resampling, Gamma Correction and Color Conversion

Ultimately, the data stream in our example needs to be converted to RGB space. We already discussed earlier how to convert between 4:4:4 YCbCr and RGB spaces, via a 3 × 3 matrix multiplication. However, up to this point, our pixel values are still in 4:2:2 YCbCr space. Therefore, we need to resample the chroma values to achieve a 4:4:4 format. Then the transformation to RGB will be straightforward, as we've already seen.

Resampling from 4:2:2 to 4:4:4 involves interpolating Cb and Cr values for those Y samples that are missing one of these components. A clear-cut way to resample is to interpolate the missing chroma values from their nearest neighbors by simple averaging. That is, a missing Cb value at a pixel site would be replaced by the average of the nearest two Cb values. Higher-order filtering might be necessary for some applications, but this simplified approach is often sufficient. Another approach is to replicate the relevant chroma values of neighboring pixels for those values that are missing in the current pixel's representation.

In general, conversions from 4:1:1 space to 4:2:2 or 4:4:4 formats involves only a one-dimensional filter (with tap values and quantities consistent with the level of filtering desired). However, resampling from 4:2:0 format into 4:2:2 or 4:4:4 format involves vertical sampling as well, necessitating a two-dimensional convolution kernel.

Because chroma resampling and YCbCr → RGB conversion are both linear operations, it is possible to combine the steps into a single mathematical process, thus achieving 4:2:2 YCbCr → RGB conversion efficiently.

At this stage, gamma correction is often necessary as well. Because of its nonlinear nature, gamma correction is most efficiently performed via a table lookup, prior to color space conversion. Then the result of the conversion process will yield gamma-corrected RGB components (commonly known as R′G′B′), the appropriate format for output display.

Scaling and Cropping

Video scaling allows the generation of an output stream whose resolution is different from that of the input format. Ideally, the fixed scaling requirements (input data resolution, output panel resolution) are known ahead of time, in order to avoid the computational load of arbitrary scaling between input and output streams.

Depending on the application, scaling can be done either upwards or downwards. It is important to understand the content of the image to be scaled (e.g., the presence of text and thin lines). Improper scaling can make text unreadable or cause some horizontal lines to disappear in the scaled image.

The easiest way to adjust an input frame size to an output frame that's smaller is simply to crop the image. For instance, if the input frame size is 720×480 pixels, and the output is a VGA frame (640×480 pixels), you can drop the first 40 and the last 40 pixels on each line. The advantage here is that there are no artifacts associated with dropping pixels or duplicating them. Of course, the disadvantage is that you'd lose 80 pixels (about 11%) of frame content. Sometimes this isn't too much of an issue, because the leftmost and rightmost extremities of the screen (as well as the top and bottom regions) are often obscured from view by the mechanical enclosure of the display.

If cropping isn't an option, there are several ways to downsample (reduce pixel and/or line count) or upsample (increase pixel and/or line count) an image that allow tradeoffs between processing complexity and resultant image quality.

Increasing or Decreasing Pixels per Row

One straightforward method of scaling involves either dropping pixels (for downsampling) or duplicating existing pixels (for upsampling). That is, when scaling down to a lower resolution, some number of pixels on each line (and/or some number of lines per frame) can be thrown away. While this certainly reduces processing load, the results will yield aliasing and visual artifacts.

A small step up in complexity uses linear interpolation to improve the image quality. For example, when scaling down an image, filtering in either the horizontal or vertical direction obtains a new output pixel, which then replaces the pixels used during the interpolation process. As with the previous technique, information is still thrown away, and again artifacts and aliasing will be present.

If the image quality is paramount, there are other ways to perform scaling without reducing the quality. These methods strive to maintain the high frequency content of the image consistent with the horizontal and vertical scaling, while reducing the effects of aliasing. For example, assume an image is to be scaled by a factor of Y:X. To accomplish this scaling, the image could be upsampled ("interpolated") by a factor of Y, filtered to eliminate aliasing, and then downsampled ("decimated") by a factor of X, in a manner analogous to Figure 5.17 for audio. In practice, these two sampling processes can be combined into a single multirate filter.

Increasing or Reducing Lines per Frame

The guidelines for increasing or reducing the number of pixels per row generally extend to modifying the number of lines per frame of an image. For example, throwing out every other line (or one entire interlaced field) provides a quick method of reducing vertical resolution. However, as we've mentioned above, some sort of vertical filtering is necessary whenever removing or duplicating lines, because these processes introduce artifacts into the image. The same filter strategies apply here: simple vertical averaging, higher-order FIR filters, or multirate filters to scale vertically to an exact ratio.

Display Processing

Alpha Blending

Often it is necessary to combine two image and/or video buffers prior to display. A practical example of this is overlaying of icons like signal strength and battery level indicators onto a cellular phone's graphics display. An example involving two video streams is picture-in-picture functionality.

When combining two streams, you need to decide which stream "wins" in places where content overlaps. This is where alpha blending comes in. It defines a variable alpha (α) that indicates a "transparency factor" between an overlay stream and a background stream as follows:

Output value = $\alpha \times$ (foreground pixel value) + $(1-\alpha) \times$ (background pixel value)

As the equation shows, an α value of 0 results in a completely transparent overlay, whereas a value of 1 results in a completely opaque overlay that disregards the background image entirely.

Sometimes α is sent as a separate channel along with the pixel-wise luma and chroma information. This results in the notation "4:2:2:4," where the last digit indicates an alpha key that accompanies each 4:2:2 pixel entity. Alpha is coded in the same way as the luma component, but often only a few discrete levels of transparency are needed for most applications. Sometimes a video overlay buffer is premultiplied by alpha or premapped via a lookup table, in which case it's referred to as a "shaped" video buffer.

Compositing

The act of compositing involves positioning an overlay buffer inside a larger image buffer. Common examples are a "picture-in-picture" mode on a video display, and placement of graphics icons over the background image or video. In general, the composition function can take several iterations before the output image is complete. In other words, there may be many "layers" of graphics and video that combine to generate a composite image.

Two-dimensional DMA capability is very useful for compositing, because it allows the positioning of arbitrarily sized rectangular buffers inside a larger buffer. One thing to keep in mind is that any image cropping should take place after the composition process, because the positioned overlay might violate any newly cropped boundaries. Of course, an alternative is to ensure that the overlay won't violate the boundaries in the first place, but this is sometimes asking too much!

Chroma Keying

The term "chroma keying" refers to a process by which a particular color (usually blue or green) in a background image is replaced by the content in an overlay image when the two are composited together. This provides a convenient way to combine two video images by purposefully tailoring parts of the first image to be replaced by the appropriate sections of the second image. Chroma keying can be performed in either software or hardware on a media processor. As a related concept, sometimes a "transparent color" can be used in an overlay image to create a pixelwise "$\alpha = 0$" condition when a separate alpha channel is not available.

Rotation

Many times it is also necessary to rotate the contents of an output buffer before display. Almost always, this rotation is in some multiple of 90 degrees. Here's another instance where 2D DMA is extremely useful. Refer to Example 3.2 for an illustration of image rotation performed exclusively through the DMA engine.

Output Formatting

Most color LCD displays targeted for consumer applications (TFT-LCDs) have a digital RGB interface. Each pixel in the display actually has 3 subpixels—one each with red, green and blue filters—that the human eye resolves as a single color pixel. For example, a 320 × 240 pixel display actually has 960 × 240 pixel components, accounting for the R, G and B subpixels. Each subpixel has 8 bits of intensity, thus forming the basis of the common 24-bit color LCD display.

The three most common configurations use either 8 bits per channel for RGB (RGB888 format), 6 bits per channel (RGB666 format), or 5 bits per channel for R and B, and 6 bits for G (RGB565 format).

RGB888 provides the greatest color clarity of the three. With a total of 24 bits of resolution, this format provides over 16 million shades of color. It offers the high resolution and precision needed in high-performance applications like LCD TVs.

The RGB666 format is popular in portable electronics. Providing over 262,000 shades of color, this format has a total of 18 bits of resolution. However, because the 18-pin (6 + 6 + 6) data bus doesn't conform nicely to 16-bit processor data paths, a popular industry compromise is to use 5 bits each of R and B, and 6 bits of G (5 + 6 + 5 = a 16-bit data bus) to connect to a RGB666 panel. This scenario works well because green is the most visually important color of the three. The least-significant bits of both red and blue are tied at the panel to their respective most-significant bits. This ensures a full dynamic range for each color channel (full intensity down to total black).

Compression/Decompression

Over the past decade or so, image, video and audio standards all have undergone revolutionary changes. As Figure 6.26 conveys, whereas historical progress was primarily based on storage media evolution, the dawn of digital media has changed this path into one of compression format development. That is, once in the digital realm, the main challenge becomes "How much can I condense this content while maximizing attainable quality?" Naturally, consumers view this format proliferation as a distraction that obscures the real prize—access to a plethora of multimedia content.

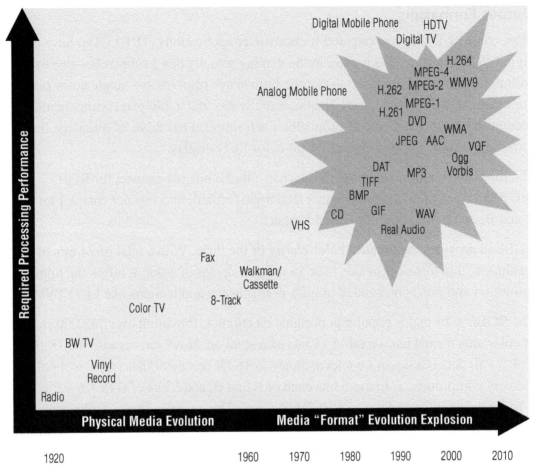

Figure 6.26 **Historical progression of media**

Lossless versus Lossy Compression

"Lossless" compression implies that the original content can be reconstructed identically, whereas "lossy" compression allows some degradation in reconstruction quality in order to achieve much higher compression ratios. In JPEG, for instance, lossless compression typically achieves ratios of perhaps 2:1, whereas lossy schemes can compress a source image by 10:1 or more.

So what does image or video "quality" really mean? Well, it really entails several different measures. For instance, what's the pixel *resolution* compared with the image size? Also, how much *color depth* (bits per pixel) exists? For video, is the frame rate high or low? Too low a frame rate will cause noticeable flicker. Finally, quality can be measured by what is sufficient for the application. Given the intensive processing that video demands, it's advantageous to strive for quality that's "good enough" for an application, but not excessively expensive.

In the compression domain, the required level of quality translates into another set of issues. For one, the bit rate of the compressed stream is directly proportional to video quality. This bit rate is bounded by real-world concerns, such as the amount of available storage space for the compressed source, the ability of the decoding processor to handle the compressed stream in real time, and the duration of the video clip. Moreover, how high can you raise the compression ratio before quality degrades unacceptably for the target application? All of these factors influence the determination of proper compression format and ratio.

The interesting thing about lossy codecs is that their net goal is to achieve the lowest bit rate possible for a desired level of quality. Yet, this perception of quality is subjective and differs from a numerical analysis performed on the reconstituted image. In other words, all that matters is that we humans think the end result looks good—it doesn't matter if the metrics tell us otherwise.

In general, there are several high-level approaches to image and video compression, most of which take advantage of the limits in human perception. For instance, as with 4:2:2 YCbCr broadcast video, we can reduce the color bandwidth in an image to account for the fact that our eyes are much more sensitive to intensity than to color. Spatial techniques reduce compressed image size by accounting for visual similarities within image regions, such that a small amount of information can be made to represent a large object or scene portion.

For video, temporal compression takes advantage of similarities between neighboring frames to encode only the differences between them, instead of considering each frame as its own separate image to be compressed.

Image Compression

Let's start by surveying some widespread image compression schemes. We'll then extend our discussion to popular video compression formats.

BMP

The BMP bitmapped file representation is known to all Microsoft Windows® users as its native graphics format. A BMP file can represent images at color depths up to 24 bits (8 bits each for R, G and B). Unfortunately, though, this format is normally an uncompressed representation, and file sizes can be quite unwieldy at 24 bits per pixel. As a result, the BMP format is not Internet-friendly. Luckily, other file formats have been devised that provide a range of "quality versus file size" tradeoffs to facilitate image transfer across a network.

GIF

GIF, or the Graphics Interchange Format, was developed by CompuServe in the 1980s for their own network infrastructure. This is still a popular Internet format today, especially for compressing computer graphics images with limited color palettes, since GIF itself is palette-based, allowing only 256 colors in a single image. GIF compresses better than JPEG does for these types of images, but JPEG excels for photographs and other images having many more than just 256 colors.

PNG

The development of the royalty-free "Portable Network Graphics (PNG)" format is a direct product of some licensing fees that beset the GIF format. Although much of the GIF-relevant patents have expired, PNG is still seen as an improvement over GIF in color depth, alpha channel support (for transparency), and other areas. It is considered a successor to GIF.

JPEG

JPEG is perhaps the most popular compressed image format on the Internet today. As noted above, it's mainly intended for photographs, but not for line drawings and other graphics with very limited color palettes. The 10x–20x compression ratios of JPEG really got people excited about digital photos and sharing their pictures over bandwidth-limited networks. Of course, the higher the compression rate, the larger the loss of information. Nevertheless, even at relatively high rates, JPEG results in a much smaller file size but retains a comparable visual quality to the original bitmapped image. We talk much more about the details of JPEG compression in Chapter 9.

JPEG2000

JPEG2000, also known as J2K, is a successor to JPEG, addressing some of its fundamental limitations while remaining backward-compatible with it. It achieves better compression ratios (roughly 30% better for excellent quality), and it performs well on binary (black and white) images, computer graphics, and photographs alike. Like JPEG, it has both lossy and lossless modes. J2K also supports "region of interest" compression, where selective parts of an image can be encoded in higher quality than other regions are.

J2K isn't DCT-based like JPEG. Instead, it's wavelet-based. Essentially, wavelets involve a frequency-domain transform like the DCT, but they also include information pertaining to spatial location of the frequency elements. Reference 35 in the Appendix offers a good overview of wavelet technology.

Video Compression

Video data is enormously space-consuming, and its most daunting aspect is that it just keeps coming! One second of uncompressed 4:2:2 NTSC video requires 27 Mbytes of storage, and a single minute requires 1.6 Gbytes! Because raw video requires such dedicated high bandwidth, the industry takes great pains to avoid transferring it in uncompressed form whenever possible. Compression algorithms have been devised that reduce the bandwidth requirements for NTSC/PAL video from tens of megabytes per second down to just a few megabits per second, with adjustable tradeoffs in video quality for bandwidth efficiency.

Compression ratio itself is highly dependent on the content of the video being compressed, as well as on the compression algorithm being used. Some encoders, like MPEG-4 and H.264, have the ability to encode foreground and background information separately, leading to higher compression than those that deal with the entire image as a whole. Images that have very little spatial variation (e.g., big blocks of uniform color), as well as video that remains fairly static from frame to frame (e.g., slow-changing backgrounds) can be highly compressed. On the other hand, detailed images and rapidly varying content reduce compression ratios.

Most embedded media processing developers tend to treat video codecs as "drop-in" code modules that the processor vendor or a third-party source has optimized specifically for that platform. In other words, most embedded multimedia designers today expect to acquire the video codec, as opposed to design it from scratch. Thus, their chief concern is which codec(s) to pick for their application. Let's review a little about some popular ones below. For detailed operation about how a particular algorithm works, refer to References 34, 35, and 75 in the Appendix.

There is no right answer in choosing a video codec—it really depends on what your end application needs are. If the content source, distribution and display are all well controlled, it may be possible to use a proprietary codec for increased performance that's not encumbered by the dictates of the standards bodies. Or, if the idea of paying royalties doesn't appeal to you, open-source codecs are very attractive alternatives. Content protection, network streaming capability, and bit rate characteristics (constant versus variable, encoding options, etc.) are other important features that differentiate one codec from another. And don't forget to consider what codecs are already ported to your chosen media processor, how many implementations exist, how well-supported they are, and what it will cost to use them (up-front and per-unit).

Table 6.3 lists many of the popular video coding standards, as well as their originating bodies. Let's review a little about each here.

Table 6.3 **Popular video coding standards**

Video Coding Standards	Year Introduced	Originating Body
M-JPEG	1980s	ISO
H.261	1990	ITU-T
MPEG-1	1993	ISO/IEC
MPEG-2 (H.262)	1994/1995	ITU-T and ISO/IEC
H.263, H.263+, H.263++	1995-2000	ITU-T
MPEG-4	1998-2001	ISO/IEC
DV	1996	IEC
QuickTime	1990s	Apple Computer
RealVideo	1997	RealNetworks
Windows Media Video	1990s	Microsoft
Ogg Theora	2002 (alpha)	Xiph.org Foundation
H.264 (MPEG-4 Part 10)	2003	ITU-T and ISO/IEC

Motion JPEG (M-JPEG)

Although not specifically encompassed by the JPEG standard, M-JPEG offered a convenient way to compress video frames before MPEG-1 formalized a method. Essentially, each video frame is individually JPEG-encoded, and the resulting compressed frames are stored (and later decoded) in sequence.

There also exists a Motion JPEG2000 codec that uses J2K instead of JPEG to encode individual frames. It is likely that this codec will replace M-JPEG at a rate similar to the adoption of J2K over JPEG.

H.261

This standard, developed in 1990, was the first widespread video codec. It introduced the idea of segmenting a frame into 16×16 "macroblocks" that are tracked between frames to determine motion compensation vectors. It is mainly targeted at video-conferencing applications over ISDN lines ($p \times 64$ kbps, where p ranges from 1 to 30). Input frames are typically CIF at 30 fps, and output compressed frames occupy 64–128 kbps for 10 fps resolution. Although still used today, it has mostly been superseded by its successor, H.263.

MPEG-1

When MPEG-1 entered the scene in the early 1990s, it provided a way to digitally store audio and video and retrieve it at roughly VHS quality. The main focus of this codec was storage on CD-ROM media. Specifically, the prime intent was to allow storage and playback of VHS-quality video on a 650–750 Mbyte CD, allowing creation of a so-called "Video CD (VCD)." The combined video/audio bit stream could fit within a bandwidth of 1.5 Mbit/sec, corresponding to the data retrieval speed from CD-ROM and digital audio tape systems at that time.

At high bit rates, it surpasses H.261 in quality (allowing over 1 Mbps for CIF input frames). Although CIF is used for some source streams, another format called SIF is perhaps more popular. It's 352×240 pixels per frame, which turns out to be about ¼ of a full 720×480 NTSC frame. MPEG-1 was intended for compressing SIF video at 30 frames/sec, progressive-scan. Compared to H.261, MPEG-1 adds bidirectional motion prediction and half-pixel motion estimation. Although still used by diehards for VCD creation, MPEG-1 pales in popularity today compared with MPEG-2.

MPEG-2

Driven by the need for scalability across various end markets, MPEG-2 soon improved upon MPEG-1, with the capability to scale in encoded bit rate from 1 Mbit/sec up to 30 Mbit/sec. This opened the door to higher-performance applications, including DVD videos and standard- and high-definition TV. Even at the lower end of MPEG-2 bit rates, the quality of the resulting stream is superior to that of an MPEG-1 clip.

This complex standard is composed of 10 parts. The "Visual" component is also called H.262. Whereas MPEG-1 focused on CDs and VHS-quality video, MPEG-2 achieved DVD-quality video with an input conforming to BT.601 (NTSC 720×480

at 30 fps), and an output in the range of 4–30 Mbps, depending on which "performance profile" is chosen. MPEG-2 supports interlaced and progressive scanning.

H.263

This codec is ubiquitous in videoconferencing, outperforming H.261 at all bit rates. Input sources are usually QCIF or CIF at 30 fps, and output bit rates can be less than 28.8 kbps at 10 fps, for the same performance as H.261. Therefore, whereas H.261 needs an ISDN line, H.263 can use ordinary phone lines. H.263 finds use in end markets like video telephony and networked surveillance (including Internet-based applications).

MPEG-4

MPEG-4 starts from a baseline of H.263 and adds several improvements. Its prime focus is streaming multimedia over a network. Because the network usually has somewhat limited bandwidth, typical input sources for MPEG-4 codecs are CIF resolution and below. MPEG-4 allows different types of coding to be applied to different types of objects. For instance, static background textures and moving foreground shapes are treated differently to maximize the overall compression ratio. MPEG-4 uses several different performance profiles, the most popular among them "Simple" (similar to MPEG-1) and "Advanced Simple" (field-based like MPEG-2). Simple Profile is suitable for low video resolutions and low bit rates, like streaming video to cellphones. Advanced Simple Profile, on the other hand, is intended for higher video resolutions and higher bit rates.

DV

DV is designed expressly for consumer (and subsequently professional) video devices. Its compression scheme is similar in nature to Motion JPEG's, and it accepts the BT.601 sampling formats for luma and chroma. Its use is quite popular in camcorders, and it allows several different "playability" modes that correspond to different bit rates and/or chroma subsampling schemes. DV is commonly sent over a IEEE 1394 ("FireWire") interface, and its bit rate capability scales from the 25 Mbit/sec commonly used for standard-definition consumer-grade devices, up beyond 100 Mbit/sec for high-definition video.

QuickTime

Developed by Apple Computer, QuickTime comprises a collection of multimedia codecs and algorithms that handle digital video, audio, animation, images and text. QuickTime 7.0 complies with MPEG-4 and H.264. In fact, the QuickTime file format served as the basis for the ISO-based MPEG-4 standard, partly because it provided a full end-to-end solution, from video capture, editing and storage, to content playback and distribution.

RealVideo

RealVideo is a proprietary video codec developed by RealNetworks. RealVideo started as a low-bit-rate streaming format to PCs, but now it extends to the portable device market as well, for streaming over broadband and cellular infrastructures. It can be used for live streaming, as well as for video-on-demand viewing of a previously downloaded file. RealNetworks bundles RealVideo with RealAudio, its proprietary audio codec, to create a RealMedia container file that can be played with the PC application RealPlayer.

Windows Media Video (WMV)/VC-1

This codec is a Microsoft-developed variant on MPEG-4 (starting from WMV7). It also features Digital Rights Management (DRM) for control of how content can be viewed, copied, modified or replayed. In an effort to standardize this proprietary codec, Microsoft submitted WMV9 to the Society of Motion Picture and Television Engineers (SMPTE) organization, and it's currently a draft standard under the name "VC-1."

Theora

Theora is an open-source, royalty-free video codec developed by the Xiph.org Foundation, which also has developed several open-source audio codecs—see Chapter 9 for further information about Speex (for speech) and Vorbis (for music). Theora is based on the VP3 codec that On2 Technologies released into the public domain. It mainly competes with low-bit-rate codecs like MPEG-4 and Windows Media Video.

H.264

H.264 is also known as MPEG-4 Part 10, H.26L, or MPEG-4 AVC ("Advanced Video Coding") profile. It actually represents a hallmark of cooperation, in the form of a joint definition between the ITU-T and ISO/IEC committees. H.264's goal is to reduce bit rates by 50% or more for comparable video quality, compared with its predecessors. It works across a wide range of bit rates and video resolutions. H.264's dramatic bit rate reductions come at the cost of significant implementation complexity. This complexity is what limits H.264 encoding at D-1 format today to only higher-end media processors, often requiring two discrete devices that split the processing load.

Encoding/Decoding on an EMP

Today, many of the video compression algorithms mentioned above (e.g., MPEG-4, WMV9 and H.264) are all competing for industry and consumer acceptance. Their emergence reflects the shift from dedicated media stored and played on a single device to a "streaming media" concept, where content flows between "media nodes" connected by wireless or wireline networks. These transport networks might be either low-bandwidth (e.g., Bluetooth) or high-bandwidth (e.g., 100BaseT Ethernet), and it's essential to match the streaming content with the transport medium. Otherwise, the user experience is lackluster—slow-moving video, dropped frames and huge processing delays.

As Figure 6.27 shows, these new algorithms all strive to provide higher-resolution video at lower bit rates than their predecessors (e.g., MPEG-1 and MPEG-2) and at comparable or better quality. But that's not all; they also extend to many more applications than the previous generation of standards by offering features like increased scalability (grabbing only the subset of the encoded bit stream needed for the application), better immunity to errors, and digital rights management capabilities (to protect content from unauthorized viewing or distribution).

However, the downside of these newer algorithms is that they generally require even more processing power than their predecessors in order to achieve their remarkable results.

Decoding is usually a much lighter processing load than encoding, by about half. Decoders have an operational flow that's usually specified by the standards body that designed the compression algorithm. This same body, however, does not dictate how an encoder must work. Therefore, encoders tend to use a lot more processing power in order to squeeze the input stream into the lowest possible output bit rate. In fact, the model of "Encode on the PC, Decode on the Device" is still common today for devices such as PDAs, MP3 players, and the like.

Estimate of compression bandwidths for equivalent picture quality

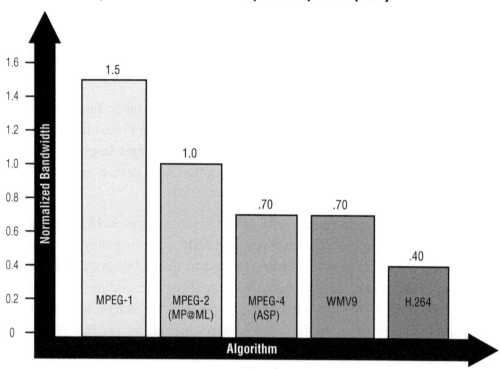

Figure 6.27 **Progress in video encode algorithms leads to lower bit rates and higher storage density for comparable video quality**

With the proliferation of video and audio standards, interoperability between systems has become increasingly challenging. Along with the burgeoning number of available formats, the numbers and types of networks and media devices have also grown significantly. As discussed above, these different network service levels result in multiple compression standards being used to fulfill the multimedia requirements of a system.

Transcoding

In the end, the consumer demands a seamless pathway through which to share, transfer and experience media. Today, "transcoding" of multimedia content is helping to remove barriers between different encoding/decoding platforms. Transcoding allows data to move transparently between and within wired and wireless networks. At the highest level, it is simply a way to convert from one encoding scheme to another. Importantly, it allows bit stream reduction with a manageable loss in content quality, appropriate for the available data channel. In other words, transcoding allows compression of a data stream to meet a target storage size or a specific transmission path. For example, MPEG-2 content from a DVD server might be transcoded into MPEG-4 before transmission across a wireless network to a PDA, thus resulting in a significant bit stream reduction (which translates into dollars saved). On the PDA, the data can then be transcoded into an appropriate format before being played.

The type of operation described above is known as "format transcoding." Another related process is "sample-rate-reduction transcoding," which lowers the streaming media bit rate by reducing the displayed resolution or frame rate. In either case, transcoding is performed in order to match the needs of the target device, and thus it can place a large burden on the system processor.

As far as transcoding is concerned, totally programmable solutions like convergent processors have an advantage over fixed-function ASICs, because they allow completely flexible conversion between arbitrary media formats. Additionally, the fast clock rates of convergent processors can enable real-time transcoding, where the processor can decode the input stream while simultaneously encoding it into the target format. This speeds up the process and saves interim storage space. That is, the entire source stream doesn't have to be downloaded to memory before starting to transcode it into the desired format. In this scenario, the processor performs what would otherwise be an effort by multiple ASICs that are each geared toward a limited set of video encoding or decoding functions.

What's Next?

You've now studied the particulars of audio and video as they apply to embedded processing. It's finally time to integrate this knowledge with that gained in our discussions on memory, DMA and system performance from previous chapters. The next chapter does just that, providing the basis for creating multimedia frameworks for embedded applications.

Media Processing Frameworks

Introduction

As more applications transition from PC-centric designs to embedded solutions, software engineers need to port media-based algorithms from prototype systems where memory is an "unlimited" resource (such as a PC or a workstation) to embedded systems where resource management is essential to meet performance requirements. Ideally, they want to achieve the highest performance for a given application without increasing the complexity of their "comfortable" programming model. Figure 7.1 shows a summary of the challenges they face in terms of power consumption, memory allocation and performance.

A small set of programming frameworks are indispensable in navigating through key challenges of multimedia processing, like organizing input and output data buffer

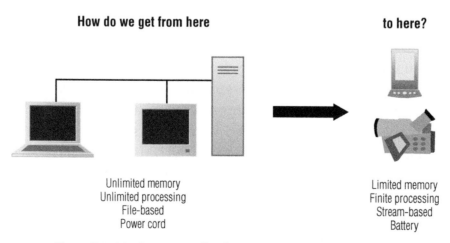

How do we get from here   to here?

Unlimited memory
Unlimited processing
File-based
Power cord

Limited memory
Finite processing
Stream-based
Battery

Figure 7.1 **Moving an application to an embedded processor**

flows, partitioning memory intelligently, and using semaphores to control data movement. While reading this chapter, you should see how the concepts discussed in the previous chapters fit together into a cohesive structure. Knowing how audio and video work within the memory and DMA architecture of the processor you select will help you build your own framework for your specific application.

What Is a Framework?

Typically, a project starts out with a prototype developed in a high-level language such as C, or in a simulation and modeling tool such as Matlab or LabView. This is a particularly useful route for a few reasons. First, it's easy to get started, both psychologically and materially. Test data files, such as video clips or images, are readily available to help validate an algorithm's integrity. In addition, no custom hardware is required, so you can start development immediately, without waiting for, and debugging, a test setup. Optimal performance is not a focus at this stage because processing and memory resources are essentially unlimited on a desktop system. Finally, you can reuse code from other projects as well as from specialized toolbox packages or libraries.

The term "framework" has a wide variety of meanings, so let's define exactly what we mean by the word. As we described in Chapter 2, it's important to harness the memory system architecture of an embedded processor to address performance and capacity tradeoffs in ways that enable system development. Unfortunately, if we were to somehow find embedded processors with enough single-cycle memory to fit complicated systems on-chip, the cost and power dissipation of the device would be prohibitive. As a result, the embedded processor needs to use internal and external memory in concert to construct an application.

To this end, "framework" is the term we use to describe the complete code and data movement infrastructure within the embedded system. If you're working on a prototype development system, you can access data as if it were in L1 memory all of the time. In an embedded system, however, you need to choreograph data movement to meet the required real-time budget. A framework specifies how data moves throughout the system, configuring and managing all DMA controllers and related descriptors. In addition, it controls interrupt management and the execution of the corresponding interrupt service routines. As implied in Chapter 4, code movement is an integral part of the framework. We'll soon review some examples that illustrate how to carefully place code so that it peacefully coexists with the data movement tasks.

So, the first deliverable to tackle on an embedded development project is defining the framework. At this stage of the project, it is not necessary to integrate the actual algorithm yet. Your project can start off on the wrong foot if you add the embedded algorithm before architecting the basic data and coding framework!

Defining Your Framework

There are many important questions to consider when defining your framework. Hopefully, by answering these questions early in the design process, you'll be able to avoid common tendencies that could otherwise lead you down the wrong design path.

Q: At what rate does data come into the system, and how often does data leave the system?

Comment: This will help bound your basic system. For example, is there more data to move around than your processor can handle? How closely will you approach the limits of the processor you select, and will you be able to handle future requirements as they evolve?

Q: What is the smallest collection of data operated on at any time? Is it a line of video? Is it a macroblock? Is it a frame or field of video? How many audio samples are processed at any one time?

Comment: This will help you focus on the worst-case timing scenario. Later, we will look at some examples to help you derive these numbers. All of the data buffering parameters (size of each buffer and number of buffers) will be determined from this scenario.

Q: How much code will your application comprise? What is the execution profile of this code? Which code runs the most often?

Comment: This will help determine if your code fits into internal memory, or whether you have to decide between cache and overlays. When you have identified the code that runs most frequently, answering these questions will help you decide which code is allocated to the fastest memory.

Q: How will data need to move into and out of the system? How do the receive and transmit data paths relate to each other?

Comment: Draw out the data flow, and understand the sizes of the data blocks you hope to process simultaneously. Sketch the flows showing how input and output data streams are related.

Q: What are the relative priorities for peripheral and memory DMA channels? Do the default priorities work, or do these need to be re-programmed? What are your options for data packing in the peripherals and the DMA?

Comment: This will help you lay out your DMA and interrupt priority levels between channels. It will also ensure that data transfers use internal buses optimally.

Q: Which data buffers will be accessed at any one time? Will multiple resources try to access the same memory space? Is the processor polling memory locations or manually moving data within memory?

Comment: This will help you organize where data and code are placed in your system to minimize conflicts.

Q: How many cycles can you budget for real-time processing? If you take the number of pixels (or audio samples, or both) being processed each collection interval, how many processor core-clock and system-clock cycles can you allocate to each pixel?

Comment: This will set your processing budget and may force you to, for example, reduce either your frame rate or image size.

We have already covered most of these topics in previous chapters, and it is important to re-examine these items before you lay out your own framework. We will now attack a fundamental issue related to the above questions: understanding your worst-case situation in the application timeline.

The Application Timeline

Before starting to code your algorithm, you need to identify the timeline requirements for the smallest processing interval in your application. This is best characterized as the minimum time between data collection intervals. In a video-based system, this interval typically relates to a macroblock within an image, a line of video data, or perhaps an entire video frame. The processor must complete its task on the current buffer before the next data set overwrites the same buffer. In some applications, the processing task at hand will simply involve making a decision on the incoming data buffer. This case is easier to handle because the processed data does not have to be transferred out. When the buffer is processed and the results still need to be stored or displayed, the processing interval calculation must include the data transfer time out of the system as well.

Figure 7.2 shows a summary of the minimum timelines associated with a variety of applications. The timeline is critical to understand because in the end, it is the fore-most benchmark that the processor must meet.

An NTSC-based application that processes data on a frame-by-frame basis takes 33 ms to collect a frame of video. Let's assume that at the instant the first frame is received, the video port generates an interrupt. By the time the processor services the interrupt, the beginning of the next frame is already entering the FIFO of the video port. Because the processor needs to access one buffer while the next is on its way in, a second buffer needs to be maintained. Therefore, the time available to process the frame is 33 ms. Adding additional buffers can help to some extent, but if your data rates overwhelm your processor, this only provides short-term relief.

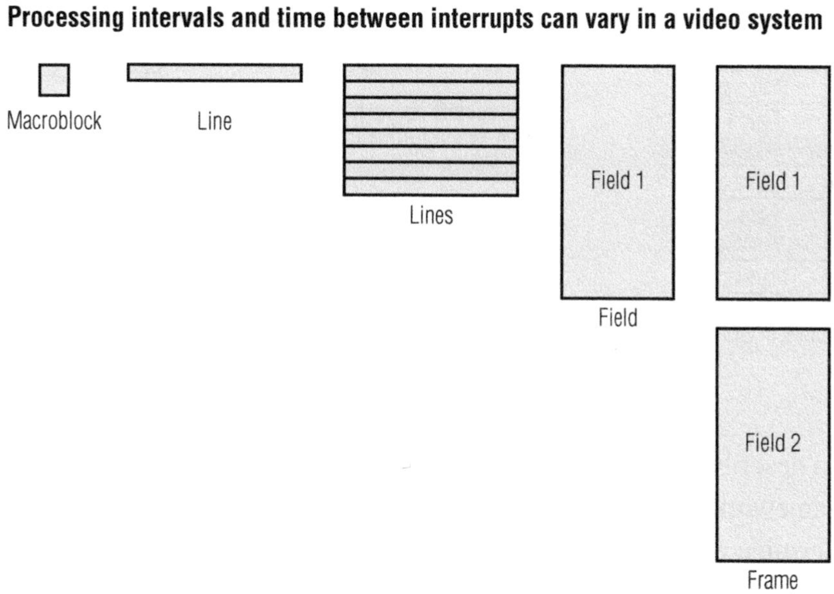

Processing intervals and time between interrupts can vary in a video system

Figure 7.2 **Minimum timeline examples**

Evaluating Bandwidth

When selecting a processor, it's easy to oversimplify the estimates for overall band-width required. Unfortunately, this mistake is often realized after a processor has been chosen, or after the development schedule has been approved by management!

Consider the viewfinder subsystem of a digital video camera. Here, the raw video source feeds the input of the processor's video port. The processor then downsamples the data, converts the color space from YCbCr to RGB, packs each RGB word into a 16-bit output, and sends it to the viewfinder's LCD. The process is shown in Figure 7.3.

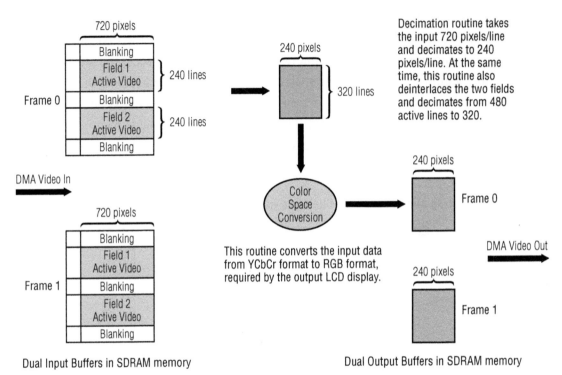

Figure 7.3 **Block diagram of video display system**

The system described above provides a good platform to discuss design budgets within a framework. Given a certain set of data flows and computational routines, how can we determine if the processor is close to being "maxed out"?

Let's assume here we're using a single processor core running at 600 MHz, and the video camera generates NTSC video at the rate of 27 Mbytes per second.

So the basic algorithm flow is:

A. Read in an NTSC frame of input data (1716 bytes/row × 525 rows).

B. Downsample it to a QVGA image containing (320 × 240 pixels) × (2 bytes/pixel).

C. Convert the data to RGB format.

D. Add a graphics overlay, such as the time of day or an "image tracker" box.

E. Send the final output buffer to the QVGA LCD at its appropriate refresh rate.

We'd like to get a handle on the overall performance of this algorithm. Is it taxing the processor too much, or barely testing it? Do we have room left for additional video processing, or for higher input frame rates or resolutions?

In order to measure the performance of each step, we need to gather timing data. It's convenient to do this with a processor's built-in cycle counters, which use the core-clock (CCLK) as a timebase. Since in our example CCLK=600 MHz, each tick of the cycle counter measures 1/(600 MHz), or 1.67 ns.

OK, so we've done our testing, and we find the following:

Step A: (27 million cycles per second / 30 frames per second), or 900,000 cycles to collect a complete frame of video.

Steps B/C: 5 million CCLK cycles to downsample and color-convert that frame.

Steps D/E: 11 million CCLK cycles to add a graphics overlay and send that one processed frame to the LCD panel.

Keep in mind that these processes don't necessarily happen sequentially. Instead, they are pipelined for efficient data flow. But measuring them individually gives us insight into the ultimate limits of the system.

Given these timing results, we might be misled into thinking, "Wow, it only takes 5 million CCLK cycles to process a frame (because all other steps are allocated to the inputting and outputting of data), so 30 frames per second would only use up about 30 × 5 = 150 MHz of the core's 600 MHz performance. We could even do 60 frames/sec and still have 50% of the processor bandwidth left."

This type of surface analysis belies the fact that there are actually three important bandwidth studies to perform in order to truly get your hands around a system:

- Processor bandwidth
- DMA bandwidth
- Memory bandwidth

Bottlenecks in any one of these can prevent your application from working properly. More importantly, the combined bandwidth of the overall system can be very different than the sum of each individual bandwidth number, due to interactions between resources.

Processor Bandwidth

In our example, in Steps B and C the processor core needs to spend 5M cycles operating on the input buffer from Step A. However, this analysis does not account for the total time available for the core to work on each input buffer. In processor cycles, a 600 MHz core can afford to spend around 20M cycles (600 MHz/30 fps)on each input frame of data, before the next frame starts to arrive.

Viewed from this angle, then, Steps B and C tell us that the processor core is 5M/20M, or 25%, loaded. That's a far cry from the "intuitive" ratio of 5M/600M, or 0.8%, but it's still low enough to allow for a considerable amount of additional processing on each input buffer.

What would happen if we doubled the frame rate to 60 frames/second, keeping the identical resolution? Even though there are twice as many frames, it would still take only 5M cycles to do the processing of Steps B and C, since the frame size has not changed. But now our 600 MHz core can only afford to spend 10M cycles (600 MHz/60 frames/sec) on each input frame. Therefore, the processor is 50% loaded (5M processing cycles/10M available cycles) in this case.

Taking a different slant, let's dial back the frame rate to 30 frames/sec, but double the resolution of each frame. Effectively, this means there are twice as many pixels per frame. Now, it should take twice as long to read in a single frame and twice as long (10M cycles) to process each frame as in the last case. However, since there are only 30 frames/second, If CCLK remains at 600 MHz, then the core can afford to spend 20M cycles on each frame. As in the last case, the processor is 50% loaded (10M processing cycles/20M available cycles). It's good to see that these last two analyses matched up, since the total input data rate is identical.

DMA Bandwidth

Let's forget about the processor core for a minute and concentrate on the DMA controller. On a dual-core Blackfin processor, each 32-bit peripheral DMA channel (such as one used for video in/out functionality) can transfer data at clock speeds up to half the system clock (SCLK) rate, where SCLK maxes out at 133 MHz. This means that a given DMA channel can transfer data on every other SCLK cycle. Other DMA channels can use the free slots on a given DMA bus. In fact, for transfers in the same direction (e.g., into or out of the same memory space), every bus cycle can be utilized. For example, if the video port (PPI) is transferring data from external memory, the audio port (SPORT) can interleave its transfers from external memory to an audio codec without spending a cycle of latency for turning around the bus.

This implies that the maximum bandwidth on a given DMA bus is 133 MHz × 4 bytes, or 532 Mbytes/sec. As an aside, keep in mind that a processor might have multiple DMA buses available, thus allowing multiple transfers to occur at the same time.

In an actual system, however, it is not realistic to assume every transfer will occur in the same direction. Practically speaking, it is best to plan on a maximum transfer rate of one half of the theoretical bus bandwidth. This bus "derating" is important in an analogous manner to that of hardware component selection. In any system design, the more you exceed a 50% utilization factor, the more care you must take during software integration and future software maintenance efforts. If you plan on using 50% from the beginning, you'll leave yourself plenty of breathing room for coping with interactions of the various DMA channels and the behavior of the memory to which you're connecting. Of course, this value is not a hard limit, as many systems exist where every cycle is put to good use. The 50% derating factor is simply a useful guideline to allow for cycles that may be lost from bus turnarounds or DMA channel conflicts.

Memory Bandwidth

As we saw in Chapter 4, planning the memory access patterns in your application can mean the difference between crafting a successful project and a building a random number generator! Determining up front if the desired throughput is even possible for an application can save lots of headaches later.

Recall our Chapter 2 discussion on hierarchical memory architectures. As a system designer, you'll need to balance memory of differing sizes and performance levels at the onset of your project.

For multimedia applications involving image sizes above QCIF (176 × 144 pixels), on-chip memory is almost always insufficient for storing entire video frames. Therefore, the system must rely on L3 DRAM to support relatively fast access to large buffers. The processor interface to off-chip memory constitutes a major factor in designing efficient media frameworks, because access patterns to external memory must be well thought out in order to guarantee optimal data throughput. There are several high-level steps to ensure that data flows smoothly through memory in any system. Some of these are discussed in Chapter 4, and they all play a key role in the design of system frameworks.

Once you understand the actual bandwidth needs for the processor, DMA and memory components, you can return to the issue at hand: what is the minimum processing interval that needs to be satisfied in your application?

Let's consider a new example where the smallest collection interval is defined to be a line of video. Determining the processing load under ideal conditions (when all code and data are in L1 memory) is easy. In the case where we are managing two buffers at a time, we must look at the time it takes to fill each buffer. The DMA controller "ping-pongs" between buffers to prevent a buffer from being overwritten while processing is underway on it. While the computation is done "in place" in Buffer 0, the peripheral fills Buffer 1. When Buffer 1 fills, Buffer 0 again becomes the destination. Depending on the processing timeline, an interrupt can optionally signal when each buffer has been filled.

So far, everything seems relatively straightforward. Now, consider what happens when the code is not in internal memory, but instead is executing from external memory. If instruction cache is enabled to improve performance, a fetch to external memory will result in a cache-line fill whenever there is not a match in L1 instruction memory (i.e., a cache-line miss occurs). As we saw in Chapter 2, the resulting fill will typically return at least 32 bytes. Because a cache-line fill is not interruptible—once it starts, it continues to completion—all other accesses to external memory are held off while it completes. From external memory, a cache-line fill can result in a fetch that takes 8 SCLKs (on Blackfin processors) for the first 32-bit word, followed by 7 additional SCLKs for the next seven 32-bit fetches (1 SCLK for each 32-bit fetch). This may be okay when the code being brought in is going to be executed. But now, what if one of the instructions being executed is a branch instruction, and this instruction, in turn, also generates a cache-line miss because it is more than a cache-line fill width away in memory address space? Code that is fetched from the second cache-line fill might also contain dual accesses that again are both data cache misses. What if these misses result in accesses to a page in external memory that is not active? Additional cycles can continue to hold off the competing resources. In a multimedia system, this situation can cause clicking sounds or video artifacts.

By this time, you should see the snowballing effect of the many factors that can reduce the performance of your application if you don't consider the interdependence of every framework component. Figure 7.4 illustrates one such situation.

The scenario described in Figure 7.4 demonstrates the need to, from the start, plan the utilization on the external bus. Incidentally, it is this type of scenario that drives the need for FIFOs in media processor peripherals, to insure that each interface has a cushion against the occurrence of these hard-to-manage system events. When you hear a click or see a glitch, what may be happening is that one of the peripherals has encountered an over-run (when it is receiving) or under-run (when it is transmitting) condition. It is important to set up error interrupt service routines to trap these conditions. This sounds obvious, but it's an often-overlooked step that can save loads of debugging time.

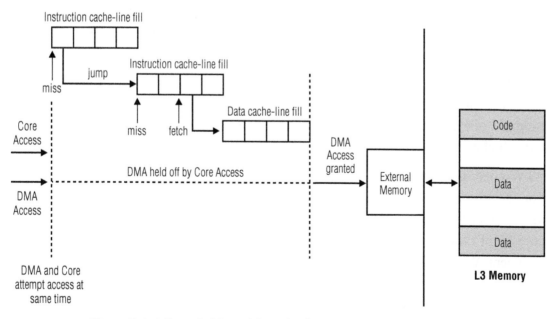

Figure 7.4 **A line of video with cache-line misses overlayed onto it**

The question is, what kinds of tasks will happen at the worst possible point in your application? In the scenario we just described with multiple cache-line fills happening at the wrong time, eliminating cache may solve the problem on paper, but if your code will not fit into L1 memory, you will have to decide between shutting off cache and using the available DMA channels to manage code and data movement into and out of L1 memory, as we discussed in Chapter 4. Even when system bandwidth seems to meet your initial estimates, the processor has to be able to handle the ebbs and flows of data transfers for finite intervals in any set of circumstances.

Asymmetric and Symmetric Dual-Core Processors

So far we've defaulted to talking about single-core processors for embedded media applications. However, there's a lot to be said about dual-core approaches. A processor with two cores (or more, if you're really adventurous) can be very powerful, yet along with the extra performance can come an added measure of complexity. As it turns out, there are a few common and quite useful programming models that suit a dual-core processor, and we'll examine them here.

There are two types of dual-core architectures available today. The first we'll call an "asymmetric" dual-core processor, meaning that the two cores are architecturally different. This means that, in addition to possessing different instruction sets, they also run at different operating frequencies and have different memory and programming models.

The main advantage of having two different architectures in the same physical package is that each core can optimize a specific portion of the processing task. For example, one core might excel at controller functionality, while the second one might target higher-bandwidth processing.

As you may figure, there are several disadvantages with asymmetric arrangements. For one, they require two sets of development tools and two sets of programming skill sets in order to build an application. Secondly, unused processing resources on one core are of little use to a fully loaded second core, since their competencies are so divergent. What's more, asymmetric processors make it difficult to scale from light to heavy processing profiles. This is important, for instance, in battery-operated devices, where frequency and voltage may be adjusted to meet real-time processing requirements; asymmetric cores don't scale well because the processing load is divided unevenly, so that one core might still need to run at maximum frequency while the other could run at a much lower clock rate. Finally, as we will see, asymmetric processors don't support many different programming models, which limits design options (and makes them much less exciting to talk about!).

In contrast to the asymmetric processor, a symmetric dual-core processor (extended to "symmetric multiprocessor," or SMP) consists of two identical cores integrated into a single package. The dual-core Blackfin ADSP-BF561 is a good example of this device class. An SMP requires only a single set of development tools and a design team with a single architectural knowledge base. Also, since both cores are equivalent, unused processing resources on one core can often be leveraged by the other core. Another very important benefit of the SMP architecture is the fact that frequency and voltage can more easily be modified together, improving the overall energy usage in a given application. Lastly, while the symmetric processor supports an asymmetric programming model, it also supports many other models that are very useful for multimedia applications.

The main challenge with the symmetric multiprocessor is splitting an algorithm across two processor cores without complicating the programming model. We will look at how this can be done with an MPEG encoder example in Chapter 9.

Programming Models

There are several basic programming models that designers employ across a broad range of applications. We described an asymmetric processor in the previous discussion; we will now look at its associated programming model.

Asymmetric Programming Model

The traditional use of an asymmetric dual-core processor involves discrete and often different tasks running on each of the cores, as shown in Figure 7.5. For example, one of the cores may be assigned all of the control-related tasks. These typically include graphics and overlay functionality, as well as networking stacks and overall flow control. This core is also most often where the operating system or kernel will reside. Meanwhile, the second core can be dedicated to the high-intensity processing functions of the application. For example, compressed data may come over the network into the first core. Received packets can feed the second core, which in turn might perform some audio and video decode function.

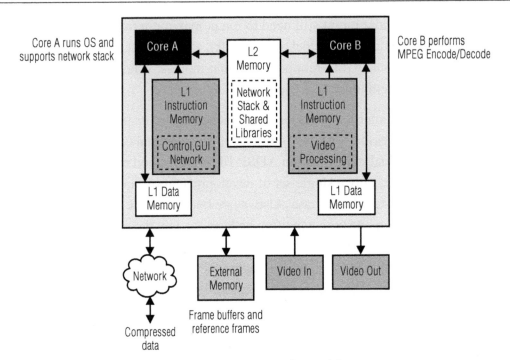

Core A runs OS and supports network stack

Core B performs MPEG Encode/Decode

Figure 7.5 **Asymmetric model**

In this model, the two processor cores act independently from each other. Logically, they are more like two stand-alone processors that communicate through the interconnect structures between them. They don't share any code and share very little data. We refer to this as the Asymmetric Programming Model. This model is preferred by developers who employ separate teams in their software development efforts. The ability to allocate different tasks to different processors allows development to be accomplished in parallel, eliminating potential critical path dependencies in the project. This programming model also aids the testing and validation phases of the project. For example, if code changes on one core, it does not necessarily invalidate testing efforts already completed on the other core.

Also, by having a dedicated processor core available for a given task, code developed on a single-core processor can be more easily ported to "half" of the dual-core processor. Both asymmetric and symmetric multiprocessors support this programming model. However, having identical cores available allows for the possibility of re-allocating any unused resources across functions and tasks. As we described earlier, the symmetric processor also has the advantage of providing a common, integrated environment.

Another important consideration of this model relates to the fact that the size of the code running the operating system and control tasks is usually measured in megabytes. As such, the code must reside in external memory, with instruction cache enabled. While this scheme is usually sufficient, care must be taken to prevent cache line fills from interfering with the overall timeline of the application. A relatively small subset of code runs the most often, due to the nature of algorithm coding. Therefore, enabling instruction cache is usually adequate in this model.

Homogeneous Programming Model

Because there are two identical cores in a symmetric multiprocessor, traditional processing-intensive applications can be split equally across each core. We call this a Homogeneous Model. In this scheme, code running on each core is identical. Only the data being processed is different. In a streaming multi-channel audio application, for example, this would mean that one core processes half of the audio channels, and the other core processes the remaining half. Extending this concept to video and imaging applications, each core might process alternate frames. This usually translates to a scenario where all code fits into internal memory, in which case instruction cache is probably not used.

The communication flow between cores in this model is usually pretty basic. A mailbox interrupt (or on the Blackfin processor, a supplemental interrupt between cores) can signal the other core to check for a semaphore, to process new data or to send out processed data.

Usually, an operating system or kernel is not required for this model; instead, a "super loop" is implemented. We use the term "super loop" to indicate a code segment that just runs over and over again, of the form:

```
While (1)
    {
    Process_data();
    Send_results();
    Idle();
    }
```

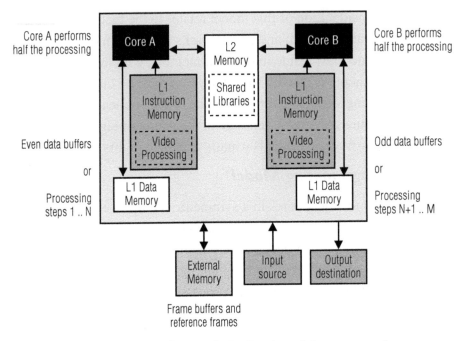

Figure 7.6 **Master-Slave and Pipelined model representations**

Master-Slave Programming Model

In the Master-Slave usage model, both cores perform intensive computation in order to achieve better utilization of the symmetric processor architecture. In this arrangement, one core (the master) controls the flow of the processing and actually performs at least half the processing load. Portions of specific algorithms are split and handled by the slave, assuming these portions can be parallelized. This situation is represented in Figure 7.6.

A variety of techniques, among them interrupts and semaphores, can be used to synchronize the cores in this model. The slave processor usually takes less processing time than the master does. Thus, the slave can poll a semaphore in shared memory when it is ready for more work. This is not always a good idea, though, because if the master core is still accessing the bus to the shared memory space, a conflict will arise. A more robust solution is for the slave to place itself in idle mode and wait for the master to interrupt it with a request to perform the next block of work.

A scheduler or simple kernel is most useful in this model, as we'll discuss later in the chapter.

Pipelined Programming Model

Also depicted in Figure 7.6, a variation on the Master-Slave model allocates processing steps to each core. That is, one core is assigned one or more serial steps, and the other core handles the remaining ones. This is analogous to a manufacturing pipeline where one core's output is the next core's input. Ideally, if the processing task separation is optimized, this will achieve a performance advantage greater than that of the other models. The task separation, however, is heavily dependent on the processor architecture and its memory hierarchy. For this reason, the Pipelined Model isn't as portable across processors as the other programming models are.

The MPEG-2 encoder example in Chapter 9 sheds more light on the Master-Slave and Pipelined models.

As Table 7.1 illustrates, the symmetric processor supports many more programming models than the asymmetric processor does, so you should consider all of your options before starting a project!

Table 7.1 **Programming model summary**

Processor	Asymmetric	Homogenous	Master-Slave	Pipelined
Asymmetric	✓			
Symmetric	✓	✓	✓	✓

Strategies for Architecting a Framework

We have discussed how tasks can be allocated across multiple cores when necessary. We have also described the basic ways a programming model can take shape. We are now ready to discuss several types of multimedia frameworks that can ride on top of either a single or dual-core processor. Regardless of the programming model, a framework is necessary in all but the simplest applications.

While they represent only a subset of all possible strategies, the categories shown below provide a good sampling of the most popular resource management situations. For illustration, we'll continue to use video-centric systems as a basis for these scenarios, because they incorporate the transfer of large amounts of data between internal and external memory, as well as the movement of raw data into the system and processed data out of the system. Here are the categories we will explore:

1. A system where data is processed as it is collected

2. A system where programming ease takes precedence over performance

3. A processor-intensive application where performance supersedes programming ease

Processing Data On-the-Fly

We'll first discuss systems where data is processed on-the-fly, as it is collected. Two basic categories of this class exist: low "system latency" applications and systems with either no external memory or a reduced external memory space.

This scenario strives for the absolute lowest system latency between input data and output result. For instance, imagine the camera-based automotive object avoidance system of Figure 7.7 tries to minimize the chance of a collision by rapidly evaluating successive video frames in the area of view. Because video frames require a tremendous amount of storage capacity (recall that one NTSC active video frame alone requires almost 700 Kbytes of memory), they invariably need external memory for storage. But if the avoidance system were to wait until an entire road image were buffered into memory before starting to process the input data, 33 ms of valuable time would be lost (assuming a 30-Hz frame rate). This is in contrast to the time it takes to collect a single line of data, which is only 63 µs.

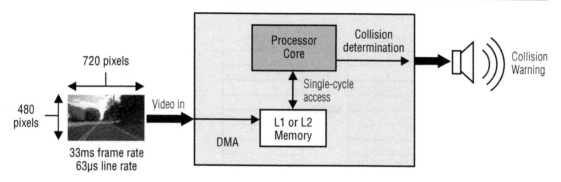

Figure 7.7 **Processing data as it enters the system**

To ensure lowest latency, video can enter L1 or L2 memory for processing on a line-by-line basis, rendering quick computations that can lead to quicker decisions. If the algorithm operates on only a few lines of video at a time, the frame storage requirements are much less difficult to meet. A few lines of video can easily fit into L2 memory, and since L2 memory is closer to the core processor than off-chip DRAM, this also improves performance considerably when compared to accessing off-chip memory.

Under this framework, the processor core can directly access the video data in L1 or L2 memory. In this fashion, the programming model matches the typical PC-based paradigm. In order to guarantee data integrity, the software needs to insure that the active video frame buffer is not overwritten with new data until processing on the current frame completes. As shown in Figure 7.8, this can be easily managed through a "ping-pong" buffer, as well through the use of a semaphore mechanism. The DMA controller in this framework is best configured in a descriptor mode, where Descriptor 0 points to Descriptor 1 when its corresponding data transfer completes. In turn, Descriptor 1 points back to Descriptor 0. This looks functionally like an Autobuffer scheme, which is also a realistic option to employ. What happens when the processor is accessing a buffer while it is being output to a peripheral? In a video application, you will most likely see some type of smearing between frames. This will show up as a blurred image, or one that appears to jump around.

In our collision-avoidance system, the result of processing each frame is a decision—is a crash imminent or not? Therefore, in this case there is no output display buffer that needs protection against being overwritten. The size of code required for this type

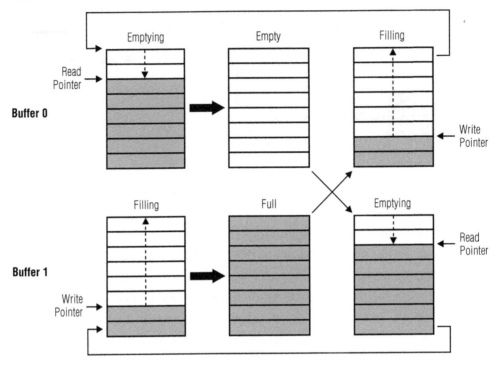

Figure 7.8 **"Ping-Pong" buffer**

of application most likely will support execution from on-chip memory. This is help-ful—again, it's one less thing to manage.

In this example, the smallest processing interval is the time it takes to collect a line of video from the camera. There are similar applications where multiple lines are required—for example, a 3 × 3 convolution kernel for image filtering.

Not all of the applications that fit this model have low system-latency requirements. Processing lines on-the-fly is useful for other situations as well. As we will see in Chapter 9, JPEG compression can lend itself to this type of framework, where image buffering is not required because there is no motion component to the compression. Here, macroblocks of 16 pixels × 16 pixels form a compression work unit. If we double-buffer two sets of 16 active-video lines, we can have the processor work its way through an image as it is generated. Again, a double-buffer scheme can be set up where two sets of 16 lines are managed. That is, one set of 16 lines is compressed while the next set is transferred into memory.

Programming Ease Trumps Performance

The second framework we'll discuss focuses entirely on using the simplest programming model at the possible expense of some performance. In this scenario, time to market is usually the most important factor. This may result in over-specifying a device, just to be sure there's plenty of room for inefficiencies caused by nonoptimal coding or some small amount of redundant data movements. In reality, this strategy also provides an upgrade platform, because processor bandwidth can ultimately be freed up once it's possible to focus on optimizing the application code. A simple flow diagram is shown in Figure 7.9.

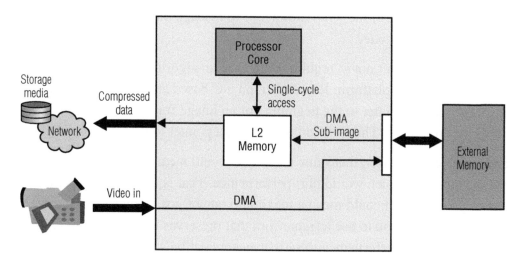

Figure 7.9 **Framework that focuses on ease of use**

We used JPEG as an example in the previous framework because no buffering was required. For this framework any algorithm that operates on more than one line of data at a time, and is not an encoder or decoder, is a good candidate. Let's say we would like to perform a 3 × 3 two-dimensional convolution as part of an edge detection routine. For optimal operation, we need to have as many lines of data in internal memory as possible. The typical kernel navigates from left to right across an image, and then starts at the left side again (the same process used when reading words on a page). This convolution path continues until the kernel reaches the end of the entire image frame.

It is very important for the DMA controller to always fetch the next frame of data while the core is crunching on the current frame. That said, care should be taken to insure that DMA can't get too far ahead of the core, because then unprocessed data would be overwritten. A semaphore mechanism is the only way to guarantee that this process happens correctly. It can be provided as part of an operating system or in some other straightforward implementation.

Consider that, by the time the core finishes processing its first sub-frame of data, the DMA controller either has to wrap back around to the top of the buffer, or it has to start filling a second buffer. Due to the nature of the edge detection algorithm, it will most certainly require at least two buffers. The question is, is it better to make the algorithm library aware of the wrap-around, or to manage the data buffer to hide this effect from the library code?

The answer is, it is better not to require changes to an algorithm that has already been tested on another platform. Remember, on a C-based application on the PC, you might simply pass a pointer to the beginning of an image frame in memory when it is available for processing. The function may return a pointer to the processed buffer.

On an embedded processor, that same technique would mean operating on a buffer in external memory, which would hurt performance. That is, rather than operations at 30 frames per second, it could mean a maximum rate of just a few frames per second. This is exactly the reason to use a framework that preserves the programming model and achieves enough performance to satisfy an application's needs, even if requirements must be scaled back somewhat.

Let's return to our edge detection example. Depending on the size of the internal buffer, it makes sense to copy the last few lines of data from the end of one buffer to the beginning of the next one. Take a look at Figure 7.10. Here we see that a buffer of 120 × 120 pixels is brought in from L3 memory. As the processor builds an output buffer 120 × 120 pixels at a time, the next block comes in from L3. But if you're not careful, you'll have trouble in the output buffer at the boundaries of the processed blocks. That is, the convolution kernel needs to have continuity across consecutive lines, or visual artifacts will appear in the processed image.

One way to remedy this situation is to repeat some data lines (i.e., bring them into the processor multiple times). This allows you to present the algorithm with "clean" frames to work on, avoiding wrap-around artifacts. You should be able to see that the

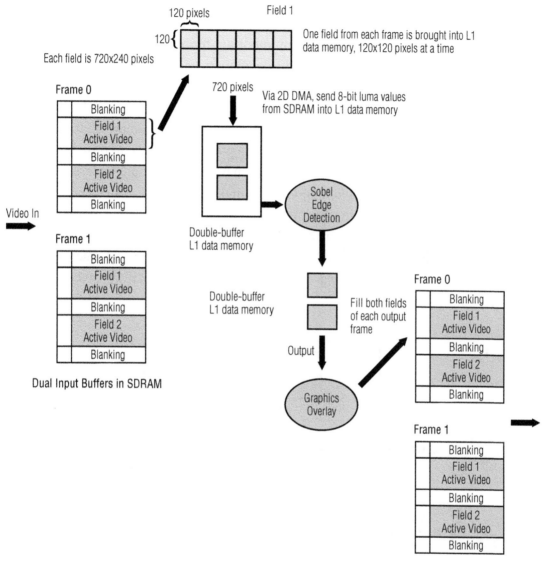

Figure 7.10 **Edge detection**

added overhead associated with checking for a wrap-around condition is circumvented by instead moving some small amount of data twice. By taking these steps, you can then maintain the programming model you started with by passing a pointer to the smaller sub-image, which now resides in internal memory.

Performance-Based Framework

The third framework we'll discuss is often important for algorithms that push the limits of the target processor. Typically, developers will try to right-size their processor to their intended application, so they won't have to pay a cost premium for an over-capable device. This is usually the case for extremely high-volume, cost-sensitive applications. As such, the "performance-based" framework focuses on attaining best performance at the expense of a possible increase in programming complexity. In this framework, implementation may take longer and integration may be a bit more challenging, but the long-term savings in designing with a less expensive device may justify the extra development time. The reason there's more time investment early in the development cycle is that every aspect of data flow needs to be carefully planned. When the final data flow is architected, it will be much harder to reuse, because the framework was hand-crafted to solve a specific problem. An example is shown in Figure 7.11.

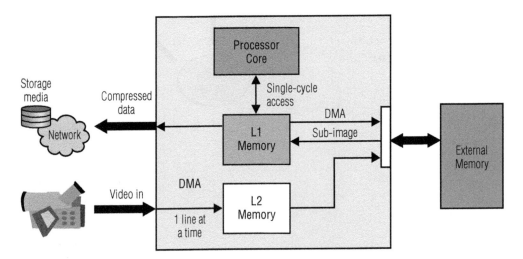

Figure 7.11 **Performance-based framework**

The examples in this category are many and varied. Let's look at two particular cases: a design where an image pipe and compression engine must coexist, and a high-performance video decoder.

Image Pipe and Compression Example

Our first example deals with a digital camera where the processor connects to a CMOS sensor or CCD module that outputs a Bayer RGB pattern. As we discussed in Chapter 6, this application often involves a software image pipe that preprocesses the incoming image frame. In this design, we'll also want to perform JPEG compression or a limited-duration MPEG-4 encode at 30 fps. It's almost as if we have two separate applications running on the same platform.

This design is well-suited to a dual-core development effort. One core can be dedicated to implementing the image pipe, while the other performs compression. Because the two processors may share some internal and external memory resources, it is important to plan out accesses so that all data movement is choreographed. While each core works on separate tasks, we need to manage memory accesses to ensure that one of the tasks doesn't hold off any others. The bottom line is that both sides of the application have to complete before the next frame of data enters the system.

Just as in the "Processing On-the-Fly" framework example, lines of video data are brought into L2 memory, where the core directly accesses them for pre-processing as needed, with lower latency than accessing off-chip memory. While the lower core data access time is important, the main purpose of using L2 memory is to buffer up a set of lines in order to make group transfers in the same direction, thus maximizing bus performance to external memory.

A common (but incorrect) assumption made early in many projects is to consider only individual benchmarks when comparing transfers to/from L2 and with transfers to/from L3 memory. The difference in transfer times does not appear to be dramatic when the measurements are taken individually, but as we discussed in Chapter 4, the interaction of multiple accesses can make a big difference.

Why is this the case? Because if the video port feeds L3 memory directly, the data bus turns around more times than necessary. Let's assume we have 8-bit video data packed into 32-bit DMA transfers. As soon as the port collects 4 bytes of sensor input, it will perform a DMA transfer to L3. For most algorithms, a processor makes more reads than writes to data in L3 memory. This, of course, is application-dependent, but in media applications there are usually at least three reads for every write. Since the video port is continuously writing to external memory, turnarounds on the external memory bus happen frequently, and performance suffers as a result.

By the time each line of a video frame passes into L2 memory and back out to external memory, the processor has everything it needs to process the entire frame of data. Very little bandwidth has been wasted by turning the external bus around more than necessary. This scheme is especially important when the image pipe runs in parallel with the video encoder. It ensures the least conflict when the two sides of the application compete for the same resources.

To complete this framework requires a variety of DMA flows. One DMA stream reads data in from external memory, perhaps in the form of video macroblocks. The other flow sends compressed data out—over a network or to a storage device, for instance. In addition, audio streams are part of the overall framework. But, of course, video is the main flow of concern, from both memory traffic and DMA standpoints.

High Performance Decoder Example

Another sample flow in the "performance-based" framework involves encoding or decoding audio and video at the highest frame rate and image size possible. For example, this may correspond to implementing a decoder (MPEG-4, H.264 or WMV9) that operates on a D-1 video stream on a single-core processor.

Designing for this type of situation conveys an appreciation of the intricacies of a system that is more complex than the ones we have discussed so far. Once the processor receives the encoded bit stream, it parses and separates the header and data payloads from the stream. The overall processing limit for the decoder can be determined by:

(# of cycles/pixel) × (# of pixels/frame) × (# of frames/second) < (Budgeted # of cycles/second)

At least 10% of the available processing bandwidth must be reserved for steps like audio decode and transport layer processing. For a D-1 video running on a 600 MHz device, we have to process around 10 Mpixels per second. Considering only video processing, this allows ~58 cycles per pixel. However, reserving 10% for audio and transport stream processing, we are left with just over 50 cycles per pixel as our processing budget.

When you consider the number of macroblocks in a D-1 frame, you may ask, "Do I need an interrupt after each of these transfers?" The answer, thankfully, is "No." As long as you time the transfers and understand when they start and stop, there is no need for an interrupt.

Now let's look at the data flow of the video decoder shown in Figure 7.12.

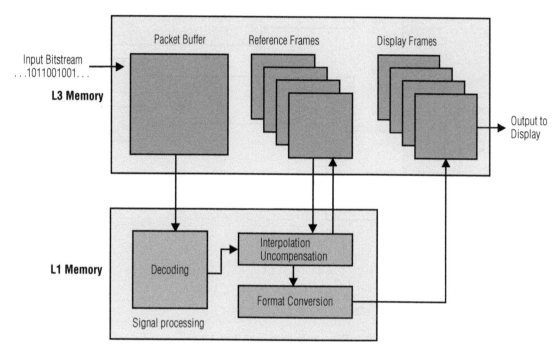

Figure 7.12 **Typical video decoder**

Figure 7.13 shows the data movement involved in this example. We use a 2D-to-1D DMA to bring the buffers into L1 memory for processing. Figure 7.14 shows the data flow required to send buffers back out to L3 memory.

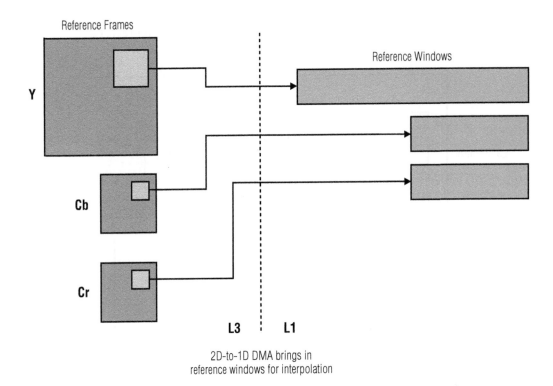

2D-to-1D DMA brings in
reference windows for interpolation

Figure 7.13 **Data movement (L3 to L1 memory)**

On the DMA side of the framework, we need DMA streams for the incoming encoded bit stream. We also need to account for the reference frame being DMA'ed into L1 memory, a reconstructed frame sent back out to L3 memory, and the process of converting the frame into 4:2:2 YCbCr format for ITU-R BT.656 output. Finally, another DMA is required to output the decoded video frame through the video port.

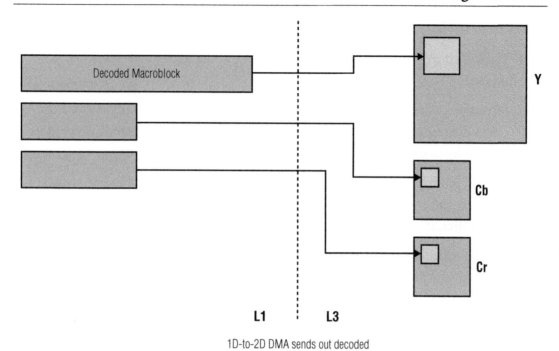

1D-to-2D DMA sends out decoded
macroblock to L3 to build reference frame

Figure 7.14 **Data movement (L1 to L3 memory)**

For this scheme, larger buffers are staged in L3 memory, while smaller buffers, including lookup tables and building blocks of the larger buffers, reside in L1 memory. When we add up the total bandwidth to move data into and out of the processor, it looks something like the following:

Input data stream: 1 Mbyte/sec

Reference frame in: 15 Mbyte/sec

Loop filter (input and output): 30 Mbyte/sec

Reference data out: 15 Mbyte/sec

Video out: 27 Mbyte/sec

The percentage of bandwidth consumed will depend on the software implementation. One thing, however, is certain—you cannot simply add up each individual transfer rate to arrive at the system bandwidth requirements. This will only give you a rough indication, not tell you whether the system will work.

Framework Tips

Aside from what we've mentioned above, there are some additional items that you may find useful.

1. Consider using L2 memory as a video line buffer. Even if it means an extra pass in your system, this approach conserves bandwidth where it is the most valuable, at the external memory interface.

2. Avoid polling locations in L2 or L3 memory. Polling translates into a tight loop by the core processor which can then lock out other accesses by the DMA controller, if core accesses are assigned higher priority than DMA accesses.

3. Avoid moving large blocks of memory using core accesses. Consecutive accesses by the core processor can lock out the DMA controller. Use the DMA controller whenever possible to move data between memory spaces.

4. Profile your code with the processor's software tools suite, shooting for at least 97% of your code execution to occur in L1 memory. This is best accomplished through a combination of cache and strategic placement of the most critical code in L1 SRAM. It should go without saying, but place your event service routines in L1 memory.

5. Interrupts are not mandatory for every transfer. If your system is highly deterministic, you may choose to have most transfers finish without an interrupt. This scheme reduces system latency, and it's the best guarantee that high-bandwidth systems will work. Sometimes, adding a control word to the stream can be useful to indicate the transfer has occurred. For example, the last word of the transfer could be defined to indicate a macroblock number that the processor could then use to set up new DMA transfers.

6. Taking shortcuts is sometimes okay, especially when these shortcuts are not visually or audibly discernable. For example, as long as the encoded output stream is compliant to a standard, shortcuts that impact the quality only matter if you can detect them. This is especially helpful to consider when the display resolution is the limiting factor or the weak link in a system.

Other Topics in Media Frameworks

Audio-Video Synchronization

We haven't talked too much about audio processing in this chapter because it makes up a small subset of the bandwidth in a video-based system. Data rates are measured in kilobytes/sec, versus megabytes/sec for even the lowest-resolution video systems.

Where audio does become important in the context of video processing is when we try to synchronize the audio and video streams in a decoder/encoder system. While we can take shortcuts in image quality in some applications when the display is small, it is hard to take shortcuts on the synchronization task, because an improperly synchronized audio/video output is quite annoying to end users.

We will look in more detail at a MPEG-2 video encoder implementation in Chapter 9, but for now let's assume we have already decoded an audio and video stream. Figure 7.15 shows the format of an MPEG-2 transport stream. There are multiple bit stream options for MPEG-2, but we will consider the MPEG-2 transport stream (TS).

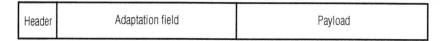

| Header | Adaptation field | Payload |

Figure 7.15 **MPEG-2 encoded transport stream format**

The header shown in Figure 7.15 includes a Packet ID code and a sequence number to ensure decode is performed in the proper order. The adaptation field is used for additional control information. One of these control words is the program clock reference, or PCR. This is used as the timing reference for the communication channel.

Video and audio encoders put out packet elementary streams (PES) that are split into the transport packets shown. When a PES packet is split to fit into a set of transport packets, the PES header follows the 4-byte Transport Header. A presentation timestamp is added to the packet. A second timestamp is also added when frames are sent out of order, which is done intentionally for things like anchor video frames. This second timestamp is used to control the order in which data is fed to the decoder.

Let's take a slight tangent to discuss some data buffer basics, to set the stage for the rest of our discussion. Figure 7.16 shows a generic buffer structure, with high and low watermarks, as well as read and write pointers. The locations of the high and low watermarks are application-dependent, but they should be set appropriately to manage data flow in and out of the buffer. The watermarks determine the hysteresis of the buffer data flow. For example, the high watermark indicates a point in the buffer that triggers some processor action when the buffer is filling up (like draining it down to the low watermark). The low watermark also provides a trigger point that signals a task that some processor action needs to be taken (like transferring enough samples into the buffer to reach the high watermark). The read and write pointers in any specific implementation must be managed with respect to the high and low watermarks to ensure data is not lost or corrupted.

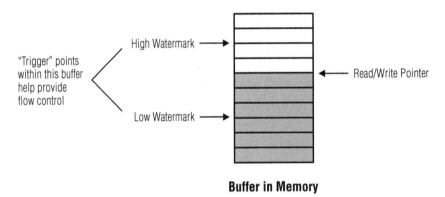

Buffer in Memory

Figure 7.16 **Buffer basics**

In a video decoder, audio buffers and video frames are created in external memory. As these output buffers are written to L3, a timestamp from the encoded stream is assigned to each buffer and frame. In addition, the processor needs to track its own time base. Then, before each decoded video frame and audio buffer is sent out for display, the processor performs a time check and finds the appropriate data match from each buffer. There are multiple ways to accomplish this task via DMA, but the best way is to have the descriptors already assembled and then, depending on which packet time matches the current processor time, adjust the write pointer to the appropriate descriptor.

Figure 7.17 shows a conceptual illustration of what needs to occur in the processor. As you can probably guess, skipping a video frame or two is usually not catastrophic to the user experience. Depending on the application, even skipping multiple frames

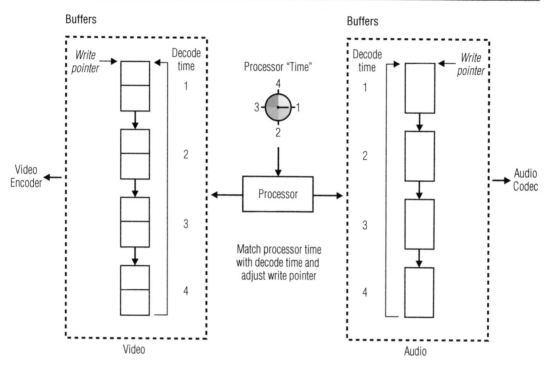

Figure 7.17 **Conceptual diagram of audio-video synchronization**

may go undetected. On the other hand, not synchronizing audio properly, or skipping audio samples entirely, is much more objectionable to viewers and listeners. The synchronization process of comparing times of encoded packets and matching them with the appropriate buffer is not computationally intensive. The task of parsing the encoded stream takes up the majority of MIPS in this framework, and this number will not vary based on image size.

Managing System Flow

We have already discussed applications where no operating system is used. We referred to this type of application as a "super loop" because there is a set order of processing that repeats every iteration. This is most common in the highest-performing systems, as it allows the programmer to retain most of the control over the order of processing. As a result, the block diagram of the data flow is usually pretty simple, but the intensity of the processing (image size, frame rate, or both) is usually greater.

Having said this, even the most demanding application normally requires some type of "system services." These allow a system to take advantage of some kernel-like features without actually using an OS or a kernel. In addition to system services, a set of device drivers also works to control the peripherals. Figure 7.18 shows the basic services that are available with the Blackfin VisualDSP++ tool chain.

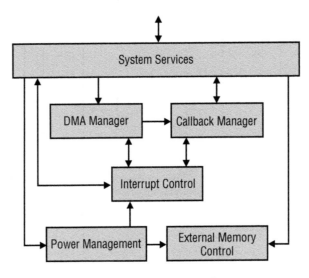

Figure 7.18 **System services**

Of those shown, the external memory and power management services are typically initialization services that configure the device or change operating parameters. On the other hand, the Interrupt, DMA and Callback Managers all provide ways to manage system flow.

As part of the DMA services, you can move data via a standard API, without having to configure every control register manually. A manager is also provided that accepts DMA work requests. These requests are handled in the order they are received by application software. The DMA Manager simplifies a programming model by abstracting data transfers.

In Chapter 4, we discussed the importance of handling interrupts efficiently. The Interrupt Manager allows the processor to service interrupts quickly. The idea is that the processor leaves the higher-priority interrupt and spawns an interrupt at the lowest priority level. The higher-priority interrupt is serviced, and the lower-priority interrupt is generated via a software instruction. Once this happens, new interrupts are no longer held off.

When the processor returns from the higher-priority interrupt, it can execute a call-back function to perform the actual processing. The Callback Manager allows you to respond to an event any way you choose. It passes a pointer to the routine you want to execute when the event occurs. The key is that the basic event is serviced, and the processor runs in a lower-priority task. This is important, because otherwise you run the risk of lingering in a higher-level interrupt, which can then delay response time for other events.

As we mentioned at the beginning of this section, device drivers provide the software layer to various peripherals, such as the video and audio ports. Figure 7.19 shows how the device drivers relate to a typical application. The device driver manages communications between memory and a given peripheral. The device drivers provided with VisualDSP++, for example, can work with or without an operating system.

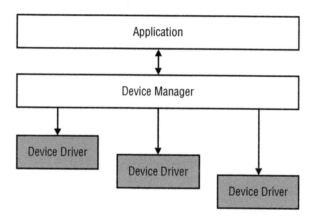

Figure 7.19 **Application with device drivers**

Finally, an OS can be an integral part of your application. If it is, Figure 7.20 shows how all of these components can be connected together. There are many OS and kernel options available for a processor. Typically, the products span a range of strengths and focus areas—for example, security, performance or code footprint. There is no "silver bullet" when it comes to these parameters. That is, if an OS has more security features, for instance, it may sacrifice on performance and/or kernel size.

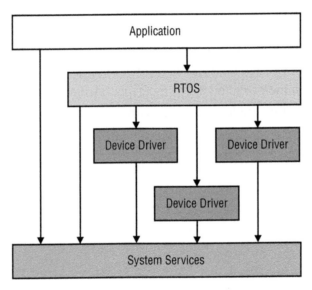

Figure 7.20 **Application with device drivers and OS**

In the end, you'll have to make a tradeoff between performance and flexibility. One of the best examples of this tradeoff is with uCLinux, an embedded instantiation of Linux that has only partial memory management unit capabilities. Here, the kernel size is measured in megabytes and must run from larger, slower external memory. As such, the instruction cache plays a key role in ensuring best kernel performance. While uCLinux's performance will never rival that of smaller, more optimized systems, its wealth of open-source projects available, with large user bases, should make you think twice before dismissing it as an option.

Frameworks and Algorithm Complexity

In this chapter we've tried to provide guidance on when to choose one framework over another, largely based on data flows, memory requirements and timing needs. Figure 7.21 shows another slant on these factors. It conveys a general idea of how complexity increases exponentially as data size grows. Moreover, as processing moves from being purely spatial in nature to having a temporal element as well, complexity (and the resulting need for a well-managed media framework) increases even further.

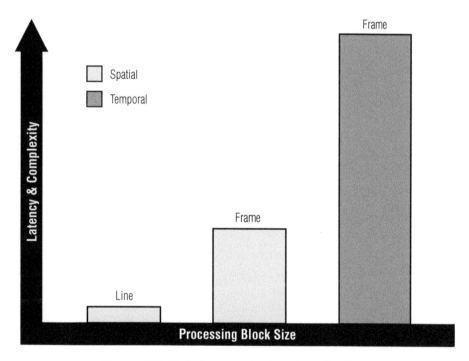

Figure 7.21 **Relative complexity of applications**

What's Next?

We will now change the focus of our media processing discussion by considering system power management. Certainly, every portable media processing application must be designed with a power-saving mentality, but there are also design aspects important to "plugged-in" applications. We'll consider many facets of system power management in Chapter 8.

Power Management for Embedded Systems

Introduction

No embedded multimedia design is complete without a thorough analysis of the power supply architecture. This goes without saying for battery-operated devices, but it also holds true for wired systems that have a constant supply of energy, because there are thermal, volumetric, and financial impacts to the power requirements of a system. The media processor and its surrounding hardware ecosystem usually consume a significant share of power, since that's where all the "heavy lifting" occurs.

There are a number of ways to tune the power profile of a system to meet application requirements. As we've done throughout the book, we will discuss concepts generically, but when we discuss specific processor features, these will be derived from Blackfin processor elements—in this case, from Blackfin's Dynamic Power Management subsystem.

This subsystem refers to a collection of architectural traits and features that allow manipulations in clock rates and voltages in order to optimize a system's power profile for a given activity level. These features include:

- A facility for dynamically changing frequency and voltage
- Flexible power management modes
- Separate power domains
- Efficient architectural constructs
- Software profiling tools
- Intelligent voltage regulation

In this chapter, we'll consider power from these angles and others, like battery choices, regulator architectures, system power dissipators, and so on. But first, let's start by studying the important relationships between frequency, voltage and power in an embedded processor.

A Processor's View of Power

Before we go any further, a discussion of terminology is in order. "Energy" relates the total amount of work performed, whereas "power" measures the rate at which the work is performed (energy per unit time). In electronics, power dissipated = (voltage across a system component) × (current flowing through that system component), and energy = power × time.

Therefore, what we usually are concerned with as system designers is total *energy* dissipated, and peak *power* dissipated. In other words, energy use is what drains a battery, but the battery needs to provide enough instantaneous energy to meet peak power demands. Our convention will be to focus on power dissipation, since this is prevalent terminology in the industry. However, we're really referring to both energy and power usage in a system.

The processor's clock generation unit controls the methods by which core and system frequencies are synthesized, thus playing an integral role in power management. Figure 1.10 of Chapter 1 introduced the Blackfin clock generation unit. Now let's take a closer look at the components of this entity, shown again in Figure 8.1 for convenience.

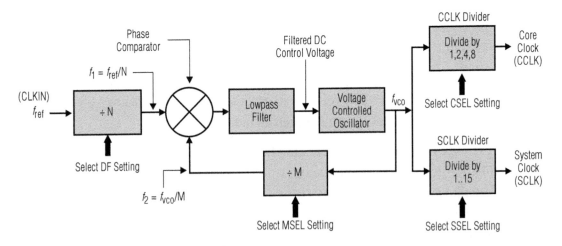

Note that when the loop is phase-locked, $f_1 = f_2$. Hence $f_{vco} = Mf_{ref}/N$.
DF, MSEL, CSEL, SSEL are Blackfin PLL configuration fields.

Figure 8.1 **Functional block diagram of Blackfin's clock generation unit**

Input Clock

The input clock into the processor, CLKIN, provides the necessary clock frequency, duty cycle and stability to allow accurate internal clock multiplication by means of an on-chip phase-locked loop (PLL) module. It connects to an external crystal or crystal oscillator in the range of 10–40 MHz. Using a crystal is usually cheaper, but oscillators, because they are buffered, provide more options for reusing the clock elsewhere in a system. For instance, a 27 MHz oscillator can serve not only as the processor clock input, but also as an NTSC video encoder or decoder clock source. Sometimes the processor itself will provide a buffered output of its crystal-based input clock, thus saving the need to purchase an oscillator.

The lower the fundamental oscillation frequency, the larger the crystal package will be. However, higher-frequency crystals cost more, because they are more fragile—the quartz inside is much thinner at higher fundamental frequencies. Another factor weighing into the crystal decision is EMI, or electromagnetic interference. It might be very important from a system perspective to avoid certain frequency multiples, in order to steer clear of spurious harmonics from the crystal that might leak into a filter or amplifier passband.

Phase-Locked Loop (PLL)

To provide the clock generation for the core and system, the Blackfin processor uses an analog PLL with programmable state machine control. Referring to Figure 8.1, let's walk through the conceptual model of the PLL circuit. Basically, the phase of an input clock f_{ref} (divided by N) is compared to that of a VCO divided by the multiplication ratio M. The difference signal generated by this comparison is filtered and then used as a closed-loop control signal to adjust the VCO frequency until f_{vco}/M exactly matches f_{ref}/N. This feedback loop provides an excellent way of generating a very accurate high-frequency clock from a stable reference signal running at a much lower frequency.

During normal operation, the external clock CLKIN is supplied at f_{ref}. Assuming (for simplicity) that the N divider is set to 1, the PLL effectively multiplies f_{ref} by the factor M, configurable between 1 and 64. This process allows a "fine adjustment" of frequency control. The resulting multiplied signal is the voltage controlled oscillator (VCO) clock f_{vco}, which serves as the reference for the processor clocks.

The core-clock (CCLK) frequency can be set by selecting a f_{vco} divide frequency of 1, 2, 4 or 8. CCLK is the reference clock for instruction execution and data processing.

Likewise, a separate programmable f_{VCO} divider configures the system clock (SCLK). The SCLK signal clocks the peripheral, DMA, and external memory buses. To optimize performance and power dissipation, these divider values, unlike the VCO multiplier settings, can be changed on-the-fly for a dynamic "coarse" frequency adjustment.

Frequency, Voltage and Power

Today's processors are normally designed in a process using CMOS FET switches, which are either fully *on* (and very lightly loaded) or fully *off* (except for leakage currents) during the steady state. The static power dissipation (quiescent power while the processor is idle) is caused by transistor leakage currents, whereas the dynamic power dissipation results from the charging and discharging of FET load capacitances at very high switching frequencies.

Let's take a look at a hypothetical transistor charging a load capacitance C. The charge (Q) stored in the device's equivalent load capacitance equals the capacitance multiplied by the voltage stored across it (which is the processor's core supply voltage, V_{DDINT}):

$$Q = CV_{DDINT}$$

Since device current to charge this capacitance is defined as the rate of change of charge with respect to time, the dynamic current, I_{dyn}, is given by

$$I_{dyn} = dQ/dt = C(dV_{DDINT}/dt)$$

Here, dV_{DDINT}/dt, or the rate of capacitor voltage change with respect to time, is a measure of how fast the capacitor is being charged and discharged. For a given clock frequency f, the fastest a charge/discharge cycle can take place is two periods, or $2/F$. Therefore,

$$dV_{DDINT}/dt = V_{DDINT}(f/2)$$

$$I_{dyn} = C(dV_{DDINT}/dt) = C(fV_{DDINT}/2)$$

Finally, dynamic power dissipated is proportional to $V_{DDINT} \times I_{dyn}$, or

$$P_{dyn} = KV_{DDINT}^2 \times f \, (K = constant)$$

Thus, it is apparent that dynamic power dissipation is proportional to the square of operating voltage and linearly proportional to operating frequency. Therefore, lowering f will decrease the dynamic power dissipation *linearly*, while reducing V_{DDINT} will lower it *exponentially* (see Figure 8.2).

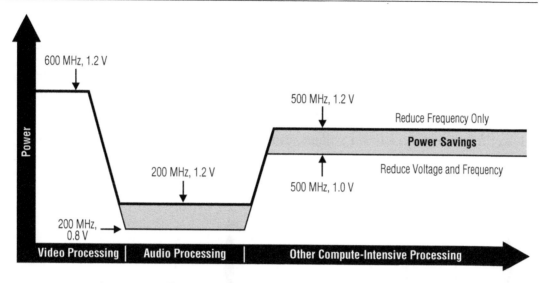

Figure 8.2 **Effects of V and F changes on power consumption**

Transistor physics dictates that higher operating voltages are necessary in order to run devices at higher frequencies. This is related to the need to charge the gate capacitance of the transistor in order to turn it on. Higher gate voltages will charge this finite capacitance faster than lower voltages.

As a practical example, a camera phone application illustrates how the ability to vary both frequency *and* voltage can be exploited to greatly extend battery life. If, for example, maximum performance (maximum core-clock frequency) is only required during a video connection, the core frequency can be lowered to some preset value when using the phone for a voice-only transaction. For operating time-insensitive value-added features only (e.g., a personal organizer), the frequency can be further reduced.

Changing just frequency (and not voltage) in a power-sensitive application is recommended only when the processor is already at its lowest voltage. In other words, it always makes sense, if possible, to run at the lowest possible voltage that supports the required frequency of operation.

Simply changing frequencies to save power dissipation does not always have the intended consequences. For example, if an application is running three sections of code, reducing the operating frequency for any one of these sections means that particular section of code will take longer to execute. But if the processor is running longer, the same amount of energy might be expended when the three sections are complete. If, for instance, the frequency is reduced by a factor of two, the code will take twice as long to execute, so (to a first degree) no net power savings is realized.

This is why, ideally, a processor will not only have a programmable operating frequency, but will also allow core voltage to be changed in concert with frequency changes. This way, less power will be consumed when running a section of code at a lower frequency *and* a lower voltage, even if execution time is longer. Figure 8.3 shows an illustration of this concept, with functions G1 and G2 running under different profiles.

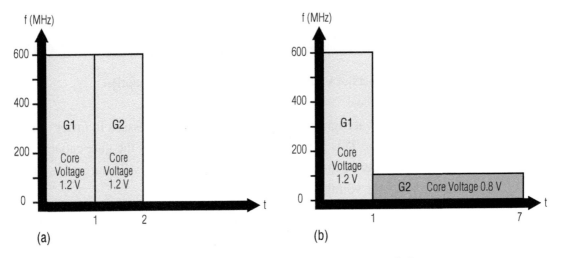

Figure 8.3 **Power dissipation vs. frequency and time**

This savings in energy consumption can be modeled by the following equation:

$$E_R/E_N = (f_{CR}/f_{CN}) \times (V_{DDR}/V_{DDN})^2 \times (t_{FR}/t_{FN})$$

where

- E_R/E_N is the ratio of reduced energy to nominal energy
- f_{CN} is the nominal core-clock frequency
- f_{CR} is the reduced core-clock frequency
- V_{DDN} is the nominal internal supply voltage
- V_{DDR} is the reduced internal supply voltage
- t_{FR} is the duration running at f_{CR}
- t_{FN} is the duration running at f_{CN}

For example, Figure 8.3 shows a scenario with the following characteristics:

- f_{CN} = 600 MHz
- f_{CR} = 100 MHz
- V_{DDN} = 1.2V
- V_{DDR} = 0.8V
- t_{FR} = 6
- t_{FN} = 1

Thus

$$(E_R/E_N) = (100/600) \times (0.8/1.2)^2 \times (6/1) = 0.44 \rightarrow 56\% \text{ savings!}$$

Processor Power Modes

Many applications involve a set of operating modes that differ markedly with respect to processing needs. Consider a battery-powered sensor that contains an embedded processor. One of the processor's peripherals might sample parameters of the surrounding environment. In this "Sleep" mode, which requires no computational power, the processor might read in sporadic packets of telemetry data. When it has read enough data to start crunching on it, the processor then enters a "Full On" mode where the entire processor is awake and running at maximum performance. There could also be a "Standby" or "Hibernate" mode that provides ultra-low power dissipation when no sensor info is expected and no processing is required.

To emerge from its various power-down modes, the processor receives some type of wakeup event. This can be triggered by an external stimulus, like a toggle of a flag pin, or by internal processor activities, like a DMA transfer completion or timer expiration.

Why would we want to bring the processor in and out of a sleep mode on a regular basis? Very simply, to reduce energy dissipation and extend battery life. In a Sleep state, the processor retains all of its internal contents because it still powered on, but at a greatly reduced current draw. Additionally, it only needs a few system clock cycles, usually an interval less than 50 ns, to wake up. This is much faster than a typical boot time (on the order of microseconds) that occurs when a processor is powered on.

Processors differ in the exact power modes they implement, but there are usually some commonalities among platforms. Blackfin processors have distinct operating modes (corresponding to different power profiles) that provide selectable performance and power dissipation characteristics. Table 8.1 summarizes the operational characteristics of each mode.

Table 8.1 **Operational characteristics of Blackfin power modes**

Operating Mode	Core-Clock	System Clock	Power Savings	Transition Time Back to Full-On
Full-On	Enabled	Enabled	Minimum	—
Active	Enabled	Enabled	Medium	Fastest
Sleep	Disabled	Enabled	High	
Deep Sleep	Disabled	Disabled	Maximum (V_{DDINT} on)	
Hibernate	Off	Off	Maximum (V_{DDINT} off)	Slowest

Full-On Mode

Full-on is the maximum performance mode. In this execution state, the processor and all enabled peripherals run at full speed. The PLL is enabled, so CCLK runs at a multiple of CLKIN.

Active Mode

In *Active* mode, the PLL is enabled but bypassed, so CCLK comes directly from CLKIN. Because CLKIN is sourced from an external oscillator input no greater than 40 MHz, this mode offers significant power savings. The system clock (SCLK) frequency is also reduced, because it never exceeds CCLK. This mode is crucial because it allows the processor to reprogram the PLL, which cannot occur when the PLL is actively generating the core and system clocks.

Sleep Mode

The *Sleep* mode significantly reduces power dissipation by disabling CCLK, which idles the processor core. However, SCLK remains enabled so that data transfer can still take place between peripherals and external memories. Activity on any of several peripherals can wake the processor from Sleep mode.

Deep-Sleep Mode

The *Deep-sleep* mode maximizes power savings while still retaining system state, by disabling the PLL, CCLK and SCLK. In this mode, the processor core and all peripherals except the real-time clock (RTC) are disabled, so only processor leakage current causes power dissipation. Only an RTC interrupt or hardware reset can wake the part from Deep-sleep mode. When used in combination with this mode, reducing the core voltage can minimize power consumption while maintaining the state of all on-chip memory.

Hibernate Mode

Whereas Deep-sleep mode can reduce power dissipation to a few milliwatts, *Hibernate* mode cuts it down to tens of microwatts. To achieve lowest possible power dissipation, this state allows the internal core supply (V_{DDINT}) to be powered down. This disables both CCLK and SCLK, and eliminates any leakage currents that would otherwise flow in the processor core and on-chip memories.

When the core is powered down, the internal state of the processor is not maintained. Therefore, any critical information stored internally (memory contents, register contents, and so on) must be written to a nonvolatile storage device prior to removing power. However, Hibernate mode provides a facility for keeping SDRAM "alive" even though the processor core has no power. By putting the SDRAM into self-refresh mode before entering Hibernate mode, and regaining control of it upon wakeup, the processor allows system state to be saved in volatile DRAM rather than nonvolatile flash memory.

The internal supply regulator can be woken up via a reset or RTC event. Powering down V_{DDINT} does not affect V_{DDEXT}, the processor's I/O supply. As long as V_{DDEXT} is still applied to the processor, external pins are maintained at high impedance to avoid compromising the integrity of other system connections. Of course, this situation implies that parts of the board are still powered on and functioning. Otherwise, it's hard to beat a powered-off board for low power dissipation!

Taking Advantage of Power Modes

As an example of how Hibernate mode is useful in a system, let's assume that for a GPS application we need the processor to wake up to obtain satellite positions on a regular basis. The real-time clock (RTC) can be set to wake up every second. In the meantime, the RTC consumes less than 30 µA, and the Blackfin processor consumes less than 50 µA of additional current. When the RTC alarm goes off, the processor wakes up, executes the algorithm that grabs the satellite coordinates, and then goes back to sleep. So in this application, with a low "on" duty cycle, only 80 μA is consumed for the majority of the operational timeline.

Let's now consider another representative situation where having different processor power modes can make a big difference. Think about a portable MP3 player that collects an input buffer, decodes the audio data into an output buffer in SDRAM, and then places the processor into Sleep mode until more data is required.

Because of MP3's low decode processing requirement, the processor can sleep during the interval when no decoding is required. For instance, the device might operate in a "25% decode, 75% sleep" profile, where 25% of the time, the core's current draw is, say, 30 mA, and 75% of the time it's only 15 mA. During its decode interval, the processor builds up decoded samples in external memory as quickly as possible. As soon as the desired buffer size is reached, the processor can go to sleep until the decoded data buffer needs to be refreshed.

So in other words, if a continuous-stream MP3 decode normally takes, say, 75 MHz, we could choose to run it at 250 MHz on a buffer collected during Sleep mode. This way, the processor's running at a higher operational level than necessary, but only for a short interval (before it goes back to sleep). By maximizing sleep time, we can save power dissipation. This approach only makes sense as part of a system like a portable media player, where video processing is needed sometimes as well. Otherwise, for just MP3 decoding, a much lower performance (and lower power) processor can be used.

How do we manage the rate at which the processor wakes up? Recall from our discussion in Chapter 3 that a 2D DMA can generate interrupts after every line. In this example, the audio buffer can be double-buffered, where each buffer is a line, from the 2D DMA perspective. The interrupt upon completion of each output line indicates that it is time for the processor to fill the buffer that was just emptied, with new data. The processor easily generates its decoded output buffer before the serial port is ready to transmit it. As soon as the processor fills this buffer, it goes back to sleep, and the process repeats continuously.

As a side note, in the above example, using an asynchronous SRAM device instead of SDRAM can provide further cost and power savings (see the "Relative Power for External Devices" section at the end of this chapter). Of course, SRAM does not offer the same performance level as SDRAM, but for audio data that is accessed in 16- or

32-bit words, SRAM performance is adequate. This is because parallel accesses by a DMA controller, even if they occur at slower SRAM rates, can easily keep the serial interface fed with decoded data.

Even if an application requires SDRAM because of a large code base or the need for increased decode performance, it may still make sense to have both SRAM and SDRAM in the design for the time intervals when only lower performance is required. While the bill of materials will increase, using both in concert intelligently can save the most power in the system. The SDRAM can be used during the portion of the application requiring highest performance, and it can be placed in self-refresh mode whenever the processor goes to sleep. During intervals of active processing, the current draw will be dominated by the processor and the SDRAM. This is because SRAM, although not as efficient as SDRAM on a mW/bit basis, is normally present in much lower bit quantities than SDRAM is.

Power Domains

Embedded processor core voltages often run at levels below typical I/O supply rails. That is, a device might run its core and PLL internally anywhere from 0.8V to 1.8V, while its I/O might be powered to a 1.8V, 2.5V, 3.3V, or even 5V supply rail. There are several reasons for this. For one, high-performance processors use small-geometry silicon processes in order to attain high speed and low dynamic power. However, these same processes are physically limited in supply voltage range.

Moreover, the processor needs to connect to standard industry interfaces and devices (like memories, peripheral bridge chips, and the like), and these overwhelmingly require 2.5V/3.3V/5V drive capability, or at least tolerance. Recently, 1.8V memories have staked their claim in the low-power memory space, offering a savings of about $(1.8V/2.5V)^2$, or 50%, in power dissipation from memory transactions.

Additionally, having separate power domains reduces noise coupling between the highly sensitive processor core realm and the sometimes unpredictable external environment. It also allows the processor core voltage to be varied without disrupting connections to external devices.

Finally, sometimes part of the processor needs to stay powered on, while other parts can be shut off to reduce power consumption. A good example of this is an RTC supply (usually powered by a battery), which can be used to wake up the rest of the processor when a preprogrammed timing event occurs.

Other Considerations

Power-Friendly Architectures

An often-overlooked means of reducing power consumption for a given application is to choose an efficient processor architecture for that application. Such features as specialized instructions and fast memory structures can reduce power consumption significantly by lessening overall algorithm execution time. Moreover, power-conscious applications make it imperative to structure algorithms efficiently, taking advantage of native architectural features like hardware loop buffers and instruction/ data caches. This is important—complex algorithms often consume more power, since they use more resources. If an algorithm is optimized, it takes fewer instructions to execute. The sooner it completes all its steps, the sooner core voltage and frequency can be reduced.

Some architectures also support selective disabling of unused functional blocks (e.g., on-chip memories, peripherals, clocks, etc.), as well as automatic disabling of unused circuits. In the case of Blackfin processors, for instance, internal clocks are routed only to enabled portions of the device.

Symmetric Multiprocessing

In Chapter 7, we discussed the notion of symmetric multiprocessing (SMP) on a dual-core processor. We mentioned that using an SMP approach can actually save power over a single-core alternative. That is, even when an application fits on a single core processor, the dual-core SMP system can be exploited to reduce overall energy consumption. As an example, if an application requires a 500 MHz clock speed to run on a single-core processor like the ADSP-BF533, it must also operate at a higher volt-age (1.1V) in order to attain that speed.

However, if the same application is partitioned across a dual-core device like the ADSP-BF561, each core can run at around 250 MHz, and the voltage on each core can be lowered significantly—to 0.8V. Because power dissipation is proportional to frequency and to the square of operating voltage, this voltage reduction from 1.1V to 0.8V (coupled with the frequency reduction from 500 MHz to 250 MHz) can have a marked impact, actually saving energy compared with the single-core solution.

Software Tools

Providing yet another way to optimize power consumption, the processor's development tools suite can offer useful features that profile applications to determine the exact processing requirements for each section of an algorithm. For example, Figure 8.4 shows the Statistical Profiler in the *Blackfin VisualDSP++* tools suite. It quantifies how much time is spent in any given code segment, thus allowing selective tuning of code blocks to improve performance. Using this technique in battery-powered applications optimizes code so that it can run for a shorter duration, thus allowing frequency and/or voltage reduction sooner than in the unoptimized case.

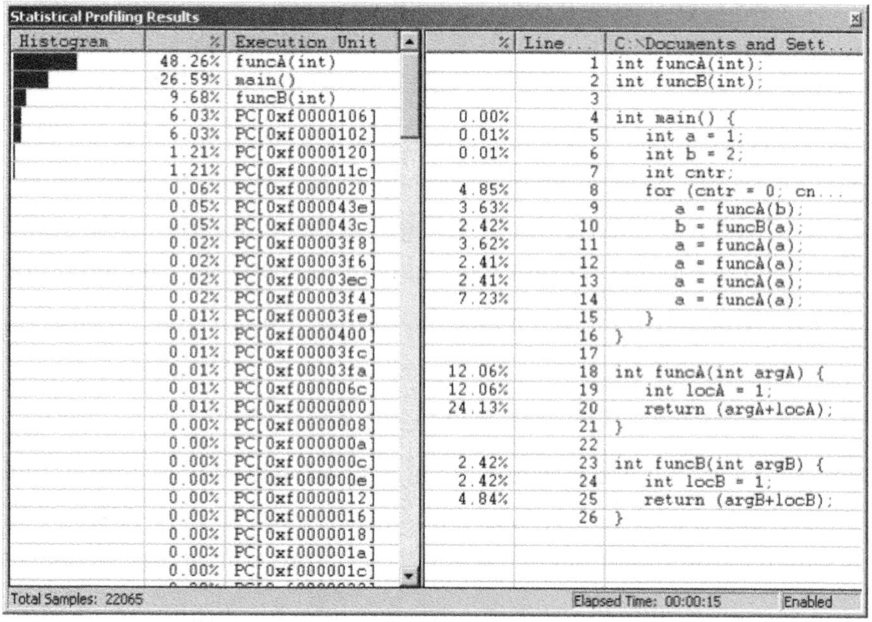

A Code Profiler shows where most time is spent during program execution.

Figure 8.4 **VisualDSP++ Statistical Profiler**

Voltage Regulation

A crucial aspect of system-level design is properly architecting the power supply subsystem. In this context, voltage regulation is key. Some processors have on-chip voltage regulation control, which assists in transitioning between different core voltage levels and power modes. The idea here is to reduce core voltage when maximum processor performance is not needed, thus lowering both the ac and dc power dissipation of the processor.

In any case, it's important to review some underlying concepts and structures of voltage regulation, with the goal of guiding you to the proper architectural and component-level choices for your system. It should be noted that much of the following discussion on linear and switching regulators originates from References 63 and 65 in the Appendix. These are excellent resources to consult for further detail.

Linear Regulators

The simplest way to provide a regulated core voltage is through a linear regulator. This device converts a wide range of input voltages to a single, well-controlled output voltage by dissipating power across a transistor switch. For instance, a linear regulator might convert a 3.3V input to a fixed 1.2V output. If the 1.2V supply draws 100 mA, then the 3.3V input must also draw 100 mA, and the difference is lost in power dissipation. In this case, it's equal to (3.3V–1.2V) × 100 mA, or 210 mW.

This kind of power loss does not excite designers of battery-operated devices. Early linear regulator designs needed the input voltage to be around 2V higher than the regulated output voltage. This "dropout voltage" is the minimum voltage differential between input and output in order for the regulator to keep doing its job properly.

Nowadays, low-dropout (LDO) regulators shrink this difference to a few hundred millivolts. So for example, if a 1.8V supply already exists in the system, using an LDO to generate a 1.2V regulated output isn't necessarily a bad idea.

Advantages of LDOs, and linear regulators in general, include low noise, minimal parts count, and general ease of use. A major disadvantage is poor efficiency for combinations of high current loads and large input-to-output voltage differentials.

Figure 8.5 shows a simplified model of a linear regulator. Most linear regulator ICs today have an integrated pass device and require only a couple of small capacitors and perhaps a voltage-setting resistor. Low-current LDOs can be quite tiny indeed, and they find wide use in portable devices.

Figure 8.6 provides a somewhat more detailed circuit diagram of a linear regulator. The onboard voltage reference V_{REF} is compared to a sample of the output voltage V_{OUT} to generate an error signal that modulates the pass device in order to keep V_{OUT} at the proper voltage. R1 and R2 set the output voltage via a simple voltage divider relationship. Depending on the regulator, they are either supplied by the user or integrated into the IC device.

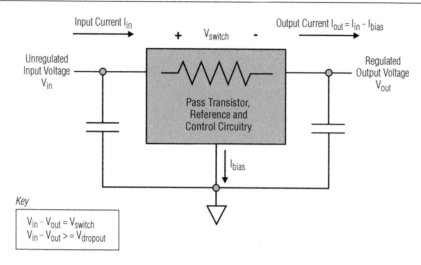

Figure 8.5 **Linear regulator**

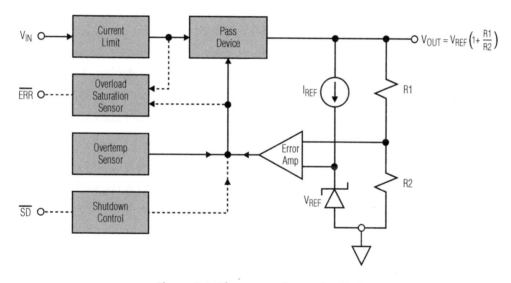

Figure 8.6 **Linear regulator, detailed**

Switching Regulators

Because of the relatively poor efficiency garnered by using LDOs at high input-to-output voltage differentials, a switching regulator ("switcher") is often the best choice for a primary regulator in battery-conscious applications. Secondarily, LDOs can be appended to switcher outputs as appropriate to provide tighter tolerances or to save board space.

Switching regulators use a clever arrangement of energy storage components and transistor switching to generate a fixed output voltage from a widely varying input voltage, without dissipating the $(V_{in}-V_{out}) \times I_{out}$ product as power loss.

There are many kinds of switching topologies. To name a few common ones, the "buck converter" regulates from a higher voltage to a lower one, the "boost converter" steps up a lower voltage to a higher one, and the "buck-boost" acts as one or the other, depending on the nature of the input and output voltages.

The boost converter is popular for applications like charge pumps, panel backlights and photo flash units, but it's not efficient for powering low-voltage, high-current loads. Because of the buck converter's wide applicability in sourcing processor power supplies, we'll focus on this topology.

Step-Down Switching Regulator

Figure 8.7 shows the basic circuit for an ideal step-down ("buck") regulator. In the Blackfin processor's case, the error amplifier and switch control are internal to the processor, but in general, these are available as stand-alone ICs that, depending on output current requirements, often integrate the FET switching device. Appropriately, these ICs often cost a little more than a "buck," but just by fortunate coincidence! All other components shown (diode, inductor, load bypass capacitor) are external to the IC, because of their sheer size and/or performance requirements.

Here's how the buck converter works. When the switch is closed, L and C_{load} are charged through the input voltage source. The Schottky diode D is back-biased in this case, so it's pretty much out of commission. The longer the switch stays closed, the more charge becomes stored. When the switch opens, the inductor cannot instantaneously stop the flow of current through itself, so it continues to pump charge into C_{load} via the now forward-conducting diode D.

The switch control circuit senses the output voltage and compares it to an expected value. The error amplifier then generates a difference signal that converts into a pulse-width modulated (PWM) waveform that drives the gate of the FET switch in order to adjust the total "on time" percentage ($t_{on}/(t_{on} + t_{off})$, also called duty ratio) of the switch. The larger the input voltage, the shorter the t_{on}. This makes sense intuitively, since a higher input voltage will cause a higher current ramp through the inductor, which charges the output capacitor faster to its target dc value.

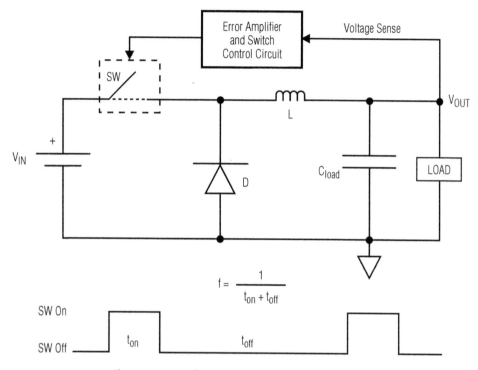

Figure 8.7 **Basic step-down (buck) converter**

The PWM waveform has a constant period ($t_{on} + t_{off}$), but a variable pulse-width that depends on the error amplifier's output. It should be noted that, although this is a common configuration, not all buck regulators have this characteristic. Some have a pulse burst modulation (PBM), or "gated oscillator" methodology. Anyway, given the PWM assumption, Figures 8.8b and c show the waveforms associated with the buck regulator's operation.

Closing the switch causes a voltage differential of $V_{IN}-V_{OUT}$ across the inductor, and this generates an inductor current slope of $(V_{IN}-V_{OUT})/L$ (see Figure 8.8b). Opening the switch causes the entire output voltage V_{OUT} to appear across the inductor. Because an inductor cannot change current through itself instantaneously, this voltage differential is negative, and current now changes according to a slope of $(-V_{OUT}/L)$.

Figure 8.8b illustrates the diode and switch currents that sum to compose the total current through the inductor. Observe that the switch current is identical to the input current, whereas the inductor current is the same as the output current.

(a) Buck Converter Waveforms

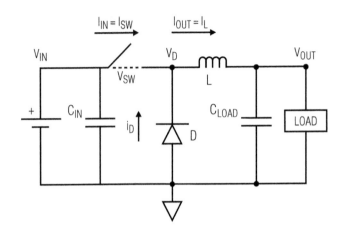

(b) Continuous Mode

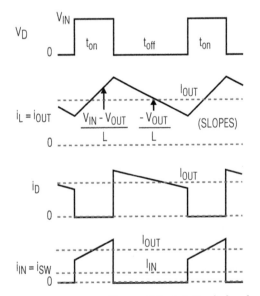

(c) Discontinuous Mode

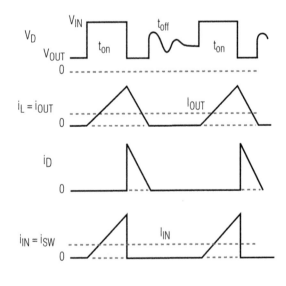

Figure 8.8 **(a) Basic buck converter (b) Continuous mode waveforms (c) Discontinuous mode waveforms**

Keep in mind these waveforms assume we're using ideal components. We'll see shortly what this means in practice, when we're forced to use nonideal parts.

In the steady state, the basic relationship between the input and output voltage is:

$$V_{OUT} = V_{IN} \times \frac{t_{on}}{t_{on} + t_{off}}$$

This is a surprisingly straightforward equation which shows that output voltage simply depends upon input voltage and the switch's duty ratio. We should note that this equation does assume that there is always at least some current flowing through the inductor, so that it is operating in *continuous* mode.

If, however, the output load current is decreased to the point where the inductor current goes to zero between cycles, this represents *discontinuous* mode, which is important to understand, given that processors tend to have widely varying output current requirements depending on the particular algorithm profiles at a given instant in time. Refer to Figure 8.8c for the slightly modified waveforms of discontinuous mode.

When the switch is closed, the circuit operates identically to the continuous case. It's when the switch opens that things get interesting. Here, the inductor current decreases all the way to zero, at which point it tries to reverse direction, but is blocked from doing so by the diode's polarity. As a result, the voltage at the input of the inductor shoots up to V_{OUT} in order to maintain zero current across itself. This causes a ringing effect between the inductor and the stray capacitances of the diode and switch, C_D and C_{SW}. The oscillation occurs at a frequency f_o indicated by:

$$f_o = \frac{1}{2\pi\sqrt{L(C_D + C_{SW})}}$$

If the ringing generates electromagnetic interference problems, it can be damped with an RC "snubber" circuit, at the cost of reduced switcher efficiency.

Viewed from another angle, we can determine at what load current the inductor will enter discontinuous operation mode. This relationship is given by the following equation:

$$I_{OUT} > \frac{V_{OUT}\left(1 - \dfrac{V_{OUT}}{V_{IN}}\right)}{2Lf}.$$

Efficiency

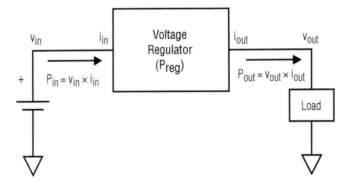

P_{reg} = Power dissipation in regulator components

Energy must be conserved, so $P_{in} = P_{out} + P_{reg}$

Efficiency $\eta = \dfrac{P_{out}}{P_{in}}$

$\eta \longrightarrow 100\%$ as $P_{reg} \longrightarrow 0$

Figure 8.9 **Efficiency**

The whole point of a voltage regulator is to convert an energy source at a given (range of) input voltage to an energy source at a stable output voltage across temperature, input conditions, and load variations. As the First Law of Thermodynamics states, energy in a closed system is conserved; that is, the energy entering a system is equal to the energy exiting the system plus the energy converted within the system (to heat, for instance). For voltage conversion, we're concerned with the efficiency (η) of a system (as in Figure 8.9), which measures how effectively the input energy was converted to output energy that's usable by the load.

In other words, we know that in a system where there's no energy dissipation through heat, $(V_{out} \times I_{out} = V_{in} \times I_{in})$. Since there's no such thing as a perfect system, the equation becomes $(V_{out} \times I_{out} = \eta(V_{in} \times I_{in}))$.

In the case of the linear regulator, input current roughly equals output current, whereas input voltage is greater than output voltage. Thus, from the equation above, we see that efficiency must decrease in a manner directly proportional to the voltage mismatch between V_{in} and V_{out}.

For a buck switching regulator, V_{in} can be much greater than V_{out}, but I_{in} can then be much less than I_{out}. This leads to much higher efficiencies when $V_{in} >> V_{out}$. Whereas LDOs often dwell in the 40%–60% efficiency range, many buck regulators today can achieve efficiencies of 95% and greater, with proper component selection.

Component Selection for Step-Down Regulators

Schottky Diode and FET Switch

The diode in buck regulator circuits is usually of the Schottky variety, because Schottkys have low forward voltage drops, low capacitance, and quick recovery time between back-bias and forward-bias operation. Power dissipation loss through the diode is roughly the average current through the diode multiplied by its forward voltage drop.

To minimize the efficiency loss that this forward drop causes during the FET switch's open state, some designs will eliminate the diode entirely, in favor of a second FET switch that is often packaged with the main switch. In this so-called "synchronous switcher" implementation, the switch control circuitry is usually modified to ensure that both FETs are not on simultaneously, as this would create a short circuit between input voltage and ground.

The main selection criteria for the FET switch are the peak current rating, gate charge, threshold voltage, and on-resistance $R_{ds,on}$. The on resistance is usually in the 5 to 100 milliohm range, and lower values lead to higher efficiency ratios, since $(I_{switch})^2 \times R_{ds,on}$ is the power dissipation loss through the FET.

The gate charge required to turn the FET on and off is an important parameter because the gate drive signal must overcome the gate capacitance, which increases with the FET's output current capability and physical size. The gate charge current must be sourced from the PWM generation circuit, and it can detract significantly from efficiency. This efficiency loss, which worsens with higher input voltages and switching frequencies, is one reason why it's best to use only a FET switch large enough for the application at hand, but not unnecessarily large.

Now that we're talking about nonideal components, let's update our basic buck regulator equation, referring back to Figure 8.8. When the switch is closed, a voltage of $V_{IN} - V_{OUT} - V_{SW}$ appears across the inductor. V_{SW} is the voltage drop across the switch due to the presence of $R_{ds,on}$. When the switch opens, the inductor current ramps down into a voltage of $(V_{OUT} + V_D)$ across the output load, where V_D represents the average forward drop across the diode. Accounting for these nonideal characteristics, the basic relationship of Figure 8.8 now becomes:

$$\left(\frac{V_{IN} - V_{OUT} - V_{SW}}{L}\right) t_{on} = \left(\frac{V_{OUT} + V_D}{L}\right) t_{off}$$

Inductor Considerations

Although we have been assuming the opposite, there is, alas, no such thing as an ideal inductor. A real inductor, modeled in Figure 8.10a, has a host of physical properties that interact with one another, causing both linear and nonlinear performance degradation. These include things like inductance value, saturation current, temperature effects, self-resonant frequency, physical material properties, operating current, ... and the list goes on.

As you can see, selecting an appropriate inductor for a switching regulator application is a function of many parameters. We'll just cover some of the salient ones here, and you can refer to Reference 63 in the Appendix for more detailed information.

Inductance Value

It is usually not necessary to specify an inductance value precisely, as long as the chosen value is bounded by design equations typically provided by the switching controller IC data sheet, which will look something like the following:

$$L = \left(\frac{1}{f}\right) \frac{V_{IN} - V_{OUT} - V_{SW}}{V_{IN} - V_{SW} + V_D} \left(\frac{V_{OUT} + V_D}{I_{PP}}\right)$$

This equation assumes that the peak-to-peak ripple current (I_{pp}) is about 20% of the average output current (I_{out}), well within the 10% to 30% common design practice.

Once you know the V_{in} extremes, you can calculate your inductance range following the guidance of the equation above. Decreasing the inductor value will increase I_{pp}, while increasing the value results in smaller ripple.

(a)

(b)

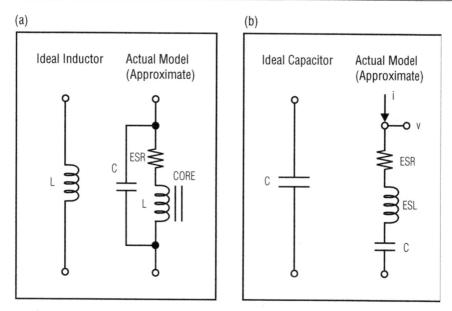

Figure 8.10 **Ideal vs. actual models for (a) inductor and (b) capacitor**

Saturation Current

One very important inductor effect to avoid is magnetic core saturation, which can compromise the entire switching regulator design and introduce noise into the regulator's load. Figure 8.11 illustrates our familiar triangular inductor waveform, charging to a maximum of I_{peak}, and then discharging to some nominal level. However, if I_{peak} were to exceed the rating of the chosen inductor, the incoming magnetic flux would saturate the inductor's magnetic core, reducing the effective inductance. This, in turn, increases inductor current exponentially. This is why it's imperative to give yourself

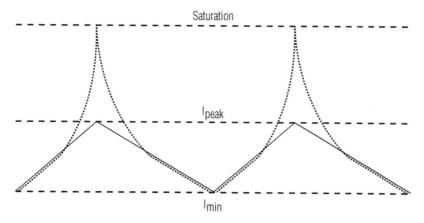

Figure 8.11 **Inductor saturation**

a wide degree of design margin (over input voltage, current load and temperature swings, for instance) when selecting an inductor with a given peak current rating.

DC Resistance

Referring to the nonideal inductor model of Figure 8.10a, we see that there's an equivalent series resistance, or ESR, connected to the inductance L. This resistance, R_{DC}, comes about as a result of physical inductor properties like number of wire turns, wire size, and volume of the magnetic core. Because this acts as a series resistance on the order of tens or hundreds of milliohms, it can have a significant bearing on regulator efficiency, causing a power loss of $(I_{out})^2 \times R_{DC}$. Therefore, it's important to choose an inductor with a low-enough ESR to minimize the impact on overall efficiency.

Self-Resonant Frequency

From the nonideal inductor model of Figure 8.10a, it is apparent that the inductor will self-resonate because of its distributed capacitance and its inherent inductance. This self-resonant frequency is calculated as follows:

$$f_{resonance} = \frac{1}{2\pi}\sqrt{\frac{1}{LC}}$$

It is good design practice to choose a switching frequency for the buck regulator that is no more than 10% of $f_{resonance}$.

Capacitor Considerations

Technology/Construction

Choosing a particular capacitor technology is quite an involved process, since there are many different dielectrics with varying physical properties that may or may not suit its use for a particular switching circuit function. Table 8.2 provides a comparison between different capacitor types and where they are most useful in switching regulator designs.

Capacitance Value

As with inductors, capacitors have nonideal qualities that result in the equivalent circuit shown in Figure 8.10b. This is why it's crucial to choose capacitors wisely in switching regulator circuits. The input capacitor serves primarily as a power supply

Table 8.2 **Capacitor technology comparison**

	Aluminum Electrolytic	Tantalum Electrolytic	Ceramic	Polymer/Film
Benefits	• Low cost • Good storage density • Adequate ESR	• Excellent storage density • Small size • Good temperature & frequency stability • Low ESR	• Very low ESR • Small • No voltage derating • Low cost for small values • Unpolarized	• Very low ESR • No voltage derating • Good temperature & Frequency stability • Unpolarized • No surge current problem
Drawbacks	• Bad cold performance • Bad frequency performance • Large size • Ultimately fail (electrolyte dries up) • Polarized	• In-rush/surge current failure mode • Can be costly • Need voltage derating • Polarized	• Poor temp stability for large values (high-k dielectrics) • Costly for large values	• Costly • Can be large (moderate storage density)
Primary Uses	• Input storage cap • Output storage cap	• Input storage cap (if surge protection present) • Output storage cap	• Input storage cap • High-frequency filter cap	• Input storage cap • Output storage cap

bypass, keeping the input voltage constant despite the spikes caused by the switching element. Because of this, it must have low impedance at high frequencies. High values provide better bypassing, but at the expense of higher ESR. The input capacitor should be placed very close to the switching element, and it should be accompanied by some high-frequency ceramic bypass capacitors.

On the output side, the capacitor must also have low impedance, because any equivalent series resistance translates directly into output voltage ripple. However, since the output current is continuous, it's not as important for the output capacitor to have good high-frequency performance. Also, some ESR is necessary to help provide feedback loop stability. Output capacitors are usually high in value, because they act as bulk storage for the target load, as well as low-pass filter elements for the switching-induced output voltage ripple.

The output capacitor, C_{load}, must be large enough so that the output voltage does not droop significantly when the switch is open. Therefore, the capacitance needed is a function of the current drawn by the load. One equation for determining minimum C_{load} value at switching frequency f_{SW} is:

$$C_{min} = \frac{\Delta I_{Lpp}}{\left(f_{SW} \times \Delta V_{out}\right)}$$

where ΔI_{Lpp} is the output ripple current, and ΔV_{out} is the acceptable output voltage ripple.

Ripple Current

It is important to specify capacitors that have appropriate ripple current ratings for the task at hand. As Figure 8.12 shows, on the input side, ripple current is roughly equivalent to a square wave of peak amplitude I_{out}, so the rms ripple is approximately $I_{out}/2$. The output current, on the other hand, looks like a sawtooth waveform with a peak-to-peak amplitude of $0.2I_{out}$ (as an example). Of course, it's wise to derate these calculated values by another 25% or more, to add design margin.

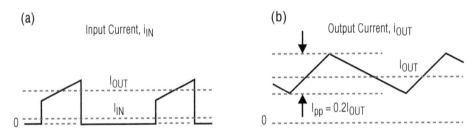

Figure 8.12 **Example input and output capacitor ripple current waveforms**

Practically speaking, it's often beneficial to parallel two or more capacitors together at the input and/or output. Not only does this help to achieve the desired capacitance value, but it also reduces ESR and ESL and shares the ripple current requirement.

Input and Output Filtering

As we have seen, switchers create ripple currents in their input and output capacitors, which translates into conducted noise via the nonideal ESR and ESL capacitor properties. Added to this is radiated noise caused mainly by parasitic inductances in board traces and circuit components, as well as by inductors with unshielded magnetic cores. Both of these types of noise will be present to some extent in any switching regulator design and must be controlled by proper component selection, good board layout, shielding and/or filtering.

Given the fact that, as Figure 8.12 shows, input ripple current is pulsating, it might be necessary to add extra input filtering to prevent the switching frequency and other high-frequency artifacts from feeding back into the input supply. A small series inductor (shown as L_{input} in Figure 8.13) is often sufficient for this filtering need.

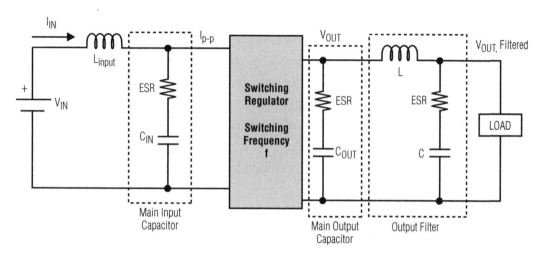

Figure 8.13 **Switching regulator input and output filtering**

On the output side, ripple filtering can be accomplished in a couple of ways. Since output ripple is directly proportional to ESR value, one way to minimize ripple is to add several parallel capacitors to reduce ESR. Another is to add a post-LC filter, as shown in Figure 8.13, that provides a sharp second-order attenuation in frequency passband. However, in going this route, it's important to choose an inductor with a low DC resistance (as well as a low-ESR filter capacitor), since any resistive loss directly reduces efficiency.

Switching Frequency

The choice of switching frequency is very important to the overall design of the buck regulator. The higher the frequency, the smaller the main inductor and load bypass capacitor can be. This is great for board layout and cost, and often for reduction of radiated emissions as well. However, a higher switching frequency causes more loss in the $R_{ds,on}$ of the FET switch and the "on" resistance of the Schottky diode. To accommodate different design needs, a switching controller IC will sometimes allow a range of different switching frequency options, programmable via an external resistor or, in the case of Blackfin processors with integrated controllers, via writing to a memory-mapped register.

Calculating System Power

Let's turn our attention now to calculating the total power dissipated by the processor subsystem. This includes the power drawn by the processor in all relevant power domains—the internal core domain (V_{DDINT}), the I/O supply (V_{DDEXT}) and any other separately powered circuit portions (a real-time clock supply, for instance, that stays battery-powered while the rest of the processor is off). We cannot overstate the importance of seeking out a thorough discussion of power dissipation for a given processor, because processors are notoriously difficult to characterize for power. Though you might wish otherwise, the silicon vendor almost certainly didn't recreate your exact configuration when taking power measurements. Here, we'll provide a general overview of the factors that you should take into account when arriving at a power estimate for your processor. For a more detailed analysis, refer to References 64 and 65 in the Appendix.

Several variables affect the power requirements of an embedded system. Measurements published in the processor data sheet are indicative of typical parts running under typical conditions. However, these numbers do not necessarily reflect the actual numbers that may occur for a given processor under nontypical conditions. The fabrication process plays a large role in estimated power calculations. In addition, ambient temperature, core-clock and system-clock frequencies, supply voltages, pin capacitances, power modes used, application code, and peripheral utilization all contribute to the average total power dissipated.

Average Power Dissipation

Assuming that a system can be in several possible states, to calculate a true average power dissipation you need to run a statistical analysis to determine what percentage of the time the processor spends in each of the defined states, apply those percentages to the estimated power draw calculated for that state, and then add each of the state averages. For example:

```
STATE1 = 20% of application
STATE2 = 10% of application
STATE3 = 70% of application
```

If statistical analysis yields the above numbers for percentage of time spent in a particular system state, the total average power (P_{TOT}) is summarized as follows:

$$P_{TOT} = (0.2 \times P_{STATE1}) + (0.1 \times P_{STATE2}) + (0.7 \times P_{STATE3})$$

The average power number that results from this equation shows how much the processor is loading a power source over time. Do not use this calculation to size the power supply! The power supply must also support peak requirements. Average power estimates are useful in terms of expected power dissipation within a system, but designs must support the worst-case conditions under which the application can be run.

Total average power consumption (P_{DDTOT}) is the sum of the average power dissipated in each power domain in an application:

Since power is defined as the product of the supply voltage and the current sourced by that supply, the power dissipated in each domain is described by the equations:

$$P_{DDINT} = V_{DDINT} \times I_{DDINT}$$
$$P_{DDEXT} = V_{DDEXT} \times I_{DDEXT}$$

where we assume average values for current and power, measured at constant voltage. The total average power dissipated by the processor is the sum of these components:

$$P_{DDTOT} = P_{DDINT} + P_{DDEXT}$$

Bear in mind that, for your application, additional power domains, such as a real-time clock domain, might also be relevant.

Average Internal Power Consumption

Internal power is composed of two components, one static and one dynamic. The static component, as its name implies, is independent of transistor switching frequency. It is a reflection of "leakage" current, which is a phenomenon that causes transistors to dissipate power even when they are not switching. Leakage is a factor in high-performance CMOS circuit design and is a function of both the supply voltage and the ambient operating temperature at which the part is expected to run. Leakage current increases as temperature and/or voltage increases.

The dynamic power component is largely independent of temperature and is a function of supply voltage and switching frequency. The faster the transistors switch, the more voltage swings occur per unit time. The higher the supply voltage, the larger the voltage swing between the on and off transistor states. Thus, the dynamic component will increase with increasing voltage and frequency.

Another major consideration in estimating average internal power is the type of application code expected to run on the processor. You need to pay careful attention to specifications provided in processor data sheets, since they usually provide data on only a targeted set of applications or operating conditions: for instance, with the processor running a 75% Dual-MAC and 25% Dual-ALU algorithm while fetching data from L1 memory. Because of the huge variability of usage scenarios, device vendors can't provide specific power data for every situation. Thus, you need to extrapolate from this data for your own system.

Average External Power Dissipation

Average external power dissipation refers to the average power dissipated in the V_{DDEXT} power domain. All enabled peripherals contribute to this overall external power value, based on several parameters:

- Number of output pins (O_P)
- Number of pins toggling each clock cycle (TR)
- Frequency at which the peripheral runs (f)
- Utilization factor → percentage of time that the peripheral is on (U)
- Load capacitance (C)
- Voltage swing (V_{DDEXT})

The equation used to approximate each component's contribution to the total external power is:

$$P_{DDEXT} = (V_{DDEXT})^2 \times C \times (f/2) \times (O_P \times TR) \times U$$

The worst external pin power scenario is when the load capacitor continuously charges and discharges, requiring the pin to toggle continuously. Since the state of the pin can change only once per cycle, the maximum toggling frequency is f/2. Table 8.3 contains data for a realistic example that runs several peripherals simultaneously. Actual results may vary, but again, the intent is to help designers size the power supplies.

This model assumes that each output pin changes state every clock cycle, which is a worst-case model, except in the case of the SDRAM (because the number of output pins transitioning each clock cycle will be less than the maximum number of output pins). Note that the SDRAM itself will also draw power from its own source supply, unrelated to its I/O power draw.

Table 8.3 **Example calculation of external I/O power dissipation**

Peripheral	Frequency in MHz (f)	# of Output Pins (O_P)	Pin Capacitance in pF (CL)	Toggle Ratio (TR)	Utilization (U)	VDDEXT (V)	Pout @ 2.5V (mW)
PPI	30	9	15	1	1.00	2.50	12.66
SPORT0	4	2	15	1	1.00	2.50	0.38
SPORT1	4	2	15	1	1.00	2.50	0.38
UART	0.115	2	15	1	0.25	2.50	0.003
SDRAM	133	36	15	0.25	0.50	2.50	28.05
Total External Power Dissipation @ 2.5V (est mW)							41.47

Battery Fundamentals

Let's talk now about batteries—those marvels of the electronics world that generate electrical energy via a chemical reaction. Battery selection is a very important process that must take into account peak and average energy needs, device form factor, time between recharges/replacements, and voltage requirements. For portable applications, energy density (gravimetric and volumetric) is crucial. Gravimetric energy density pertains to energy per unit weight, whereas volumetric relates to energy per unit volume.

Actually, a battery consists of one or more *cells* configured in a uniform form factor. The chemical reaction within each cell generates a nominal output voltage. Cell capacity is measured in units of milliamp-hours, or mAh. A cell with a "C rate" of 100 mAh can supply 100 mA of current at its rated voltage for 1 hour. It's important to note that a cell is normally rated at a typical discharge rate (specified as a fraction of the "C rate"), and deviations from this rate alter the expected lifetime (or time between charges) of the battery.

For instance, if a cell has a "C rate" of 1000 mAh at a C/5 discharge rate, then it can run for 5 hours at a current load of C/5, or 200 mA. However, if this battery were used for an application requiring a 500-mA load, its capacity would run out before 2 hours (= 1000 mAh/500 mA), because the discharge rate of C/2 far exceeds the 1000-mAh rating at C/5. Conversely, if the battery load were 100 mA, it would last longer than the expected 10 hours, because the discharge rate is lower than the C rating of the device.

Connecting several identical cells in series creates a battery with a voltage corresponding to the sum of all cell voltages, but with a capacity corresponding to that of a single cell. For instance, connecting three 1.5V, 400-mAh cells in series creates a 4.5V, 400-mAh battery.

On the other hand, connecting cells in parallel creates a battery with the same voltage as a single cell, but with a capacity corresponding to the sum of all cells. So connecting our same 3 1.5V, 400 mAh cells in parallel creates a 1.5V, 1200 mAh battery.

There are two types of battery cells: primary and secondary. Primary cells are meant for single use, after which point they're discarded. Secondary cells, on the other hand, are rechargeable, and they're often good for several hundred charge-discharge cycles before they lose their ability to store charge. Primary cells usually have higher volumetric efficiency and energy density than secondary cells, as well as longer shelf lives. That said, rechargeable batteries are of more interest for portable embedded multimedia systems, because it's not practical to buy new batteries for every 4 hours of movie viewing, unless your last name is Duracell.

Battery geometries are varied, with a wide range of common cylindrical and button form factors. Fortunately, both disposable and rechargeable batteries tend to come in several mainstream sizes. Generally, the larger sizes correspond to higher storage capacities.

It's very important to understand that a battery actually puts out a range of voltages throughout its life (or between charges). The "open-circuit voltage" is the voltage with nothing connected, and it's usually higher than the rated voltage of the battery. The "working voltage" refers to the battery voltage during normal operation, under varying loads. Under heavier current loads, the voltage will droop to some level below the rated voltage, but the battery will still function until it loses the capacity to generate a usable voltage for the system. At this point, it needs to be recharged (or thrown out, if it's a primary battery system).

Based on the above discussion, it should be clear that we cannot presume that a battery outputs a regulated voltage, and thus it's often necessary to condition a battery's output and have appropriate circuit mechanisms in place to detect undervoltage conditions.

Primary Batteries

Alkaline

Primary batteries for most portable devices are either alkaline-based or lithium-based. Alkaline cells are inexpensive and have long shelf life, and they're good for high-drain applications. They have an open-circuit voltage around 1.6V, and a nominal operating voltage of 1.5V. However, their output voltage can droop as they discharge.

Lithium

Lithium disposables, on the other hand, have good retention of output voltage across the discharge cycle, and they also have outstanding energy density, peak current capability, shelf life and performance across temperature. Their nominal voltage is 3.0V, which allows a single cell to replace a pair of alkaline cells. Lithium batteries are generally more expensive than alkalines, but their long operating life and high peak current abilities (essential for digital camera flashbulbs, for instance) make them the primary cell of choice for handhelds.

Silver Oxide

This common "button cell" is an excellent choice for small electronic devices requiring relatively low current drain. With a nominal voltage around 1.5V and C ratings of 100–200 mAh, these cells can power watches, miniature games, and the like. They exhibit very stable voltage over their discharge interval, and they have long shelf life and good performance across temperature as well.

Zinc Air

These batteries are most commonly found in hearing aids and other medical and monitoring devices. They offer stable output voltage of 1.4V, and have the highest volumetric energy density for miniature batteries. They're activated by peeling off an adhesive tab to start the chemical reaction by exposing the cathode to air. Once exposure occurs, the battery is typically at its peak performance for several weeks.

Rechargeable Batteries

Nickel Cadmium (NiCd)

NiCd is the oldest rechargeable technology, and its energy density and volumetric efficiency are somewhat low by today's standards. Additionally, NiCd cells suffer from the "memory effect," which reduces overall capacity of the battery if it isn't fully discharged before recharging. That said, they support many more charge-discharge cycles than most newer technologies. Also, they can deliver very high peak current, and thus they still find use in many products today, such as power tools and laptop computers.

Nickel Metal Hydride (NiMH)

NiMH, while lacking NiCd's peak current capability, improves on the older technology in several respects. First, it has about 50% higher energy density while outputting the same nominal 1.25V, which means that a NiMH battery stores significantly more energy than does a NiCd in an equivalent form factor. Moreover, NiMH doesn't contain environmentally unfriendly cadmium. Finally, it doesn't share the NiCd curse of the "memory effect" to nearly the same extent.

Lithium Ion (Li+ or Li-Ion)

Lithium ion batteries provide excellent energy density per unit volume and weight, and they exhibit no memory effect. Furthermore, their rated voltage output is 3.6V, which is very convenient for systems based on 3V logic, and they tend to stay in the 3.6V range for most of their discharge cycle. These properties combine to make Li+ a very attractive technology for portable multimedia devices. On the downside, they are more temperamental than NiMH or NiCd in terms of their operating and charge/ discharge profiles, so they require special circuitry to keep them well-controlled and safe. This, in turn, adds to overall cost.

Lithium Polymer

Lithium polymer cells use a different type of electrolyte than lithium ion cells, resulting in a safer, much thinner battery structure. This lightweight, flexible form factor is the primary advantage (aside from improved safety, of course!) that lithium polymer technology has over lithium ion, but so far the higher manufacturing cost and lower energy density of the polymer-based cell have slowed its introduction into portable markets.

Table 8-4 shows a comparison of the main rechargeable battery types and their chief characteristics.

Table 8.4 **Comparison of rechargeable battery technologies**

	NiCd	NiMH	Lithium Ion	Lithium Polymer
Volumetric Energy Density	Low	High	High	High
Gravimetric Energy Density	Low	High	Very high	Exceptionally high
Charge-discharge cycle life	Very Long	Long	Moderate	Short
Shelf life	Very long	Long	Very long	Exceptionally long
Environment friendly?	No -- Cadmium	Yes	No: Lithium is very reactive	Yes
Safe?	No -- Cadmium	Yes	No: Lithium electrode can spontaneously combust, battery can explode	Yes
Temperature performance	Very good	Fair	Very good	Very good
Nominal voltage	1.25V	1.25V	3.6V	3.6V
Load current capability	Very high	Moderate	High	Low
Price	Low	Moderate	High	Very high
Comments	Exhibits Memory Effect	Needs protection against overcharge and overdischarge	Needs controlled charging and discharging	Excellent form factor Flexibility

Relative Power for External Devices

As an appropriate end to this chapter, we'd like to put processor power dissipation into the perspective of a representative multimedia system. For all the talk of low-power processing, we sometimes lose track of the large amounts of power burned by other system components. It is often these subsystems that determine the ultimate battery life of a system, but every component contributes an important part. Table 8.5 gives a rough idea of some other key energy users in a typical portable multimedia application.

Table 8.5 **Approximate power dissipation for other key components in a portable multimedia system**

Component	Approximate Power Dissipation (mW)
3.3V SDRAM, 100 MHz, 128 Mb, 1Meg x32 x4 banks	
Active power	600
Standby power (Active)	200
Standby power (Power-Down) / Self-refresh power	7
2.5V Mobile SDRAM, 100 MHz, 128 Mb, 1Meg x32 x4 banks	
Active power	400
Standby power (Active)	115
Standby power (Power-Down) / Self-refresh power	1
3.3V SRAM, 1 MB, 55nS access time	
Active power	80
Standby power	.03
QVGA TFT-LCD Panel (320x240 pixels)	
Backlight	500-3000
Pixel Array	500
Hard drive:	
Motor not spinning	200
Motor spinning, but no data transfer	500
Data actively read or written	1000-4000
Optical drive:	
Initial spin-up	3000
Steady spin	2000
Reading data	5000
Stereo Audio Codec	50
NTSC Video Decoder	100–500
NTSC Video Encoder	100–600

Application Examples

Introduction

If you've made it this far in the book (without cheating and skipping ahead), you now have an appreciation for the workings of the interrelated structural components of an embedded media processing system. Throughout the book, we've tried to inject examples involving pieces of real systems, in an attempt to solidify the somewhat abstract knowledge that's being conveyed. In this chapter, we have a chance to delve a little further into some sample systems, in more detail than we could afford elsewhere. It is our hope that this chapter adds value by viewing things more at a practical application level, and by relating the inner workings of a processor to tangible functionality in the system.

We'll first look at an automotive driver assistance application, seeing how a video-based lane departure warning system can utilize a media framework identical to one we discussed in Chapter 7. Then, we'll turn our attention to implementation of a JPEG algorithm, which contains a lot of the key elements of more complex image and video codecs. Next, we'll extend this discussion to the MPEG realm, outlining how an MPEG-2 video encoder algorithm can be partitioned efficiently across a dual-core processor. Finally, we'll switch gears and talk about the porting of open-source C code to the Blackfin processor environment. In doing so, we'll undergo an enlightening analysis of the code optimization process—which optimization steps give you the most "bang for your buck."

So let's get started…

Automotive Driver Assistance

With the dozens of processors controlling every aspect of today's automobiles, not a single aspect of the "vehicle experience" remains untouched by technology. Whether it's climate control, engine control or entertainment, there has been constant evolution in capabilities and manufacturer offerings over the last decade. One of the drivers for this evolution, the rapidly increasing performance trend of media processors, is set to have a profound impact on another critical automotive component—the safety subsystem.

While most current safety features utilize a wide array of sensors—most involving microwaves, infrared light, lasers, or acceleration and position detection—only recently have processors emerged that can meet the real-time video requirements that make image processing a viable safety technology. Let's look at the roles for embedded media processing in the emerging field of video-based automotive safety, using the Blackfin processor as a basis for discussion.

Automotive Safety Systems

The entire category of car safety demands a high-performance media processor for many reasons. For one, since the response times are so critical to saving lives, video filtering and image processing must be done in a real-time, deterministic manner. There is a natural desire to maximize video frame rate and resolution to the highest level that a processor can handle for a given application, since this provides the best data for decision making. Additionally, the processor needs to compare vehicle speeds and relative vehicle-object distances against desired conditions, again in real time. Furthermore, the processor must interact with many vehicle subsystems (such as the engine, braking, steering and airbag controllers), process sensor information from all these systems in real time, and provide appropriate audiovisual output to the driver interface environment. Finally, the processor should be able to interface to navigation and telecommunication systems to log accidents and call for assistance.

Smart Airbags

One emerging use of media processors in automotive safety is for an "intelligent airbag system," which bases its deployment decisions on who is sitting in the seat opposite the airbag. Presently, weight-based systems are most popular, but video sensing will soon become prevalent. Either thermal or regular cameras may be used, at rates up to 200 frames/sec, and more than one might be employed to provide a stereo image of the occupant. In any case, the goal is to characterize not only the size of the occupant, but also her position or posture. Among other things, image processing algorithms must account for the differentiation between a person's head and other body parts in determining body position. Ultimately, in the event of a collision the system may choose to restrict deployment entirely, deploy with a lower force, or fully deploy.

In this system, the media processor reads in multiple image streams at high frame rates, processes the images to profile a seat's occupant size and position under all types of lighting conditions, and constantly monitors all the crash sensors placed throughout the car in order to make the best deployment decision possible in a matter of milliseconds.

Collision Avoidance and Adaptive Cruise Control

Another high-profile safety application is Adaptive Cruise Control (ACC)/Collision Avoidance. ACC is a convenience feature that controls engine and braking systems to regulate distance and speed of the car relative to the vehicle ahead. The sensors involved employ a combination of microwave, radar, infrared and video technology. A media processor might process between 17 and 30 frames/sec from a roadway-focused camera mounted near the rear-view mirror of the car. The image processing algorithms involved include frame-to-frame image comparisons, object recognition and contrast equalization for varying lighting scenarios. Goals of the video sensor input include providing information about lane boundaries, obstacle categorization and road curvature profiling.

Whereas ACC systems are promoted as a convenience feature, collision avoidance systems aim to actively avoid accidents by coordinating the braking, steering and engine controllers of the car. As such, they have been slower to evolve, given the legal ramifications of such an endeavor. The estimated widespread deployment of these systems is 2010. However, since the automotive design cycle is typically a five-year span, the design of such systems is ongoing.

Collision warning systems are a subset of the collision avoidance category. They provide a warning of an impending accident, but don't actively avoid it. There are two main subcategories within this niche:

Blind spot monitors—Cameras are mounted strategically around the periphery of the car to provide visual display of the driver's blind spots, as well as to sound a warning if the processor senses another vehicle is present in a blind-spot zone. These systems also serve as back-up warnings, cautioning the driver if there is an obstruction in the rear of the car while it is shifted in reverse. The display might be integrated directly into the rear-view mirror, providing a full unobstructed view of the car's surroundings. Moreover, video of "blind spots" within the car cabin may also be included, to allow the driver to, say, monitor a rear-facing infant.

Lane departure monitors—These systems can act as driver fatigue monitors, as well as notify drivers if it is unsafe to change lanes or if they are straying out of a lane or off the road. Cameras facing forward monitor the car's position relative to the center-line and side markers of the roadway up to 50–75 feet in front of the car. The system sounds an alarm if the car starts to leave the lane unintentionally.

Figure 9.1 gives an indication of where image sensors might be placed throughout a vehicle, including how a lane departure system might be integrated into the chassis. There are a few things to note here. First, multiple sensors can be shared across the different automotive safety functions. For example, the rear-facing sensors can be used when the vehicle is backing up, as well as to track lanes as the vehicle moves forward. In addition, the lane departure system might accept feeds from any number of camera sources, choosing the appropriate inputs for a given situation. At a minimum, a video stream feeds the embedded processor. In more advanced systems, other sensor information, such as position data from GPS receivers, also weighs in.

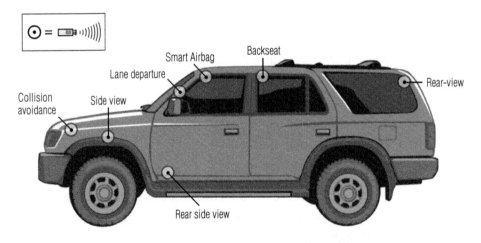

Figure 9.1 **Basic camera placement regions for automotive safety applications**

Lane Departure—A System Example

Having discussed the role that a media processor can play in video-based automotive safety applications, it is instructive to analyze typical components of just such an application. To that end, let's probe further into a lane departure monitoring system. Figure 9.2a shows the basic operational steps in the system, while Figure 9.2b illustrates the processor's connection to external subsystems within the car.

The overall system diagram of Figure 9.2a is fairly straightforward, considering the complexity of the signal processing functions being performed. What is interesting about a video-based lane departure system is that, instead of having an analog signal chain, the bulk of the processing is image-based, carried out within the processor.

(a)

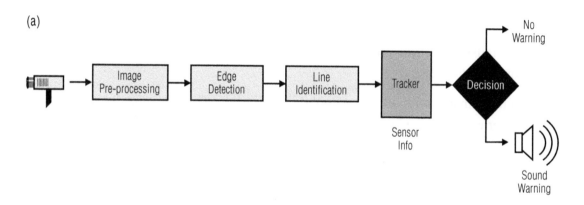

(b)

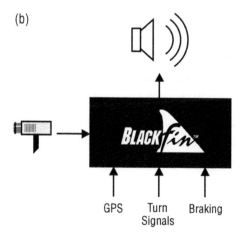

Figure 9.2 **(a) Basic steps in a lane departure algorithm and (b) how the processor might connect to the outside world**

This is very advantageous from a system bill-of-materials standpoint. The outputs of the vehicle-based system consist of some indication to the driver to correct the car's path before the vehicle leaves the lane unintentionally. This may be in the form of an audible "rumble strip" warning, or perhaps just a cautionary chime or voice.

The video input system to the embedded processor must perform in harsh environments, including wide and drastic temperature shifts and changing road conditions. As the data stream enters the processor, it is transformed instantaneously into a form that can be processed to output a decision. At the simplest level, the lane departure system looks for the vehicle's position with respect to the lane markings in the road. To the processor, this means the incoming stream of road imagery must be transformed into a series of lines that delineate the road surface.

Lines can be found within a field of data by looking for edges. These edges form the boundaries that the vehicle should stay within while it is moving forward. The processor must track these line markers and determine whether or not to notify the driver of irregularities.

Keep in mind that several other automobile systems also feed the lane departure system. For example, the braking system and the turn signals will typically disable warnings during intentional lane changes and slow turns.

Let's now drill deeper into the basic components of our lane departure system example. Figure 9.3 follows the same basic operational flow as Figure 9.2a, but with more insight into the algorithms being performed. The video stream coming into the system needs to be filtered to reduce noise caused by temperature, motion, and electromagnetic interference. Without this step, it would be difficult to find clean lane markings. The next processing step involves edge detection, and if the system is set up properly, the edges found will represent the lane markings. These lines must then be matched to the direction and position of the vehicle. For this step, we will describe something called the Hough transform. The output of this step will be tracked across frames of images, and a decision will be made based on all the compiled information. The final challenge is to send a warning in a timely manner without sounding false alarms.

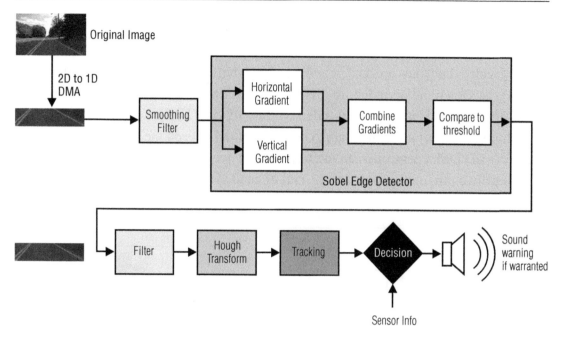

Figure 9.3 **Algorithm flow showing results of intermediate image processing steps**

Image Acquisition

For automotive safety applications, image resolutions typically range from VGA (640 × 480 pixels/image) down to QVGA (320 × 240 pixels/image). Regardless of the actual image size, the format of the data transferred remains the same, but because less data is transferred, lower clock speeds can be used. Moreover, for applications like lane departure warning systems, sometimes only grayscale images are required. Therefore, data bandwidth is halved (from 16 bits/pixel to 8 bits/pixel), because no chroma information is needed.

Memory and Data Movement

Efficient memory usage is an important consideration for system designers, because external memories are expensive and their access times are slow. Therefore, it is important to be judicious in transferring only the video data needed for the application. By intelligently decoding ITU-R BT.656 preamble codes, an interface like Blackfin's PPI can aid this "data filtering" operation. For example, in some applications, only the active video fields are required. In a full NTSC stream, this results in a 25% reduction in the amount of data brought into the system, because horizontal and vertical blanking data is ignored and not transferred into memory. What's more, this lower data rate helps conserve bandwidth on the internal and external data buses.

Because video data rates are so demanding, frame buffers must be set up in external memory, as shown in Figure 9.4. In this scenario, while the processor operates on one buffer, a second buffer is being filled by the PPI via a DMA transfer. A simple semaphore can be set up to maintain synchronization between the frames. With the Blackfin's 2D DMA controller, an interrupt can be generated virtually anywhere, but it is typically configured to occur at the end of each video line or frame.

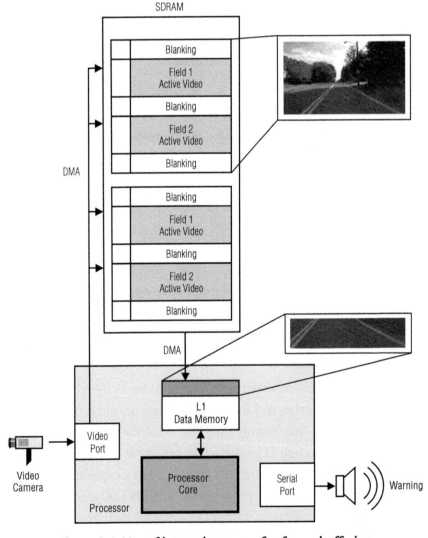

Figure 9.4 **Use of internal memory for frame buffering**

Once a complete frame is in SDRAM, the data is normally transferred into internal L1 data memory so that the core can access it with single-cycle latency. To do this, the DMA controller can use two-dimensional transfers to bring in pixel blocks. Figure 9.5 shows how a 16 × 16 macroblock, a construct used in many compression algorithms, can be stored linearly in L1 memory via a 2D DMA engine.

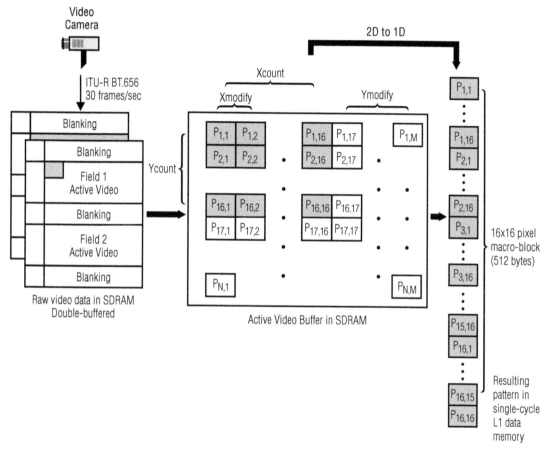

Figure 9.5 **A 2D-to-1D transfer from SDRAM into L1 memory**

From a performance standpoint, up to four unique internal SDRAM banks can be active at any time. This means that in the video framework, no additional bank activation latencies are observed when the 2D-to-1D DMA is pulling data from one bank while the PPI is feeding another.

Projection Correction

The camera used for the lane departure system typically sits in the center-top location of the front windshield, facing forward. In other cases, the camera is located in the rear windshield and faces the road already traveled. In some systems, a "bird's eye" camera is selected to give the broadest perspective of the upcoming roadway. This type of camera can be used in lieu of multiple line-of-sight cameras. In this case, the view is warped because of the wide-angle lens, so the output image must be remapped into a linear view before parsing the picture content.

Image Filtering

Before doing any type of edge detection, it is important to filter the image to smooth out any noise picked up during image capture. This is essential because noise introduced into an edge detector can result in false edges output from the detector.

Obviously, an image filter needs to operate fast enough to keep up with the succession of input images. Thus, it is imperative that image filter kernels be optimized for execution in the fewest possible number of processor cycles. One effective means of filtering is accomplished with a basic 2D convolution operation. We introduced the 2D convolution in Chapter 6. Now let's look in some detail at how this computation can be performed efficiently on a Blackfin processor.

The high-level algorithm can be described in the following steps:

1. Place the center of the mask over an element of the input matrix.

2. Multiply each pixel in the mask neighborhood by the corresponding filter mask element.

3. Sum each of the multiplies into a single result.

4. Place each sum in a location corresponding to the center of the mask in the output matrix.

Figure 9.6 shows three matrices: an input matrix F, a 3×3 mask matrix H, and an output matrix G.

After each output point is computed, the mask is moved to the right by one element. When using a circular buffer structure, on the image edges the algorithm wraps around to the first element in the next row. For example, when the mask is centered on element F2m, the H23 element of the mask matrix is multiplied by element F31 of

$$g(x,y) = \sum_{i=-1}^{i=1} \sum_{k=-1}^{k=1} h(i,k)f(x-i,\ y-k)$$

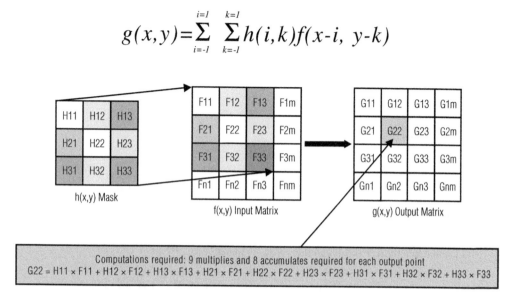

Figure 9.6 **Computation of 3 × 3 convolution output**

the input matrix. As a result, the usable section of the output matrix is reduced by one element along each edge of the image.

By aligning the input data properly, both Blackfin multiply-accumulate (MAC) units can be used in a single processor cycle to process two output points at a time. During this same cycle, multiple data fetches occur in parallel with the MAC operation. This method, shown in Figure 9.7, allows efficient computation of two output points for each loop iteration, or effectively 4.5 cycles per pixel instead of the 9 cycles per pixel of Figure 9.6.

G11	G12	G13	G1m
G21	G22	G23	G2m
G31	G32	G33	G3m
Gn1	Gn2	Gn3	Gnm

g(x,y) Output Matrix

$$G22 = H11 \times F11 + H12 \times F12 + H13 \times F13 + H21 \times F21 + H22 \times F22 + H23 \times F23 + H31 \times F31 + H32 \times F32 + H33 \times F33$$

$$G23 = H11 \times F12 + H12 \times F13 + H13 \times F14 + H21 \times F22 + H22 \times F23 + H23 \times F24 + H31 \times F32 + H32 \times F33 + H33 \times F34$$

Loop Cycle (F11 Loaded into R0.H, F12 Loaded into R0.L, H11 Loaded into R1.L)

1	A1 = R0.H * R1.L,	A0 = R0.L * R1.L	|| R0.L = w[I0++] || R2 = [I3++]; //I0-I3 are index regs
2	A1 += R0.L * R1.H,	A0 += R0.H * R1.H	|| R0.H = w[I0--]; // w[ ] is 16-bit access
3	A1 += R0.H * R2.L,	A0 += R0.L * R2.L	|| R0 = [I1++] || R3 = [I3++];
4	A1 += R0.H * R2.H,	A0 += R0.L * R2.H	|| R0.L = w[I1++];
5	A1 += R0.L * R3.L,	A0 += R0.H * R3.L	|| R0.H = w[I1--] || R1 = [I3++];
6	A1 += R0.H * R3.H,	A0 += R0.L * R3.H	|| R0 = [I2++];
7	A1 += R0.H * R1.L,	A0 += R0.L * R1.L	|| R0.L = w[I2++] || R2 = [I3++];
8	A1 += R0.L * R1.H,	A0 += R0.H * R1.H	|| R0.H = w[I2--] || R1 = [I3++];
9	R6.H = (A1 += R0.H * R2.L),	R6.L = (A0 += R0.L * R2.L);	//Accumulate for 2 outputs

Each time through this loop yields two output points
Total Cycles = 9 for every 2 pixels => 4.5 cycles per pixel

Figure 9.7 **Efficient implementation of 3 × 3 convolution**

Edge Detection

A wide variety of edge detection techniques are in common use. Before considering how an edge can be detected, we must first settle on a definition for what constitutes an edge. We can then find ways to enhance the edges we are seeking to improve the chances of detection. Because image sensors are non-ideal, two factors must be considered in any approach we take: ambient noise and the effects of quantization errors.

Noise in the image will almost guarantee that pixels with equal gray-scale level in the original image will not have equal levels in the output image. Noise will be introduced by many factors that can't be easily controlled, such as ambient temperature, vehicular motion, and outside weather conditions. Moreover, quantization errors in the image will result in edge boundaries extending across a number of pixels. Because of these factors, any appropriate image-processing algorithm must keep noise immunity as a prime goal.

One popular edge detection method uses a set of common derivative-based operators to help locate edges within the image. Each of the derivative operators is designed to find places where there are changes in intensity. In this scheme, the edges can be modeled by a smaller image that contains the properties of an ideal edge.

We'll discuss the Sobel Edge Detector because it is easy to understand and illustrates principles that extend into more complex schemes. The Sobel Detector uses two convolution kernels to compute gradients for both horizontal and vertical edges. The first is designed to detect changes in vertical contrast (S_x). The second detects changes in horizontal contrast (S_y).

$$S_x = \begin{bmatrix} -1 & 0 & 1 \\ -2 & 0 & 2 \\ -1 & 0 & 1 \end{bmatrix} \quad S_y = \begin{bmatrix} -1 & -2 & -1 \\ 0 & 0 & 0 \\ 1 & 2 & 1 \end{bmatrix}$$

The output matrix holds an "edge likelihood" magnitude (based on horizontal and vertical convolutions) for each pixel in the image. This matrix is then thresholded in order to take advantage of the fact that large responses in magnitude correspond to edges within the image. Therefore, at the input of the Hough Transform stage, the image consists only of either "pure white" or "pure black" pixels, with no intermediate gradations.

If the true magnitude is not required for an application, this can save a costly square root operation. Other common techniques to build a threshold matrix include summing the gradients from each pixel or simply taking the larger of the two gradients.

Straight Line Detection—Hough Transform

The Hough Transform is a widely used method for finding global patterns such as lines, circles and ellipses in an image by localizing them in a parameterized space. It is especially useful in lane detection, because *lines* can be easily detected as *points* in Hough Transform space, based on the polar representation of Equation 9.1:

$$\rho = x \cos \Phi + y \sin \Phi \qquad \qquad \text{Equation 9.1}$$

The meaning of Equation 9.1 can be visualized by extending a perpendicular from the given line to the origin, such that Φ is the angle that the perpendicular makes with the abscissa, and ρ is the length of the perpendicular. Thus, one pair of coordinates (ρ, Φ) can fully describe the line. To demonstrate this concept, we will look at the lines L1 and L2 in Figure 9.8. As shown in Figure 9.8a, L1's location is defined by Φ_1 and the length of the perpendicular extending from the X-Y origin to L1, while L2's position is defined by Φ_2 and the length of the perpendicular extending from the X-Y origin to L2.

Another way to look at the Hough Transform is to consider a possible way that the algorithm could be implemented intuitively:

1. Visit only white pixels in the binary image.

2. For each pixel and every Φ value being considered, draw a line through the pixel at angle Φ from the origin. Then calculate ρ, which is the length of the perpendicular between the origin and the line under consideration.

3. Record this (ρ, Φ) pair in an accumulation table.

4. Repeat steps 1–3 for every white pixel in the image.

5. Search the accumulation table for the (ρ, Φ) pairs encountered most often. These pairs describe the most probable "lines" in the input image, because in order to register a high accumulation value, there had to be many white pixels that existed along the line described by the (ρ, Φ) pair.

The Hough Transform is computationally intensive, because a sinusoidal curve is calculated for each pixel in the input image. However, certain techniques can speed up the computation considerably. First, some of the computation terms can be computed ahead of time, so that they can be referenced quickly through a lookup table. In a fixed-point architecture like Blackfin's, it is very useful to store the lookup table only for the cosine function. Since the sine values are 90 degrees out of phase with the cosines, the same table can be used for both, with an offset as appropriate. Given the lookup tables, the computation of Equation 9.1 can be represented as two fixed-point multiplications and one addition.

Another factor that can improve Hough performance is a set of assumptions about the nature and location of lane markings within the input image. By considering only those input points that could potentially be lane markings, a large number of unnecessary calculations can be avoided, since only a narrow range of Φ values need be considered for each white pixel.

(a)

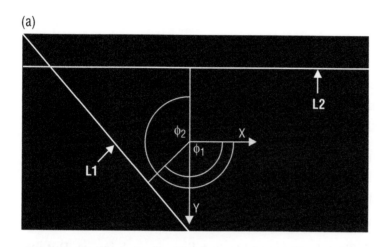

(b)

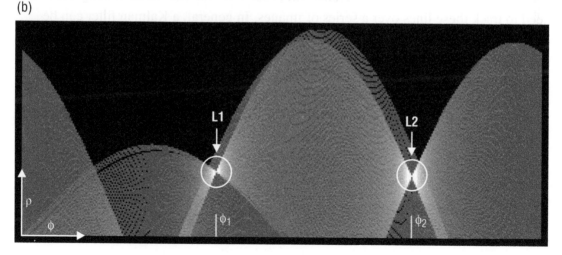

Figure 9.8a **Line segments L1 and L2 can be described by the lengths and angles of perpendicular lines extending from the origin**

Figure 9.8b **The Hough Transform of the two line segments in Figure 9.8a. The two bright regions correspond to local maxima, which can be used to reconstruct the two segments L1 and L2 of Figure 9.8a.**

Among the parameters useful for further analysis are the offset from the camera's center axis, the widths of the detected lines, and the angles with respect to the position of the camera. Since lane markings in many highway systems are standardized, a set of rules can eliminate some lines from the list of lane-marking candidates. The set of possible lane-marking variables can then be used to derive the position of the car.

Lane Tracking

Lane information can be determined from a variety of possible sources within an automobile. This information can be combined with measurements of vehicle-related parameters (e.g., velocity, acceleration, etc.) to assist in lane tracking. Based on the results of these measurements, the lane departure system can make an intelligent decision as to whether an unintentional departure is in progress.

The problem of estimating lane geometry is a challenge that often calls for using a Kalman filter to track the road curvature. Specifically, the Kalman filter can predict future road information, which can then be used in the next frame to reduce the computational load presented by the Hough Transform.

As described earlier, the Hough Transform is used to find lines in each image. But we need to track these lines over a series of images. In general, a Kalman filter can be described as a recursive filter that estimates the future state of an object. In this case, the object is a line. The state of the line is based on its location and its motion path across several frames.

Along with the road state itself, the Kalman filter provides a variance for each state. The predicted state and the variance can be used to narrow the search space of the Hough Transform in future frames, which saves processing cycles.

Decision Making

From experience, we know that false positives are always undesirable. There is no quicker way to have a consumer disable an optional safety feature than to have it indicate a problem that does not really exist.

With a processing framework in place, system designers can add their own intellectual property to the decision phase of each of the processing threads. The simplest approach might take into account other vehicle attributes in the decision process. For example, a lane-change warning could be suppressed when a lane change is perceived to be intentional—as when a blinker is used or when the brake is applied. More complex systems may factor in GPS coordinate data, occupant driving profile, time of day, weather and other parameters.

Clearly, we have only described an example framework for how an image-based lane departure system might be structured. The point is, with a flexible media processor in the design, there is plenty of room for feature additions and algorithm optimizations.

Baseline JPEG Compression Overview

Image compression, once the domain of the PC, is now pervasive in embedded environments. This trend is largely a result of the increased processing power and multimedia capabilities of new embedded processors. Consequently, it now becomes advantageous for embedded designers to gain a better grasp of image algorithms in an effort to implement them efficiently. This section examines the Baseline JPEG compression standard, one of the most popular image compression algorithms. While not covered explicitly here, the JPEG decode process is a straightforward inversion of the encode process.

Although there are many specified versions of JPEG, Baseline JPEG compression (referred to herein simply as "JPEG") embodies a minimum set of requirements. It is lossy, such that the original image cannot be exactly reconstructed (although a "Lossless JPEG" specification exists as well). JPEG exploits the characteristics of human vision, eliminating or reducing data to which the eye is less sensitive. JPEG works well on grayscale and color images, especially on photographs, but it is not intended for two-tone images. Figure 9.9 shows the basic encode process, which we'll examine below in some detail.

Preprocessing

Color Space

The incoming uncompressed image might be stored in one of several formats. One popular format is 24 bit/pixel RGB—that is, 8 bits each of red, green and blue subpixels. However, in viewing these separate R, G and B subchannels for a given image, there is usually a clear visual correlation between the three pictures. Therefore, in order to achieve better compression ratios, it is common to decorrelate the RGB fields into separate luma (Y) and chroma (Cb, Cr) components. As discussed in Chapter 6, the equations to do this are:

$$Y' = (0.299)R' + (0.587)G' + (0.114)B'$$
$$Cb = -(0.168)R' - (0.330)G' + (0.498)B' + 128$$
$$Cr = (0.498)R' - (0.417)G' - (0.081)B' + 128$$

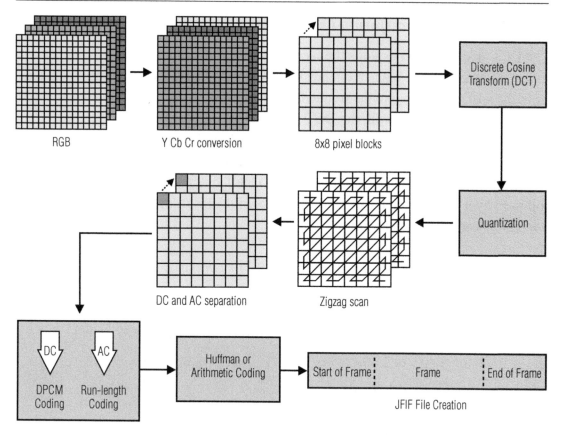

Figure 9.9 **Sample Baseline JPEG encode data flow**

Spatial Filtering

Whichever format is chosen, the image needs to be separated into Y, Cb and Cr buffers, because the JPEG algorithm acts on each component individually and in identical fashion. If the chroma are subsampled, this is simply akin to running the JPEG algorithm on an image of smaller size.

JPEG operates on 8 × 8-byte blocks of data, as shown in Figure 9.9. Therefore, in each image buffer the data is partitioned into these blocks, from left to right and top to bottom. These blocks do not overlap, and if the image dimensions are not multiples of 8, the last row and/or column of the image is duplicated as needed.

Discrete Cosine Transform (DCT)

The DCT stage of JPEG exploits the fact that the human eye favors low-frequency image information over high-frequency details. The 8 × 8 DCT transforms the image from the spatial domain into the frequency domain. Although other frequency transforms can be effective as well, the DCT was chosen because of its decorrelation features, image independence, efficiency of compacting image energy, and orthogonality (which makes the inverse DCT very straightforward). Also, the separable nature of the 2D DCT allows the computation of a 1D DCT on the eight column vectors, followed by a 1D DCT on the eight row vectors of the resulting 8 × 8 matrix. The 8 × 8 DCT can be written as follows:

$$Y_{mn} = \frac{1}{4} K_m K_n \sum_{i=0}^{i=7} \sum_{j=0}^{j=7} x_{ij} \cos\left((2i+1)m\pi/16\right) \cos\left((2j+1)n\pi/16\right), \text{ where}$$

Y_{mn} = the output DCT coefficient at row m, column n of the 8×8 output block

x_{ij} = the input spatial image coordinate at row i, column j of the 8×8 input block

$K_m = 1/\sqrt{2}$ for $m = 0$, or 1 otherwise

$K_n = 1/\sqrt{2}$ for $n = 0$, or 1 otherwise

For uniform handling of different image components, the DCT coder usually requires that the expected average value for all pixels is zero. Therefore, before the DCT is performed, a value of 128 may be subtracted from each pixel (normally ranging from 0 to 255) to shift it to a range of –127 to 127. This offset has no effect on the ac characteristics of the image block.

It is instructive to take a visual view of the DCT transform. Refer to the DCT basis functions shown in Figure 9.10. In performing a DCT on an 8 × 8 image block, what we are essentially doing is correlating the input image with each of the 64 DCT basis functions and recording the relative strength of correlation as coefficients in the output DCT matrix.

For example, the coefficient in the output DCT matrix at (2,1) corresponds to the strength of the correlation between the basis function at (2,1) and the entire 8 × 8 input image block. The coefficients corresponding to high-frequency details are located to the right and bottom of the output DCT block, and it is precisely these weights which we try to nullify—the more zeros in the 8 × 8 DCT block, the higher

Input to DCT:
8x8 pixel block

DCT Basis Functions

Output from DCT:
8x8 coefficient block

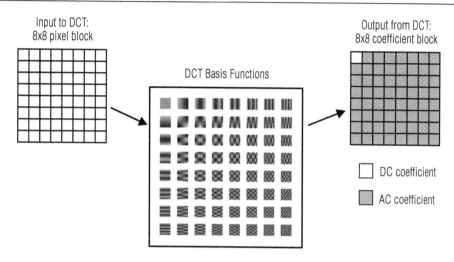

☐ DC coefficient

▨ AC coefficient

Figure 9.10 **DCT basis functions**

the compression achieved. In the quantization step below, we'll discuss how to maximize the number of zeros in the matrix.

Quantization

After the DCT has been performed on the 8×8 image block, the results are quantized in order to achieve large gains in compression ratio. Quantization refers to the process of representing the actual coefficient values as one of a set of predetermined allowable values, so that the overall data can be encoded in fewer bits (because the allowable values are a small fraction of all possible values).

Remember that the human eye is much more attuned to low-frequency information than high-frequency details. Therefore, small errors in high-frequency representation are not easily noticed, and eliminating some high-frequency components entirely is often visually acceptable. The JPEG quantization process takes advantage of this to reduce the amount of DCT information that needs to be coded for a given 8×8 block.

Quantization is the key irreversible step in the JPEG process. Although performing an inverse DCT will not exactly reproduce the original input 8×8 input matrix because of rounding error, the result is usually quite visually acceptable. However, after quantization, the precision of the original unquantized coefficients is lost forever. Thus, quantization only occurs in lossy compression algorithms, such as the Baseline JPEG implementation we're discussing here.

The quantization process is straightforward once the quantization table is assembled, but the table itself can be quite complex, often with a separate quantization coefficient for each element of the 8×8 DCT output block. Because this output matrix corresponds to how strongly the input image block exhibits each of the 64 DCT basis functions, it is possible to experimentally determine how important each DCT frequency is to the human eye and quantize accordingly. In other words, frequencies towards the bottom and right of the basis functions in Figure 9.10 will tend to have large values in their quantization table entries, because this will tend to zero out the higher-frequency elements of the DCT output block. The actual process of quantization is a simple element-wise division between the DCT output coefficient and the quantization coefficient for a given row and column.

A "Quality Scaling Factor" can be applied to the quantization matrix to balance between image quality and compressed image size. For the sample tables mentioned in the JPEG standard, typical quality values range from 0.5 (high recovered image quality) to 5 (high compression ratio).

Zigzag Sorting

Next, we prepare the quantized data in an efficient format for encoding. As we have seen from the DCT output, the quantized coefficients have a greater chance of being zero as the horizontal and vertical frequency values increase. To exploit this behavior, we can rearrange the coefficients into a one-dimensional array sorted from the dc value to the highest-order spatial frequency coefficient, as shown in Figure 9.11. This is accomplished using *zigzag sorting,* a process which traverses the 8×8 block in a back-and-forth direction of increasing spatial frequency. On the left side of the diagram, we see the index numbers of the quantized output DCT matrix. Using the scan pattern shown in the middle of the figure, we can produce a new matrix as shown in the right side of the figure.

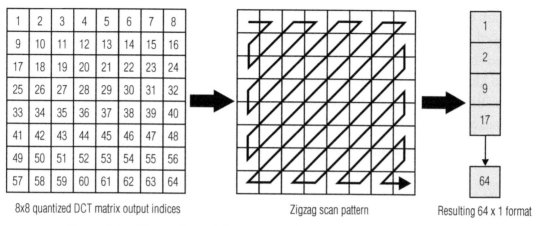

| 8x8 quantized DCT matrix output indices | Zigzag scan pattern | Resulting 64 x 1 format |

Figure 9.11 **Illustration of zigzag scan for efficient coefficient encoding**

Each quantized DCT output matrix is run through the zigzag scan process. The first element in each 64 × 1 array represents the dc coefficient from the DCT matrix, and the remaining 63 coefficients represent the ac components. These two types of information are different enough to warrant separating them and applying different methods of coding to achieve optimal compression efficiency.

All of the dc coefficients (one from each DCT output block) must be grouped together in a separate list. At this point, the dc coefficients will be encoded as a group, and each set of ac values will be encoded separately.

Coding the DC Coefficients

The dc components represent the intensity of each 8 × 8 pixel block. Because of this, significant correlation exists between adjacent blocks. So, while the dc coefficient of any given input array is fairly unpredictable by itself, real images usually do not vary widely in a localized area. As such, the previous dc value can be used to predict the current dc coefficient value. By using a differential prediction model (DPCM), we can increase the probability that the value we encode will be small, and thus reduce the number of bits in the compressed image.

To obtain the coding value we simply subtract the dc coefficient of the previously processed 8 × 8 pixel block from the dc coefficient of the current block. This value is called the "DPCM difference." Once this value is calculated, it is compared to a table to identify the symbol group to which it belongs (based on its magnitude), and it is then encoded appropriately using an entropy encoding scheme such as Huffman coding.

Coding the AC Coefficients (Run-Length Coding)

Because the values of the ac coefficients tend towards zero after the quantization step, these coefficients are run-length encoded. The concept of run-length encoding is a straightforward principle. In real image sequences, pixels of the same value can always be represented as individual bytes, but it doesn't make sense to send the same value over and over again. For example, we have seen that the quantized output of the DCT blocks produces many zero-valued bytes. The zigzag ordering helps produce these zeros in groups at the end of each sequence.

Instead of coding each zero individually, we simply encode the number of zeros in a given "run." This run-length coded information is then variable-length coded (VLC), usually using Huffman codes.

Entropy Encoding

The next processing block in the JPEG encode sequence is known as the *entropy encoder*. In this stage, a final lossless compression is performed on the quantized DCT coefficients to increase the overall compression ratio achieved.

Entropy encoding is a compression technique that uses a series of bit codes to represent a set of possible symbols. Table 9.1a shows an obvious 2-bit encode sequence with four possible output symbols (A, B, C and D).

In this example, we can uniquely describe each symbol with two bits of information. Because each symbol is represented as a 2-bit quantity, we refer to the code as "fixed length." Fixed length codes are most often applied in systems where each of the symbols occurs with equal probability.

Table 9.1 **(a) Example of entropy encoding with equal symbol probabilities (b) Example of entropy encoding with weighted symbol probabilities**

(a)

Symbol	Bit Code
A	00
B	01
C	10
D	11

(b)

Symbol	Probability	Bit Code
A	0.50	0
B	0.30	10
C	0.10	110
D	0.10	111

In reality, most symbols do not occur with equal probability. In these cases, we can take advantage of this fact and reduce the average number of bits used to compress the sequence. The length of the code used for each symbol can be varied based on the probability of the symbol's occurrence. By encoding the most common symbols with shorter bit sequences and the less frequently used symbols with longer bit sequences, we can easily improve on the average number of bits used to encode a sequence.

Huffman Coding

Huffman coding is a variable-length encoding technique that is used to compress a stream of symbols with a known probability distribution. Huffman code sequences are built with a code tree structure by pairing symbols with the two least probabilities of occurrence in a sequence. Each time a pair is combined, the new symbol takes on the sum of the two separate probabilities. This process continues with each node having its two probabilities combined and then being paired with the next smallest probable symbol until all the symbols are represented in the coded tree.

Once the code tree is constructed, code sequences can be assigned within the tree structure by assigning a 0 or a 1 bit to each branch. The code for each symbol is then read by concatenating each bit from the branches, starting at the center of the structure and extending to the branch for which the relevant symbol is defined. This procedure produces a unique code for each symbol data size that is guaranteed to be optimal.

Even though the codes can have different lengths, each code can be unambiguously decoded if the symbols are read beginning with the most significant bit. The JPEG standard provides a number of Huffman code tables to describe the different ways of encoding the input quantized data—for instance, depending on whether luminance or chrominance information is being processed.

Table 9.1b uses the same example as in Table 9.1a, but with differently weighted symbol probabilities. The Bit Code column shows the modified encode sequence. As we can see, the most likely symbol is encoded with a single bit, while the least likely symbols require 3 bits each.

With this table, we can determine the average bit length for a code per symbol.

$$(0.5 \times 1 \text{ bit}) + (0.3 \times 2 \text{ bits}) + (0.1 \times 3 \text{ bits}) + (0.1 \times 3 \text{ bits}) = 1.7 \text{ bits/symbol}$$

In this example, the variable length encode scheme produces an average of 1.7 bits/symbol, which is more efficient than the 2 bits/symbol that the fixed-length code of Table 9.1a produced.

Another entropy encoding scheme used in JPEG is Arithmetic Coding. While this algorithm provides for better compression than Huffman coding because it uses adaptive techniques that make it easier to achieve the entropy rate, the additional processing required may not justify the fairly small increase in compression. In addition, there are patent restrictions on Arithmetic Coding.

JPEG File Interchange Format (JFIF)

The encoded data is written into the JPEG File Interchange Format (JFIF), which, as the name suggests, is a simplified format allowing JPEG-compressed images to be shared across multiple platforms and applications. JFIF includes embedded image and coding parameters, framed by appropriate header information. Specifically, aside from the encoded data, a JFIF file must store all coding and quantization tables that are necessary for the JPEG decoder to do its job properly.

MPEG-2 Encoding

As a natural outgrowth of JPEG's popularity for still image compression, Motion JPEG (M-JPEG) gained acceptance as a "barebones" method of video compression. In M-JPEG, each frame of video is encoded as a JPEG image, and frames are transmitted or stored sequentially.

As we discussed in Chapter 6, MPEG-1 soon emerged to satisfy the requirement to transmit motion video over a T1 data line, as well as to match the access times of CD-ROMs. MPEG-2 soon followed, and it further improved attainable compression ratios and provided more flexibility on image quality and bandwidth tradeoffs. MPEG-1 and MPEG-2 differ from M-JPEG in that they allow temporal, in addition to spatial, compression. Temporal compression adds another dimension to the encode challenge, a realm that is addressed using motion estimation techniques.

Both MPEG-1 and MPEG-2 have asymmetric encode and decode operations. That is, the encoding process is much more computationally intensive than the decoding process. This is why we'll choose a dual-core processor as the basis for describing the framework for an MPEG-2 encoder implementation.

One point to note about MPEG algorithms—the encoder is not specifically defined by the MPEG organization, but rather the encoded bit stream is specified. This means that the encoder can be implemented in a variety of ways, as long as it creates a compliant bit stream. The decoder, however, must be able to handle any MPEG-compliant bit stream.

Figure 9.12 provides a block diagram for a sample MPEG-2 encoder. Some of the steps it shows are very similar to the ones we described earlier in this chapter for JPEG. The biggest difference is in how motion within frames is handled, so let's start our discussion there. Once you understand these basics, we'll proceed to examine some possible algorithm partitions on a dual-core processor.

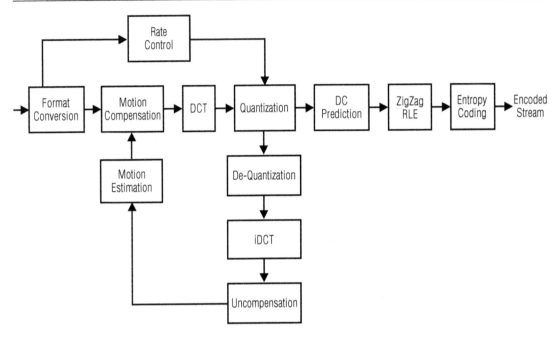

Figure 9.12 **Block diagram for sample MPEG-2 encoder**

Motion Estimation/Compensation

M-JPEG encodes only the information contained in one image frame at a time. As a result, the algorithm does not take advantage of any correlation between frames. In reality, there can be a high degree of correlation between frames, and if we're able to take this fact into account, we can greatly reduce the rate of the encoded bit stream.

You can imagine that if you look at consecutive frames of a video stream and only encode (and thus transmit) the "differences," you can conserve a lot of bandwidth over an approach like M-JPEG, which has no frame-to-frame "memory." A simple example illustrates this point. Consider a video sequence with a constant background but a small moving object in the foreground. Substantially, the frames are identical except with regard to the position of this foreground object. Therefore, if the background is encoded only once, and subsequent frames only encode the new position of this object, the output bit rate needed to faithfully reproduce the original sequence is markedly reduced.

However, now consider the case where the inter-frame data is largely identical, but the whole image might shift slightly between frames. Since this amounts to a slowly moving background image with no foreground objects, it seems that we'd have to revert to M-JPEG-style encoding, because for all intents and purposes, one frame is different from the next on a pixel-for-pixel basis.

But, if we could instead calculate the movement of a macroblock between frames, we can transmit information that tells the decoder to use the macroblock from the previous frame, along with a motion vector, to derive the proper macroblock location for the current frame. The motion vector informs the decoder where the macroblock was located in the previous frame. To obtain the vector, we employ an algorithm called "motion estimation." When the decoder uses this vector to account for motion, it employs "motion compensation."

The challenge is detecting motion between frames on a macroblock basis. In an ideal world, the macroblock would be identical between frames, but shifted in the image. In reality, things like shading and lighting may alter the macroblock contents, in which case the search must be adjusted from an exact match to something that is "close enough." This is where the "Subtract/Absolute/Accumulate (SAA)" instruction we mentioned in Chapter 6 can come in handy. Using SAA, the encoder can compare macroblocks against their positions in a reference frame, created using the feedback loop shown in Figure 9.12.

You might be saying, "Well, that sounds fine, but how do you go about searching for the match?" The more you search the reference frame, the more cycles are required to perform the encoding function. The challenge is determining where to search within the next frame. This is a system consideration and really depends on how many cycles you have available to allocate to this function. If an encoder is used in a real-time application such as a videoconferencing system or a video phone, the processor performing the encode function must be sized assuming the maximum amount of processing each frame. Several outstanding resources are available to help you select your search algorithm; Reference 74 in the Appendix is a particularly useful source of information. Some common methods include searching only a subset of the frame, and searching through various levels of pixel-reduced image frames.

Frame Types

MPEG-encoded frames are classified into I, P and B frames.

I frames represent *intra-coded* frames. Each of these macroblocks are encoded using only information contained within that same frame. The I frame is similar in this respect to a JPEG frame. I frames are required to provide the decoder with a place to start for prediction, and they also provide a baseline for error recovery.

There are two types of *inter-coded* frames, P frames and B frames. Inter-coded frames use information outside the current frame in the encode process.

P frames represent *predicted* frames. These macroblocks may be coded with forward prediction from references made from previous I and P frames, or they may be intra-coded.

B frames represent *bidirectional* predicted frames. The macroblocks within these frames may be coded with forward prediction based on data from previous I or P references. Or, they may be coded with backward prediction from the most recent I or P reference frame.

Note that in P and B pictures, macroblocks may be skipped and not sent at all. The decoder then uses the anchor reference pictures (I frames) for prediction with no error. B pictures are never used as prediction references.

There are many techniques that can be used to space out I, B and P frames. These are detailed in sources such as References 74 and 77 in the Appendix. Our purpose here is only to provide some background on the general concepts. As an example, one technique involves using something similar to a histogram to help determine when a new I frame needs to be generated. If the difference in histogram results between frames exceeds a certain threshold, it may make sense to generate another I frame.

Format Conversion

All profiles of MPEG-2 support 4:2:0 coding. In this system, data comes from an ITU-R BT.656 source in 4:2:2 interleaved format. The first step in the encoding process involves converting the data to the 4:2:0 format we described in Chapter 6.

The first frame in every group of pictures (GOP) in the sequence is an intra frame (I-frame), which is independently coded. As such, the macroblocks from these frames go through the stages of a discrete cosine transform (DCT), quantization, zigzag scan, and run-length encoding (RLE). These algorithms all follow the descriptions we provided in our JPEG discussion earlier in this chapter.

The DCT converts the input so it can be processed in the frequency domain.

The encoder quantizes the DCT coefficients to reduce the number of bits required to represent them. Higher-frequency coefficients have larger quantized step sizes than lower frequency coefficients, for the reasons we described in the JPEG section.

A reference frame is created by "de-quantizing" the output of the quantization step.

Quantization scales down the input, and the zigzag scan and RLE both take advantage of spatial correlation in order to compress the input stream into the final bit stream.

During the encoding process, frames are reconstructed for reference. These reference frames are used during the predictive coding of future frames. To reconstruct a reference frame, the input results of the quantization stage are de-quantized. Next, an inverse DCT is performed. If a predictive frame is currently being encoded, the final stage of reconstructing the reference is uncompensation.

The encoding of predictive frames calls for the extra stages of motion estimation and motion compensation, which compute temporal correlation and produce a motion vector. Information is gathered at different stages so that the rate control task can update the quantization stage, which will in turn stabilize the output bit rate.

The table and pie chart of Figure 9.13 provide a representative cycle distribution of the algorithm on a Blackfin processor.

MPEG-2 Encoder Task Workload (Cycles per pixel)

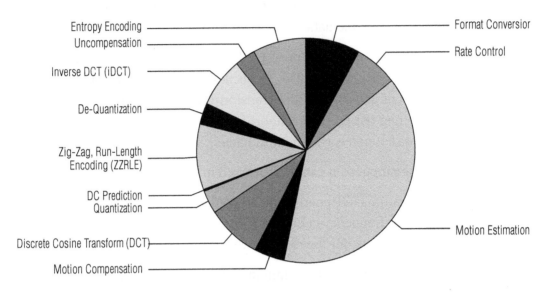

Task Name	Percentage of total algorithm	Parallelism possible?
Format Conversion	8%	Yes
Rate Control	7%	No
Motion Estimation	39%	Dependent on Algorithm
Motion Compensation	4%	Yes
Discrete Cosine Transform (DCT)	8%	Yes
Quantization	3%	Yes
DC Prediction	1%	No
Zig-Zag, Run-Length Encoding (ZZRLE)	9%	Yes
De-Quantization	3%	Yes
Inverse DCT (iDCT)	7%	Yes
Uncompensation	3%	Yes
Entropy Encoding	8%	No

Figure 9.13 **MPEG-2 encoder task workload**

MPEG-2 Encoder Frameworks

Now that you have a basic understanding of the MPEG-2 Encoder implementation on a single-core processor, let's add a twist. How can this algorithm be partitioned across a dual-core symmetric multiprocessor like the ADSP-BF561? The framework models and discussions from Chapter 7 will be helpful references here.

To achieve maximum processing speed for the encoder, we want to utilize both cores efficiently by partitioning code and data across each core. There are many ways to split the algorithm in a parallel pattern, taking into account task dependency and data flow. An efficient parallel system will have multiple execution units with balanced workloads. We can partition the tasks so that both cores are in an execution phase most of the time.

The first model we will demonstrate is the Master-Slave model. It treats both cores as thread execution units. The program flow is almost the same as for a single-core processor implementation. One of the cores is designated the "master," and it handles the host processing and signal processing. The program running on the master is similar to the code base for a single-core program, except that it parallelizes tasks wherever possible and assigns a portion of the parallel workload to the "slave." After it completes a given task, it waits for the slave to finish the same task, and then it resynchronizes the system.

For example, the DCT stage in the MPEG-2 encoder needs to perform the discrete cosine transform on N 8 × 8 input blocks. These DCTs can be executed independently. The master can create a thread request to the slave, assigning it $N/2$ of the blocks, so that each core ends up only doing $N/2$ DCTs. After both of them finish executing, they will re-synchronize with each other, and the master will continue processing the next task.

For those tasks that have to execute sequentially, the master core has two options. It either continues executing instructions itself while the slave is left idle, or it assigns the task(s) to the slave core, during which time the master can handle I/O or host data transfer. The master-slave model achieves speedup from those tasks that can be executed in parallel. In the MPEG-2 encoder, 75% of the tasks can be executed in parallel. Figure 9.14 indicates this graphically. The tasks in the left column execute on the master, while the tasks in the right column execute on the slave. The speedup of this model is approximately 1.75.

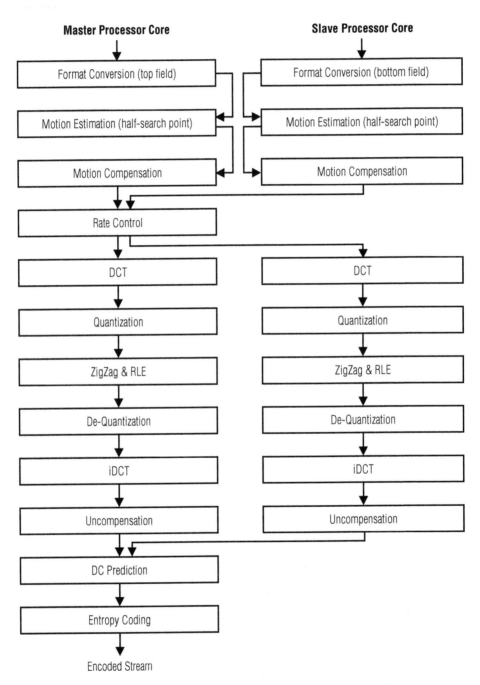

Figure 9.14 **Master-slave MPEG-2 encoder implementation on dual-core processor**

While the Master-Slave model is easy to implement and is scalable, it does not fully utilize processor resources. When the task is not able to run in parallel, one core has to idle and wait for the other core to send another request. When the slave processor is not finished with a task, the master core may have to wait to resynchronize.

Let's now consider how things change if we use the pipelined model of Figure 9.15 instead of the master-slave configuration. Here, the task flow is separated vertically by the two cores. The first portion of the algorithm runs on the first processor core, and the remainder executes on the second core. Because the two processor cores are "peers" to each other, there is no concept of master-slave in this model. The division of the tasks needs to be balanced between the two cores such that both have almost the same workload. Due to the data dependency between the two cores, typically one core will process the data that feeds into the other core—hence the term "pipelined."

In the task flow diagram, we see that the first processor will perform format conversion and motion estimation. This is about 46% of the overall workload. After motion estimation, the first processor will save the motion vectors in a shared memory region. The second processor will then use these motion vectors to complete the remaining 54% of the algorithm.

In this pipelined model, the two processor cores are much more loosely synchronized than in the master-slave model. Consequently, the pipelined model has lower communication overhead, which makes it much more efficient. However, when more than two processor cores are involved, the master-slave model has an advantage, because the pipelined model is not very scaleable, due to the nature of the code partitioning.

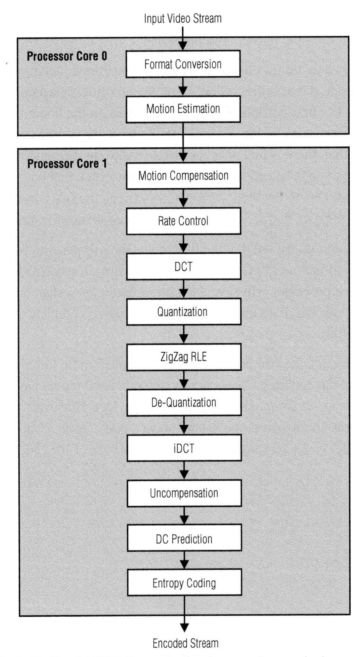

Figure 9.15 **Pipelined MPEG-2 encoder implementation on dual-core processor**

Code Optimization Study Using Open-Source Algorithms

Although "open source" C/C++ code is becoming an increasingly popular alternative to royalty-based algorithms in embedded processing applications, it carries with it some challenges. Foremost among these is how to optimize the code to work well on the chosen processor. This is a crucial issue, because a compiler for a given processor family will cater to that processor's strengths, at the possible expense of inefficiencies in other areas. This leads to uneven performance of the same algorithm when run out-of-the-box on different platforms. This section will explore the porting of open source algorithms to the Blackfin processor, outlining in the process a "plan of attack" leading to code optimization.

What Is Open Source?

The generally understood definition of "open source" refers to any project with source code that is made available to other programmers. Open source software typically is developed collaboratively among a community of software programmers and distributed freely. The Linux operating system, for example, was developed this way. If all goes well, the resulting effort provides a continuously evolving, robust application. The application is well-tested because so many different applications take advantage of the code. Programmers do not have to pay for the code or develop it themselves, and they can therefore accelerate their project schedule.

The certification stamp of "Open Source" is owned by the Open Source Initiative (OSI). Code that is developed to be freely shared and evolved can use the Open Source trademark if the distribution terms conform to the OSI's Open Source Definition. This requires that the software must be redistributed to others under certain guidelines. For example, under the General Purpose License (GPL), source code must be made available so that other developers will be able to improve or evolve it.

What Is Ogg?

There is a whole community of developers who devote their time to the cause of creating open standards and applications for digital media. One such group is the Xiph.org Foundation, a nonprofit corporation whose purpose is to support and develop free, open protocols and software to serve the public, developer and business markets. This umbrella organization (see Figure 9.16) oversees the administration of such technologies as video (Theora), music (the lossy Vorbis and lossless Flac), and speech (Speex) codecs.

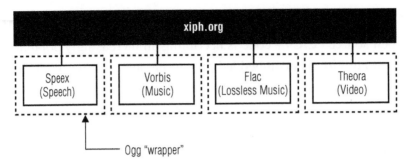

Figure 9.16 **Xiph.org open-source "umbrella"**

The term *Ogg* denotes the container format that holds multimedia data. It generally serves as a prefix to the specific codec that generates the data. One audio codec we'll discuss here is called Vorbis and uses Ogg to store its bit streams as files, so it is usually called "Ogg Vorbis." In fact, some portable media players are advertised as supporting OGG files, where the "Vorbis" part is implicit. Speex, a speech codec discussed below, also uses the Ogg format to store its bit streams as files on a computer. However, VoIP networks and other real-time communications systems do not require file storage capability, and a network layer like the Real-time Transfer Protocol (RTP) is used to encapsulate these streams. As a result, even Vorbis can lose its Ogg shell when it is transported across a network via a multicast distribution server.

What Is Vorbis?

Vorbis is a fully open, patent-free, and royalty-free audio compression format. In many respects, it is very similar in function to the ubiquitous MPEG-1/2 layer 3 (MP3) format and the newer MPEG-4 (AAC) formats. This codec was designed for mid- to high-quality (8 kHz to 48 kHz, >16 bit, polyphonic) audio at variable bit rates from 16 to 128 kbps/channel, so it is an ideal format for music.

The original Vorbis implementation was developed using floating-point arithmetic, mainly because of programming ease that led to faster release. Since most battery-powered embedded systems (like portable MP3 players) utilize less expensive and more battery-efficient fixed-point processors, the open-source community of developers created a fixed-point implementation of the Vorbis decoder. Dubbed *Tremor*, the source code to this fixed-point Vorbis decoder was released under a license that allows it to be incorporated into open-source and commercial systems.

Before choosing a specific fixed-point architecture for porting the Vorbis decoder, it is important to analyze the types of processing involved in recovering audio from a compressed bit stream. A generalized processor flow for the Vorbis decode process (and other similar algorithms) is shown in Figure 9.17. Like many other decode algorithms, there are two main stages: front-end and back-end.

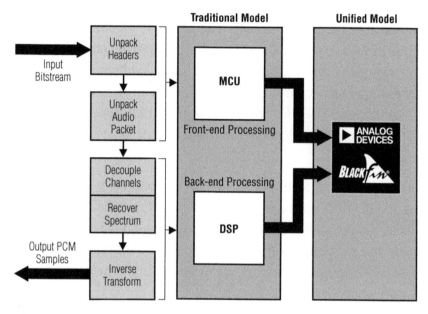

Figure 9.17 **Generalized processor flow for the Vorbis decode process**

During the front-end stage, the main activities are header and packet unpacking, table lookups, Huffman decoding, etc. These types of operations involve a lot of conditional code and tend to take up a relatively large amount of program space. Therefore, embedded developers commonly use microcontrollers (MCUs) for this stage.

Back-end processing is defined by filtering functions, inverse transforms, and general vector operations. In contrast to the front-end phase, the back-end stage involves more loop constructs and memory accesses, and it is quite often smaller in code size. For these reasons, back-end processing in embedded systems has historically been dominated by full-fledged DSPs.

The Blackfin processor architecture unifies MCU and DSP functionality, so there is no longer a need for two separate devices. The architecture allows for an efficient implementation of both front-end and back-end processing on a single chip.

What Is Speex?

Speex is an open-source, patent-free audio compression format designed for speech. While Vorbis is mostly aimed at compressing music and audio in general, Speex targets speech only. For that reason, Speex can achieve much better results than Vorbis on speech at the same quality level.

Just as Vorbis competes with already existing royalty-based algorithms like MP3 and AAC, Speex shares space in the speech codec market with GSM-EFR and the G.72x algorithms, such as G.729 and G.722. Speex also has many features that are not present in most other codecs. These include variable bit rate (VBR), integration of multiple sampling rates in the same bit stream (8 kHz, 16 kHz, and 32 kHz), and stereo encoding support. Also, the original design goal for Speex was to facilitate incorporation into Internet applications, so it is a very capable component of VoIP phone systems.

Besides its unique technical features, the biggest advantages of using Speex are its (lack of) cost and the fact that it can be distributed and modified to conform to a specific application. The source code is distributed under a license similar to that of Vorbis. Because the maintainers of the project realized the importance of embedding Speex into small fixed-point processors, a fixed-point implementation has been incorporated into the main code branch.

Optimizing Vorbis and Speex on Blackfin

"Out-of-the-box" code performance is paramount when an existing application, such as Vorbis or Speex, is ported to a new processor. However, there are many techniques available for optimizing overall performance, some requiring only minimal extra effort. Software engineers can reap big payback by familiarizing themselves with these procedures.

The first step in porting any piece of software to an embedded processor is to customize the low-level I/O routines. As an example, the reference code for both Vorbis and Speex assumes the data originates from a file and the processed output is stored into a file. This is mainly because both implementations were first developed to run and be easily tested on a Unix/Linux system where file I/O routines are available in the operating system. On an embedded media system, however, the input and/or output are often data converters that translate between the digital and real-world analog domains. Figure 9.18 shows a conceptual overview of a possible Vorbis-based media player implementation. The input bit stream is transferred from a flash memory, and the decoder output is driven to an audio DAC. While some media applications like the portable music player still use files to store data, many systems replace storage with a network connection.

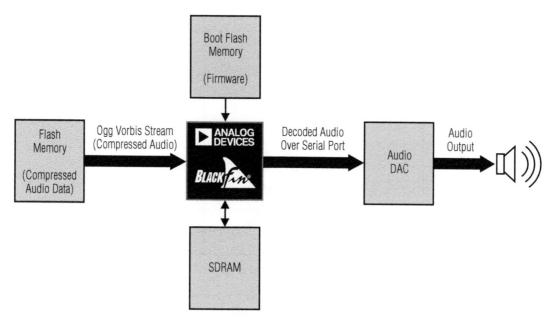

Figure 9.18 Example Vorbis media player implementation

When it comes to actually optimizing a system like the Vorbis decoder to run efficiently, it is a good idea to have an organized plan of attack. One possibility is to focus first on optimizing the algorithm from within C, then move on to streamlining system data flows, and finally tweak individual pieces of the code at an assembly level. To show the efficacy of this method, Figure 9.19 illustrates a representative drop in processor load through successive optimization steps.

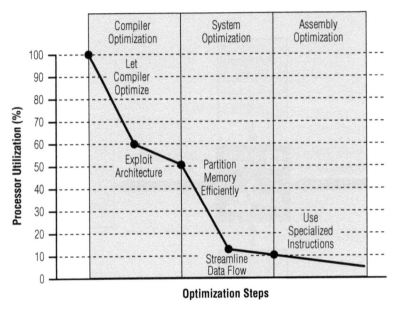

Figure 9.19 **Steps in optimizing Vorbis source code on Blackfin, leading to significantly reduced processor utilization**

Compiler Optimization

Probably the most useful tool for code optimization is a good profiler. Using the Statistical Profiler in VisualDSP++ for Blackfin allows a programmer to quickly focus on hotspots that become apparent as the processor is executing code. A generally accepted rule of thumb states that 20% of the code takes 80% of the processing time. Focusing on these critical sections yields the highest marginal returns. It turns out loops are prime candidates for optimization in media algorithms like Vorbis. This makes sense, given that DSP-centric number-crunching usually occurs inside loops.

There are also global approaches to code optimization. First, a compiler can optimize for memory conservation or for speed. Functions can also be considered for automatic inlining of assembly instructions into the C code. This, again, creates a tradeoff between space and speed. Lastly, some compilers can use a two-phase process to derive relationships between various source files within a single project to further speed up code execution (inter-procedural analysis).

As mentioned above, most reference software for media algorithms uses floating-point arithmetic. Those that are written with fractional fixed-point machines in mind are actually still missing a critical component. The language of choice for the majority of codec algorithms is C, but the C language doesn't natively support the use of fractional fixed-point data. For this reason, many fractional fixed-point algorithms are emulated with integer math. While this makes the code highly portable, it doesn't approach the performance attainable by rewriting some math functions with machine-specific compiler constructs for highest computational efficiency.

A specific example of this is shown in Figure 9.20. The left column shows the C code and Blackfin compiler output for emulated fractional arithmetic that works on all integer machines. One call to perform a 32-bit fractional multiplication takes 49 cycles. The right column shows the performance improvement by utilizing a Blackfin compiler intrinsic function (mult_fr1x32x32NS) that takes advantage of the underlying fractional hardware. With this straightforward modification, an 88% speedup is achieved.

```
Original

union magic {
  struct {
    int lo;
    int hi;
  } halves;
  long long whole;
};

int MULT31_original(int x, int y) {
  union magic magic;
  magic.whole = (long long)x * y;
  magic.whole = magic.whole << 1;
  return magic.halves.hi;
}

R1 = R0 >>> 31 ;
R3 = R2 >>> 31 ;
[ SP + 0xc ] = R3 ;
CALL ___mulli3 ; // 43 cycles
R1 <<= 0x1 ;
R0 >>= 0x1f ;
R0 = R1 | R0 ;

49 cycles
```

```
Improved

int MULT31_improved(int x, int y) {
  return mult_fr1x32x32NS(x,y);
}

A1 = R0.L * R1.L ( FU ) ;
A1 = A1 >> 16 ;
A1 += R0.H * R1.L ( M ) , A0 = R0.H * R1.H ;
A1 += R1.H * R0.L ( M ) ;
A1 = A1 >>> 15 ;
R0 = ( A0 += A1 ) ;

6 cycles (12% of original)
```

Figure 9.20 **Compiler intrinsic functions are an important optimization tool**

System Optimization

System optimization starts with proper memory layout. In the best case, all code and data would fit inside the processor's L1 memory space. Unfortunately, this is not always possible, especially when large C-based applications are implemented within a networked application.

The real dilemma is that processors are optimized to move data independently of the core via DMA, but MCU programmers typically run using a cache model instead. While core fetches are an inescapable reality, using DMA or cache for large transfers is mandatory to preserve performance.

Let's review several memory attributes discussed in detail earlier in the book. The first is the ability to arbitrate requests without core intervention. Because internal memory is typically constructed in sub-banks, simultaneous access by the DMA controller and the core can be accomplished in a single cycle by placing data in separate sub-banks. For example, the core can be operating on data in one sub-bank while the DMA is filling a new buffer in a second sub-bank. Under certain conditions, simultaneous access to the same sub-bank is also possible.

When access is made to external memory, there is usually only one physical bus available. As a result, the arbitration function becomes more critical. When you consider that, on any given cycle, external memory may be accessed to fill an instruction cache-line at the same time it serves as a source and destination for incoming and outgoing data, the challenge becomes clear.

Instruction Execution

As you know by now, SDRAM is slower than L1 SRAM, but it's necessary for storing large programs and data buffers. However, there are several ways for programmers to take advantage of the fast L1 memory. If the target application fits directly into L1 memory, no special action is required, other than for the programmer to map the application code directly to this memory space. In the Vorbis example described above, this is the case.

If the application code is too large for internal memory, as is the case when adding, say, a networking component to a Vorbis codec, a caching mechanism can be used to allow single-cycle access to larger, less expensive external memories. The key advantage of this process is that the programmer does not have to manage the movement of code into and out of the cache.

Using cache is best when the code being executed is somewhat linear in nature. The instruction cache really performs two roles. First, it helps pre-fetch instructions from external memory in a more efficient manner. Also, since caches usually operate with some type of "least recently used" algorithm, instructions that run the most often tend to be retained in cache. Therefore, if the code has already been fetched once, and if it hasn't yet been replaced, the code will be ready for execution the next time through the loop.

Data Management

Now that we have discussed how code is best managed to improve performance, let's review the options for data movement. As an alternative to cache, data can be moved in and out of L1 memory using DMA. While the core is operating on one section of memory, the DMA is bringing in the next data buffer to be processed.

Wherever possible, DMA should always be employed for moving data. As an example, our Vorbis implementation uses DMA to transfer audio buffers to the audio converter.

For this audio application, a double-buffer scheme is used to accommodate the DMA engine. As one half of the circular double buffer is emptied by the serial port DMA, the other half is filled with decoded audio data. To throttle the rate at which the compressed data is decoded, the DMA interrupt service routine (ISR) modifies a semaphore that the decoder can read in order to make sure that it is safe to write to a specific half of the double buffer. On a system with no operating system (OS), polling a semaphore equates to wasted CPU cycles; however, under an OS, the scheduler can switch to another task (like a user interface) to keep the processor busy with real work.

Using DMA can, however, lead to incorrect results if data coherency is not considered. For this reason, the audio buffer bound for the audio DAC should be placed in a noncacheable memory space, since the cache might otherwise hold a newer version of the data than the buffer the DMA would be transferring.

Assembly Optimization

The final phase of optimization involves rewriting isolated segments of the open-source C code in assembly language. The best candidates for an assembly rewrite are normally interrupt service routines and reusable signal processing modules.

The motivation for writing interrupt handlers in assembly is that an inefficient ISR will slow the responses of other interrupt handlers. As an example, some schemes must format in the audio ISR any AC97 data bound for the audio DAC. Because this happens on a periodic basis, a long audio ISR can slow down responses of other events. Rewriting this interrupt handler in assembly is the best way to decrease its cycle count.

A good example of a reusable signal processing module is the modified discrete cosine transform (MDCT) used in the back-end Vorbis processing to transform a time-domain signal into a frequency domain representation. The compiler cannot produce code as tightly as a skilled assembly programmer can, so the C version of the MDCT won't be as efficient. An assembly version of the same function can exploit the hardware features of the processor's architecture, such as single-cycle butterfly add/subtract and hardware bit-reversal.

APPENDIX

Sources and Further Reading

Chapter 1

1. Analog Devices, Inc., *ADSP-BF533 Blackfin Processor Hardware Reference*, Rev 3.0, September 2004.

2. Analog Devices, Inc., *Blackfin Processor Instruction Set Reference*, Rev 3.0, June 2004.

3. Analog Devices, Inc., *Blackfin Embedded Processor ADSP-BF531/ADSP-BF532/ADSP-BF533 Data Sheet*, Rev. B, April 2005.

4. *The McClean Report*, Chapter 10, "Microcontrollers and Digital Signal Processors," IC Insights, 2005 Edition.

Chapter 2

5. Arie Tal, "Two Technologies Compared: NOR vs. NAND White Paper," M-Systems, Revision 1.1, July 2003.

6. J. Hennessy and D. Patterson, *Computer Architecture: A Quantitative Approach*, Morgan Kaufmann, Third edition, 2002.

7. Atsushi Inoue and Doug Wong, *NAND Flash Applications Design Guide*, Toshiba America Electronic Components, Inc., Revision 1.0, April 2003.

8. Doug Wong, "NAND Flash Performance White Paper," Toshiba America Electronic Components, Inc., Revision 1.0, March 2004.

9. Steve Heath, *Embedded Systems Design*, Elsevier (Newnes), Second edition, 2003.

10. Technical Note: TN-46-05. "General DDR SDRAM Functionality," Micron Corporation.

11. V. Pietikainen and J. Vuori, *Memories ITKC11* "Mobiilit sovellusalustat (Mobile Application Platforms)," http://tisu.mit.jyu.fi/embedded/itkc11/itkc11.htm.

12. "DDR2 SDRAM," http://www.elpida.com/en/ddr2/advantage.html.

13. "Mobile-RAM" Application Note, V1.1 Feb 2002, Infineon Technologies.

14. "Innovative Mobile Products Require Early Access to Optimized Solutions," A Position Paper by Samsung Semiconductor, Inc.

15. Application Note 23710, Rev A: "Understanding Burst Mode Flash Memory Devices," Spansion, March 23, 2000.

16. C. MacNamee and K. Rinne, "Semiconductor Memories," http://www.ul.ie/~rinne/et4508/ET4508_L9.pdf.

17. "DDR2—Why Consider It?", Micron Corporation, 2005, http://download.micron.com/pdf/flyers/ddr_to_ddr2.pdf.

17a. Brian Dipert, "Pick a Card: Card Formats," *EDN*, July 8, 2004.

Chapter 3

18. Analog Devices, Inc., *ADSP-BF533 Blackfin Processor Hardware Reference*, Rev 3.0, September 2004.

19. Steve Heath, *Embedded Systems Design*, Elsevier (Newnes), Second edition, 2003.

Chapter 4

20. Analog Devices, Inc., *ADSP-BF533 Blackfin Processor Hardware Reference*, Rev 3.0, September 2004.

21. Analog Devices, Inc., *VisualDSP++ 4.0 C/C++ Compiler and Library Manual for Blackfin Processors*.

22. Steve Heath, *Embedded Systems Design*, Elsevier (Newnes), Second edition, 2003.

Chapter 5

23. K.C. Pohlmann, *Principles of Digital Audio*, McGraw-Hill, 2000.

24. E.C. Ifeachor and B.W. Jervis, *Digital Signal Processing: A Practical Approach*, Addison-Wesley, 1999.

25. Steven Smith, *Digital Signal Processing: A Practical Guide for Engineers and Scientists*, Elsevier (Newnes), 2002.

26. B. Gold and N. Morgan, *Speech and Audio Signal Processing: Processing and Perception of Speech and Music*, Wiley & Sons, 2000.

27. Analog Devices, Inc., *Digital Signal Processing Applications Using the ADSP-2100 Family*, Prentice Hall, 1992.

28. J. Tomarakos and D. Ledger, "Using the Low-Cost, High Performance ADSP-21065L Digital Signal Processor for Digital Audio Applications," Analog Devices.

29. J. Sondermeyer, "EE-183: Rational Sample Rate Conversion with Blackfin Processors," http://www.analog.com/processors/resources/technicalLibrary/appNotes.html.

30. Analog Devices, Inc., "EE-186: Extended-Precision Fixed-Point Arithmetic on the Blackfin Processor Platform," http://www.analog.com/processors/resources/technicalLibrary/appNotes.html.

31. "Digital source coding of speech signals," http://www.ind.rwth-aachen.de/research/speech_coding.html.

32. L. Dumond, "All About Decibels, Part I: What's your dB IQ?," ProRec.com.

32a. Don Morgan, "It's All About Class," *Embedded Systems Programming*, August 31, 2001.

Chapter 6

33. Charles Poynton, *Digital Video and HDTV: Algorithms and Interfaces,* Boston: Morgan Kaufman, 2003.

34. Keith Jack, *Video Demystified,* Fourth edition, Elsevier (Newnes), 2004.

35. Peter Symes, *Video Compression Demystified*, New York: McGraw-Hill, 2001.

36. ITU-R BT.601-5 — *Studio Encoding Parameters of Digital Television for Standard 4:3 and Wide-Screen 16:9 Aspect Ratios*, 1995.

37. ITU-R BT.656-4 — *Interfaces for Digital Component Video Signals in 525-Line and 625-Line Television Systems Operating at the 4:2:2 Level of Recommendation ITU-R BT.601* (Part A), 1998.

38. Analog Devices, Inc., *ADSP-BF533 Blackfin Processor Hardware Reference*, Rev 3.0, September 2004.

39. Keith Jack, "BT.656 Video Interface for ICs," Intersil, Application Note AN9728.2, July 2002.

40. "Digital CCD Camera Design Guide," Cirrus Logic, Application Note AN80, December 1998.

41. Andrew Wilson, "CMOS Sensors Contend for Camera Designs," *Vision Systems Design,* September 2001.

42. Rajeev Ramanath, Wesley E. Snyder, Youngjun Yoo, and Mark S. Drew, "Color Image Processing Pipeline," *IEEE Signal Processing Magazine* (22:1), 2005.

43. Bahadir K. Gunturk, John Glotzbach, Yucel Altunbasak, Ronald W. Schafer, and Russl M. Mersereau, "Demosaicking: Color Filter Array Interpolation," *IEEE Signal Processing Magazine* (22:1), 2005.

44. Gary Sullivan and Stephen Estrop, "Video Rendering with 8-Bit YUV Formats," MSDN Library, August 2003, http://Msdn.microsoft.com/library/default.asp?url=/library/en-us/dnwmt/html/yuvformats.asp.

45. G. de Haan and EB Bellers, "Deinterlacing—An overview," *Proceedings of the IEEE*, Vol. 86, No. 9, Sep. 1998.

46. Matthias Braun, Martin Hahn, Jens-Rainer Ohm, and Maati Talmi, "Motion-Compensating Real-Time Format Converter for Video on Multimedia Displays," Heinrich-Hertz-Institut and MAZ Brandenburg, Germany, http://www.ient.rwth-aachen.de/engl/team/ohm/publi/icip971.pdf.

47. Dan Ramer, "What the Heck is 3:2 Pulldown?," www.dvdfile.com/news/special_report/production_a_z/3_2_pulldown.htm).

48. LeCroy Applications Brief, "Video Basics," Number LAB 1010. Revision 4, 2001, http://www.lecroy.com/tm/library/LABs/PDF/LAB1010.pdf.

49. Rajeev Ramanath, "Interpolation Methods for the Bayer Color Array," Master of Science Thesis, Department of Electrical and Computer Engineering, North Carolina State University, 2000, http://www.lib.ncsu.edu/theses/available/etd-20001120-131644/unrestricted/etd.pdf.

50. Martyn Williams, "Benefits of Future Displays Debated," *PC World Online*, April 9, 2003, http://www.pcworld.com/news/article/0,aid,110209,00.asp.

51. National Instruments, "Anatomy of a Video Signal," http://zone.ni.com/devzone/conceptd.nsf/webmain/0C19487AA97D229C8625685E00803830?OpenDocument.

52. Kelin J. Kuhn, "EE 498: Conventional Analog Television — An Introduction," University of Washington, http://www.ee.washington.edu/conselec/CE/kuhn/ntsc/95x4.htm.

53. Wave Report, "OLED Tutorial," 2005, http://www.wave-report.com/tutorials/oled.htm.

54. Gary A. Thom and Alan R. Deutermann, "A Comparison of Video Compression Algorithms," Delta Information Systems, 2001, http://www.delta-info.com/DDV/downloads/Comparison%20White%20Paper.pdf.

55. Jan Rychter, "Video Codecs Explained," 2003, http://www.sentivision.com/technology/video-codecs/codecs-explained-en.html.

56. Robert Currier, "Digital Video Codec Choices, Part 1," 1995, http://www.synthetic-ap.com/qt/codec1.html.

57. Robert Kremens, Nitin Sampat, Shyam Venkataraman, and Thomas Yeh, "System Implications of Implementing Auto-Exposure on Consumer Digital Cameras," New York, http://www.cis.rit.edu/~rlkpci/ei99_Final.pdf.

58. Scott Wilkinson, "An Eye for Color, Part 1," Ultimate AV Magazine, February 2004, http://ultimateavmag.com/features/204eye/index1.html.

59. Keith Jack, "YCbCr to RGB Considerations," Intersil, Application Note AN9717, March 1997.

Chapter 7

60. Analog Devices, Inc., *ADSP-BF561 Blackfin Processor Hardware Reference*, Preliminary Rev 0.3, January 2005.

61. Ke Ning, Gabby Yi, and Rick Gentile, "Single-Chip Dual-Core Embedded Programming Models for Multimedia Applications ECN," 2/1/2005.

62. K. Sanghai, D. Kaeli, and R. Gentile. "Code and data partitioning on the Blackfin 561 dual-core platform."

Chapter 8

63. Walt Kester, et. al., *Practical Design Techniques for Power and Thermal Management*, Chapters 2 and 3, Analog Devices, Inc., 1998.

64. Analog Devices, Inc., "EE-229: Estimating Power for ADSP-BF533 Blackfin Processors," Revision 1.0, February 2004.

65. Bob Libert, Brian Erisman, and Joe Beauchemin, "EE-228: Switching Regulator Design Considerations for ADSP-BF533 Blackfin Processors," Analog Devices, Inc., Revision 1.0, February 2005.

66. Analog Devices, Inc., *ADSP-BF533 Blackfin Processor Hardware Reference*, Rev 3.0, September 2004.

67. "Comparisons in Chemistry," *Nickel Metal Hydride Batteries Handbook*, Harding Energy, Inc., Section 3, Revision 1.1, 2001, http://www.cell-expert.com/Comparisons%20of%20rechargeable%20technologies.pdf.

68. "Increasing Battery Life in Laptops," Micron Technology, Inc., Technical Note TN-48-06, Rev. 2/00, http://download.micron.com/pdf/technotes/ZT06.pdf.

69. "A Simple Method of Estimating Power in XC4000XL/EX/E FPGAs," Xilinx Corporation, Application Brief XBRF 014, Revision 1.0, June 30, 1997.

70. Luca Benini, Alessandro Bogliolo, and Giovanni De Micheli, "A Survey of Design Techniques for System-Level Dynamic Power Management," *IEEE Transactions on VLSI Systems*, Vol. 8, No. 3, June 2000.

71. Carlos Martinez, Yossi Drori, and Joe Ciancio, "Smart Battery Primer," Xicor AN126, October 1999.

72. John Brophy Jr., "Batteries 101: A primer on cells, batteries, and battery packs ..." Radio Accessory Headquarters, Inc., Revision 4, 2001, http://www.rahq.com/images/batteries_101/Batteries_101.htm

73. Isidor Buchmann, "The Lithium-Polymer Battery: Substance or Hype?," Darnell Group, Inc., 2001, http://www.powerpulse.net/powerpulse/archive/pdf/aa_080601a.pdf

Chapter 9

74. Peter Symes, *Video Compression Demystified*, McGraw-Hill: New York, 2001

75. Vasudev Bhaskaran and Konstantinos Konstantinides, *Image and Video Compression Standards,* Second edition, Kluwer Academic Publishers: Boston, 1997.

76. Cliff Parris and Phil Wright, *Implementation Issues and Trade-Offs for Digital Audio Decoders*, Monmouthshire, UK: ESPICO Ltd.

77. Ke Ning, Gabby Yi, and Rick Gentile, *Single-Chip Dual-Core Embedded Programming Models for Multimedia Applications, ECN*, 2/1/2005.

Index

Printed and bound by CPI Group (UK) Ltd, Croydon, CR0 4YY
03/10/2024
01040338-0005